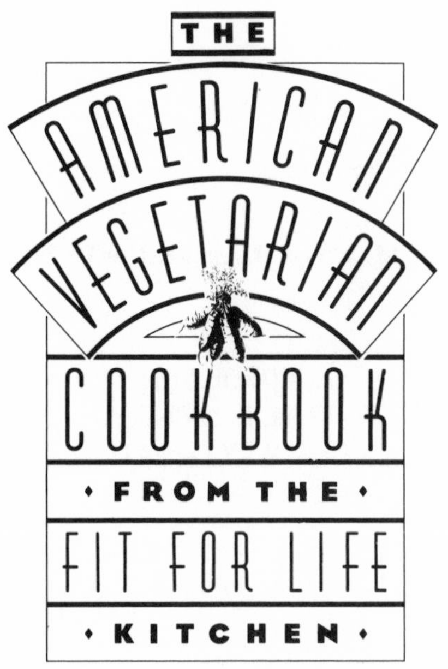
THE
AMERICAN
VEGETARIAN
COOKBOOK
FROM THE
FIT FOR LIFE
KITCHEN

Other Books by Marilyn Diamond with Harvey Diamond

FIT FOR LIFE
FIT FOR LIFE II: LIVING HEALTH
A NEW WAY OF EATING

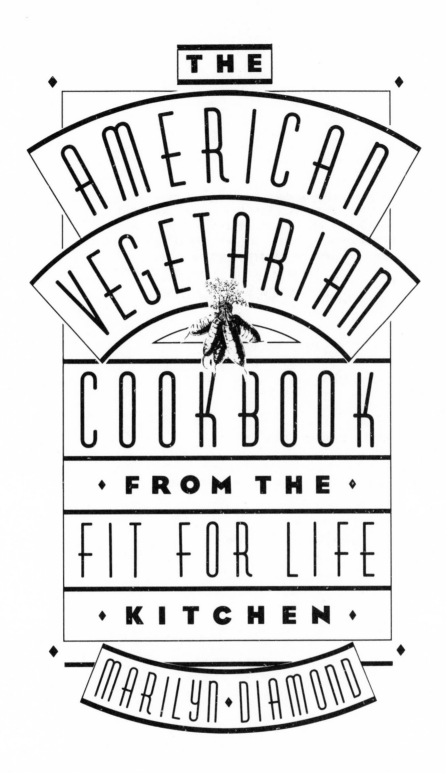

THE AMERICAN VEGETARIAN COOKBOOK FROM THE FIT FOR LIFE KITCHEN

MARILYN DIAMOND

WARNER BOOKS

A Time Warner Company

I have recommended certain brand-name products in this book. These products were selected on the basis of their value as perceived by me while I conducted my research for this book in 1987–89. When manufacturers of such products publicize my authorized recommendations, I want the reader to understand that these efforts did not in any way influence my selection of these products.

—Marilyn Diamond

A Time Warner Company

Warner Books, Inc., 1271 Avenue of the Americas, New York, NY 10020

Printed in the United States of America
First printing: April 1990
10

Library of Congress Cataloging-in-Publication Data

Diamond, Marilyn.
American vegetarian cookbook : from the fit for life kitchen / by Marilyn Diamond.
p. cm.
ISBN 0-446-51561-2
1. Vegetarian cookery. 2. Cookery, American. I. Title.
TX837.D46 1990 89-40456
CIP

Book Design: H. Roberts

With great respect and great love,
this book is dedicated to
you who are now holding it
in your hands

To Dr. C. Everett Koop, America's forward-thinking and courageous former Surgeon General, for guiding us to a new level of awareness.

We wish to share with you the encouraging words of health care professionals from all over the country who have endorsed the *Fit for Life* approach and ideals that inspired this book:

"Marilyn Diamond's new cookbook leads us with a gigantic step forward as we enter the last decade of this 20th century in pursuing this country's goals toward 'health and happiness.' "

Glenn H. Koepke, M.D.
Emergency Physician
St. Joseph Hospital
Tucson, Arizona

"Marilyn Diamond shares with us a sensible way to feed our kids and ourselves so that we can all be *Fit for Life*."

Joseph Girone, M.D.
Professor of Pediatrics
Temple University Medical School
Philadelphia, Pennsylvania

"The most important advice I can give my patients to improve their health and lifestyle would be to change their eating habits and follow the *Fit for Life* philosophy set forth in this book."

Toni Manos, M.D.
Emergency Medicine
Yonkers, New York

"This book is a masterpiece! I recommend this to my patients and to all others for optimal health. The wonderful recipes and ideas make for a simple, delicious nutritional lifestyle."

Victoria Arcadi, D.C.
Los Angeles, California

"The majority of chronic and life-threatening diseases most prevalent in our society can be prevented by adherence to a wholesome vegetarian diet as so very effectively set forth in Marilyn Diamond's new cookbook."

Joel Fuhrman, M.D.
St. Joseph's Medical Center
Yonkers, New York

"Marilyn Diamond's new vegetarian cookbook is the guidebook for the nutritional revolution of the '90s. The service that the Diamonds have performed in spreading nutritional wisdom through *Fit for Life* is immeasurable."

Terry Grossman, M.D.
Granby Medical Center
Granby, Colorado

"Marilyn Diamond's new cookbook celebrates the joy of good food in a way that is perfectly in tune with all our latest up-to-date medical knowledge and then soars beyond it by overcoming all the confusion about good and bad cholesterol, triglycerides and lipids, because in these recipes, it is just not there. Use this book with peace of mind."

Edward Taub, M.D.
University of California Medical School
Irvine, California

"Clearly, vegetarian and near vegetarian diets have medical, economic, political and humanitarian benefits that are enormous in their scope. I applaud Marilyn Diamond for 'carrying the torch' with this fine book."

Joshua Leichtberg, M.D.
Medical Director
Suma Medical Group
Beverly Hills, California

"This new book provides a wonderful 'how to' approach for the novice in nutrition as well as the veteran. This book will inspire you to be bolder in the kitchen. *Fit for Life* principles have had a tremendously favorable impact on my patients and on me."

Barbara Beuckman, D.C.
Beuckman Chiropractic Center
Belleville, Illinois

"More than ever nutrition counseling plays a key role in diagnosis and treatment planning for the achievement of optimum dental health. I emphasize the *Fit for Life* principles set forth in Marilyn Diamond's new book. Personally I look forward to experiencing the health adventures therein."

Stanley Corwin, D.D.S.
Fellow of the Academy of General Dentistry
Los Angeles, California

"I cannot extol the virtues of this book enough. It is excellent! The recipes are delectable. With this book, offering food to others is a form of love."

Phyllis Terry-Gold, Ph.D.
Clinical Psychologist
Hofstra University
Hempstead, New York

"There is no illness, no condition that would not be improved—oftentimes dramatically—by a proper vegetarian diet. Marilyn Diamond has combined the best of traditional vegetarian knowledge with up-to-date touches that make vegetarianism extraordinarily enjoyable and readily available to all, regardless of previous eating habits."

Henry Golden, D.C.
International Sports Medicine Consultant,
Naturopathic Physician,
Licensed Acupuncturist, West Hills, California

"Vegetarianism through the *Fit for Life* approach is an exciting, healthy way of life. My own health experiences are a living testimony to me of the benefits of the lifestyle that Marilyn Diamond has set forth in this book."

Lynn Freeman, R.N.
Medical Center of North Hollywood
North Hollywood, California

"Cleverly disguised as a cookbook, Marilyn Diamond's new work is really a doorway to a future of vibrant physical health for you. It is a world-class collection of nutritional pearls and entertaining food lore. As a physician I have repeatedly observed *Fit for Life* proponents experiencing profound improvements in their health."

Michael Klaper, M.D.
Santa Cruz, California

ACKNOWLEDGMENTS

With all my love and gratitude, I wish to thank my family, for helping me and supporting me during the years of work that went into this book.

Harvey, *for setting the example of commitment and dedication...*
Lisa, *for the endless hours of work with me to get the job done...*
Beau, *for the cheerful independence when Mom was too busy...*
Greg, *for saying "You can do it, Mom," when those words were much needed...*
Mom, *for teaching me how to cook... and advising me to write this book...*
Dad, *for the fatherly advice and moral support...*
Linda, *for willingly sharing recipes when so much else demanded attention...*
Doris, *for showing me there is always time to do something nice for someone else...*
Grandma Ida, *for being so inspiring and young at heart at 90 years of age...*

To all the dear friends who were willing to lend assistance or expertise, I thank you, with love and appreciation...

Patti Breitman, Paul Obis, Jo Dawson, William Shurtleff, Richard Rose, Deo *and* ***John Robbins, Jae Duckhorn, Albert Lusk, Alan Goldhammer, Cheryl Mitchell,*** *and especially:*
Nansey Neiman, *my publisher, for believing in the book...*
Fredda Isaacson, *my editor, for helping to trim, organize and clarify...*
Chuck Ashman, *my friend, for saying "This is my life too."*

Contents

A Personal Letter

Dear Reader,

In the four years that have passed since the release of *Fit for Life I* and *Fit for Life II,* many of you have written to us asking for more recipes. There have also been questions regarding the feeding of children and other family members who seem a little resistant to dietary improvement. People have asked about food products and kitchen equipment, and some have sent personal recipes that I have included in the following pages, whenever possible, for all to enjoy. Thank you all for taking the time to tell us about your successes, experiences, and concerns. You have been the inspiration for this book.

I am excited to welcome you to my vegetarian kitchen, a wonderfully happy kitchen devoted to great taste and good health!

Wonderful? Because the recipes you find on these pages are truly that. They really taste good!

Happy? You bet! When your kitchen is dedicated not only to pleasing your taste buds but also to supporting your health—and the health of those you love—here's what happens:

You feel happy!

Because the food tastes so good, and because you know it is good for you,

You really DO feel happy!

"Eating should be fun." That is a direct quote from our eleven-year-old Beau. I add, "Food should be delicious." Sometimes I feel that in an endeavor to make food healthier, many people have lost sight of both those important qualities. The psychological and emotional environment that surrounds a meal is just as important as what is on the plate. If we make our food choices from the wide variety of wholesome foods that are available to us and we approach the eating experience with the joy, reverence, and gratitude our food abundance deserves, we can reap all the health we desire. But taste is equally important. If you and your family and friends aren't truly *loving* what comes out of your kitchen, no amount of explanation about how *healthy* it is is going to evoke enthusiasm. FOR FOOD TO DO GOOD FOR PEOPLE, IT HAS TO TASTE GOOD FIRST!

You who are avid FIT FOR LIFERS, living faithfully by its principles, reaping the benefits of doing so, will find a world of new recipes and new information that can broaden your horizons. There are new techniques and ingredients to incorporate, valuable new options and possibilities that can help make vegetarian cooking the most exciting, innovative, relevant, and gourmet of all the present-day cuisines.

If you are one of the many people in today's world who have determined that it is time for you to remove certain harmful foods from your diet and eat more healthfully, you can be certain that this book supports your worthy determination. All cholesterol and saturated animal fat, all refined sugar and fiberless grains and almost all salt have been eliminated in this book to help you take a new step to a higher level of health in a pleasurable way, as you prepare one exciting new dish after another, all of which are based on healthful ingredients.

Fit for Life is a fluid philosophy, based solidly on physiological principles but necessarily flexible to accommodate psychological and social situations. For those times when food combining, fruit in the morning, or omission of certain favorite ingredients may not be useful, this book offers good-tasting, viable options. As I include these recipes, I think specifically of health-minded mothers with children who are now out of the "trusting" toddler years. At seven, eight, or nine years of age, these children are voicing the need to "fit into life" with their peers. This is a *very important* need that must be acknowledged. Children at this time of life want their food to look like everyone else's. No "weird stuff"—know what I mean? While I in no way imply that you should condone a junk-food diet, I do suggest that for those relatively few precious years your children spend in your kitchen, go out of your way to prepare the foods they like as healthfully as you can, and avoid allowing food to become an issue that gives anybody "a stomachache." But all the while, *educate* them. Tell them what you've learned. Few adults realize that, given the knowledge, many children begin to make food choices to perpetuate their own health.

By including as much variation as possible in the recipes, I also think of all the letters I have received from people in relationships—people who are personally motivated to make changes but who find their friends or spouses reluctant to embrace the idea that the health, happiness, and energy that come from better eating are worth a "little" improvement at the dinner table. Like children, these "resistant ones" need familiar food, and they resent having what they like "taken away" from them and replaced by something they don't understand. The broader, more forgiving recipes included here will work well to keep them satisfied and enthusiastic, to get their energy up and their cholesterol level down, and help them pull in their belts a few notches. There are also lots of wholesome, festive foods that you can offer to friends and family willing to eat anything delicious but unwilling to jump on a philosophical bandwagon. For all of you—mothers and others—who *want* to cook more healthfully but have simply thrown in the towel because it involves too much change from what you may be accustomed to, this book is for you.

For those who feel they don't have the necessary talent in the kitchen to be effective, this book is for you, too! Men and women who never cooked before in their lives have become wonderfully proficient—even creative—because of the simplicity of recipes like these and the "I feel so good" results from eating better. For all those active and energetic "seasoned citizens" in their sixties, seventies, and eighties, who wrote to us to express their appreciation for the improvements in their lives, here are more easy recipes to keep you feeling confident about your health.

For those who don't have time for food preparation—I know there are millions of you out there in this predicament—there are the many "FIX-IT-FAST" recipes that take from ten minutes to just under one hour for *a whole meal.*

In other words, this is a book for EVERYBODY! As an inveterate nourisher, I can't bear to leave anyone out, even if it means stretching fundamental principles now and then or combining two or three philosophies at a time to be inclusive. Food is a personal issue. There are many food philosophies, all with something good to contribute, but no *one* food philosophy works for *everyone all the time.* The best we can do in our eclectic society is to learn to become eclectic about food. I urge you to do what works for you at all times, without ever feeling apologetic or guilty. Those are two emotions that have no place around food!

In these changing times, flexibility is the key to success in anyone's kitchen. Since as a species we are physiologically similar but psychologically and emotionally diverse as snowflakes, the mentality of a short order cook, open to all desires, will help us when we prepare foods for others. Your willingness to accept that everybody is at a different level of evolution will be greatly appreciated. When you've thought to include "something for everyone," your gratification will come when they smile and say, "That was really good!" When your child exclaims, "All right, Mom!" (or "All right, Dad!") after enjoying the "healthiest" meal possible for that moment in time, you'll know a sense of achievement.

Thank you, once again, dear reader, for motivating this work. May the recipes and ideas on the pages that follow make your life easier. May they make you and your loved ones healthier and happier. Working together, may we revitalize what has always united our species in joyous celebration—the food on our tables. And, in doing so, may we revitalize ourselves and our planet. With LOVE as our main ingredient, it is our power to bring forth from our kitchens the very substance of LIFE—and the right nourishment to lead us into a future full of LOVE!

I love you,

Marilyn

May the seeds of love be planted
In the hearts of your children who gather,
With the water of forgiveness,
May they grow . . .

Dispeller of Darkness,
Lord of Creation,
Mother of Humanity,
Ruler of all Nations,
Master of the starry skies,
Creator of the wind's caress,
Shine a little tenderness,
On your children in the Wilderness.

—Eliza Gilkyson

Legends of the Rainmaker
Gold Castle Records
Los Angeles, California

Introduction

THE *Fit for Life* principles are an international phenomenon. With over 7 million copies in print, translated into sixteen languages our books have reached millions of people and the ideas we have shared have had worldwide impact. People have experienced an immensely enhanced quality of life through improvement in diet; yet the question arises over and over again: How can we eat better and still *love* what we're eating? The answer is in this book.

The food we Americans have loved over the last several decades has brought us some pretty serious trouble, and we have exported our problem as well. Our fads and customs have set trends around the world. We wear jeans; the world wears jeans. We eat junk; people clamor for it from the Ginza to the Champs-Elysées! One Middle Eastern family who moved to the United States proudly put their three-year-old in an American preschool, where his teeth decayed and he gained a great deal of weight. Why? The teachers reported that every lunchbox the child brought was filled with sodas, sugary pastries, potato chips, and cookies. His parents honestly thought that these items represented the good foods that made Americans big and strong. They certainly made us big; because of those foods many Americans don't or can't fit into their jeans. As other populations increasingly embrace American junk food, their jeans are likely to get tighter, too. But Americans can set better trends. When books like *Fit for Life* become popular around the world, and Americans go through the process of getting back into shape, the world watches with a vested interest. That's very good news for the future of the planet.

Having accepted for years the disenfranchising idea that when health eluded us it was not in our power to understand the causes or do something about them, today "we the patients" of the past decades have become "we the participants." At the beginning of the decade of the '90s, we have responded to the challenge made in 1979 by the Secretary of Health, Education, and Welfare, Joseph Califano; and the Surgeon General, Julius Richmond, that the health of the American people depends on what they are willing to do for *THEMSELVES,* and not on what others are willing to do for them. Open to all empowering ideas, we are now far more motivated than ever before to learn what individuals can do to become fit and well, and stay that way. We value our health. We value health for our loved ones. And we are willing to do whatever we can to ensure both.

Doing whatever we can certainly spills over into our behavior in the kitchen; but for those who cook, these exciting times can also be confusing and frustrating. In the world of cooking, everything is changing. Many "red, white, and blue" ingredients—which were once the mainstay of American food preparation—have been discredited. But although we are willing to stop using them, we are not quite sure what to use instead. How can we put together palate-pleasing meals that our families and friends will enjoy and request *without* the refined oils, white sugar, white flour, and abundance of butter, milk and cheese, eggs, red meat, bacon and sausage, salt, and canned and processed staples that once we used so routinely and nonchalantly? Now that we know such a diet not only forced us into larger and larger sizes but also brought us the dubious premiums of heart disease, cancer, and stroke, we need to adopt a new approach to cooking.

This new approach comes to you from the *Fit for Life* kitchen. The solutions are easy and rewarding, quick and exciting. These good and good-for-you foods are *not* difficult to prepare and certainly do not demand a big investment of your time. Every recipe has been timed, and you will be pleased to find that most of them fall into the "Fix-it-Fast" range of ten to thirty-five minutes. In this book, the techniques are deliberately simplified to save time and effort, so that even the least experienced cook will be guided toward healthful creativity.

The ingredients needed are, for the most part, readily available in the fresh-food section of your supermarket, with an occasional trip to your local health food store for some staples. On pages 35–44, I have prepared an up-to-date shopping list that will introduce you to the excellent ingredients and products now available from the natural foods industry and from the more progressive commercial food manufacturers. These healthful substitutes for many of the common, chemical-laden ingredients are of superb quality. There is also a list of mail order houses that can supply many useful items when marketing time and access are limited. In addition, a chart of food values shows you unequivocally that everything your body needs to be healthy is available from natural sources.

Synthesizing today's popular trends in healthful eating and our natural love of many different cuisines, the recipes on the following pages transform French, Chinese, Japanese, Italian, and Mexican favorites into up-to-date versions of our national favorites. You'll find innovation and excitement in even the simplest of recipes, and you'll learn how to bring wholesomeness, balance, and artistry to each meal.

This book contains everything you need to know about preparing delectable meals that will keep you and your family in shape and bursting with high energy for maximum harmony, productivity, and creativity. In fact, you will find that this food makes you joyful, for it supports, rather than undermines, the integrity of your body and the sanctity of your life. Big promises? Wait and see what results you get!

The fact that so many people are interested in preparing good food that is also *good for them* heralds the possibility of what many people are already calling the "Twenty-first Century of Health." We are brother and sister pioneers in the kitchen! Certainly our interest in preparing this high-quality food will affect the health and happiness of future generations.

Since "we are what we eat," this book is my affirmation that wholesome and healthful food can help bring out all that is strong, beautiful, and harmonious in the human species. So let's tie on our aprons and begin to discover together a new path we can follow that will affect the very fiber of our existence. Whatever you do, do it from the heart. Then you can invite your family and friends to join you at a table full of Love and Life! It is an honor for me to share this experience with you.

Let's proceed together now into the rewarding endeavor of preparing food that is *Fit for Life!*

What This Book Can Do for You

by Harvey Diamond

THE American people need support to follow more seriously the recommendations of the former U.S. surgeon general, Dr. C. Everett Koop. In his "Report on Nutrition and Health," published in October 1988, Dr. Koop left no doubt about the urgent need to alter our eating habits to stem the growth of disease that besets our population. Presently in the United States, 2.1 million people die annually from *all* causes of death. Diet plays a role in a full 68 percent of these deaths! If you remove suicide and unintentional injuries such as auto accidents from the list of causes, the number of deaths to which diet is a contributing factor is a whopping 80 percent! Those are numbers that *demand* our immediate attention. Fortunately, Dr. Koop had the wisdom and dedication as surgeon general to take the appropriate measures to help protect the American people from further unnecessary suffering and death.

This landmark report is a comprehensive compilation of over 2,000 scientific studies of the most rigorous nature. It states categorically that our standard, fat-laden American diet is, in Dr. Koop's words, "killing millions prematurely and ruining the lives of tens of millions." In discussing the wealth of research leading to this conclusion, Dr. Koop said that "the depth of the science underlying this report's findings is even more impressive than that for tobacco and health in 1964."

Diet is at present a factor in heart disease, cancer, stroke, diabetes, atherosclerosis, high blood pressure, obesity, dental disease, osteoporosis, and gastrointestinal diseases. The report states that "it is now clear that diet contributes in substantial ways to the development of these diseases and that modification of diet can contribute to their prevention." And while the report acknowledges that many food factors are involved, it also states that "the chief culprits are saturated fats and cholesterol eaten in disproportionate amounts, often at the expense of fruit, vegetables and grains which are high in complex carbohydrates and fiber." The source of all this saturated fat and cholesterol certainly is no mystery. It is animal products: meat, poultry, fish, eggs, and dairy foods. The surgeon general's recommendations are simple and succinct: reduce your intake of animal products while increasing your intake of fruit, vegetables, and whole grains. The same conclusion has been reached by the National Cancer Institute, the American Cancer Society, the American Heart Association, and virtually every health-related institution in the academic community. After all the years of talk about prevention to curb ill health in our country, we now have a defined direction to take to achieve that goal.

So huge and obvious is the body of evidence substantiating our need to cut back on animal products in order to prevent disease that many people have opted to give up their meat-based diets altogether and become vegetarians; but for some this may seem too drastic or even unwise for health reasons. For quite some time vegetarianism was grossly misperceived. Many thought it sprang from the days of granola eating in the 1960s or that it was practiced as a statement for animal rights or simply misguided fanaticism. Although frequently misunderstood, vegetarianism has been practiced for centuries. Leonardo da Vinci, Benjamin Franklin, Albert Einstein, Buddha, George Bernard Shaw, Socrates, Plato, and St. Francis of Assisi were just a few of its celebrated proponents. Today there is a mass of scientific medical evidence attesting to and confirming the benefits of a meatless life-style. So many studies prove this statement that it is virtually impossible to cite them all.

One recent study was of such magnitude that it deserves at least some mention. It was presented at the First International Congress on Vegetarian Nutrition in Washington, D.C., in March 1987. Nearly 400 medical doctors, scientists, and health researchers heard testimony from around the world, affirming the health benefits of a vegetarian diet. One report conducted by the University of Minnesota followed 25,000 vegetarians for twenty-one years; the results were decisive and unassailable. Across the board, all these individuals experienced a higher level of health in all categories than nonvegetarians. The keynote address was delivered by Dr. Johanna Dwyer of Tufts University. In her talk she stated that: "Vegetarianism has gotten a bad rap; it has been considered something odd that some people got into, something one tolerated." The authors of the report wrote in *Nutrition Today* (July/August 1987), "The congress demonstrated that vegetarian dietary practices have come into the mainstream of scientific and medical thinking." The traditional dietary and nutritional organizations now agree.

All this talk of vegetarianism might lead you to think that the goal of this book is to make you a vegetarian. If you think so, you're wrong. Our goal is to assist you in escaping the ravages of heart disease and cancer by supplying you with appealing, innovative, and delicious foods that you can enjoy in place of foods that have been medically proved to do harm. You don't have to become a vegetarian to enjoy freedom from disease. You do, however, have to move *to some degree* in that direction. Every health-related area of the scientific community implores us to do so, but they do not tell us *how.* This book fills that crucial need. When you wish to prepare dishes that are entirely in line with the surgeon general's recommendations, here is a bookful from which to choose.

Now that the evidence is in and the most prestigious, highly qualified, and well-respected authorities in our country have told us that the safest and smartest course is to move away from animal products, here are the tasty, tantalizing recipes you need to help you in that endeavor. These recipes will not only excite *you* but will be irresistible to your family as well.

That's what this book is all about, and we could not be more delighted that you have chosen to make it a part of your life.

1

Nutrition Update

VEGETARIANISM, cholesterol, saturated fats, protein, fiber, calories, whole foods, refined foods, vitamin B_{12}, salt, pesticides, food irradiation... these are the buzzwords of a national preoccupation with nutrition that is historically unprecedented. The layperson is being asked to absorb data that heretofore was the domain of the "specialists." As we are continually barraged by the latest findings, we are, in fact, light-years ahead of where we were only a decade ago. Still, at times, the average individual can feel overwhelmed and confused, to say the least.

This chapter has been included to clarify and define some of the concepts and terms that are in the news daily and that enter into any up-to-date debate of nutritional issues. Rather than offer a final point of view, which is impossible in a field that is so young and so quickly evolving, I instead relay information that can help you to evaluate the data and determine for yourself what is true for you.

RECENT FINDINGS ON VEGETARIANISM

> **The average age [longevity] of a meat eater is 63. I am on the verge of 85 and still work as hard as ever. I have lived quite long enough and I am trying to die; but I simply cannot do it. A single beef-steak would finish me, but I cannot bring myself to swallow it. I am oppressed with a dread of living forever. This is the only disadvantage to vegetarianism.**
>
> **—George Bernard Shaw**

Few people realize that there are currently some 10 million vegetarians in the United States, and a far larger number of people who are changing their diets in that direction. Yet only a few years ago, the vegetarian life-style was frowned upon, belittled, ridiculed, and totally misunderstood. Today, being vegetarian is just as mainstream, if not more "in," than eating a meat-based diet, as we find increasing numbers of trendsetters becoming vegetarian.

Based on the most recent government research, the U.S. surgeon general's office, leading dietary and nutritional organizations, and many, many doctors have now concluded that:

1. Since the most up-to-date dietary guidelines for Americans recommend a reduction in fat intake and increased consumption of fruits, vegetables, and whole grains, well-planned vegetarian diets *can* effectively meet these guidelines and the recommended dietary allowances. Vegetarianism can confidently be embraced as a healthy dietary alternative.[1]

2. A vegetarian diet reduces the risk of obesity.

3. Vegetarians generally have lower mortality rates from several chronic degenerative diseases than do nonvegetarians.

4. Vegetarians generally have lower blood pressure, lower rates of diabetes, and suffer less from hypertension, lung cancer, osteoporosis, kidney stones, gallstones, and diverticular diseases.

5. A varied vegetarian diet consumed daily provides adequate amounts of amino acids and satisfies or exceeds the body's protein requirements. (Lower protein intake in vegetarian diets as opposed to meat-based diets may be beneficial and may be associated with lower risk of osteoporosis in vegetarians.)

6. Plant-based diets are lower in total fat, saturated fat, and cholesterol than meat-based diets, an important facter in the lower risk of heart disease and some cancers.

7. Calcium deficiency in vegetarians is rare. There is evidence that vegetarians absorb and retain more calcium from foods than do nonvegetarians.

8. In addition to health aspects, there are other valid reasons for the adoption of a vegetarian diet. These include: (a) preservation of the environment by eating foods low on the food chain (plants instead of animals); (b) a solution to world hunger by decreasing the demand on the world's food resources; (c) low cost, since diets low in animal proteins typically are less expensive than meat-based diets; and (d) philosophical or ethical concerns, including opposition to cruelty to animals and attitudes toward violence.

WHAT YOU SHOULD KNOW ABOUT CHOLESTEROL

Cholesterol is a hard, waxy, fat-soluble (as opposed to water-soluble) substance that is synthesized in all cells of the body but primarily in the liver. It is part of every cell of the body as a building block of the cell membrane, and it is critically important—so important that Nature has equipped each cell with the means to synthesize its *own* cholesterol. This cholesterol made by our bodies keeps the membranes of our cells functioning at optimum level. Our bodies produce between 500 and 1,000 milligrams of cholesterol every day, and that amount is plenty to supply our needs.[2] In fact, we create such an ample supply that the *dietary* requirement for cholesterol is zero. The cholesterol that we create in our bodies is not the problem cholesterol about which there is so much publicity. The problem cholesterol is manufactured in the bodies of animals for their needs, but we take it in when we eat these animals as food. When we live on a diet of animal products (meat, poultry, fish, dairy, and eggs), we consume 500 to 1,000 milligrams of *dietary* cholesterol a day, most of which cannot be easily removed (excreted) and is, instead, deposited in the tissues of our body, particularly in the arteries. It is well established that this accumulated

[1]Position paper of the American Dietetic Association, "Vegetarian Diets—Technical Support Paper," March 1988.
[2]John A. McDougall, *The McDougall Plan* (Piscataway, N.J.: New Century Publishers, 1983), p. 63.

excess of dietary cholesterol (that which the body has not manufactured for itself) is a contributing factor to the high rate of cardiovascular disease and other degenerative diseases that afflict North Americans.

The cholesterol that contributes to heart disease comes from the animal products we eat. A tablespoon of butter contains 35 mg of cholesterol; a cup of low-fat cottage cheese contains 23 mg of cholesterol; 3 ounces of cream cheese contains 94 mg of cholesterol; an egg yolk contains 252 mg of cholesterol; 6 ounces of beef contains 160 mg of cholesterol; a whole chicken breast contains 126 mg of cholesterol; a cup of liver contains 744 mg of cholesterol; and a fillet of halibut contains 175 mg of cholesterol; 6 ounces of light-meat turkey contains 130 mg of cholesterol and a cup of shrimp has 192 mg of cholesterol. In contrast, apples, bananas, grapes, almonds, cashews, coconut, tofu, avocados, garbanzo beans, oats, corn, carrots, lettuce, potatoes, and *all other plant foods* contain zero mg of cholesterol, no matter how large a quantity you eat.

Serum cholesterol is the level of cholesterol in your blood, measured by a test which has been found to be one of the least accurate any patient can take. So, if you have your cholesterol checked, you should probably have the results verified. As an example of this inaccuracy, a blood sample with a known cholesterol value of 262.6 was sent to 5,000 of the nation's top labs. Readings came back ranging from 101 to 524![1] The average serum cholesterol level in the U.S. population is 220 milligrams per milliliter. At this "average," a male American has a 50 percent or greater chance of dying of heart disease! So it's not a comfortable level to strive for. If your serum cholesterol level is 240, you have a four-times-greater risk of dying of cardiovascular disease than average. At 260, your risk is *six* times greater![2] Six times greater than 50 percent is too-o-o much. What you must realize is that it is so *easy* to raise cholesterol levels: Just consume a diet high in animal fat and protein (meat, poultry, fish and shellfish, eggs, and dairy) and low in fiber, as many routinely do in this country. In all likelihood, your serum cholesterol level will be average or above average as a result. In countries where people live primarily on grains, legumes, vegetables, and fruit, with practically no animal foods in their diet, average cholesterol levels are in the 120 to 160 range, and cardiovascular disease is virtually unknown.[3]

There are other ways to lower cholesterol that also are totally in your control. The elimination of refined sugar, refined grains, refined fats, and oils will also lower cholesterol. In other words, a diet of whole foods, made from unprocessed ingredients, lowers cholesterol to the point where you won't even have to think about it. Aerobic exercise (walking, dancing, swimming, running, cycling, and jumping on a minitrampoline) will also lower cholesterol. And so will laughter. In short, dietary improvements, exercise that you enjoy, and a good, positive feeling about life will help get your cholesterol level under control. None of these activities costs you money nor does it have the harmful side effects inherent in cholesterol-lowering drugs.

> An average American male with a cholesterol level of 220 has an over 50 percent risk of dying of heart disease; an average vegetarian male has a 15 percent risk and a pure vegetarian male (no animal products whatsoever) has a 4 percent risk.[4] The numbers are equally impressive for women. You can lower your cholesterol level by as much as *100 milligrams in one month* by switching to the pure vegetarian diet laid out for you in this book!

[1]*Wall Street Journal,* June 14, 1988, p. 25.
[2]Udo Erasmus, *Fats and Oils* (Vancouver, B.C.: Alive Books, 1986), pp. 310–11.
[3]Erasmus, *Fats and Oils,* pp. 310–11.
[4]John Robbins, *Diet for a New America* (Walpole, N.H.: Stillpoint, 1987).

CLEARING UP THE CONFUSION ABOUT FATS AND OILS

No society in the world has ever eaten as much total fat as ours. In fact, our government has targeted reduction in fat intake as the number one *dietary priority* of the nation.

In the "Report on Nutrition and Health," Surgeon General Koop cited fat as a leading cause of disease that should be avoided in most people's diets and terms the overconsumption of fat "a national health problem." Dr. Koop further noted:

> **Of greatest concern is our excessive intake of dietary fat and its relationship to risk for chronic diseases such as coronary heart disease, some types of cancers, diabetes, high blood pressure, strokes and obesity.**[1]

In his work, Nathan Pritiken demonstrated that reducing dietary fat intake to 10 percent or less of total calories not only would prevent heart disease but would also *cure* it, even in the most severe stages. That we need to lower our fat intake is one of the most necessary and universally supported messages of the day.

Because there are several kinds of fats, it's important to understand their differences and what they mean to you:

Fatty acids are the building blocks of fats in the same sense that amino acids are the building blocks of protein. We *need* fatty acids in our diet.

Essential fatty acids are those that we get from food rather than synthesize in our body. The most important—linoleic acid—is abundant in almonds, tofu, avocados, barley, cashews, garbanzo beans, peanut butter, rice, corn, and so many other common foods. You don't have to worry about essential fatty acids. You get them in your food.

Saturated fats are the most harmful. They are found almost exclusively and highest in animal products and are highest in beef, chicken, pork, and dairy products. Plant sources of saturated fats, primarily coconut oil and palm oil, are contained mostly in processed foods. Saturated fats are solid or semisolid at room temperature. They have been proved to raise blood cholesterol levels and increase your chances of dying of heart disease.

Monounsaturated fats, in extracted form as oils, are liquid at room temperature and tend to thicken slightly under refrigeration. The most popular and highly recommended monounsaturated fat comes from olives, in the form of olive oil. Whole foods such as cashews, peanuts, and avocados also contain monounsaturated fats in reasonable quantities. Monounsaturated fats do *not* raise blood cholesterol, and some research indicates they may lower it.

Polyunsaturated fats are liquid, whether at room temperature or refrigerated. They are found in high concentrations in a wide variety of foods in the plant kingdom, specifically in vegetables. In extracted form in sesame, sunflower, safflower, and other oils from nuts and seeds, these fats were highly touted some years ago for their ability to reduce cholesterol levels. Most researchers no longer believe that's true; rather, the supposed benefits relative to cholesterol reduction are now in doubt. In fact, since these oils are highly refined and the polyunsaturated fats they contain

[1]C. Everett Koop, *New York Times,* July 12, 1988, p. 1.

in extracted form no longer resemble those present in whole foods, researchers feel they should not be consumed in large quantities.

How to Lower Your Fat Intake to Safe Levels, Thereby Reducing Your Risk of Heart Disease and Cancer

1. Be aware that *all animal products are high in saturated fat,* and try to cut back—gradually, if necessary, but consistently.

2. Understand that even when meats are "engineered" to be *lean,* they are still in no way low-fat choices.

3. Increase your intake of fruits, vegetables, and whole grains, which are low-fat choices, containing *zero* saturated fat. Even the "fatty" plant foods such as avocados and raw nuts and seeds are very low in harmful *saturated* fat, containing primarily helpful *monounsaturated* and *polyunsaturated* fat, which are both acceptable in our diets. Do not overeat on these foods, however, since a diet low in fat *of any kind* is ideal.

4. Decrease your intake of refined foods, most of which contain much hidden fat, especially saturated fat.

5. Get your fats and oils naturally, in whole foods such as vegetables, grains, seeds, nuts, and legumes. Avoid trusting any pitch that tells you that an extracted or engineered fat or oil is good, since it is not natural fat eaten as part of a whole food. Use processed fats and other oils *minimally* as condiments or additives that contribute flavoring, moisture, or improved texture.

6. Use only vegetable oils that contain minimal amounts of saturated fat, from peanut oil at approximately 15 percent saturated fat to olive, safflower, corn, soybean, canola, and sunflower oil at 11 percent or less.[1] Keep your intake of vegetable oils at a low level and work continuously to reduce *all* animal products in your diet. *No oil-reduction diet will give you the results you'll achieve from lowering your animal product intake!*

Tips on Vegetable Oil Selection and Use

When you go to the supermarket and stand in front of the oil displays, you may wonder which one to buy. Which is best? Frankly, most of the oils on those shelves are not useful in your diet; and, with the exception of some olive oils, *none* is "good for you," despite advertising claims. All commonly used oils, with the exception of extra-virgin olive oil, have been expelled with heat, (even if they are labeled "cold-pressed"), bleached, and subjected to other de-naturing processes that leave them empty of nutritional benefit. Treat them, therefore, *not* as nutritional additives but as condiments, to be used sparingly.

Cold-pressed extra-virgin olive oil, made from the first pressing of the choicest olives, is the one exception. In Greece and southern Italy, where this oil is consumed in quantity, people have much lower blood cholesterol levels and a much lower rate of heart disease than people elsewhere in Europe and in the United States. A large amount of the fat they consume comes from olive oil.[2]

[1]Chicken fat, lard, and butterfat range from 24 to 100 percent saturated fat.
[2]Tufts University, "Diet and Nutrition Letter," May 1986.

Many recent research studies indicate that the high level of monounsaturated fats in cold-pressed olive oil actually brings down blood cholesterol levels. Remember, however, that this is only true when the oils are cold-pressed, because once they have been heated (tantamount to cooking), they are altered in quality and structure. "Virgin" olive oil of lesser quality is usually the second pressing. "Pure" olive oil is a blend of inferior oils, which is not recommended.

In answer to the question, "Which oils should I use?"

1. Use extra-virgin olive oil for all your salads and on any dish where it will not be heated. It will be beneficial in your diet, since it has a very low ratio of saturated fat and high ratios of monounsaturated and polyunsaturated fats.

2. Substitute sunflower or safflower oil for olive oil in homemade mayonnaise, where a large quantity of oil is required.

3. In cooking, use virgin olive oil except for gourmet dishes, for special meals, or for entertaining, when you may elect to use extra-virgin olive oil throughout.

4. For wok cooking, use sunflower, safflower, or light sesame oil—all of which are relatively stable at high temperatures. Use a touch of roasted sesame oil (sometimes called oriental sesame oil) in wok cooking for flavor.

5. Use extra-virgin olive oil as a substitute for butter on potatoes, grains, vegetables, and even toast.

6. For baking, use sunflower, safflower, or corn oil. Use pure soy margarine occasionally when a buttery texture is required. All these oils contain less saturated fat than butter and no cholesterol whatsoever.

7. If you are deep-fat frying, be aware that oils kept at 215° C for fifteen minutes or more consistently have produced atherosclerosis in laboratory animals.[1] What does that tell you about commercial french fries, potato chips, doughnuts, and the like? If you must deep-fry, cook very small quantities quickly and drain them well. My solution is to avoid deep-frying entirely. It's simply not good for us. The choice of oils is not going to make that much difference; it's the process that's the killer.

8. When pan-frying or sautéing, avoid heat breakdown of oil by placing the food in the pan before adding the oil, then heat them together. Use less oil rather than more. A teaspoon of oil will go a long way with today's nonstick cookware. Many chefs use a little vegetable broth instead of oil for sautéing, which also works well.

9. To ensure freshness, prepare oil-based salad dressings just before using instead of making a large quantity and storing it. (See page 122 for Two-Minute Dressings you'll love.)

10. Always refrigerate a product that contains oil after it has been prepared.

Remember, oils are sensitive to heat and light and become rancid quickly:

1. Buy all oils in small rather than large bottles for freshness.

2. Store olive oil in a dark place, not in the refrigerator where it will become cloudy.

3. Store all other oils in the refrigerator after opening to prevent rancidity—and keep them cold! Measure out the amount of oil you need and return the remainder to the refrigerator immediately.

[1]Erasmus, *Fats and Oils,* p. 117.

Margarine or Butter?

In previous books, I have recommended butter over margarine, since butter is a less synthetic food than most margarines. However, since that time I have discovered pure soy margarines, made from soy oil, soy beans, lecithin, and carotene with a minimum of hydrogenated oil, which respond in the way butter does in baking recipes and have the advantage of being lower in saturated fat than butter is and totally devoid of cholesterol. I do not recommend regular or continuous use of margarine as a butter substitute; olive oil makes a far healthier replacement. Pure soy margarine can, however, be helpful for those who need to reduce cholesterol. In some dishes, many will feel that only butter will do. I know, because even now I still have those feelings. It is a very personal choice that you can make for yourself. All options are indicated, where appropriate, in the recipes.

THE IMPORTANCE OF PROTEIN

> **Think of the fierce energy concentrated in an acorn! You bury it in the ground, and it explodes into a great oak. Bury a sheep, and nothing happens but decay.**
>
> **—George Bernard Shaw**

In school, we were all taught the importance of getting our protein at every meal. We learned about the basic four food groups: meat, dairy, grains, fruits, and vegetables. (In fact, originally there were *twelve* food groups rather than four, giving us a much broader range of choices in healthful meal planning.) As trusting children and adults, we absorbed these teachings, never considering that they might be less directly connected to health education than to industry profits. Why, after all, would we question? The information came via our trusted teachers and professors, and the presentation did not seem to be advertising propaganda. It was couched in some pretty official terms. But now we learn that food industries are the *foremost suppliers* of "nutritional education" materials to classrooms in the United States and that most teachers, although they believe what they are teaching, are merely used to relay information on nutrition that will sell products. What products, specifically? With *two* out of four supposed food groups being meat and dairy (suggesting that it is healthful for our diet to contain at least 50 percent of those two foods), it's not hard to guess what products are being sold.

Well, we all bought the concept, and we lived for decades with the idea that protein deficiencies were likely if we didn't eat some meat and dairy every day, at every meal. People who leaned toward other foods—grains, legumes, vegetables, or fruits—because they liked them better or because they felt better when they ate them were criticized by well-meaning family members, friends, nutritionists, and doctors who insisted that protein deficiency was inevitable. Even those who cut back on meat and dairy products as recently as the late sixties and early seventies worried that they were not getting enough protein—so complete was the indoctrination. (I know, because I was one of those people.)

In fact, by honoring as nutritional guidelines the pretty charts that told us what industry wanted us to hear, our population has overconsumed on meat and dairy to the point where *the average American male has an over 50 percent risk of dying of atherosclerosis* (clogging of the arteries with the cholesterol and saturated fat from meat and dairy consumption). In addition, we have the added risk of developing several types of cancer, diabetes, high blood pressure, stroke, and obesity.[1]

Let's not make the same mistake again. If we're going to talk about protein, let's turn to recent unbiased scientific research to get a clearer understanding of our protein needs, not to the industries that produce protein. The information in this section on our protein needs has been taken from studies by individuals and organizations who have *no product to sell.*

How Much Protein Do We Need

First let's consider how much protein we actually need. Not all authorities agree on a precise figure. Scientific estimates differ, but the range is calculated to be from 2½ to a little over 8 percent of our total daily caloric intake:

1. Reports in the *American Journal of Clinical Nutrition* estimate that we need 2½ percent of our daily calories from protein. "Many populations have, in fact, lived in excellent health on this amount."[2]

2. The World Health Organization sets protein requirements at 4½ percent of caloric intake per day for men, with similar requirements for women.[3]

3. The Food and Nutrition Board of the National Academy of Sciences gives a 4½ percent figure as a minimum daily requirement and then adds 30 percent for "safety." This basic figure of slightly less than 6 percent meets the needs of 98 percent of the U.S. population.[4]

4. The National Research Council also figures a safety margin and cites a figure of 8 percent of our daily calories needing to come from protein. This, again, is not a minimum daily requirement, but it is recommended as more than adequate for 98 percent of the population.[5]

Some in the scientific community are concerned about these "safety" allowances. When asked who *needs* the extra allowances, Dr. David Reuben replied:

> **The people who sell meat, fish, cheese, eggs, chicken and all the other high prestige and expensive sources of protein. Raising the amount of protein you eat raises their income by 30%. It also increases the amount of protein in the sewers and septic tanks of your neighborhood 30% as you merrily urinate away everything that you can't use that very day. It also deprives the starving children of the world of the protein that would save their lives. Incidentally, it makes you pay 30% of your already bloated food bill for protein that you will never use. If you are an average American family, it will cost you about $40 a month to unnecessarily pump up your protein intake. That puts another $36 billion a year into the pockets of the protein producers.**[6]

[1]C. Everett Koop, *Los Angeles Times,* July 28, 1988, p. 1.
[2]D. Hegsted, "Minimum Protein Requirements of Adults," *American Journal of Clinical Nutrition,* 21 (1968), p. 3250.
[3]"Protein Requirements," Food and Agricultural Organization, World Health Organization Expert Group, United Nations Conference, Rome, 1965.
[4]Food and Nutrition Board, "Vegetarian Diets," Washington, D.C., National Academy of Sciences, 1974.
[5]National Research Council, *Recommended Dietary Allowances,* 9th ed. (Washington, D.C.: National Academy of Sciences, 1980), p. 46.
[6]David Reuben, *Everything You've Always Wanted to Know About Nutrition* (New York: Avon Books, 1978), pp. 154–55.

And it will bring you 30 percent closer to atherosclerosis.

Individual needs differ as well. Roger Williams, a biochemist and nutrient researcher, sums it up in his suggestion that the range of protein needs among people may vary as much as fourfold![1] Note, however, how *low* these protein figures actually are. Think of how much meat and dairy people are eating and then realize how little 2½ to 8 percent of that total caloric intake really is.

Let's turn to nature as a source of enlightenment on this issue.

- When in your life do you grow most? In infancy we double our birth weight in six months. Never again in our lives do we do that.
- What food is created for us by Nature at birth? Mother's milk.
- Since protein is what is used to *build* our bodies, doesn't it make sense that, at the time of most rapid growth, we would need the most protein? Yes!
- How much protein is contained in mother's milk? Approximately 3 percent.
- What is Nature then telling us? Little babies, whose bodies are growing the fastest they will ever grow, and whose protein needs are therefore at maximum, do best at the very modest level of approximately 3 percent.

Where *Do* We Get Our Protein?

That question comes up all the time. Let's face it. We're brainwashed. Even when people accept that we have overconsumed protein for years, which has made a lot of us very sick, and even when they realize that we are still doing it—even when they hear from the most prestigious sources that all the protein we need in a day is between 2½ and 8 percent of the calories we take in—they'll still ask, "But where do you get your protein?"

The animal-products industry has succeeded beyond its wildest dreams. This entire population (with the exception of a few thousand people, I would imagine) absolutely *believes* that the only foods that give us protein are meat, eggs, and dairy. What an incredible propaganda coup!

Do you know how thoroughly brainwashed we are? Let me give you an example. I recently went to an excellent medical doctor for a checkup. This man has been a vegetarian for fourteen years. He's quite knowledgeable, and I consider him a very good practitioner. What do you think was one of the first questions he asked me? You guessed it. "Where do you get your protein, Marilyn?"

I couldn't *believe* it. Even he suffers from the same knee-jerk protein reflex that afflicts the rest of the population. And I didn't call him on it, but proceeded to answer him as if it were a legitimate question. I've got the knee-jerk protein reflex, too!

How to Get Rid of the Knee-Jerk Protein Reflex

We must learn some new data, that's how. Even if we find our protein needs to be at the very top of the spectrum, a full 8+ percent, not for one minute do we have to worry about filling those needs. Since we've only heard for decades that protein is found exclusively in animal products,

[1]R. J. Williams, "We Abnormal Normals," *Nutrition Today,* 2 (1967), 19–28.

it's difficult for many people to grasp that it exists in abundance in so many other foods. For example, in computing the percentage of calories coming from protein in common plant foods, we find:

spinach	49% protein
broccoli	45% protein
lettuce	34% protein
cabbage	22% protein
potatoes	11% protein
strawberries, oranges, cherries, apricots, watermelon, grapes	8% protein
wheat germ	31% protein
oatmeal	15% protein
tofu	43% protein
lentils	29% protein

Far more than 2½ to 8 percent of your daily calories is *automatically* protein. It's in everything you eat from the plant kingdom. You get it in spite of yourself, without trying. The issue is not how we get enough, but rather, how we avoid getting too much! The problem arises when your protein comes from animal sources (meat, chicken, fish, eggs, and dairy products), because they provide a dangerous side order of saturated fat and cholesterol—which *everybody* (except, of course, the industries that produce animal protein) is telling you to stop eating.

The chart on page 15 from the *U.S. Department of Agriculture Handbook No. 456* shows how many of the foods you eat contain *at least* the 8 percent allowance and usually much more.

How Are Fish and Chicken Different from Beef?

Many people, including dietitians and doctors, claim that fish and chicken are to be preferred over red meat, such as beef, pork, and lamb, because fish and chicken contain less saturated fat than do red meats, and fish and chicken contain more polyunsaturated fat. Polyunsaturated fats, in the opinion of some researchers, tend to lower blood cholesterol; as a matter of fact, saturated fats raise cholesterol about twice as much as polyunsaturated fats lower it.[1]

Here, however, is where many people who favor the fish and chicken advice err. Chicken and fish contain *cholesterol*, and the higher cholesterol content cancels out the effect of lower saturated fat. The end result is the same rise in blood cholesterol that you get from red meat.[2] In this case, it is not the saturated fat that pushes up your cholesterol; it is the *added dietary cholesterol* in the food that causes it to rise.

SIGNIFICANT NEW FINDINGS ON CALORIE COUNTING

For well over a decade we've been attempting to press home the point that calories, in and of themselves, do not make people fat. *Fats* make people fat. After all, a calorie is nothing more than a degree of heat, and heat does not make you fat. It is most encouraging for us to now get some support on this issue from the scientific community.

[1]John McDougall, *McDougall's Medicine* (Piscataway, N.J.: New Century, 1985), p. 109.
[2]Ibid., p. 129.

PERCENTAGE OF CALORIES FROM PROTEIN

LEGUMES

Soybean sprouts	54%
Mungbean sprouts	43%
Soybean curd (tofu)	43%
Soy flour	35%
Soybeans	35%
Soy sauce	33%
Broad beans	32%
Lentils	29%
Split peas	28%
Kidney beans	26%
Navy beans	26%
Lima beans	26%
Garbanzo beans	23%

VEGETABLES

Spinach	49%
New Zealand spinach	47%
Watercress	46%
Kale	45%
Broccoli	45%
Brussels sprouts	44%
Turnip greens	43%
Collards	43%
Cauliflower	40%
Mustard greens	39%
Mushrooms	38%
Chinese cabbage	34%
Parsley	34%
Lettuce	34%
Green peas	30%
Zucchini	28%
Green beans	26%
Cucumbers	24%
Dandelion greens	24%
Green pepper	22%
Artichokes	22%
Cabbage	22%
Celery	21%
Eggplant	21%
Tomatoes	18%
Onions	16%
Beets	15%
Pumpkin	12%
Potatoes	11%
Yams	8%
Sweet potatoes	6%

GRAINS

Wheat germ	31%
Rye	20%
Wheat, hard red	17%
Wild rice	16%
Buckwheat	15%
Oatmeal	15%
Millet	12%
Barley	11%
Brown Rice	8%

FRUITS

Lemons	16%
Honeydew melon	10%
Cantaloupe	9%
Strawberry	8%
Orange	8%
Blackberry	8%
Cherry	8%
Apricot	8%
Grape	8%
Watermelon	8%
Tangerine	7%
Papaya	6%
Peach	6%
Pear	5%
Banana	5%
Grapefruit	5%
Pineapple	3%
Apple	1%

NUTS AND SEEDS

Pumpkin seeds	21%
Peanuts	18%
Sunflower seeds	17%
Walnuts, black	13%
Sesame seeds	13%
Almonds	12%
Cashews	12%
Filberts	8%

Data obtained from Nutritive Value of American Foods in Common Units, U.S.D.A. Agriculture Handbook No. 456

Reprinted from John Robbins, *Diet for a New America* (Walpole, N.H.: Stillpoint Publishing, 1986), p. 177 (by permission of the author).

FIBER CONTENT OF COMMON FOODS

FOOD ITEM	FIBER (g/kg)	FOOD ITEM	FIBER (g/kg)
Blueberries	15.2	Ground Beef	0
Brussels Sprouts	13.5	Sirloin Steak	0
Oat Flakes	13.5	Lamb Chops	0
Pumpkin	12.0	Pork Chops	0
Cooked Carrot	9.6	Chicken	0
Brown Rice	8.1	Ocean Perch	0
Swiss Chard	6.8	Salmon	0
Lettuce	6.3	Cheddar Cheese	0
Cucumber	5.7	Whole Milk	0
Applesauce	5.3	Eggs	0

Source: Nutritional Almanac (Revised), Nutritional Research, Inc., John D. Kirshmann, McGraw Hill Book Co., New York, 1979.

Reprinted from John Robbins, *Diet for a New America* (Walpole, N.H.: Stillpoint Publishing, 1986), p. 257 (by permission of the author).

Studies at the Stanford Center for Research in Disease Prevention and the Harvard Medical School both indicate that there was *no link at all* between the number of calories eaten and amount of body fat. Our "data suggests that dietary fat can be a contributor to obesity, independent of its calories."[1] In other words, if your calories come from foods high in fat, you have a greater possibility of becoming fat than if your calories come from foods low in fat.

WHOLEFOODS VS. REFINED

So much that we hear about nutrition these days emphasizes the necessity for whole food. After decades of consuming the most highly refined food products, as a nation we are learning that we need *all* of what food provides, not just the fragmented remains. We have been shown that, if a food is processed, every part of it should be available for the consumer. For example, when apple juice is pressed, the pressings, which are predominantly fiber, could be dried and ground to produce "apple fiber," which could then be utilized in "apple crackers" to be eaten with the juice. In processing of most of the foods commonly eaten, however, industry discards the important elements, including fibers, or uses them in animal feeds; the animals are getting the better end of the deal as we dine on empty foods.

[1]*American Journal of Clinical Nutrition,* 47 (1988), pp. 406, 995.

The *wholefood concept* is at the heart and soul of the natural food industry, where currently products of the highest quality, highest purity, and greatest nutritional integrity are being created using only wholefood ingredients. Until the giant food manufacturers measure up to this level of production, it is incumbent on us to be active, outspoken consumers of superior natural food products.

At present only a small percentage of foods in supermarkets is made from unrefined ingredients. This is because the food giants have not yet fully understood how serious American consumers are about wholefood products. They still think we don't *really* care. But they're mistaken! As more and more supermarkets experience the attrition in sales while consumers increasingly patronize natural foods stores all over the nation, the food giants—via their customers, the supermarkets—are getting the word. Supermarkets are bound to be feeling the effects of competition from natural foods stores since, in major population centers throughout the country, there are growing numbers of full-on "natural foods" supermarkets, bustling with sophisticated and enthusiastic shoppers more than willing to spend their dollars on food of the highest quality.

Clearly, the food giants are facing a challenge, but they are not to be blamed entirely if their products do not meet our present demands. Over the past 100 years, they have found willing consumers for practically anything they have produced. They have spent the better part of a century overcoming spoilage of *natural ingredients* by the addition of preservatives and chemicals, by coloring and overprocessing wholefoods and discarding that which we now know is essential. They have done so, you must realize, to *please* the consumer who, until recently, always demanded the prettiest, sweetest, most palate-stimulating convenience food. In fact, since most people have made their food choices based on marketing hype, slick packaging, prizes, and coupons, why

For Fiber, Eat Fruits and Vegetables

According to *Science News*, December 3, 1988 (Volume 134, no. 23):

In the past, studies have linked diets high in fiber with a reduced risk of colon cancer—a cancer whose incidence in the United States trails only that of lung and breast. But dietary fiber comes in many forms. While many breakfast cereal makers have extolled the potential anti-cancer benefits their products' fiber may offer, a new study now suggests that it's fruit and vegetables—not grains—that offer the most beneficial fiber.

In terms of actual food, decreased colon-cancer risk was most strongly associated with men eating diets high in fruit, and with women eating many vegetables, according to a report of the study in the Nov. 16th *Journal of the National Cancer Institute.* Somewhat unexpectedly, notes epidemiologist Martha L. Slattery, who headed this study at the University of Utah School of Medicine in Salt Lake City, neither group experienced any apparent protective effect from eating grains.

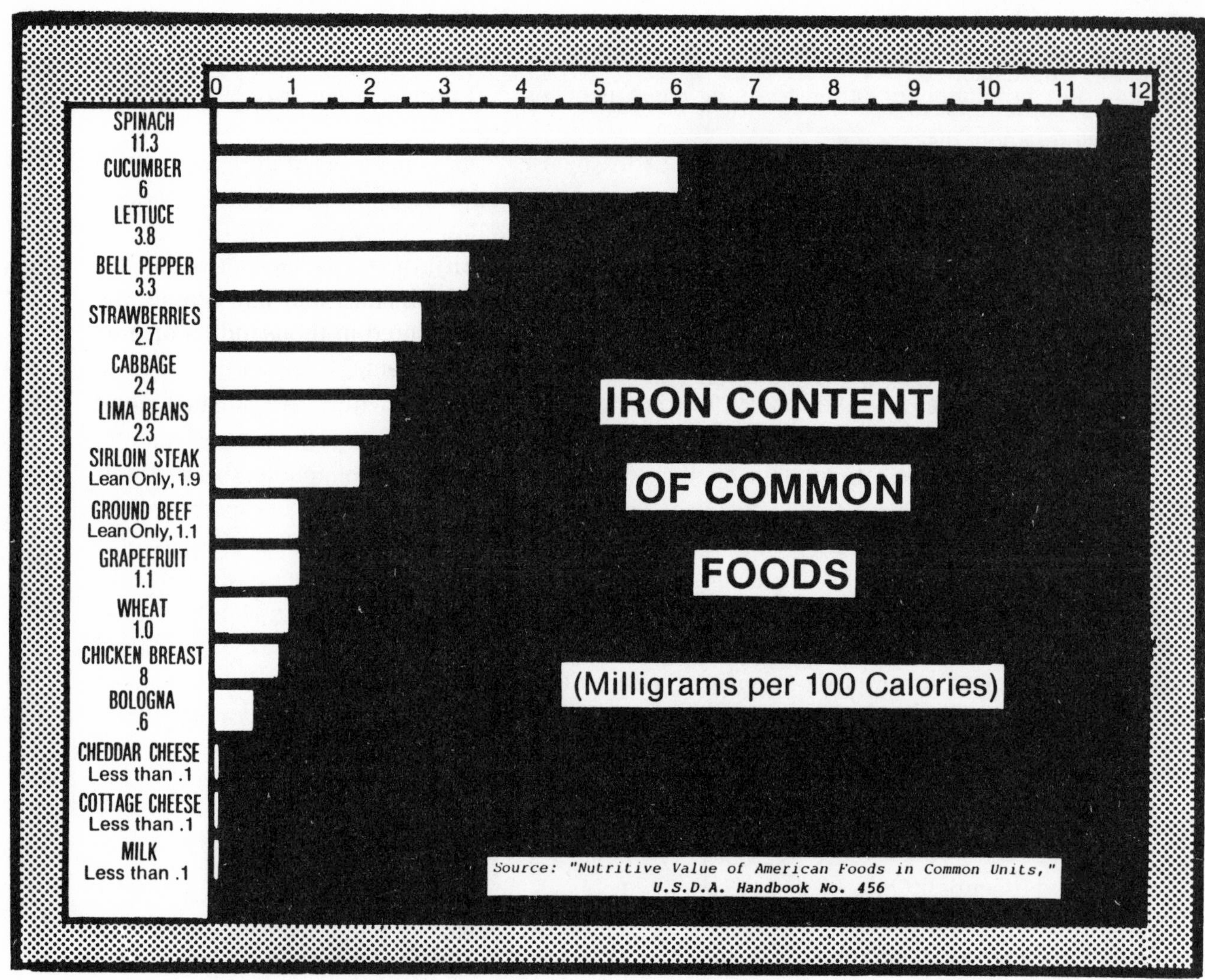

Reprinted from John Robbins, *Diet for a New America* (Walpole, N.H.: Stillpoint Publishing, 1986), p. 165 (by permission of the author).

shouldn't the food giants think they will continue to do so? Industry may be banking on past experience, holding out to discover if this trend toward wholesomeness warrants their acknowledgement. They must be made to understand: we are *serious!* And we will only buy what meets our *standards!* We are the economic force that can bring about revolutionary change in the food industry!

The largest food manufacturing companies control 100 percent of the shelf space in most supermarkets. You can communicate with them through your supermarket manager. Be vocal about what products you would like to see on the shelves. Avoid purchasing products that contain refined ingredients, and let the manager know you are doing so. The message will get to the food giants that your needs are significant, and they can and *will* respond!

Good News!

At the time of writing this book, we find that many of the largest supermarket chains are responding enthusiastically to creating wholefood departments in their stores. At the same time, major food manufacturers are in discussion with representatives of the wholefood movement, so as to develop widely distributed wholefood products for the American consumer.

THE DEBATE OVER VITAMIN B_{12}

For the last few years, as vegetarianism has grown in popularity, there has been a continuing, unresolved debate over vitamin B_{12}. There is total agreement on both sides that our vitamin B_{12} requirement is surprisingly small. Whereas other nutrients are measured in thousandths or millionths of grams required, vitamin B_{12} is measured in *billionths* of a gram.

One side of the debate says you can get B_{12} only from animal products; the other side maintains that the tiny amount of B_{12} required is produced by bacteria in the mouth and intestines, as with all other mammals. They also explain that the vitamin is additionally available in the required infinitesimal amounts from the plant kingdom, specifically from microscopic particles of soil clinging to home-grown vegetables and from the fermentation that occurs in preparing certain soy products.

In its "Technical Support Paper on Vegetarianism," the American Dietetic Association stated that deficiencies may be due more to the difficulty of *assimilating* vitamin B_{12} than to its lack of availability in the diet. In *Vegan Nutrition: Pure and Simple,*[1] Dr. Michael Klaper writes, "Most of the concerns over vitamin B_{12} adequacy in the vegan diet [those eating no animal products whatsoever] seem to be more theoretical than real, and most vegan people seem to grow and function very well without ever taking a vitamin B_{12} supplement." Dr. Klaper is a vegan medical doctor who has been treating vegans for over a decade. His recommendation is that "because vitamin B_{12} deficiency, *though unlikely,* can be serious, and because the measures to prevent it are simple and essentially risk-free, all people using the vegan nutritional approach should ensure that they ingest a reliable source of vitamin B_{12} at least three times weekly." He cites as reliable sources B_{12}-fortified foods such as breakfast cereals, breads, pastas, soy milks, soy meat "analogs," and texturized vegetable protein (TVP). Other specialists recommend adding fermented soy products to the list, as well as homegrown vegetables whenever available. They also maintain that fresh sprouts or microalgae such as spirulina, blue green algae, or chlorella supply vitamin B_{12}. (These are wholefood supplements available in health food stores.) If a person worries about vitamin B_{12} and wishes to be sure this nutrient is present in his or her diet, Dr. Klaper recommends that a vitamin B_{12} supplement, from vegetable sources and averaging 25 micrograms, be taken once a week. For children, tablets (in crushed form) or powders can be added to gravies, soy milk, fruit juices, or smoothies.

These are the more conservative, precautionary measures I present. In my opinion, the research has up until now focused too heavily on animal sources of Vitamin B_{12}, as has been the case with many other nutrients we were once told we could not get from the plant kingdom (protein, for example). What is necessary is further research on plant sources after which the Vitamin B_{12} issue will very quickly become a non-issue. Concerns over this nutrient will be laid to rest, just as worries over adequate sources of protein and calcium from the plant kingdom have been laid to rest.

[1]Michael Klaper, M.D., *Vegan Nutrition* (Umatilla, Fla.: Gentle World, Inc. 1987).

WHY I USE GROUND ROCK SALT WHENEVER I USE SALT...

I take into consideration this passage from *Fresh Fruit and Vegetable Juices* written by one of my mentors, Dr. N. W. Walker, when he was over 100 years old. Success leaves clues!

> **Regular table salt is composed of insoluble inorganic elements.... In the commercial production of TABLE SALT, extremely high temperatures are used running around 1500°F to solidify the salt with additives and adulterants to coat the salt crystals to cause [them] to pour readily under nearly all conditions. Such salt is not completely water soluble....**
>
> **To overcome this handicap, whenever we use salt, we use ROCK SALT, the pure rock salt used in water purifiers. Rock salt is obtained from soil sodium rock formations and is not subjected to heat. This salt we have found to be soluble in water and its use, in moderation, of course, is found to be compatible and satisfactory. In order to use it we grind it to the fineness we desire.... Such rock salt is a natural catalyst which the enzymes in the body can cause to be utilized constructively.**
>
> **Rock salt will usually be found to contain the following elements:**

Sodium chloride	**90–95%**
Calcium sulphate	**.05–1%**
Magnesium sulphate	**.05–1%**
Magnesium chloride	**.05–1%**

> **The "regular Table Salt" is likely to contain in addition to the above elements in quite different proportions:**

Potassium chloride	**Sodium sulphate**
Potassium sulphate	**Barium chloride**
Magnesium bromide	**Strontium chloride**
Calcium chloride	

> **Most of these elements tend to inhibit the dissolving of the salt in water.**[1]

Since table salt, with all the additives it contains, is insoluble in water, it also settles out in the bloodstream and hardens the arteries.

[1]N. W. Walker, *Fresh Vegetable and Fruit Juices* (Phoenix, Ariz.: Norwalk Press, 1978), pp. 48, 49.

PESTICIDES: PRODUCE VS. ANIMAL PRODUCTS

We hear much about pesticides on fruits and vegetables, and it is absolutely true that, in whatever concentration they are found on our produce, that amount is too much. However, most people would be shocked to learn that less than 10 percent of the pesticides ingested in our country come from produce. Over 90 percent are found in animal products. How is that possible?

Produce is treated with pesticides a set number of times during its growth. Factory farm animals, however, are fed regularly and repeatedly pesticide-laden crops. The pesticides in animal feeds are administered every day for the life of the animal and are absorbed into its tissues and stored there. For example, a large fish will accumulate in its flesh the total amount of pesticides or toxins stored in the flesh of the thousands of smaller fish it has eaten. And each of those smaller fish will have collected in its tissues all the pesticides ingested by thousands of even smaller fish that they have eaten.

In the same way, factory farm animals (cows, chickens, and pigs) retain in their flesh all the pesticides they have ever absorbed from their feed. They build up extremely high levels of chemical pesticides and toxins because their food consists exclusively of pesticide-laden fish meal and feed grown on lands sprayed repeatedly with many more dangerous chemicals. In addition, to combat disease, factory farm animals are dipped and sprayed with extremely toxic compounds and are fed massive doses of toxic drugs never given to animals raised naturally, in levels that are undoubtedly dangerous for humans.

All of these poisons are retained in the flesh and fat of the animals you eat. When you eat these animals or the milk products they produce, you are consuming concentrated doses in uncontrolled combinations of many of the most deadly chemicals ever known.

The *Pesticides Monitoring Journal,* published by the Environmental Protection Agency, reports numerous studies that confirm that *"foods of animal origin (are) the major source of... pesticide residues in the diet."*[1] Recent studies indicate that at least 90 percent and as much as 99 percent of all residues from pesticides and other toxic chemicals come from meat, fish, eggs, and dairy products,[2] with less than 10 percent coming from fruits, vegetables, and grains.

If it's pesticides you are worried about in your diet, know that the greatest concentrations are to be found in animal products. The valid desire to reduce the amount of deadly chemicals you are ingesting is just one more good reason to reduce your intake of animal products (see table on page 24).

[1]R. Duggan, "Dietary Intake of Pesticide Chemicals in the United States, June 1966–April 1968," *Pesticides Monitoring Journal,* 2 (1969), pp. 140–52.
[2]S. Harris, "Organochlorine Contamination of Breast Milk," *Environmental Defense Fund,* November 7, 1979.

ORGANIC PRODUCE IS A BARGAIN

The price of organically grown food reflects the true cost of raising food—what it costs for a farmer simply to make a living. This current U.S. farm crisis, with 35 to 40 percent of all family farms in foreclosure, is a symptom of our unrealistic agricultural economy. The payments farmers receive for their crops are not enough to cover the cost of farming. These payments have not changed much in the last fifteen years, while costs have increased as much as four or five times. Oil, gasoline, agricultural chemicals, food, energy, and real estate prices as well as interest rates have all skyrocketed, while farmers still get the same range of prices for their products! Often, the grower sells the product at a loss.

When we buy lettuce, the grower may receive $2.50 to $3 for twenty-four heads. The labor to pick and pack a box of twenty-four heads is, say, $1.50 and the box itself costs $1.25. What the farmer gets paid may scarcely cover the picking and packing costs, while costs for planting, cultivation, fertilization, weed, pest, and disease control, machinery upkeep, fuel, seed, and irrigation are not covered at all. No wonder the farmer's reward is foreclosure.[1]

The prices for organic food are fair in terms of giving the farmer a chance to make a living. Organic food practices, in other words, are not only sustainable agriculturally but also economically. The price we pay for organic food allows the farmer to put more back into the soil, rather than using the fastest and cheapest "fertilizers" (which do the opposite of making the land fertile). The organic matter used by organic growers brings fertility back to the soil, which had been neglected by conventional farmers. While the rise of pesticides and synthetic fertilizers has increased *tenfold* in the last forty years, crop losses to insects have *doubled.* Organic methods, on the other hand, build up the soil, creating stronger, more disease-resistant plants.

That seems fair to me! What good does it do any of us if farming techniques turn our once-vital farmlands to empty desert? Given the price of soil abuse and the price of commercial produce anywhere else in the world, organic food in America is an *incredible bargain.*

On March 20, 1989, the *Los Angeles Times* carried this story:

> **An overwhelming majority of Americans say they would buy organically grown food if it cost the same as fruits and vegetables treated with pesticides or synthetic fertilizers and nearly half would pay more, according to a new survey. The strong preference for chemical-free fruits and vegetables showed up in a survey conducted even before the recent scare over poisoned grapes from Chile and apples treated with Alar. The Louis Harris Poll conducted for *Organic Gardening* magazine found that 84.2% of those surveyed would choose organically grown food if given the choice, and 49% said they would pay more for organic food.**

[1]"Organic Advocate," *Albert's Organics*, 1 (December 1988), p. 4.

When we request and buy organic produce we are lending our support to the replenishing of the lands that yield our food. Why would anyone want those lands to be depleted? Organic produce is not only safe and pesticide-free, but also an investment in our future.

FOOD IRRADIATION

According to a study conducted by the National Institute of Nutrition at the Medical Research Center in Hyderabad, India, children fed freshly irradiated wheat developed polyploidy, a defect in the chromosomes of the blood cells. Once the children were taken off the irradiated wheat diet, their blood patterns returned to normal. Polyploidy, frequently seen in cancerous tumor cells, is a significant health issue.[1]

No discussion of pesticides would be complete without some comments on food irradiation. It is clear that treating foods with chemicals hasn't reaped rewards for anyone but the chemical manufacturers. The sanctity of our land, the integrity of our food, and our inalienable right to health have all been undermined by this regrettable tactic. Undoing the damage will require initiative, perseverance, and massive public support.

Having experienced the damage chemicals have caused in food production, let us be on guard against new solutions to make chemical farming obsolete. After World War II, the chemical industry needed to find new markets for its chemicals, and so it expanded into food production. Many people were up in arms. How will these chemicals affect our health? What will they do to the land and to the other creatures who share it with us? After run-off, what will happen to the oceans, lakes, and rivers? These people were branded alarmists by the chemical industry. They were standing in the way of "progress." Progress? *Profits* would be the more appropriate word.

We appear to be at the brink of that scenario again, only this time we are playing with even more dangerous substances. One of the ways to lower the amounts of chemicals in foods according to the nuclear power industry, the U.S. Department of Agriculture, and the Department of Energy is to irradiate our food. Proponents say that bombarding our food with large doses of gamma rays will prolong its shelf life; inhibit sprouting in vegetables; delay the ripening of fruits; kill insects and pests in vegetables, fruits, and grains; eliminate parasites in pork; and reduce bacteria in meat and seafood.

Should we ignore the research—plenty of it, all over the world—that tells us that irradiated food causes dangerous changes in human physiology? In 413 studies reviewed by the U.S. Food and Drug Administration, only *five* supported radiation technology. Others found links to cancer, lower birth weights, kidney disease, and changes in white blood cells and chromosomes.

[1]Press release for *Food Irradiation: Who Wants It?* by Tony Webb, Tim Lang, and Kathleen Tucker (Rochester, Vt: Healing Arts, 1987).

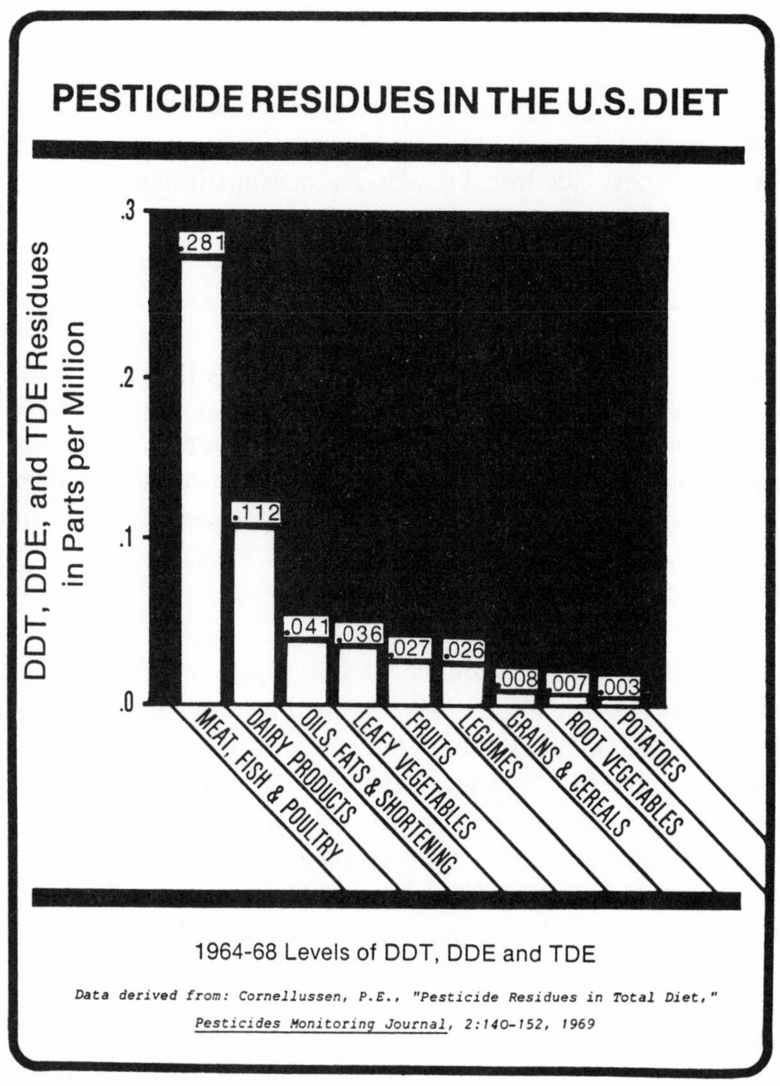

Reprinted from John Robbins, *Diet for a New America* (Walpole, N.H.: Stillpoint Publishing, 1986), p. 317 (by permission of the author).

Should we ignore the fact that it does *not* eliminate pesticides? Should we ignore that killing of bacteria does not remove the toxins made by that bacteria, which results in increased aflatoxins in the food? (Aflatoxins are powerful agents that cause liver cancer.) Should we ignore that irradiated food contains "free radicals," which form new and dangerous chemical compounds in the food? Some of these are benzene, hydrogen peroxide, and formaldehyde! Neither the presence of these new chemicals nor their ramifications has been adequately tested.

And are we to disregard the vast body of scientific literature that assures us food irradiation destroys up to 80 percent of vitamins A, B, C, D, and K, while vitamin E is almost completely destroyed? These losses are sustained *in addition to* other cooking and storage losses.

Who Wants It?

Now—at the early stages of inception, before food irradiation is in place and the reasons why are lost forever in history—it is imperative to know why, in spite of all the health warnings, there is such an effort to force this technology upon our food and our population. First, understand what it means. When you receive a standard chest X-ray, you get a fraction of 1 rad of radiation. The F.D.A. permits food irradiation in doses as high as 100,000 rads! Food irradiation plants are powered by Cobalt 60 and Cesium 137. These are nuclear wastes. The true motivation behind food irradiation, in the opinion of many who have thoroughly studied the issue, is the need by the Department of Energy to develop a waste-management program for nuclear wastes! Disposal of radioactive Cesium 137, a by-product of nuclear technology, presents a particularly sticky problem. The large quantities produced for the Department of Energy take thirty years to decay. It is this Cesium 137 that the Energy Department is most eager to find a commercial use for. As part of its waste-management program, the Department of Energy is preparing to finance six irradiation demonstration plants (at a cost of $10 million). This is a developmental scenario similar to the dumping of chemicals in our food. When World War II ended, the chemical companies needed a place to dump their chemicals to keep profits high, and that place ended up being our food supply. Now the Department of Energy wants us to "eat" its waste. What next?

Here are the questions we need to ask:

1. Who wants food irradiation?

2. Why do they want it?

3. Could it be that the whole program to promote food irradiation is nothing more than a thinly disguised attempt to find a commercial use for radioactive waste?

The FDA has, so far, approved irradiation for pork, fruit, spices, and vegetables. Presently, the U.S. Department of Agriculture and the Department of Energy defend food irradiation. They are funding new irradiation plants in California, Hawaii, Iowa, Oklahoma, and Washington. Meanwhile, consumer rights and freedom of choice are quietly being circumvented, manipulated, and ignored. *There is no test that shows whether a food has been irradiated. There is no test to show what dose a food has received or how many times it has been irradiated. Nor is there adequate labeling so that we can tell which foods have been irradiated, and boycott them if we so choose.* Irradiated foods *look* fresh longer, so consumers will be fooled into perceiving them as healthy and wholesome. In reality, they are older and more depleted of nutrients.

Because of improved "cosmetic" effect and longer shelf life, many giant food manufacturers are solidly behind food irradiation which enables them to sell more old food. Thus, the "Coalition for Food Irradiation" includes some of the world's leading food manufacturers!

Before this technology is in place, we have a choice. Many experts predict that at least 40 percent of our food will be irradiated by the year 2000. We must exert the power to abort this idiotic, cynical, and malevolent campaign against our health NOW.

Knowledge Is Power

Contact the citizens' nonprofit organization:

Food and Water
225 Lafayette St. Suite 612
New York, N.Y. 10012
(212) 941-9341

2

The Fit for Life *Kitchen*

SIGNIFICANT boost to your cooking can come from a well-set-up kitchen. With this in mind, I list for you the components of the *Fit for Life* kitchen. Even the simplest of tools or cookware materials can decidedly affect your efficiency in the kitchen, as well as your health.

MACHINES AND APPLIANCES

The tools you use in cooking are very personal, and frequently it takes time, substantial investment, and trial and error to find those that most suit your needs. From my own experience I can recommend many of the kitchen tools and appliances by Braun[1] as practical, well-designed, and effective. These include their convenient hand blenders, juicers, citrus juice squeezers, juice extractors, food processors, grinders, and kitchen scale.

Essential Equipment

Hand blender. A convenient alternative to a traditional blender, the Braun unit has as its basic function a high-speed capacity for thoroughly blending fruit drinks, cream soups, salad dressings, and some sauces. The Braun hand blender also comes with a mincer-chopper attachment.

Blender. The larger stand-up models with multi-speed capacity can handle greater quantities and the intense whipping required for nut milks, but they do take more time to clean.

Juicer. Making your own fresh fruit and vegetable juices is a major plus for your health. With your Braun juice extractor, you can make exotic juice blends not readily available in the market, such as melon juice nectars and vegetable juice cocktails.

Citrus juice squeezer. Citrus juices can always be squeezed by hand, but electric citrus juicers make the process faster and are more efficient.

[1]See Mail Order Directory, page 405.

Range and oven. Gas ranges permit quicker and more finely tuned temperature changes; electric stoves are less toxic. If your oven sweats, does not heat uniformly, or the temperature gauge is inaccurate, have it repaired. Does 350°F on the knob really mean 350°F within? Test with an oven thermometer if you have any doubts.

If you use a microwave oven, be aware that such ovens pose hidden dangers, since they have the potential to leak harmful radiation. Make sure yours has no cracks, scratches, or chips on the interior surface and that the door seals are in good shape. Test your microwave *regularly* with a microwave leakage detector. Call for service if there is even the slightest indication of leakage. At present there are over 100 research studies ongoing, funded by the U.S. government, on the safety of microwave radiation. The question we ought to be asking is, if microwaves are safe enough to warrant the vast popularity they have achieved, why is so much research still going on? Were they adequately tested prior to marketing and distribution? Do we, unknowingly, want to be part of the test?

Toaster. Since we recommend that you eat your breads lightly toasted, a good toaster is needed. Nothing fancy!

Drinking Water System. Tap water throughout much of the United States is not suitable for drinking. While there are many different systems available, we have found that the most effective with respect to health and environment and the one that produces the best-tasting water is the combined reverse osmosis and carbon purification system. A new countertop FIT FOR LIFE Drinking Water System utilizing this state-of-the-art technology is now available.[1]

Nice-to-Have Items and Luxuries

Food processor. For me, and many others, this appliance is no longer a luxury. It saves time in chopping, slicing, mixing, pureeing, shredding, and dough preparation—and some models even allow you to set the slicing thickness. I frequently choose to do these things by hand, but I use my Braun food processor just as often. It's invaluable.

Electric spice or coffee grinder. Its lightweight blade instantly pulverizes garlic, seeds, and herbs. Slightly heavier grinders work well for nuts.

Food dehydrator. Available in various shapes and sizes, the dehydrator basically consists of enclosed trays and produces dried fruits and vegetables that may be used as is, stored, and/or rehydrated. All come with instructions and recipes.

Kitchen scale. When recipe instructions are given in pounds or ounces rather than cups, you can make the conversion arithmetically, but a simple kitchen scale tells you instantly if you have measured the right amount. (I find the Braun Multipractic Scale is a compact tool that makes measuring easier.)

Pasta machine. A definite luxury, but homemade pasta is so good!

Popcorn popper. The new oil-free hot-air poppers are clean, fast, and more desirable than the pot-with-oil type and are great for kids.

Toaster oven. Saves time and energy for baking, toasting, reheating, browning, and broiling.

Waffle iron. Not a necessity at all, but a fun item for baking special "feasting"-type food, especially with the new eggless recipes.

[1]To find out where you can get more information about the FIT FOR LIFE DRINKING WATER SYSTEM, call 800–767–5511.

COOKWARE

Saucepans, soup pots and skillets. Farberware's Millennium™ is a remarkable breakthrough in nonstick, stainless steel cookware. Millennium's surface is the first "never-stick" coating to be reinforced with stainless steel. As a result, it is so scratch-resistant that you can cook with metal utensils, and it carries a 20-year guarantee! I find that food browns without the use of fat or oil, cooking is easier because the pans are lightweight, and clean-up is a breeze! This product is a dream come true for the busy, health-aware cook.

Wok. A never-stick wok is indispensable for preparing vegetables, pastas, and many other dishes.

Steamer (pot or tray). Buy the simple steamer tray to put into pots of your own, or a better investment is a steamer pot outfitted with its own insert. Do have one or the other for easily steaming vegetables.

Tea kettle. Stainless steel or enamel. One that sings adds a homey touch.

Pressure cooker. Some swear by them; others don't. I happen to be of the latter group.

OVENWARE AND BAKEWARE

Ovenproof casserole dishes and covers. Of glass, earthenware, ceramics, or enamel are great for baking lasagna, braising vegetables, roasting potatoes, or preparing casseroles.[1]

Roasting pans. Of stainless steel or pyrex.

Baking dishes. Of assorted sizes.

Cookie sheets and muffin tins. In assorted sizes, stainless or tinned steel rather than aluminum.

Muffin papers. Enable you to eliminate oil required for greasing muffin cups. Use paper rather than aluminum.

Pie plates. Of stainless or tinned steel.

Cake pans and bread or loaf pans. Of stainless or tinned steel, or glass.

Bundt or tube pan. Of enamel or tinned steel for making beautiful cakes or molds of rice or potatoes.

Springform pan. Used for dense cakes that need special handling to unmold.

Cooling racks. To allow air to circulate under hot cookie sheets or cake pans so immediate cooling will begin, and for cooling of baked items once they have been removed from pans.

MEASURING TOOLS AND CUTLERY

Measuring cups. Calibrated glass cups are handy for liquids in one- to 8-cup sizes. Plastic or metal sets in ¼, ⅓, ½, and 1 cup sizes are more convenient for measuring dry ingredients.

Measuring spoons. ¼, ½, and one teaspoon and one tablespoon sets. Having more than one set is convenient.

[1]FIT FOR LIFE ceramic coordinates are made in the U.S. by Treasure Craft. They travel beautifully from oven to table to freezer, and they clean like a dream. The products bearing the FIT FOR LIFE name are tested and certified by independent laboratories to pass all FDA food and lead-safe standards. For more information about these earthenware items, write to: Susan Levin, Consumer Service, TREASURE CRAFT, 2320 N. Alameda St., Compton, California 90222–2803.

Cutlery. A knife sharpener, hand steel or electric device, should be used routinely on the knives you rely on. Professional chefs pass their knives over a sharpening steel before each use.

Knife set. A chef's knife or chopping knife for cutting and chopping, with an 8-inch blade and handle that allows room for your hand as you move the knife up and down in chopping. An all-purpose tool, the one I use the most. Also, a carving knife for opening melons, squashes, and other large fruits and vegetables, and a spreader for buttering or for spreading condiments. You'll need a serrated 8-inch blade for bread and a 6-inch one for tomatoes. Lastly, a paring knife for peeling, trimming, and other "detail" tasks; the convenient sizes are 3- or 4-inch blades. A grapefruit knife is useful, too.

Cake cutter (knife-type). Not sharp, but does the job.

Scissors. For snipping fresh herbs, string, etc.

FOOD PREPARATION UTENSILS

Bean slicer for julienning string beans.

Crinkle chip cutter for potatoes and decorative crudités.

Strawberry huller—best way to trim strawberries without losing any of the fruit.

Peeler/Paring utensil for carrots, potatoes, asparagus, and broccoli stalks, etc.

Spatulas—flat, to keep the food moving as you sauté or stir-fry; wooden or plastic to protect nonstick pans.

Slotted spoons to remove vegetables from blanching water, potatoes from boiling water, etc.

Rubber spatulas—the soft rubber blade on a handle allows you to clean out a bowl, a can, a blender, or other container.

Sifter for thoroughly combining dry baking ingredients.

Wooden and plastic spoons are essential for all nonstick cookware.

Whisks are important for salad dressing and sauce preparation.

Basting brushes for broiling, grilling, and baking.

Garlic press for pressing out the pulp of garlic or ginger.

Hand graters in assorted sizes for whole nutmeg and vegetables.

Potato masher for potatoes and refried beans.

Rolling pin for pie crusts and keeping your spouse in line (since pie crusts will usually please the most out-of-line spouse).

Zester to pare thin, decorative strips from citrus, carrots, daikon; use the holes for zesting and the tooth for cutting decorative grooves in radishes, zucchini, cucumbers, mushrooms, etc.

"V" or "U" cutter for decorative cuts on melon "baskets" and baked winter squashes.

Small Equipment—Other Aids

Can opener (manual). For the small number of cans used in wholefood cooking; we can use the exercise and save energy.

Cheesecloth. For straining nut milks or tying bundles of fresh or dried herbs for soups or stews.

Colander(s). Of plastic or stainless steel. For draining fruits and vegetables, or pouring off liquids from pastas or legumes. They come in assorted sizes; 1-quart to 1-gallon capacities are handy.

Cookie cutters of various sizes and shapes. For cutting not only cookies but also slices of hard vegetables into interesting shapes—for example, red pepper or jicama hearts for dips!

Cutting board(s). Wood is preferable as long as it is kept well scoured with a solution of lemon, baking soda, or bleach and water. Keep one separate board that is used *only* for fruit and juice preparation; a second board can be designated for general purposes. This will enable you to keep strong garlic and onion flavors from your fruit. Any board where meat, chicken, or fish are cut must be *thoroughly* scoured regularly to prevent bacterial (salmonella) contamination.

Funnel. For pouring from bowl to narrow-mouth container.

Herb tea infusion ball or spoon. Have several in case you have requests for more than one flavor and use bulk rather than bagged teas.

Mandoline. The simple plastic version or the elaborate metal device used by professional chefs. This little machine is great for quickly slicing, shredding, or julienning small amounts. I like the plastic one, which has three slicing options and two julienne blades. I use it for salads, to julienne cucumber, or for thinly slicing celery or cucumbers. This special cutting method adds a nice touch to an "everyday" salad. Kids especially respond to the way things are cut in salads. The thinnest slicing setting is also great for cutting paper-thin cucumber for sandwiches or for finely sliced onion for gravies and garnishes. Use a mandoline with caution and as directed. They are extremely *sharp!*

Melon baller. Especially helpful for enticing children to fruit salads. Also useful for cutting potatoes into tiny balls prior to roasting or seeding cucumbers to make seedless cucumber "crescents."

Mixing bowls. Assorted sizes, in plastic, stainless steel, ceramic, or glass. They are extremely important and have many uses: mixing, stirring, marinating, cooling, folding, tossing, storing, serving, and heating. Deep, narrow bowls are best for combining, folding, or beating large amounts, since the high sides keep ingredients in. Wide, shallow bowls are good for whisking small amounts (like salad dressings or marinades) and allow you to see everything that is in them. Choose bowls that sit flat on the counter. Melamine plastic with rubber washers on the bottom are useful in this respect. Avoid bowls that are too heavy to move around easily or too large to store conveniently.

Apron. To keep you spotless. An important item for your own mental attitude in the kitchen. Helps you switch roles and take cooking as seriously as you do your other endeavors (for which you have special items of clothing). A selection of (bib) chef's aprons to suit your changing moods and meals is a good investment and they actually do complement many outfits.

Pot holders. Glove-type or pads to ward off burns.

AIDS TO FOOD SERVING

Cake and pie servers.

Chopsticks. For Asian food enthusiasts and people who just like to eat with them.

Divided platter. For serving hors d'oeuvres, dips, or nibbles.

Glass pitchers with lids. For serving and storing fresh juices.

Lazy Susan. A round platter that *turns.* It is easier to reach condiments or other meal items when there is a lazy Susan in the middle of the table. It originated in China, where it is customary for guests to help themselves from platters in the center of the table.

Salad servers. With long handles for convenience.

Salad bowls. For both preparation and serving: wood or ceramic, in assorted sizes including one very large one to feed a lot of people.

Sauce server or gravy boat. Passing sauce in its own bowl allows each person to have the amount preferred.

Ladles. Large for soup, small for sauces.

Trays. For serving, setting up, and clearing at a distance from the kitchen.

Hot pads and trivets. To keep your tables from being burned or marred with hot serving dishes, platters, and casseroles.

STORAGE/DISPLAY ITEMS

Baskets. Hanging or countertop, baskets serve well to hold ripening fruits, bags of chips, and innumerable other food items that do not lend themselves to refrigerator or pantry-shelf storage.

Large countertop ceramic bowls. Excellent for storing your fruit supply and double as mixing bowls or even as serving or salad bowls.

Freezer proof, airtight containers. Invaluable for food storage in cupboards, refrigerator, or freezer. Can be plastic for freezer; glass is preferable for refrigerator since plastic flavors the food. Most handy are ovenproof bowls with plastic lids that move from table to refrigerator.

Large, wide-mouth jars with lids. Excellent for storage of grains, legumes, flours, nuts, and other foods that you want to see and to keep fresh at the same time.

Lucite book or recipe holder. Free-standing see-through recipe holder that is handy for keeping book open to desired page and free from kitchen drips and stains.

Masonry or ceramic jars. At least one, for cookies!

Spice jars and rack. Herbs and spices are hard to use if they are not organized in some way. A rack to hold the bottles and an alphabetical system work well to keep these seasonings at your fingertips. Set rack well away from heat to preserve flavor of spices.

Wraps and bags. A word to the wise: Do not use aluminum foil directly on any dish containing cooked tomatoes, peppers, or eggplant. The acid from the tomatoes will cause the aluminum to leach directly into the food. A friend of mine who cooks at a neighborhood health food restaurant recently told me that all the cooks there know not to cover the tomato spaghetti sauce with aluminum foil. When they did, they found that the sauce had flecks of leached aluminum floating on the top. A solution to this problem is first to cover the bowl or casserole with parchment paper and then top it with aluminum foil to hold the paper or waxed paper in place. See page 33 for a fuller explanation. Also, avoid excessive dependence on plastic bags. It takes twenty-five years for them to break down in the environment. Waxed paper is a good product and should be used more than it is. Durable plastic and glass storage containers with lids are the best and cleanest solution environmentally!

Masking tape. A roll of tape is handy to keep in the kitchen for creating instant labels that are easily removed later.

Gummed labels. For keeping track of frozen foods (label and *date* them) and for identifying storage jars of grains, beans, flours, and meals.

WHY YOU SHOULD AVOID ALUMINUM COOKWARE[1]

I have been a medical man for forty years and because of the work I have done in relation to the aluminum question I can state, without a shadow of a doubt, and with all the urgency of my command, that the use of aluminum in the preparation of food and food products is one of the most harmful factors in modern civilization.

—H. Tomlinson,
M.B., Ch.B, M.R.C.S., L.R.C.P.
London, England

I have always known that aluminum and food do not mix, and when I read Dr. Tomlinson's book, *Aluminum Utensils and Disease,* published in England in 1958 and reprinted in 1978, I felt I had to share with you some of his findings.

No matter how much denial we get from the aluminum industry, aluminum cookware leaches aluminum into our food. In spite of protests that the quantity is small or that aluminum already exists in some foods (as part of the molecular structure, *not* as an inorganic metal), aluminum from cookware negatively affects the health of as many as one in every three people.[2]

As far back as 1913 the orthodox British medical journal *Lancet* reported that aluminum cookware, acted on by food, could be injurious to health. Since then, studies by medical researchers on the harmful effects of aluminum cookware have appeared in *Biochemical Journal,* the *British Medical Journal,* the *American Journal of Physiology,* and in German medical journals as well. Books linking aluminum cookware to cancer and other diseases have been published in Canada, France, Germany, Great Britain, and the United States. Aluminum cookware is banned in many countries of the world, but here it is a multimillion-dollar industry.

The problem is that aluminum cookware dissolves into food. You can actually see the cookware become pitted. Even tap water, boiled in aluminum, becomes charged with aluminum. Aluminum is easily dissolved by the acids and alkalies that most foods contain in abundance. Cleansers will dissolve aluminum and so will hard water.

Studies have shown that aluminum poisoning can cause a whole range of serious health problems, from migraines to cancer, severe intestinal disorders, and pain to a deterioration of the intellect resembling Alzheimer's disease. Using aluminum for cooking certainly is not worth the risk, since there are so many other fine substitutes. Stainless steel, enamel, Pyrex, cast-iron, and lead-free earthenware are all safe and excellent. These materials may cost more initially, but they all certainly outlast aluminum and you will not be putting your health in jeopardy unnecessarily.

Unfortunately, restaurants and the processed food industry are heavily invested in aluminum. Their products are therefore tainted with the metal. You can control aluminum contamination in your home, but when you eat out or buy food prepared outside your home, you are at the mercy of the commercial kitchens that prepare it.

[1] Specifically, *non-anodized* aluminum cookware is to be avoided. Unfortunately, manufacturers of anodized aluminum cookware frequently use non-anodized aluminum for lids, so the problem persists.

[2] H. Tomlinson, *Aluminum Utensils and Disease* (Essex, England: L. N. Fowler Ltd., 1958), p. 11.

FREEZER HINTS

Freezers should be at 0°–5°F. Even 10°F cuts storage life in half. Periodically check the freezer temperature with a freezer thermometer.

1. Freeze foods only when they have cooled to room temperature. It is not a good idea to overload your freezer. In any 24-hour period, freeze only 3 lb. per cubic foot of freezer space. Foods that freeze too slowly have a tendency to spoil.

2. Use airtight wrapping and containers designed for freezing. Label each item and date it.

3. Quick-freeze by placing items close to the outside freezer walls and in a single layer with air space all around them. Don't stack items until they have been frozen 24 hours.

4. Tray-freeze (for cookies, pastries, stuffed crepes, etc.) by placing unwrapped food on baking sheets in freezer so they remain separate until frozen. This allows them to hold their shape and not stick together during the freezing process. As soon as they are firm, you can package them and will be able to remove as many as you want as you need them.

5. You will know foods have been frozen too long if their colors change and become faded.

6. Foods that are wrapped poorly will suffer freezer burn (gray and white spots), which means the dry air of the freezer has drawn out some of their moisture.

7. If there is ice inside the package, food has been partially defrosted and then refrozen.

8. When starches in the food break down, it has been frozen too long. The same is true when sauces change consistency or when vegetables become limp.

9. To avoid spoilage, whenever possible, thaw food in the refrigerator. Foods thawed at room temperature have a higher spoilage risk. During thawing, microorganisms are no longer inhibited by cold, and they begin to grow again in the food.

10. All foods can be thawed in wrappers except cakes, which may absorb the moisture that accumulates on the inside of the wrapper. For cakes, loosen wrappers.

11. Never refreeze food that has thawed completely. Cook it before you refreeze it. Any food that has an off odor when defrosted should be discarded.

3

The Vegetarian Shopping List

THIS is a very important list, and I suspect it will come as a surprise to more than a few of my readers. I have so often found that people have the erroneous impression that vegetarian means "spartan." That is a common misconception that I love to correct. This shopping list will give you a good idea of the many raw materials that can go into creating the luscious array of foods you can include in vegetarian meals.

There are many delicious foods and products that can be used in the preparation of vegetarian meals, and in all cases the key word is purity.

SHOPPING LIST

Avoid all prepared foods with chemical additives and preservatives. Avoid anything that contains salt as a major component, refined sugar, dyes, or MSG. If you are buying canned foods, take advantage of the products from companies that are now lining the inside of the cans with enamel, or whenever it is possible, buy prepared foods in glass jars. Always look for wholefood products, rather than those that are made from refined ingredients. Refined means only that most of the essential nutrients have been processed out of the food, so you are wasting your money and your energy when you include refined products in your shopping cart. Nearly all of the foods you presently enjoy are available in high-quality form from excellent natural food companies, some of whom have now gained shelf space in the supermarkets. When you consistently purchase these foods, and avoid those that are not manufactured with your health in mind, you will be forcing your supermarkets to become more responsive to your needs. They are in the business of making money, so they will stock what you buy. If you cannot find what you are looking for at the supermarket, shop at natural food stores. The supermarkets will notice. Vote with your dollars for foods and products that support your health.

PANTRY ITEMS

(These items would not generally require refrigeration.)

Flours, Powders, Meals, and Mixes (See Baking with Love, p. 325.)

corn meal (yellow, white, and blue)
buckwheat flour
oat flour (or oatmeal that can be ground to flour in food processor)
rye flour
whole-wheat flour*
whole-wheat pastry flour*
millet flour
soy flour*
soy powder*
whole-grain pancake or biscuit mixes
whole-grain cake or muffin mixes
falafel mix—Middle Eastern sandwich pattie made from chick peas and spices

Whole Grains (See Foods for the Planet, p. 283.)

barley—Pearl barley is refined. Scotch barley is a whole grain.
bulgur—Cracked whole wheat, parboiled and dried; available from coarse to fine.
couscous—Refined semolina grain, pasta-like flavor. Precooked so only has to be rehydrated.
kasha (buckwheat groats)—Seed grain, high in protein, B vitamins, an excellent source of calcium. Available in fine, medium, or coarse grind.
millet—The only nonacid-forming grain. A tiny yellowish seed that swells in cooking, bland in flavor, filling, lends itself to gravies. Rich in protein, iron, potassium, calcium, and B vitamins. Staple of Hunzas, renowned for longevity.
rice: basmati (white or brown). Distinctive rice with nutty flavor, originally from India, now available in Calmati and Texmati varieties. White basmati, although popular, is a refined grain.
long-grain brown
short-grain brown
sweet brown—short grain rice, sweet in flavor, sticky in texture, ideal for sushi.
wild rice
quinoa—Easy-to-prepare seed grain from South America now grown in Colorado. Complete protein (16 percent), has 10 times as much absorbable iron as corn or wheat. High in B vitamins.
Packaged whole-grain mixes, such as tabouli, rice blends, and pilafs.

*May be refrigerated to prevent rancidity, or store in a cool place.

Pastas and Noodles

artichoke pastas of all kinds—Made from refined durum wheat and Jerusalem artichoke powder. Slightly more nutritious than refined pastas. Widely distributed.
vegetable pastas of all kinds—Made from refined wheat with powdered beets, spinach, tomato, carrot, mushroom, or herbs added. No eggs.
Asian pastas
  udon—Broad Japanese spaghetti made from wheat and/or brown rice, superior nutritionally to refined pastas, better texture than domestic whole-grain pastas
  soba—Thin Japanese spaghetti, usually containing wheat and buckwheat and other flavoring ingredients, such as mugwort (green Japanese herb) or jinenjo (wild mountain yam). Superior nutritionally to refined pastas and in texture to domestic whole-grain pastas.
whole-grain pastas of all kinds
  amaranth—Complete and high protein
  lupini—Complete and high protein. Grain cultivated by every civilization since Babylon. Highly nutritious pasta with 400 percent more fiber, 225 percent more protein, and 1500 percent more calcium than refined pastas.
  wheat
  quinoa—Complete and high protein
Italian pastas of all kinds—If you are a pasta d'Italia aficionado, but most of these are highly refined.

Dried or Prepared Legumes (See Foods for the Planet, p. 283.)

Dried—

adzuki beans
black-eyed peas
garbanzo beans (chick-peas)
Great Northern beans
navy beans
kidney beans
lima beans (large and baby)
pinto beans
mung beans
split peas (yellow and green)
lentils (brown and red)

Prepared—

Great Northern beans
pinto beans, adzuki beans, garbanzo beans
refried beans

Canned Soups or Packaged Soup Mixes—Look for enamel-lined cans when purchasing soups.

"Meatless Meats"

vegieburger mixes
breakfast pattie mixes
tofu burger mixes, which can be added to tofu to turn it into delicious burgers.
seitan meat alternative—Wheat gluten, packed in jars or barbecue-flavored in the freezer or dairy section of many national food stores, made from wheat, water, and seasonings. Useful as meat substitute in spaghetti sauces and chilies.
tofu—firm or soft in non-refrigerated vacuum-packed boxes

Whole Grain Crackers—Without cheese, chemical additives, preservatives, or sugar.

honey grahams
rice cakes
crisp breads
bread sticks

Chips—Salt-free or low salt.

(Those that are baked are preferable to those that are deep fried.)

corn or tortilla chips
blue corn chips
black bean chips
sesame or sunflower chips
brown rice chips
seaweed chips
vegetable chips
carrot chips
potato and sweet potato chips
taco shells

Cereals—Whole grain, hot and cold.

Nuts and Seeds (raw)—All may be refrigerated or frozen for better storage or keep in a cool, dry place.

almonds
cashews—Even those labeled raw have been exposed to some heat to remove them from their outer shells.
caraway seeds
sesame seeds
sunflower seeds
poppy seeds
Brazil nuts
filberts
macadamias
pecans
pine nuts or pignolas
walnuts
pistashios
shredded coconut or coconut flakes (unsweetened)

Dried Fruits (unsulfured)—Keep cool or refrigerate. Freeze for long storage.

apples
apricots
figs
pineapple (unsweetened)
papaya
raisins
prunes
dates
currants

Sweeteners

Descriptions of sweeteners below are to be found in Baking with Love, page 325.

date sugar
raw honey
barley malt syrup
maple syrup or sugar
brown rice syrup
sorghum
carob powder

Sauces, Vinegars, and Oils—Should be kept in a cool, dark place.

extra-virgin olive oil
virgin olive oil
mirin—Sweet cooking wine made from rice, used in Japanese cooking to mellow salty dishes, commonly used in stir-fries and marinades.
rice vinegar (white or brown)
apple cider vinegar
umeboshi plum vinegar—Highly alkaline vinegar made from a Japanese *vegetable.* Agreeable, pickled flavor.
soy sauce (low sodium)
tamari (low sodium)—Concentrated Japanese soy sauce, wheat free, aged.
all-purpose teriyaki sauce
all-purpose tofu sauce
(see also Refrigerator Items, page 42)

Vegetable Bouillon, Powdered Broths, and Other Seasonings

pure vegetable bouillons
natural vegetable seasonings and instant gravies

"chicken"-flavored vegetable broth—Pure vegetable product, made to taste like chicken broth.

Fantastic Foods Tofu Scrambler—Packaged blend of dry seasonings that turns tofu into a scrambled egg substitute.

nutritional yeast—Flavorful, yellow powder, grown as a food and food supplement, concentrated in amino acids and B vitamin complex. Not a by-product like "brewer's yeast" (from beer industry). Taste is slightly "cheesy."

Seasoned Salts and Salt-Free Seasonings—Based on onion, garlic, sea vegetables, sesame seeds, vegetables, herbs, and spices with no chemical additives or preservatives.

"chicken"-flavored
Mexican blends
Indian blends
barbecue blends
dulse flakes
nori flakes
kelp powder

Spices—Look for Spice Gardens *nonirradiated* spices by Modern Products.

allspice
asafetida (hing—in Indian markets, substitute for garlic and onions)
cardamon
cayenne
chile powder
cinnamon
cloves
coriander
cumin (ground or seeds)
curry
ginger
mace
mustard (dry)
nutmeg (whole and ground)
paprika (sweet Hungarian)
peppercorns (white and black)
red pepper flakes
saffron
turmeric
black mustard seeds
fennel seeds
garlic powder
onion powder

Herbs and Herb Blends—Look for Spice Gardens nonirradiated herbs.

basil
bay leaf
celery salt
chervil
dill weed
fennel leaf
marjoram
mushroom powder
oregano
parsley
pepperment
poultry seasoning
red pepper flakes
rosemary
sage
savory
tarragon
thyme

Sea Vegetables and Dried Mushrooms

nori sheets—Sun-dried red sea algae, pressed into sheets, used in sushi.
dulse—Dried purple sea vegetable, used in soups, salads, vegetables, or ground as a salt substitute.
sun-dried kombu—Flat, chewy sea vegetable, used as flavoring in soups and to tenderize beans.
agar-agar—White gelling agent made from sea vegetables, replaces gelatin.
dehydrated mushrooms:
Asian—shiitake, straw, oyster, black forest
French—morels or chanterelles
Italian—porcini

Herbal Teas—All those that are caffeine-free are recommended.

Coffee Substitutes (caffeine free)

grain coffee—Made from roasted and ground grains and roots.

Baking Ingredients: Binders and Thickeners— (See Baking with Love, p. 325.)

egg replacer—Powdered mixture of starches that simulates an egg in baked food when mixed with water.
aluminum-free baking powder
baking soda
arrowroot—Powdered starch from the root of tropical plant. Replaces cornstarch as thickener. Dissolves in cold water, thickens at relatively low temperature. Use one teaspoon arrowroot for each one cup of liquid. Easily digestible. Interchangeable with kuzu (wild mountain vine), but kuzu is more alkalinizing. Both make glossy, light sauces.

Miscellaneous

hearts of palm—Tender inner heart of palm shoots, used in salads.
sun-dried tomatoes—Packed in olive oil in jars or dried in packages for reconstituting in water.
coconut milk or cream—unsweetened
vacuum-packed or canned tomatoes and tomato sauces
artichoke hearts
popcorn

REFRIGERATOR AND FREEZER ITEMS

All Fresh Fruits and Fresh Fruit Juices

All Fresh Vegetables and Fresh Vegetable Juices

Fruit Jams, Jellies and Preserves (refined sugar-free)

Breads (whole grain or sprouted grain)—Keep refrigerated or frozen, since those without chemical preservatives are naturally more perishable.

seven grain
whole wheat
rye
oat bran
unleavened, sprouted breads
pocket pita breads
whole-wheat chapatis—Soft whole grain flatbread popular in Indian cooking.
whole-wheat tortillas
corn tortillas
rolls
bagels
English muffins
muffins
burger buns

Condiments and Sauces

olives
pickles and pickle relish (sweet or dill)
mustards
eggless mayonnaises
hickory barbecue sauces
prepared tomato sauces for pasta
prepared salsas
ketchups

Misos (unpasteurized)

Fermented paste used as soup base and seasoning, made from soy beans and other grains, such as brown rice or barley. Highly alkaline, felt to be strengthening to the blood, stomach, and intestines in Japan and, for that reason, taken on a daily basis by many people as a coffee or tea substitute or as a soup. Light misos can be used in place of dairy. Pastes are not to be confused with powdered misos, which are inferior in taste and practically devoid of nutritional benefit. (See Soups Make the World Go 'Round!, page 189.)

Nut Butters and Seed Butters

peanut butter
almond butter
cashew butter
sunflower butter
sesame butter (tahini)—Commonly used as a dairy substitute in Middle Eastern cooking.

Oils

sunflower
sesame
safflower
avocado
canola

Prepared Salad Dressings—Any that are pure (containing no sugar, cheese, or chemicals).

Soy Products (See How to Replace Animal Products, p. 93.)

firm tofu
soft tofu
silken tofu—Japanese variety of soft, delicate nature.
soy milk (vacuum-packed)—Will keep unopened in pantry for six months, opened in refrigerator for seven days.
tofu or other soy burgers (from dairy cases in natural food stores)
pure soy margarine—Made from soybeans, partially hydrogenated soybean oil, lecithin, and carotene.

FREEZER ITEMS

Vegetables and Fruits (salt and sugar-free)

Prepared Quick-Foods

vegie burgers
burritos
tofu dogs (delicious frankfurter substitute)
soy burgers
tamales
vegie pies

Whatever you would like to try from the freezer case of your natural food store! There are some truly delicious prepared foods to be found there.

Frozen Desserts

nondairy ice creams, pops and cones—Made from tofu, brown rice, or soy milk instead of dairy. Excellent in flavor and texture.
fruit pops—Made from fresh fruit juice.
pies
cookie doughs
pie crusts

I have included this shopping list, not because I expect that you will purchase all that is on it, but because I want you to know what is available to you. In some regions it may be difficult to find all of the items I have listed. Remember that these are not required items, but merely suggestions based on my experience with all that is available. In recipes where an unusual item is listed, a more readily available one is also presented as an alternative, whenever possible. Since the natural food industry is growing at such a rapid pace, however, I am telling you about as many good products as I can so that you can be on the lookout for them as distribution improves.

4

The Friendly Thirst Quenchers

THERE is so much to drink that is delicious and good for you, and that will improve your health and vitality and help you stay in shape. When I serve some of the beverages in this chapter to friends who are unused to them, I am surprised by the level of their excitement, enthusiasm, and interest. I realize then that *most people never drink anything of a truly positive nature.* It's a category of food that has been grossly underplayed and overlooked.

The wide variety of fresh, thirst-quenching juices—alone and in mouth-watering combinations—are a big discovery for most people. After they have sampled what's possible, they go out and buy their own juicer so they can have these drinks as often as they like. People don't know about icy, thick smoothies and creamy almond milkshakes. Once they learn, they are converts and advocates. I have a feeling you are going to react in the same way.

Here, then, are the friendly thirst quenchers. They are luscious. They are luxurious. They are affordable! *And* you don't have to limit yourself to a mandated safe amount. These are only my suggestions; given a little time, you—like everyone else—will come up with some winners of your own!

Cheers! And good health!

HOW TO QUENCH YOUR THIRST

Soft Drinks and Thirst

Americans drink more soft drinks than water! The quenching of thirst is among the most important of our biological needs, second only to the intake of air. Beverages are basics in the diet, but we have gone way beyond basics in our beverage selection. For the basic thirst quencher for the human species, people have, for the first time in history, found a substitute—and that substitute is a synthetic chemical compound with very high sugar or chemical sweetener content. (A 12-ounce can of Coke contains *9.2 teaspoons* of sugar.[1] Imagine dissolving that much sugar in a tall glass of iced tea!) The health ramifications of this choice are catastrophic. Our army of

[1]*Nutrition Action,* August 1981, p. 8.

natural defenses, which we call the immune system, is continuously on call to ward off the effects of so many chemicals coursing through our bodies. It seems an unfair, unintelligent, and unnecessary drain.

What About Water?

Next to oxygen, water is the most important factor in your survival. The cells of your body consist of between 60 and 90 percent water. Your brain cells are particularly high in water; clear thinking actually depends on having adequate amounts of water in the brain.[1] The blood requires ten pounds of water to be in circulation constantly. Without water to moisten the surface of the lungs, there can be no intake of oxygen and no expulsion of carbon dioxide. Water is the vehicle for food absorption, the regulator of body temperature, the lubricant of the joints. In addition, water aids in waste elimination. Although it is imperative that you get enough water every day, most of us do not drink enough.

There's no way to exaggerate the importance of water in your life. You should drink water whenever you are thirsty so that you have not even the slightest symptom of dehydration. I've given you a sense of how much your body depends on water, but you lose water all day long through the skin, intestines, lungs, and kidneys. You must replace this water by drinking. Sometimes people who don't feel as well as they should look for complicated reasons when what they are experiencing are symptoms of dehydration. You may be slightly dehydrated if:

1. Your voice becomes scratchy or high pitched.
2. Your mouth and lips are dry.
3. You feel weak.
4. You experience a "wilting" feeling (much like a plant).
5. You are tired, although you have had adequate rest.
6. You have just done a considerable amount of perspiring.
7. The amount of your urine decreases but the concentration increases.

If you have any of these symptoms regularly, there is a possibility that you aren't drinking enough water.

I'm not recommending that you drink tap water because it's far too polluted to be healthful, and fortunately, there are adequate and affordable solutions to that problem. In the past, we have recommended distilled water—water that is transformed into steam, leaving behind all its impurities, and then condensed back into water. Distillation when combined with activated carbon produces high quality water, but it lacks oxygen, which leaves it tasting flat. This is also a health disadvantage, since richly oxygenated bodies are healthy bodies. My own recent research and personal experience have satisfied me that equal quality, superior taste and other health advantages from high levels of oxygen can best be obtained using the reverse osmosis/activated carbon process. We have examined closely the wide variety of home drinking water systems available, and we are convinced that Water Factory Systems, one of the leading companies in water purification, have developed the best example of this technology in their new FIT FOR LIFE Drinking Water System. This exciting new appliance is attractive, affordable, and functional and is the ideal centerpiece of a *Fit for Life* kitchen.

[1]Thrash and Thrash, *Nutrition for Vegetarians,* p. 87.

But Aren't Juices, Fruits, and Vegetables Full of Water?

Yes, they are and if you consume lots of them, you won't be as thirsty as you would be if you didn't and ate lots of other foods instead. However, these very fine high-water content foods are just that. They are *food.* Water is a pure fluid with no nutritional content. When your body asks for water, it is not necessarily at that moment requesting food, and it is not appropriate to attempt to meet the body's fluid requirements only with food. Water is our *basic fluid.* High-water-content foods are important. So is water. Both have their places; one does not replace the other.

When to Drink

The *worst* time to drink water—or any other fluid, for that matter—is with your meals. Water taken with food cuts down on saliva production. It also washes down the food prematurely, before it has been adequately chewed, and adequate chewing is critical to complete and efficient digestion. Water with food also dilutes the digestive enzymes in the mouth and stomach, interfering with starch and protein digestion and causing fermentation and gas in the digestive tract.

Drink water before meals or at least one hour after meals, but not with your meals. The same is true—even more so—for other beverages that, because they are essentially more complicated than water, will interfere even more with digestion.

Fresh Juices

A question that often is asked is, "Why drink the juice? Why not just eat the whole food?"

Fresh juices differ greatly from whole foods, and they are as useful and important in your diet. Each has its place. Whole fruits and vegetables contain a wide array of nutrients, enzymes, water, and fiber. Fresh fruit and vegetable juices contain all the same nutrients and enzymes *and* the water, but the juicing process has removed the fiber. This liquid food in the form of juice digests in a matter of minutes. On the other hand, when you eat the whole food, the body has to perform this process of removing the fiber for itself, and this may take several hours. The reason that fresh juices command a place in your diet is that your body can get nutrition more easily from them than from any other food.

In short, fresh juices are a *quick dose* of high-quality nutrients, enzymes, and water that your body can use without expending any energy. They should be consumed in a daily balance with whole fruits and vegetables, so that your body will also get the fiber it needs. This fiber is your intestinal broom, used by the colon to sweep out whatever is not beneficial. A balance of fresh juices and whole foods helps you maintain your body in a clean, healthy condition.

Juices put back what is missing in your body.

In his "Report on Nutrition and Health," Surgeon General Koop stated that "adequate nutrient and energy intake is critical to the maintenance of optimum immune function." The body's call for nutrients is continuous. It is a living organism that must consistently be maintained. No food other than fruit juice will give you those nutrients in such a readily available, *highly concentrated,* and enjoyable form.

Since the purpose of this book is to help you understand how to better nourish your body, the best place to start is with fresh juices. Accept the important role they play in health and longevity, enjoy their lovely natural flavors, and become an *active* fresh-juice consumer.

For maximum benefit, fresh juices should always be consumed on an *empty* stomach—not with or immediately following any other food.

Remember that juices are *food.* Do not guzzle them! Drink them *slowly,* mixing them in your mouth with your saliva in a "chewing" fashion. This will give your body a chance to get the most from them.

THE DAILY BASIC JUICES

So that you can enjoy fresh juices every day, purchase your own juicer. The varieties of juice you will then be able to drink are many and they change with the seasons. We so often hear from people that they feel themselves "in the lap of luxury" because of all the fresh, delightful great-tasting juices and juice blends they are able to have any time they wish, now that they own a juicer. Open yourself up to a whole new world of delicious, good-for-you thirst quenchers.

Getting the Most from Your Juicer

Fruits are seasonal and so are their juices. Just as the fruits of the season are freshest and best for you at that particular time, so it is with their juices. For example, you will probably find citrus juices most satisfying with their full-bodied flavors in the cool winter weather. Melon juices are most effective in warm weather. Vegetable juices work well all year round, but become quite special with the addition of lots of fresh tomatoes in the summer. In addition, juices made from fruits that are in season are economical, too.

The following basic juices cover all the seasons. Start the day with one of the fruit juices. Have vegetable juices as a snack in the afternoon or as a cocktail before dinner. Whenever you are low on energy or "under the weather," use fresh juices to cleanse and replenish your body.

FRESH CITRUS JUICES

orange
tangerine
mandarin
tangelo
grapefruit

On the cloudiest days, with a simple hand or electric juicer, you can squeeze a glass of "liquid sunshine." It's a perfect way to get a running start on the day's activities. Citrus juice is best consumed immediately or at least within a few hours; it tends to lose sweetness and turn quite bitter or sour the longer it sits.

Use juicy Valencia oranges for juicing and the less juicy navels primarily for eating. Satsuma, honey, and Kinnow tangerines, as well as tangelos and mandarins are *all* ideal for juicing. Use the sweeter pink grapefruits for juice by themselves or in combination with other varieties of citrus. For obvious reasons, avoid all citrus fruits stamped "color added."

MANY MELON JUICES

In the summer, when melons are in season and inexpensive, you will find that they make *unbelievable* juices. If you have never tasted melon juices, you are in for a big surprise. In hot weather, there is nothing more refreshing than a cold glass of sweet and cooling melon juice. In summer, I serve melon juice blends as an apértif to lunch or dinner guests. The response is usually, "What is *this?*" accompanied by an expression of delight.

Watermelon Juice

¼ large watermelon

Cut the watermelon from the rind; you may leave the seeds. Cut in long segments, thin enough to pass through the juicer. Pass fruit through juicer, stir, and serve.

Yields approximately 1–1½ quarts.

Watermelon-Cantaloupe Juice

¼ large watermelon
½ medium cantaloupe

Cut the watermelon from the rind, then cut in long strips, thin enough to pass through juicer (you can leave seeds). Cut cantaloupe in half and scoop out seeds. Cut cantaloupe in thin wedges that will pass through juicer. Remove cantaloupe rind and then pass both melons through juicer. Stir and serve.

Yields 1⅓ quarts.

Variation: Add ¼ medium honeydew melon. Process as for cantaloupe.

Notes on Melon Juice

- Melon juices are *not* expensive. The key is to make them when melons are in season and abundant. That is when they are appropriate and that is when they do the most good for your body.
- Drink melon juices *alone,* on an empty stomach. Never serve them with or after other foods unless you wish to accompany them with a fresh fruit salad or platter. That is all they should ever accompany. Melons are a cleansing fruit with the highest water content of any fruit. They pass through the empty stomach, washing it, and then cleanse the digestive tract. If melon juice is trapped in the stomach with foods that are already there or that are eaten at the same time, the entire contents of the stomach immediately spoil—actually ferment—causing indigestion, bloating, and pain. The best time for melon juice is in the morning or whenever your stomach has been empty for hours.
- Introduce fresh melon juice to breastfeeding infants after six months of age—just an ounce or two at first, diluted with purified water, as the first food of the day. This is a *favorite* for babies, toddlers, and children of all ages.
- Serve melon juices immediately after preparation for maximum benefit. If you make more than you can consume and wish to store the juice in the refrigerator, expect it to separate slightly; simply stir with a spoon before serving.
- In particularly hot weather, put some of your melon juices into popsicle forms and freeze. It's a sure way to win medals (and kisses) from the kids.

OTHER JUICES

Apple-Celery Juice

Wait until you try this combination! The celery adds a tang to the apple juice that is absolutely delightful. The highly alkaline celery will neutralize acids in your stomach that may be causing discomfort. It helps maintain your blood in its delicate alkaline balance, so that you feel wonderful and mellow rather than acid and irritated. In addition, celery is very high in natural sodium. When you perspire heavily during a workout or feel wilted because of the heat, Apple-Celery Juice will put back the sodium you have lost. It actually raises your heat tolerance! (It should be the "secret" of professional athletes who compete in the heat!)

Make your Apple-Celery Juice in a 3 to 1 ratio: 3 parts apple juice to 1 part celery juice.

6 apples, cored, quartered

2 celery stalks, leaves removed

Make sure you have cut all the seeds from the apples to prevent the bitterness they create in the juice. Peeling is not necessary. Run apples and celery through the juicer. Stir well to combine. Spoon off any foam that may form on the top, if desired.

Yields about 1 cup.

Note: If storing the juice in the refrigerator, expect that it may separate slightly and simply stir before serving. A nice touch is to serve it with a thin stalk of celery as a swizzle stick.

Variation: You can add celery juice directly to fresh bottled apple juice for excellent results!

Creamy Carrot Juice

This full-bodied "milky" juice is like a meal in a glass—a glassful of beta-carotene. There are local juice companies in many regions that produce excellent fresh carrot juice. However, it is only excellent when first made; with each passing hour, carrot juice loses its good flavor and texture. It doesn't have much of a shelf life. The date of juicing should be stamped on the bottle so you can check for freshness. It is especially nice to have a juicer on hand to prepare this juice. When you make it yourself, you *know* it's fresh.

7 or 8 medium carrots

Thoroughly wash the carrots and trim off *both* ends, which can make the juice slightly bitter. Run the carrots through your juicer.

Yields 1 glass.

Carrot-Celery Juice

The addition of celery alters the sweetness of carrot juice, making it less filling, more thirst quenching, and a little tangier. Your blend should be a 3:1 carrot to celery ratio.

2 celery stalks, ends trimmed and leaves removed
6 medium carrots, ends trimmed

Wash the vegetables well and run them through the juicer. If your carrots aren't very "juicy," add a few more.

Yields 1 glass.

Vegetable Juice Cocktail

This refreshing glass of juice could not be better for you, and the bonus is how *delicious* it tastes. It contains enzymes in abundance, vitamins, minerals, amino acids—all the essentials for vitality and Life! It's a good idea to make this your regular before-dinner cocktail.

Fresh vegetable juices have a very short shelf life. Make and drink them immediately (but slowly!) for best flavor and most benefit. You may find that they will separate, particularly when tomato is one of the ingredients, so add a thin celery swizzle stick to each glass as you serve it.

6 to 7 medium carrots, ends trimmed
4 to 5 celery stalks, ends trimmed
3 medium tomatoes, quartered
1 medium green or red bell pepper, quartered with seeds removed
Handful of spinach, parsley, or lettuce
1 tiny wedge of beet, about ½ a small beet (optional)
A squeeze of lemon (optional)

Wash all the vegetables thoroughly before you juice them. Run the vegetables through the juicer in mixed order. Stir juice well and remove foam on top, if desired. Season with a squeeze of lemon. Serve with a carrot or celery swizzle stick.

Serves 3.

JUICE BLENDS FOR SPECIAL OCCASIONS

Here are some suggestions for using juices for entertaining, or when you feel like having something different.

Frothy Summer Lemonade

Use thick white clover honey, if available, for extraordinary results.

½ cup lemon juice
3 heaping tablespoons honey
1 cup cold water
2–3 cups ice cubes
12 fresh mint leaves

1. Place lemon juice, honey, water, and ice cubes in blender. Blend on high until mixture is light and frothy and ice cubes are finely crushed.

2. Place additional ice cubes and mint leaves in four 12-ounce glasses. Add lemonade and serve immediately.

Yields 4 servings.

Strawberry-Mint Lemonade

This pleasantly refreshing drink is nice to serve on hot summer afternoons instead of the old standard, iced tea. Since it contains fresh fruit, it's a good accompaniment to a platter of fresh, sliced fruit.

2 quarts water
2 mint tea bags
8 sprigs fresh mint, plus 4 additional for garnish
12 strawberries
Juice of 2 lemons (approximately ¼ cup)
¼ cup honey

1. Bring 2 quarts of water to a boil. Place tea bags and mint leaves in a large nonmetallic bowl or heatproof pitcher. Pour water over mint and steep 10 minutes.

2. Puree strawberries, lemon juice, and dissolved FruitSource with a hand blender.

3. Remove and discard sprigs and tea bags from steeping solution. Stir in strawberry-lemon mixture and mix well. Chill before serving.

4. When ready to serve, pour into individual glasses and garnish with additional mint sprigs.

Serves 4 to 6.

Apple Spritzer

This is a good drink for those trying to eliminate alcoholic beverages before dinner. Use a low-sodium mineral water for the fizz.

1 cup fresh apple juice
Ice cubes
½ cup low-sodium mineral water
A squeeze of lime juice
A slice of lime, for garnish

Pour apple juice over ice cubes. Add mineral water and lime juice. Garnish with a slice of lime.

Serves 1.

Green Power

More than a juice, this is a power drink for those who really want an extra boost of nutrients and haven't the time or inclination to eat all the foods that contain them. This drink includes a pure, naturally occurring blue-green microalgae. There are several on the market. Blue-green algae is a rich source of many nutrients, including the elusive vitamin B_{12}, and Harvey and I are enthusiastic about it. Some people find the taste very strong. Use only a little at first and increase the amount as your palate adapts. It gives you so many nutrients in such instant form that you find yourself less hungry. This is a perfect addition to a living food day.

1 cup fresh apple juice
¼ to ½ teaspoon powdered algae
1 tablespoon fresh lemon juice

Blend the ingredients with a hand blender for 10 to 15 seconds to dissolve the algae. Drink immediately...slo-o-owly!

Serves 1.

Summer Vegemato

In summer, when tomatoes are so good and so abundant, this is the best! When the weather is hot, it's a terrific cooler. The high-sodium content increases your heat tolerance. The alkalinity neutralizes the acids accumulating in your body in the course of day-to-day living. This juice will make you feel good!

6 ripe medium tomatoes
3 medium carrots, ends trimmed
5 celery stalks, ends trimmed and leaves removed
2 red bell peppers, quartered with seeds removed
¼ small beet
A squeeze of lemon

1. Wash all vegetables thoroughly. Quarter tomatoes and prepare other vegetables.
2. Run the vegetables through the juicer. Place in a blender to thoroughly combine.
3. Season with a squeeze of lemon. Pour into glasses and serve with a celery swizzle stick.

Serves 2.

Tropical Ambrosia

What a great fruit punch when you are entertaining. It's also a good solution for using up lots of summer fruits.

4 cups watermelon chunks, seeded
2 cups cantaloupe chunks
2 cups cubed fresh pineapple
1½ cups apricot halves
1 cup plum halves
2 cups Red Flame grapes, or another seedless variety
6 to 8 oranges or 2 cups fresh orange or apple juice
1 large banana

1. Run all the fruit except the oranges and the banana through the juicer.

2. Juice oranges in a citrus juicer. Place orange juice and banana in a blender and liquefy.

3. Combine melon juice blend and orange-banana blend in a large container with a tight-fitting lid. Shake well, then refrigerate until serving time.

Serves 8 to 10, depending on juice content of fruit.

Note: If you use Tropical Ambrosia as a punch for parties, place it in a punch bowl with several trays of watermelon or orange juice ice cubes. You might also add sprigs of fresh mint.

SMOOTHIES

People who love smoothies tend to count on them. They substitute them for meals, especially when they need a filling breakfast or a lunch on the run. Although smoothies have that creamy, satisfying consistency so many people love, they normally contain nothing more than blended fruit and fresh fruit juice. They give us all the same good feelings we used to get from thick dairy drinks with *none* of the negatives—no fat, no cholesterol, no guilt—just loads of rich sweetness and icy smoothness. They're so delicious, they seem sinful, but as long as you drink your smoothies *on an empty stomach,* you'll gain no weight and get nothing but energy and good nutrition. On a hot day, on *any* day, a smoothie is a real treat.

It's easy to make a smoothie. All you need is some fresh or frozen fruit, fresh juice, and a blender.

1 cup fresh apple or orange juice
1 or 2 fresh or frozen bananas, depending on how thick you like your smoothies
1 cup fruit, such as strawberries, raspberries, blueberries, mango, papaya, peaches, apricots, cherries, or apples

1. Place juice in the blender with the fruit.

2. Blend for 15 to 30 seconds, or until smoothie is creamy with no chunks of fruit remaining.

3. For best flavor, drink your smoothie right after you make it. The flavor will change with time, as the banana oxidizes.

Yields 1 large smoothie.

Tips to Make Your Smoothies Great

1. Frozen bananas make icier, creamier smoothies. Peel your bananas *before* freezing and pack them in an airtight container or double plastic bags. Frozen bananas will last 7 to 10 days in your freezer before they begin to turn brown and lose their appeal.

2. If you have no frozen bananas but you want an icy smoothie, add other frozen fruit you may have on hand—for example, frozen strawberries. Be sure to still add a fresh banana for creaminess.

3. If iciness is not your preference (the digestive tract prefers room temperature), make your smoothies with fresh, unfrozen fruit and cold juice. The result is a perfect temperature.

4. Some people add ice cubes to their smoothies. The problem with this is twofold: (a) unless you make ice cubes from purified water, the ice cubes are tap water, with all its unhealthful impurities; (b) ice cubes, being frozen water, dilute your smoothie as they melt. You have to drink it fast (too fast) to avoid dilution.

5. For extra smoothie sweetness, add a few dates.

6. Although many people believe that smoothies contain dairy in the form of milk, ice cream, or frozen yogurt, this is a perversion of a healthful concept. Dairy cancels out the digestibility of the fruit, intrudes with its fat and cholesterol, acidifies your stomach, and makes your slenderizing and energizing smoothie "fattening" and unhealthful. If it's milk you're craving, see page 65 for Almond Milkshakes. You're in for a real surprise!

Favorite Smoothie Recipes

To make all the recipes that follow, the instructions are the same: Combine ingredients in a blender and blend for 15 to 30 seconds on high. Pour into a glass and enjoy!

Yields 1 to 2 servings.

Strawberry

1 cup fresh apple or orange juice
6 to 8 medium strawberries, fresh or frozen
1 medium banana, fresh or frozen

Dutch Apple

1 cup fresh apple juice
1 large sweet apple, peeled, quartered, and cored
2 to 3 dates, seeds removed
1 small banana, fresh or frozen
Dash of ground cinnamon

Orange Sunrise

1 cup fresh orange juice
1 frozen large banana
4 dates, seeds removed

Strawberry-Papaya Delight

1 cup fresh apple, orange, or pineapple juice
1 small ripe papaya, peeled and seeded
(remove every seed; they are bitter)
6 medium strawberries
1 small ripe banana
3 dates, seeds removed (optional)

Banana-Peach

1 cup fresh apple or orange juice
1 large banana, fresh or frozen
2 ripe peaches, peeled, seeds removed, cut in chunks

"Das" (Date, Apple, Strawberry)

1 cup fresh apple juice
1 small apple, peeled, cored, and quartered
2 large dates, seeds removed
5 medium strawberries, fresh or frozen

Persimmon Pleasure

1 cup fresh apple or orange juice
2 medium Hychia persimmons, stems removed, quartered, seeds removed
3 to 4 soft dates, seeds removed
6 to 8 apple-juice ice cubes or plain ice cubes

Watermelon-Raspberry

1 cup fresh watermelon juice
1 cup fresh raspberries
1 frozen medium banana or 8 frozen strawberries

Mango Paradise

1 cup fresh orange juice
2 cups mango cubes
1 tablespoon shredded coconut
1 frozen medium banana or 6 orange-juice ice cubes

Apple-Melon

1 cup fresh apple juice
2 cups seeded watermelon
2 frozen medium bananas

Melonberry

1 cup watermelon juice
2 cups cantaloupe
6 frozen strawberries

Tutti-Frutti

1 cup fresh apple or orange juice
1 apple, peeled, quartered, and cored
6 strawberries, fresh or frozen
1 medium banana, fresh or frozen
½ papaya, peeled and thoroughly seeded

Pineapple-Mint

1 cup iced mint tea
2 cups ripe pineapple chunks
½ frozen medium banana
1 small apple, peeled, quartered, and cored

Papabanana

1 cup fresh orange or apple juice
1 papaya, halved, peeled, and thoroughly seeded
1 small banana, fresh or frozen
Dash of grated nutmeg

Appleberry

1 cup fresh apple juice
2 apples, peeled, quartered, and cored
½ cup blueberries, fresh or frozen
1 medium banana, fresh or frozen
2 dates, seeds removed (optional)

FRUIT MILKS

Some fruits, when "blended," become just as creamy as a thick fruit-flavored milk. You will enjoy these when the particular fruits are in season, as an alternative to juice. The advantage of fruit milks is that you lose none of the fiber. You get the whole food, just in a "predigested" form. Fruit "milks" should be consumed right after they have been prepared. The blenderizing whips a lot of air into them. If they sit, they will separate and oxidize rather quickly.

Banana Milk

This is a nourishing alternative to juice, and a good replacement for dairy. Since bananas are available all year round, this "milk" has no seasonal limitations. Always use *very* ripe bananas with lots of brown spots or your milk will not be sweet. This is an excellent food for young children and the very elderly in particular, and all the rest of us, too!

1 date, peeled and seeded or 1 teaspoon maple syrup (optional)
1 cup water
1 large ripe banana, peeled

Blend the date in a little water first, then add the banana and remaining water.

Serves 1.

Cantaloupe Milk

When we discovered Cantaloupe Milk, we went absolutely wild! It was right before we left to film the *Fit for Life* video aboard a cruise ship, so we took a case of cantaloupes *and* our blender with us.

1 ripe cantaloupe, halved and seeded

Use a spoon to scoop the fruit directly into the blender container. Turn the blender on high and watch your cantaloupe transform into beautiful creamy milk.

Serves 1.

Note: For an icy version of Cantaloupe Milk, freeze some chunks of cantaloupe and add them to the blender with the fresh cantaloupe—about half-fresh, half-frozen is a good blend.

Honeydew Milk

This is exactly the same principle as for Cantaloupe Milk, but the result is a lovely soft shade of green. Follow the directions for Cantaloupe Milk. Since honeydew melons generally are larger than cantaloupes, you probably will not want to "milk" a whole one, unless there are several people waiting with glasses.

Serves 1.

Watermelon Cream

Blend 2 to 3 cups of watermelon chunks (seeds removed).

Serves 1.

"STEDDA" DAIRY BEVERAGES

Most people find dairy foods very hard to give up. Practically all of us, at some point in our lives, have been hooked on dairy beverages like milk, chocolate milk, and milk shakes. People love the thick, creamy, icy cold, and smo-o-o-th consistency, especially in combination with sweet flavorings.

What isn't so appealing about dairy, however, is its effect on the body. High in cholesterol, high in saturated fat, concentrated in pesticides, and pasteurized to death, dairy has little to offer after the brief moments of enjoyment. In the last several years it has been linked directly throughout the scientific literature to practically *every* degenerative disease, and it is a major contributing cause of the most serious health problem of the day—the clogging of America's arteries.

All across the country there are millions of people trying earnestly to reduce their dairy intake, in line with the surgeon general's recommendations. I have some good news for those people. In this life, there are not many instances when you can "have your cake and eat it, too," but here's one.

Most people are unaware that milk can come from sources other than a cow. However, long before we ever owned cows in great numbers, people made milk from nuts, seeds, and even corn! You can use Almond Milk "stedda" cows' milk.

Almond Milk

I would like to introduce you to Almond Milk. It has a thick, creamy, smo-o-o-th consistency. You can drink it instead of cows' milk and love it just as much, if not more. It has *no cholesterol,* has *good fat* rather than bad, has little or *no pesticide residue,* and is *not pasteurized.* You can make it icy cold and add all kinds of sweet flavorings to make the most incredible milkshakes. You can have almond milk whenever you want it, because you make it right in your own kitchen, in your own blender, quickly and easily!

Almond Milk is delicious plain as a beverage. It can be substituted for dairy milk measure-for-measure in baking. It can be added to soups and sauces at the end of the cooking and heated gently rather than boiled. (Since it is not homogenized it will have a tendency to break down if boiled intensely.) Add it to strong tea or coffee substitutes for a real treat. Pour it over your children's cereals or fruit salads. After they are weaned, give your toddlers Almond Milk blended with banana or strawberries and freeze these for creamy pops.

You'll need the following equipment:

a simple blender or Vita-Mix
one medium-size fine strainer
cheesecloth to line the strainer (optional)
a large bowl
a pitcher with lid, for storage

Blanch almonds by placing them in 1 cup boiling water. Allow them to stand until the water has cooled slightly, and then peel off skins, or prepare milk with unblanched almonds. (Milk from blanched almonds will be slightly whiter in color and smoother in consistency with no difference in flavor.) Dry almonds well.

½ cup shelled raw almonds
2 cups water
1 tablespoon maple syrup (optional)

1. Place almonds in blender and grind to a fine powder. Add sweetener and 1 cup water. Blend again for 1 to 2 minutes to form a smooth cream.

2. With blender running on high, add remaining cup of water slowly through opening of blender lid. Blend 2 minutes.

3. Place the strainer over a large bowl; to ensure a smooth milk, line the strainer with cheesecloth. (If you do not have cheesecloth, you can simply strain your milk twice, using an even finer strainer the second time.)

4. Pour almond milk slowly into strainer and allow to filter through. Add liquid to strainer in increments and just let it drain naturally, or stir the milk in the strainer with a spoon to encourage it to pass through more rapidly.

5. When all the milk has passed through the strainer, there will be approximately ½ cup of almond fiber accumulated. If you have used a cheesecloth liner, you can pull the edges together and gently squeeze the remaining milk out of the fiber, or use a spoon to gently press the remaining milk through the strainer. (The fiber can be stored in the refrigerator for a few days and used as a moisturizing body scrub when you shower.)

Makes about 2 cups.

Note: The amount can be doubled if you need a quart of Almond Milk. Almond Milk will keep in the refrigerator for 4 or 5 days, but it will probably not *last* that long once you discover the milkshake recipes on pages 65–67. Store it in a jar or pitcher with an airtight lid.

Almonds for Goodness Sake

Botanically, almonds are a fruit—the ancient ancestor of later fruits that have large stones for seeds, like nectarines, peaches, plums, and apricots. The almond itself has a tough, greenish gray hull that looks very much like a small, elongated peach. At maturity, this hull splits open, revealing the familiar almond shell, which encases the nut.

Almonds are available all year round. They are an excellent source of plant protein, B vitamins, essential minerals, unsaturated fats, and fiber. They are also low in sodium, and are such a concentrated food that people who are underweight should consider almonds as an excellent "building" food with great nutritional benefits.

Buy almonds in bulk and store them, in airtight containers or plastic bags, in the refrigerator or freezer. Almonds are a complete protein, containing all 8 of the essential amino acids (see table on page 396). In addition to their high protein value, they provide ample amounts of many other important nutrients.

I have found the price of almonds to vary with the season and the region, ranging from $2 a pound at peak season to $6 out of season. There are approximately 4 cups of almonds in a pound. Since it takes 1 cup of almonds to make a quart of Almond Milk, the price ranges from 50¢ to

NUTRITIONAL VALUE OF ONE OUNCE OF ALMONDS

Nutrient	Amount (in Grams)
protein	5.65 gm
carbohydrates	5.78 gm
fat	14.8 gm
saturated fat	1.40 gm
oleic fatty acid	9.44 gm
linoleic fatty acid	2.97 gm
cholesterol	0
thiamine (B_1)	.06 mg
riboflavin (B_2)	.22 mg
niacin	.95 mg
vitamin B6	.032 mg
vitamin E	6.78 mg
folic acid	15.64 Ug
calcium	75.45 mg
iron	1.04 mg
phosphorus	147.4 mg
zinc	.83 mg
copper	.27 mg
pantothenic acid	.13 mg
manganese	.64 mg
fluoride	25.52 Ug
dietary fiber	2.64 gm

$1.50 a quart. You can cut the expense by buying bulk almonds when they are well-priced and storing them in the freezer. I use my almonds directly from the freezer to ensure freshness. I always try to keep at least 5 pounds on hand year-round, and much more than that in late fall, after the almond harvests when the prices are most reasonable.

Other Nut and Seed Milks

Using the same equipment, ratio of ingredients, and procedure, you can make wonderful milks from sesame seeds, sunflower seeds, or cashews. Almond Milk is the most popular and the most versatile, but these other milks also have their important uses.

Sesame Milk has a robust sesame flavor. It is very rich in *calcium*. According to *Agriculture Handbook No. 34,* published by the U.S. Department of Agriculture, sesame seeds contain approximately 1,125 milligrams of calcium in every cup. This is much higher content than other calcium-rich foods such as soybeans (227 milligrams), dairy milk (295 milligrams), or almonds (604 milligrams). Sesame seeds are also high in protein, lecithin (which keeps the fatty acids in the body low and in a fluid state), several of the B vitamins, and vitamin E.

Sunflower Milk is also highly nutritious. It has a strong flavor like Sesame Milk, and lends well to added flavorings like carob, cinnamon, nutmeg, and sweeteners.
Tip: Take advantage of the high nutritional values and low cost of sesame and sunflower seeds by making "milk blends" containing almonds, sesame, and sunflower seeds in the proportions you desire.

Cashew Milk

½ cup raw cashew pieces
2 cups water
1 tablespoon FruitSource or maple syrup

1. Combine cashews with 1 cup water and sweetener in blender. Blend on high to form a thick cream.

2. Slowly add remaining water and blend on high for 2 minutes. Strain if unnecessary.

Yields 2 cups.

Cashew Milk is very rich. I do not recommend that it be consumed "straight." Instead, use it as if it were cream (see page 96).

Food-Combining with Almond Milk

Food-combining enthusiasts may question how this fine high-protein beverage can cross borders and share itself with fruit, grains, all kinds of baking ingredients, and so on. However, notice that you do not use the whole nut, but rather a liquid made from it, with much of the fiber removed. This makes it more versatile, since it is less concentrated. Almond milk is an "extract" of the almond rather than the whole nut.

If you are wondering about the appropriateness of mixing almond milk with fruit, be advised that many proponents of food-combining strongly advocate mixing nuts with fruits, given that nuts are botanically classified as fruit. I do not recommend mixing nuts with fruit, or even almond milk with fruit, *if you are trying to lose weight,* however. When weight loss is a concern, you need the *cleansing* benefit of the fruit unhampered by other factors. Once you have lost the weight you desire, you can add a little Almond Milk to your fruit salads.

MILKS OF MANY FLAVORS

If creamy drinks are your choice, there are plenty to choose from.

Strawberry Milk

The toddlers love this.

1 cup Almond Milk (page 60)
6 ripe strawberries
1 to 2 teaspoons maple syrup (depending on sweetness of berries)

Place milk and strawberries in blender container. Add sweetener, if necessary, then blend and serve. Have some with your child.

Serves 1.

Almond-Banana Milk

A good breakfast drink.

1 cup Almond Milk (page 60)
1 fresh banana

Place milk and banana in blender container and blend until creamy.

Serves 1 to 2.

Papaya Pleasure

An aromatic, thick and creamy drink.

1 papaya, halved, peeled, and thoroughly seeded
1½ cups Almond Milk (page 60)

Blend papaya with Almond Milk in blender container until smooth. Chill or serve at room temperature.

Serves 1 to 2.

Apple Milk

This is a smooth and mellow treat. It also makes fantastic pops.

1 cup fresh apple juice
1 cup Almond Milk (page 60)
1 medium banana
¼ teaspoon ground cinnamon

Combine all the ingredients in your blender container and blend on high for 15 seconds.

Serves 3.

Yuletide "Eggnog"

Make and serve this immediately. Banana changes flavor when it sits after blending, so don't try to keep this in the refrigerator.

2 cups Almond Milk (page 60)
2 fresh bananas
¼ teaspoon grated nutmeg or to taste
½ teaspoon vanilla extract
Grated nutmeg

Place all ingredients in a blender and blend until smooth. Serve with a dash of nutmeg on top.

Serves 4.

ALMOND MILKSHAKES

This is the *big payoff* after you have made Almond Milk. It is so good that a first-time almond milkshake enthusiast told me, "Now I know there is something *better* than ice cream."

That's true! Almond milkshakes replace ice cream. They're thick—so thick you can eat them with a spoon, if you choose. They're creamy and satisfying, leaving you with a full but not heavy "I've eaten" feeling. Their delicious, mouth-watering flavors are numerous.

I developed almond milkshakes seven years ago, when my youngest was almost four. At that age of innocence, he didn't know about ice cream, but I knew that he soon would find about it as he began running barefoot on hot summer days with the neighborhood kids. I didn't wait for that discovery. I introduced almond milkshakes before he found out about ice cream, so he would already have *something better.* Over the next few years, I served almond milkshakes to little children so frequently I often felt as if I were "in the business." I can tell you without reservation that children of all ages and all nutritional backgrounds *love* almond milkshakes!

And it is "something better": no ugly fat, cholesterol, additives, or preservatives of any kind and no refined sugar; just plenty of high-quality protein, balanced sugars, vitamins, and minerals—pure goodness with every gulp!

To make successful shakes, you always need frozen bananas. The almond milk supplies the creaminess; the frozen banana turns it into *iced creaminess,* so keep plenty on hand. Your "theme" fruit, which determines the flavor of the shake, can be added fresh or frozen.

The Best Date Shake in the World

Not a very humble name, but this shake deserves the accolade. You'll see what I mean when you taste it.

1½ cups Almond Milk (page 60)
2 frozen medium bananas
6 large dates, fresh or frozen, seeds removed

Place milk and fruit in a blender. Blend until thick and creamy. If you like a thinner shake, use 1½ bananas.

Serves 2.

Strawberry Shake

Strawberry shakes are a great summer flavor when strawberry season is at its height, but you can have these all year round too, since frozen strawberries without added chemicals or sugar are available.

1½ cups Almond Milk (page 60)
2 frozen medium bananas
6 fresh or frozen large strawberries
1 tablespoon maple syrup, if you like a really sweet shake (optional)

Place milk and fruit in a blender. Blend until thick and creamy.

Serves 2 or makes 6 to 8 frozen pops.

Peach Shake

Also known as Your Iced Creaminess, this is the "king of the shakes."

1 cup Almond Milk (page 60)
1 large ripe peach, peeled and quartered
1½ frozen medium bananas

Place milk and fruit in a blender. Blend until thick and creamy. For an "iced creamier" consistency, add more frozen banana and eat with a spoon.

Serves 1 or 2 lucky people immediately!

Banana Shake

If you like bananas, this creamiest of the shakes will probably win your heart.

1 cup Almond Milk (page 60)
2 frozen medium bananas (for a thick shake)

Blend and serve, then drink slowly. Something special happens as this shake begins to melt.

Serves 1 or 2.

Carob Shake

Chocolate lovers who reject carob are making a big mistake. They shouldn't compare the two. Carob tastes different from chocolate but it is in the same family of flavors. Carob is milder, not quite as sweet; it's lighter, creamier, and very good. And carob is far superior to chocolate from a nutritional standpoint. Unlike chocolate, which is high in fat, caffeine, and oxalic acid (which inhibits calcium absorption), carob has negligible amounts of fat, has no caffeine, and has no oxalic acid. In addition, carob contains calcium, phosphorus, iron, and some B vitamins; its pectin seems to soothe stomach upsets. All in all, carob certainly is worth approaching with an open mind (or should I say "mouth"?).

1 cup Almond Milk (page 60)
2 teaspoons unsweetened carob
1 tablespoon maple syrup
1½ frozen medium bananas

Place milk, carob, and sweetener in a blender and blend to dissolve carob. Add frozen bananas and blend until smooth and creamy.

Serves 2.

Note: For a carob-chip freeze, add an additional frozen banana and 1 tablespoon carob chips and blend. Devour with a spoon.

CAFFEINE-FREE WARM BEVERAGES

When you drink hot beverages (and eat hot food, for that matter), you kill millions of cells on your tongue and along your esophagus. Ultimately, you destroy your taste buds, and crave more and more highly seasoned food because you just can't taste anything. It's not worth it. Let your hot beverages cool down a little bit. Drink warm beverages instead.

And now for caffeine. If you are having trouble living without coffee or diet sodas, don't be surprised. They contain pretty heavy doses of caffeine, as do most nonherbal teas, chocolate, and many over-the-counter drugs. Caffeine overworks the kidneys and causes twice as much calcium to be excreted (eliminated from the body) than is normal.[1] In so doing, it is a major cause of osteoporosis.

The reason it is so hard to give up anything containing caffeine is because caffeine is such an addictive drug. It is debilitating, deprives you of sleep, and stresses your nervous system to the point of exhaustion and breakdown. Please *don't* give sodas that contain caffeine to children!

Millions of people have licked the caffeine habit, so it certainly can be done. The usual symptom of caffeine detoxification is a severe headache as the drug is eliminated by the body. The headache passes, and it's a reasonable price to pay in order to be free of caffeine. Then you can begin to really enjoy some of the caffeine-free beverages that follow.

[1]Robert P. Hearney et al., "Effects of Nitrogen, Phosphorus and Caffeine on Calcium in Women," *Journal of Laboratory and Clinical Medicine,* 99 (1982), p. 46.

Teas from Herbs and Other Ingredients

Herbs are excellent in teas and in foods. In addition to being fragrant and soothing, they are remedies for the body. Many natural foods stores carry complete lines of herbs in bulk, and there are also some mail order sources listed in the back of this book. Herbs are best when they are fresh or freshly dried. If you grow them yourself, you can have a constant supply. I harvest some of the herbs I grow regularly, hang them on a rack to dry, and use them directly from there. Herbs that you buy in bulk should be stored in airtight glass jars. It is better to buy small quantities to ensure a fresh supply.

Many readily available herbs or roots make wonderful soothing teas. Some holistic medical doctors recommend the following as helpful for the conditions indicated:

chamomile—for fevers and colds, upset stomach, and diarrhea
fennel—for digestion
alfalfa—for a real nutrient boost; relieves bloating
comfrey—for inner healing, soothing, and loosening mucus
nettle—for iron
ginger—for sore throats and upset stomachs, to warm the body
mint—for digestion, acid neutralization, and calcium
peppermint—for digestion, acid neutralization, and calcium
spearmint—for digestion and calcium
red clover—to soothe the nerves and purify the blood
sage—for sore throat, fevers, and congestion
lobelia—to relax
red raspberry—for female problems and pregnancy
mullein—to loosen mucus

In making herb teas, steep the leaves and seeds but boil the roots. Use about 1 teaspoon of herb per cup of water. Many of these herbs are available in tea bags, alone or in combination with complementary herbs. There are many powerful herbs other than those just listed; these are the ones I use and enjoy most frequently. You can find many excellent books on how to use herbs.

Warm Lemon Water

Many people like to drink this in the morning to flush and cleanse their bodies. If you have eaten anything oily, it is an excellent way to "degrease."

1 cup water (or use the soaking water from dried fruit)
1 tablespoon fresh lemon or lime juice

Boil the water, add the lemon juice, and allow to cool slightly before drinking.

Serves 1.

Herbal Tonic

1 cup water
½ teaspoon comfrey
¼ teaspoon alfalfa
¼ teaspoon peppermint
1 teaspoon honey
2 teaspoons lemon juice
1 thin slice fresh ginger

Bring water to a boil, then steep comfrey, alfalfa, and peppermint for 10 minutes. Add honey and lemon juice. Place ginger slice in a clean garlic press and squeeze juice into tea. Stir well, drink warm.

Serves 1.

Cinnamon-Peppermint Tea

1 peppermint tea bag
2 teaspoons lemon juice
1 chunk cinnamon stick
1 heaping teaspoon honey
1 cup water, heated to boiling

Place the tea bag, lemon juice, cinnamon stick, and honey in a mug. Add boiling water and steep 2 to 3 minutes, stirring to dissolve the honey. Drink this slowly if your throat feels a little sore, and rest in bed after a warm bath. Your body may be warning you that its defenses are lowered.

Serves 1.

Ginger Tea

This simple tea is an excellent remedy for a grumbly stomach, and is especially soothing for flu and cold symptoms. Fresh ginger is required; the rest is easy. Sip this hot and feel its warming and settling effects.

1 (2-inch) piece ginger, finely chopped or grated
2 cups water

Place ginger and water in a saucepan and boil for 10 minutes. Strain and drink immediately.

Serves 1.

Tea to Raise Your Spirits

This is a very stimulating tea. It will wake you up!

5 (1/8-inch thick) slices fresh ginger
5 cardamom pods
4 black peppercorns
3 whole cloves
1 cinnamon stick
2 cups water

Place all ingredients in a saucepan and bring to a boil. Remove pan from heat and allow to steep for 40 minutes. Strain and serve warm or cold. (You can reheat this tea if you want it warm.)

Serves 2.

OTHER HOT BEVERAGES

Café Santé

Do you like the flavor of coffee? Of cocoa? Try this delicious substitute for both.

2 cups water
3 teaspoons grain coffee substitute
2½ teaspoons roasted carob powder
Dash of grated cinnamon
Dash of grated nutmeg
Dash of vanilla
2 teaspoons maple syrup (or to taste)
½ cup soymilk (see note), Cashew Milk (page 63), or Almond Milk (page 60)

1. Bring the water to a boil in a saucepan. Add coffee substitute and stir to dissolve.
2. Add remaining ingredients. Stir in milk and reheat gently, stirring continuously.
3. Serve in individual cups, with a dash of nutmeg on top.

Serves 2–3.

Note: Vacuum-boxed soymilk, in plain, vanilla, carob, or chocolate flavors is now available in most supermarkets and all natural food stores. It's another good milk to use instead of dairy.

Carrot Leaf Tea

Those lovely fresh leaves topping a bunch of carrots have a wonderful use. Wash them and chop them coarsely. Place in a pot with water to cover. Boil for several minutes, strain, and serve hot or allow to steep and cool. Strain and pour over ice. Refreshing and clean tasting!

Spiced Almond Milk

3 cups Tea to Raise Your Spirits (see page 70) or another spicy tea blend

½ cup soaked almonds (see page 60)

Prepare tea. Place almonds in blender, and add 1 cup of tea. Blend to form a smooth cream. Slowly add the remaining tea with blender running on high. Blend for approximately 2 minutes, then strain and reheat gently, but do not allow to boil.

Serves 3.

Red Miso Tea

Red miso is a concentrated paste made from soybeans. It makes a hearty, alkaline tea or coffee substitute. Miso is extremely high in easily assimilated amino acids, iron, calcium, phosphorus, and B vitamins. Since it is most frequently used as a soup base, I discuss it more fully in Chapter 7. I want to share this tea with you because I find it a very nutritious and soothing tea substitute. Miso is a "radioprotective" food; it binds with radioactive elements in the body and escorts them out![1]

1¼ cups water
1 tablespoon red miso
1 teaspoon chopped green onions (optional)
1 teaspoon lemon juice

Bring water to a boil, then add miso and green onions. Stir and simmer over low heat for 1 minute, until miso is dissolved. Add lemon juice and pour into a mug.

Serves 1 to 2.

ALCOHOL—A WORD TO THE WISE

EXTRA! EXTRA! Read All About It! In the Report on Nutrition and Health, the surgeon general of the United States mandates a new limit on alcohol intake: *no more than two drinks a day!* Pregnant women are urged to avoid alcohol entirely!

That *should* have been a headline in all the newspapers in October 1989, but it wasn't. So I made a headline for you. The public should not be deprived of appropriate headlines.

Excessive alcohol use is linked to three leading causes of death:

1. Cirrhosis of the liver
2. Accidents
3. Suicides

[1]Sara Shannon, *Diet for the Atomic Age* (Wayne, N.J.: Avery Publishing Group, 1987), pp. 48–49.

Eight thousand American teenagers die every year from alcohol-related accidents. Former Surgeon General Koop's important mandate should result in public pressure to *at least* curtail television advertising lauding the "tremendous social advantages" of alcohol consumption. Commercials imply that young people are "uncool," "out of it," if they don't indulge. Cigarette commercials did the same disservice until public pressure insisted they be banned.

Happily, as health awareness increases, alcohol consumption drops. "If a guy is going to jog five miles, he's not going to come home and get drunk," says John Maxwell, a beverage industry spokesman.[1] More and more people today are into Life! Alcohol *kills*—quickly, when it causes accidents and suicides, or slowly, as it degenerates mind and body. It also suppresses the immune system, which we hardly need in this day and age. The new limit of two drinks a day takes a lot more into consideration than health alone, but for the surgeon general to place even *this* limit, the data he considered against alcohol had to be pretty convincing.

If you still drink, mind the nationally mandated level. Some days, stay below the level. Other days, don't drink at all.

Your body will thank you.
These times demand sobriety.

[1]*Nutrition Action*, December 1984, p. 6.

5

What to Do with Fruit

*F*RUIT! Glorious fruit! In all its brilliant hues and succulent varieties, fruit is perhaps the truest expression of our bountiful earth—its accessibility, its perfect form, and its infinitely pleasurable effect. Who among us, even the greatest of chefs, could concoct a treat more luscious and fulfilling than a freshly picked raspberry? A cool, crisp melon? Or a juicy sun-blessed orange?

Only in the fruit family do we find a food that *continues to ripen* after it is picked. If you place a tomato on your windowsill in the sun, it will grow deeper in color and sweeter in flavor. A pineapple will turn golden and become juicier and more pungent in flavor. Bananas will go from green to bright yellow as they sit in a bowl on your table. Not all fruits will do this, of course. Oranges, grapes, and apples must be refrigerated to hold their freshness. But avocados, melons, cherimoyas, pears, mangos, papayas, guavas, pomegranates, kiwis, loquats, peaches, nectarines, plums, and apricots all improve in flavor, texture, and nutrient content *after* picking. Fruit virtually *lives* with us! This delectable family of foods works synergistically with human needs, ripening before our eyes and adding its cheerful colors and tempting aromas to our living space. It does all this for us and more—supplying the abundant enzymes, vitamins, minerals, amino acids, sugars, and fibers that are its *very essence* and are the *essentials of Life* for us.

Although in present times we find news of growing practices to sometimes upset us and cloud our good feelings toward fruit, perhaps you would like to consider a thought about that situation. You know that commercial growers, in misguided efforts to provide consumers with year-round harvests of appetizing fruits, have gone to unreasonable lengths with hormones and chemicals to "protect," alter, polish, color, preserve, enlarge, and further "enhance" their fruit. Now that the undesirable effects of all this inappropriate and unnatural manipulation have come to light, it is encouraging to witness the supply of organic produce steadily increasing. In the interim, I recommend that you adopt a certain approach. Shop at whatever market or supermarket has the *freshest* and *best-quality* produce. Shop at natural foods stores and farmers' markets that supply organic or farm-fresh produce. *Always shop for quality.* There is no substitute for quality at any price. If the cost is higher, it is both safer and more economical in the long run.

PRACTICAL STEPS TO INCREASE AND IMPROVE YOUR FRUIT SUPPLY

1. Know that the word *organic* is important. Ask for organic produce regularly; be on the lookout for it, and buy it whenever it is available.

2. When you go to the market, ask the produce manager for specific information on the produce. Find out which fruits have been tampered with the least and buy accordingly. Request organic produce and clear labeling of imported produce (which usually contains heavier pesticide residues).

3. Visit natural foods stores that stock organic produce. If they are distant, make your visit a weekly or bimonthly outing involving friends and family.

4. Special order cases of organic produce from your natural foods store (i.e., oranges and apples) and store them for eating and juice. Case prices are frequently slightly discounted, and you can share costs with friends or another family if a case seems to be more than you need. Eat these fruits, supplemented with bananas, dried fruits, juice, and vegetables, without feeling you must have a wide variety of fruit *every day.* Variety comes with the seasons.

5. Wash all produce thoroughly with a mild detergent or pesticide wash; rinse it well and dry it when possible. Peel all produce that you suspect has been heavily sprayed to remove surface pesticides.

6. Look into growing one or more fruit trees on your own or your family's property. In the last two years we have planted nearly fifty fruit and nut trees, and are already eating the harvests.

7. Speak out at every opportunity to be a contributing voice to the rising pressure that is forcing change in the agri-chemical industry.

8. Join Mothers and Others for Pesticide Limits, a project of the National Resources Defense Council, which is a nonprofit organization dedicated to environmental protection. It has a full-time staff of more than eighty lawyers, scientists, and environmental specialists and a membership of over 100,000. Its pesticide campaign is focusing national attention on the pesticides in children's food, pressing for reforms in pesticide enforcement and regulation, and working to ensure that safe produce is widely available. Write Mothers and Others, P.O. Box 96641, Washington, D.C. 20090.

9. Write to government officials. Write to the U.S. Environmental Protection Agency, the Food and Drug Administration, and your U.S. senators and representatives to press for reform.

FRUIT IN THE MORNING

For a clean, energized body, we highly recommend fruit in the morning in place of traditional heavier breakfast foods, especially in warm regions where fruit is plentiful year-round. However, in colder locales where the winter winds blow through you and good fruit is not always on hand, robust breakfasts to warm the body may be a more realistic and attractive choice. In this spirit, later chapters of this book have recipes for French toast, pancakes, muffins, scramblers, and rancheros—all wholesomely dairy free. When eating heavier breakfasts, at least *start* with some fresh juice or juicy fruit to cleanse your digestive tract and give your body the balanced simple sugars for the instant fuel it is craving. When the sun shines warmly and the seasons change, take advantage of "fruit in the morning" to lighten, cleanse, and rejuvenate your body.

ALL ABOUT FRUIT

Fruit lends itself to food preparation in a variety of ways. In addition to being easy to just pick up and eat, fruit can also be the basis of luscious creations. Since an important key to enjoying fruit is knowing how to select it, the following should help you buy the very best fruit from that which is available. I have included among those types that are familiar some not as well known to encourage you to broaden your experience. For example, did you know that the best juice oranges have thin, shiny skins and a sweet aroma? Or that the sweetest watermelon should look dull and slightly waxy?

How to Select the Best Fruit

Common Fruits

Apples. Avoid those that are waxed to appear shiny and seek out the untreated varieties (but naturally occurring wax sometimes resembles artificial waxes). Look for unblemished apples, cold to the touch. Red Delicious, Fuji, New Zealand Gala, Granny Smith, and Pippin apples should be rock hard. Best Red Delicious are elongated and slightly heart shape. Yellow Delicious, McIntosh, Jonathan, and Rome Beauty will give to light pressure. Store in refrigerator.

Apricots. Unripe if yellow; best are deep orange with red blush, slightly soft to the touch. Refrigerate once ripe; will spoil rapidly.

Avocados. Vary widely in size, shape, and texture. Best Haas and Fuerte varieties are pear shape, elongated, dull and waxy in color rather than shiny; skin should be smooth rather than pebbly. Bacon variety is large, bright green, round, and shiny with watery rather than oily flesh and a sweeter flavor. All should yield slightly to gentle pressure when ripe; rancid if too soft. Best purchased ripe or allowed to ripen in a closed paper bag. Refrigerate immediately when ripe, unbagged.

Berries. All should be unblemished, deep in color, without any runny or bleeding spots. Avoid strawberries with green or white tips, or overly large varieties that lack sweetness. Sniff the berry containers for pesticide odor; if present, do not buy. Berries should smell clean and sweet. Refrigerate rinsed and dried in a covered container.

Cherries. Should be hard rather than soft to the touch, and plump. Avoid dark stems, indicating age. The deepest red cherries will be the sweetest. Yellow varieties should also be firm and plump rather than soft. Very perishable. Wash and refrigerate in open container. Do not store well for more than 2 to 3 days.

Figs. Should be plump and tear-drop shaped, occasionally slightly wrinkled or cracked. Softness, moistness, oozing of nectar all indicate perfect ripeness. Hard and dry figs are unripe and inferior in flavor. Very perishable; refrigerate uncovered.

Grapes. Should be firm to the touch. Sniff for pesticides. Look for grapes with powdery "bloom," indicating freshness. Wash *thoroughly,* since pesticide use is extreme. Organic grapes are now widely available. Red Flame is best when round and hard as a marble. Green grapes should be firm, and usually are sweeter when they have a yellow-green, rather than lime-green color. Puckering at stem indicates that they are old. Stems should be green; if they are dry, brown, or black grapes will lack flavor. Refrigerate open to the air.

Nectarines. Should be firm but not hard, slightly soft along seam, and golden with a red blush. Avoid immature, green fruit which will be low in sugar. Ripe and sweet when aroma is fragrant. Refrigerate when ripe.

Peaches. Should yield to pressure when ripe. White-fleshed Babcock with pale pink and yellow skin will be softest when ripe; Indian Red is dark, rusty red. All peaches should be softly colorful, not washed out or dull. Avoid those tinged with green. Fragrant aroma indicates ripeness. Fuzzy peaches are less likely to have been heavily sprayed since fuzz indicates they have escaped commercial "bathhouse." Refrigerate once ripe, open to the air.

Pears. Purchase hard and allow to slightly soften. Large, yellow-skinned Comice is eaten softest. Anjou and Bartlett can be eaten semisoft to hard. Bosc should have golden brown rather than greenish skin, and can be eaten hard like an apple. Avoid overripe Boscs with soft end at stem. Asian Pears are firm, crisp, and eaten like apples. Refrigerate once ripe.

Plums. Many varieties. Generally eaten when tender, although some are eaten when firm. Avoid shriveling, splitting, or signs of mold. Peel if skin is overly tart. Consult produce dealer because signs of ripeness differ with variety. Refrigerate once ripe.

Citrus

Oranges. Commercial oranges can be particularly overtreated; avoid those that are stamped "color added." Skin should be smooth, thin, and shiny. Fruit should have weight, firmness, and sweet, fragrant aroma. Ranges in color from green-flecked yellow for smaller juice oranges to deep orange for navels and mandarins. Good Temple oranges will be red-orange with dull skin. Sniff all oranges for pesticides; they should smell like citrus, not like chemical sprays. Seek out organic oranges whenever possible.

Tangerines. Honey is smooth, with shiny skin, flat shape, and yellow-orange color; fragrance will indicate sweetness. Satsuma is bright orange, with loose, dullish skin; smaller ones are usually sweetest. Kinnow has bright orange, tight skin; difficult to peel but excellent for juice. Mineola is oval with protrusion at one end; can be shiny or dull with high color and difficult to peel. Tangy flavor can be very tart or very sweet. Store at cool room temperature.

Grapefruit. White, pink, or ruby should all have smooth, thin, shiny skins and feel weighty. Ugli fruit, a cross of grapefruit, orange, and tangerine, looks like a big, lumpy grapefruit and should be golden yellow; gives to pressure when ripe and segments easily; eat like an orange. Store at room temperature for a few days or refrigerate if kept longer.

Lemons. Thick-skinned have least juice. Should be semisoft or slightly firm, with golden yellow color. Meyer is sweetest, with an orangy, rather than lemony flavor. Refrigerate if you are keeping them for more than a few days.

Limes. Not interchangeable with lemons; have a sweeter flavor. Should be firm and bright in color. Refrigerate if you are keeping them for more than a few days.

Melons

Ripen all melons at room temperature before refrigerating. When possible, purchase local melons or those grown in the United States to avoid heavy chemical saturation of Central and South American imports.

Cantaloupe. Uniform cream color rather than greenish netting indicates ripeness. Stem end should be smooth, slightly depressed, and yield slightly to pressure. Good aroma indicates good flavor. Should be heavy for size. Ripen at room temperature before refrigerating.

Crenshaw. Must feel soft to pressure all over to be ripe, especially at enlarged end. Golden orange skin with minimum green streaking and heady aroma indicate good flavor and sweetness. Ripen at room temperature before refrigerating.

Honeydew. Orange-flesh and green-flesh honeydews should give to pressure all over, but especially at stem end to be ripe. Brown veins in skin usually indicate high sugar content. Greenish cast on skin indicates that melon is ripe. Green honeydew should not have white skin. Orange honeydew should have golden orange cast to skin and musky aroma when ripe. Should be heavy for size. Ripen at room temperature before refrigerating.

Watermelon. Skin should be dull and slightly waxy. Ends should be rounded and well filled out, rather than pointy. Melon should be very heavy for its size and bottom should be pale, creamy yellow, not white. Thumping should produce a deep, hollow sound rather than a dull thud. When cut, look for bright red flesh with dark brown or black seeds, rather than whitish ones. Avoid white streaks in flesh or deep colored "mealy" areas around seeds. Store at room temperature, then wrap and refrigerate once cut.

Tropical and Exotic Fruits

Bananas. Avoid green bananas. Leave them in a closed paper bag to hasten ripening. Do not eat until all the green is gone and banana is generously flecked with brown spots, indicating starches have been converted to sugar. Should be firm and unbruised. If skin will not break readily at stem end for peeling, banana is not ripe. If skin adheres to flesh, banana is still too starchy to eat. Red bananas must be swollen, slightly soft, and color turned from red to orange. Skin may be split. Do not refrigerate bananas as they will turn brown.

Cherimoyas. If purchased when hard, ripen in a paper bag at room temperature. When ripe, will give to pressure all around like an avocado or papaya. Do not cut until uniformly soft. Best when skin is smooth, rich green in color, and slightly flecked with brown. Flesh will be creamy, custardlike, white and juicy, with black seeds in edible chewy membranes. Peel and dice or cut in halves or quarters and eat with a spoon. Refrigerate as soon as they give to pressure.

Dates. Not a dried fruit, although they resemble one. Medjool is largest and should be plump, or only slightly shriveled. Honey, Barhi, Kadrawi, and Deglet Noor are smaller and rounded or elongated. Avoid excessive shriveling, flaky or dry appearance, or fermented aroma which indicates dates are old or have not been well stored. Store in airtight container in refrigerator or freezer.

Guava. Choose unblemished fruit which shows no signs of shriveling at ends. When ripe, will yield to pressure. Store at room temperature. Peel and dice or cut in half and eat with spoon.

Kiwifruit. Should be slightly soft rather than mushy, which indicates overripeness. Avoid if bruised or rock hard. Refrigerate when ripe. Peel and slice, or cut in half and eat with spoon.

Lychees. Round, the size of a walnut, with rough brown or rosy red skin. Avoid those that are cracked, leaking, or give off fermented aroma. Should be plump, with tight skin, and semifirm to touch. Refrigerate.

Mangos. Many colors—can be yellow-green to golden yellow, red-orange to deep red. Will be elongated or rounded in shape, as large as a small cantaloupe or as small as a juice orange. On all, avoid large black blemishes which indicate spoilage. Ripe when yields easily under pressure and fragrance is sweet and aromatic. Overripe when soft and aroma is heady and slightly fermented.

Papaya. Choose fruit that is at least half-yellow or yellow-orange rather than green. Should be heavy for size and very aromatic. Smaller stem end should yield to pressure when ripe. Avoid overly soft or bruised fruit, or any with soft or hard spots. Flesh will be bright orange or strawberry color (indicating a strawberry papaya). Refrigerate when ripe.

Persimmons. Fuyu is yellow-orange, tomato shaped, hard, and eaten crisp like apple. Peel and cut in slices across fruit to reveal beautiful flower formation in center of slice; excellent addition to fruit plates. Hychia is deep orange and slightly tear-drop shape; size of nectarine or large plum. Must be very soft to be ripe, puddinglike in consistency. Add to fruit salads as a sauce or eat whole. Purchase firm and allow to ripen in a closed paper bag.

Pineapples. Base should be slightly soft when ripe, with sweet, not fermented, aroma. When ripe, skin will turn from green to yellow-gold, and leaves will pop out easily. Ripen fruit uniformly by removing leaves and allowing pineapple to stand *inverted* at room temperature so sweet juices concentrated at base can run throughout fruit. Refrigerate when ripe.

Dried Fruits

Apples, apricots, bananas, currants, raisins, figs, mangos, papayas, peaches, pears, pineapple rounds, plums, and grapes can be dried.

1. Buy only *sun-dried* fruit.
2. Avoid sulfur-dried fruit. (Sulfur is used only to lighten the color of the fruit, after the fruit has been blanched, which causes loss of flavor and nutrients.) Unsulfured fruit will be darker, chewier, and devoid of the negative effects of added sulfur.
3. Avoid honey-dipped or sugared dried fruit.
4. Store dried fruit in airtight containers in a cool place, refrigerate, or freeze.
5. Eat it sparingly. This is a highly concentrated food, with a high ratio of simple sugars. Soak dried apricots, peaches, pears, plums, figs, grapes, currants, and raisins for several hours in pure water before eating. Rehydrated, they are quite filling, so you won't overeat. Drink the juice or use it in fruit sauces or smoothies.

FRUIT SALADS AND SAUCES

Fruit salads are fun to eat. They are pretty, a pleasing blend of colors and flavors. They contain many versions of "sweetness" all in one serving, and they leave you feeling light yet full. They quench your thirst, turn off your appestat,* and leave your mouth and body feeling clean and sweet. A child will rarely, if ever, turn down a pretty fruit salad. In fact, as I search my memory for the thousands of times I have served fruit salads, I cannot remember an instance when someone declined—unless, of course, that person had a stomach full of other food.†

Sauces for Fruit Salads

As good as fruit salads are, however, they are that much better with sauces. Fruit sauces as dips, toppings, or mixed into the salad are so special and delicious, yet so remarkably easy to make. They turn even the simplest fruit salad into an "experience," keeping the salad concept always new and exciting. Fruit sauces are the element of surprise at any fruit meal.

These recipes yield approximately 1½ cups of sauce.

Apple-Date Sauce. Blend 12 dates in 1 cup apple juice for a dark, rich sauce.

Creamy Peach Sauce. Blend 1 banana and 2 peaches with ½ cup orange or apple juice.

Apricot-Cashew Cream. Blend 2 tablespoons cashews in ½ cup water or apple juice until smooth. Add 3 ripe, juicy apricots and 2 dates, and blend again.

Icy Cantaloupe. Freeze ¼ cantaloupe, then cut in 1-inch wedges. Process or blend with a small amount of apple juice to get a thick, orange icy sherbet. Place dollops of this sherbet on fruit salads.

Icy Honeydew. Same as for Icy Cantaloupe.

Creamy Blueberry Freeze. Place 1 cup fresh or frozen blueberries in a blender with Cashew Milk (page 63) to cover. Blend until you have a thick, icy sauce. Spoon dollops onto fruit salad.

Strawberry-Banana Sauce. Blend 8 ripe strawberries with ½ banana and a little orange juice.

Rainbow Sherbet. Freeze 8 large strawberries, 1 large peeled banana, and 1 medium mango, peeled and cubed. Process or blend each individually with a small amount of orange juice. Serve in dollops over fruit salads.

Papaya Cream. Blend 1 papaya in ½ cup Almond or Cashew Milk (pages 60 and 63) or ½ cup orange juice.

Banana-Peach Sauce. Blend 1 ripe fresh or frozen banana, ¼ cup raisin water (from soaked raisins) or fresh orange juice, 1 fresh or frozen peach, and dashes of nutmeg and cardamom. (If both banana and peach are frozen, you may need ¼ cup extra liquid.)

Papaya-Fig Sauce. Blend 1½ ripe papayas with 6 very ripe fresh figs.

Piña-Banana Sauce. Blend 1 cup fresh pineapple cubes with 1 fresh or frozen banana. (Add a little fresh orange juice if liquid is needed for processing.)

Apple-Persimmon Sauce. Blend 1 large peeled Red Delicious apple, 1 very ripe Hychia persimmon, ⅓ cup fresh apple juice, and cinnamon and nutmeg to taste.

Applecado Sauce. Blend 1 cup apple juice with 1 ripe avocado.

Sweet Avocado Sauce. Blend 1 cup fresh grape juice with 1 avocado.

*The "appestat" is a tiny "alarm" at the base of your brain that signals when the bloodstream is in need of nutrients, which results in hunger pangs. It takes 30 minutes from the time you begin eating for your appestat to react, so eat your fruit salads slowly and you'll see they deal with your hunger.

†Remember that fruit, which is 90 percent water, should be eaten on an empty stomach.

"Stewed" Pears and Persimmons

10 minutes

In Asia, persimmons are the most popular fruit eaten, and they are now quite readily available in many American supermarkets. They are a very special fruit, well worth searching out and featuring in the fall, which is their season.

2 large pears, peeled and cubed
2 Hychia or Fuju persimmons
2 tablespoons currants, soaked until plump
4 dates, pitted and quartered
1 cup apple juice
6 dates, pitted
A pinch of ground cloves or allspice
¼ teaspoon ground cinnamon
1 small seedless tangerine, peeled

1. Place pear cubes in a medium bowl. Slice persimmons on top. (Peel Fuju persimmons before slicing.) Add currants and dates.

2. Combine apple juice, dates, cloves, cinnamon, and tangerine in a blender and blend until smooth.

3. Pour sauce over fruit. Allow to sit for 1 hour before serving. Spoon fruit into soup bowls.

Serves 3.

Useful Tips on Bananas

—As a Garnish

Run the prongs of a fork lengthwise down a peeled banana, then slice crosswise for dainty, crinkle-edged rounds.

—To Preserve Color

Coat sliced bananas for salads with lemon, orange, or pineapple juice to keep from browning.

—Ripeness

Use bananas when they are spotted brown, not green *anywhere* (even at the tips). When bananas are very ripe, use them in baking as a substitute for eggs.

—Freezing

Freeze extra bananas for shakes and smoothies. Always peel the banana before freezing, then freeze in airtight bags or plastic containers. Frozen bananas keep well for 2 to 3 weeks and then begin to brown.

Strawberries with Pink Almond Cream

This makes a wonderful breakfast for kids of all ages. Remember, strawberries are best when deep red.

½ cup Almond Milk (page 60)
2 pints large strawberries, preferably with hulls on
½ cup date sugar (or maple sugar or maple syrup)

1. Place milk and 6 to 8 large strawberries (hulls removed) in a blender and blend to a smooth cream.

2. Place remaining strawberries in a large bowl. Pour blended cream and date sugar into separate smaller bowls. Strawberries are dipped into the cream and then into the date sugar.

Serves 3.

Fruit Salad Parfait

15 minutes

Prepare your fruit salad, lace it with your favorite sauce, and spoon it into parfait glasses or large goblets. Top it with a spoonful of Cashew Cream and a fresh blueberry or strawberry "flower." Serve your parfaits as a first course to be followed by a salad meal.

2 cups cantaloupe balls
2 cups honeydew balls
1 cup raspberries or sliced strawberries
1 cup fresh blueberries
1 papaya, peeled, seeded, and cubed
1 mango, peeled and cubed
½ cup currants, soaked until plump (optional)
¼ cup coconut shreds (optional)
1½ to 2 cups fruit sauce of your choosing (Creamy Peach, Strawberry-Banana, Apricot-Cashew, or Papaya Cream [page 79] all suit)
½ cup Cashew Cream (page 96)
Strawberry Flowers (see Note) and mint leaves, for garnish

1. Place the fresh fruit in layers in the glasses, alternating colors to achieve a rainbow effect, and sprinkle each layer with currants and coconut.

2. Spoon the fruit sauce and some Cashew Cream over the fruit and allow to drizzle down around the layers. Top with a spoonful of remaining Cashew Cream, a strawberry flower, and some mint leaves.

Serves 6.

How to Make a Strawberry Flower:

1. Wash the strawberry and dry it gently. *Do not remove* the hull.

2. With a sharp paring knife, make 4 or 5 parallel cuts from the top of the strawberry to just above the base. The cuts should be close together, no more than ⅛ inch apart.

3. Gently fan the strawberry "petals" into a flower.

Cherimoya Berry Salad with Cashew Cream

20 minutes

Cherimoya is a luxurious fruit that adds a touch of the exotic to any fruit meal. If you have never had one, look for them in the spring. Cherimoyas are a pudding fruit, soft and creamy like custard in a green skin, with black seeds. The chewy "membranes" around the seeds are the best part, so be sure and eat them. Since these fruits are still fairly rare and therefore quite costly, you can get the best mileage out of them in fruit salad. Combined with other white-fleshed fruits, colorful berries, and Cashew Cream, the effect is quite spectacular.

2 bananas, sliced
1 medium cherimoya, peeled and sliced (approximately 1½ to 2 cups)
1 cup fresh blueberries or sliced strawberries
1 Bartlett or Comice pear, peeled and sliced
⅓ cup raw cashews
2 teaspoons maple syrup
1 cup water

1. Combine the bananas, cherimoya, berries, and pear.

2. Place the cashews, maple syrup, and water in a blender and blend on high for two to three minutes until smooth.

3. Divide salad into 3 or 4 servings. Spoon Cashew Cream over each serving or pass it separately.

Serves 3 or 4.

Honeyberry Salad

10–15 minutes

A hot-weather pick-me-up. The icy sauces make the day!

3 cups honeydew melon balls
1 cup fresh blueberries
2 ripe peaches, sliced
8 large frozen strawberries
1 large frozen banana
Fresh fruit juice as needed

1. In a bowl, gently combine the melon balls, blueberries, and peaches, taking care not to smash the berries and spoil the clear colors of the other fruit.

2. Place frozen strawberries and frozen bananas separately in your blender or food processor with a little fresh juice and blend to a smooth, icy cream.

3. Spoon frozen fruit sherbet over salad.

Serves 3.

Variation: Spoon salad into cantaloupe halves. Top with frozen fruit sherbet for an exotic fruit meal.

Minted Melon Compote

10 minutes

Mint and melon are two summer refreshers. In addition, the mint supplies lots of calcium, neutralizes acids in your stomach, and acts as a digestive aid; it's much more than a mere flavoring or decoration.

1 small honeydew melon
1 medium cantaloupe or one small Persian melon
¼ medium or ½ small watermelon
¼ cup chopped fresh mint leaves

1. Cut honeydew and cantaloupe in half and remove seeds. Remove as many seeds as possible from the watermelon.
2. Use a melon baller to cut melons into balls.
3. Toss melon balls with mint. Cover and refrigerate for at least 3 hours, to allow flavors to blend.

Serves 6 to 8.

Summer Fruit Salad

10–15 minutes

This is such a rich fruit salad that I recommend a simple sauce of fresh juice like orange juice, but for those who love dipping, the Strawberry-Banana or Banana-Peach Sauces complement the salad nicely.

1 banana, cut in thin diagonals
1 cup strawberries, sliced
3 ripe peaches, peeled and sliced
2 kiwi, peeled and sliced
1 cup red seedless grapes, halved
¼ cup shredded coconut (optional)
½ cup fresh orange juice
Butter lettuce leaves, to be eaten with the fruit
1 cup cherries, sliced off the seeds

1. Combine the banana, strawberries, peaches, kiwi, grapes, and coconut in a bowl. Toss gently in orange juice.
2. Arrange lettuce leaves on salad plates. Spoon salad into leaves, then sprinkle with cherries.

Serves 3.

Peachberry in a Melon Bowl

10 minutes

When Babcock peaches are in season, in the middle of summer, this salad, with its delicate flavors, is the one to make.

2 small cantaloupes
4 ripe Babcock peaches, peeled and cubed
1 cup ripe blueberries (or raspberries, if blueberries aren't available)
Mint leaves, for garnish

1. Halve the cantaloupes and remove the seeds.

2. Gently combine the peach cubes and berries in a bowl. Spoon into the cantaloupe "bowls." Garnish with mint leaves.

Serves 4.

FRUIT PLATES

The only difference between fruit salads and fruit plates is presentation. In salads the pieces of fruit are smaller and are eaten with a salad fork or spoon. Fruit on plates is eaten most conveniently with a knife and fork, since the fruit is cut in larger slices. Serve fruit plates for lunches and dinners, especially when your body is telling you to "lighten up" or when the weather is warm. All of the following suggestions go well with lettuce and celery.

Citrus with Avocado. Peel oranges, pink grapefruit, and avocado. Cut avocado in slices and citrus in wheels.

Papaya with Avocado and Banana. Halve and seed the avocado and papaya, then peel and cut in slices. Slice the banana in thick diagonals.

Banana and Avocado. A filling complement of flavors, sliced.

Banana, Avocado, and Pear. The pear adds water and fiber.

Pears, Persimmons, Kiwis, and Dates. Peel, core, and slice the pears. Peel and slice the kiwi. Halve the dates and remove the seeds. If using a soft Hychia persimmon, cut a deep cross in the top, open it like a flower, and set it in the center of the plate with other fruit around it. If using a hard Fuju persimmon, peel and cut it crosswise in rounds.

Mango, Papaya, Pineapple, and Avocado. Peel the mango and slice it off the seed or cut it in cubes. Halve, seed, peel, and slice the papaya. Cut the ends from the pineapple, remove the skin in lengthwise cuts, and slice into spears. Halve, seed, slice, and peel the avocado.

Apple, Grape, Celery, and Nuts. Peel (if waxed), core, and slice the crisp apple, arrange with bunches of red and green grapes. Add celery and a bowl of almonds, pecans, or walnuts.

Melon. Alternate slices of cantaloupe, honeydew, and seeded watermelon. Or substitute slices of Crenshaw, Persian, and Casaba melons.

Honeydew, Peach, Plum, Apricot, and Blueberry. Line the plate with thin slices of honeydew. Arrange peach, plum, and apricot slices on top like a flower. Mound blueberries in the middle.

Berry Plate with Nut Milk. Place mounds of fresh berries around a bowl of nut milk for dipping. Sprinkle berries with date sugar, if desired.

Summer Fruit Plate with Melon Sherbet

20 minutes

In the summer, when there is an abundance of fruit, take advantage of all of it. Understand that fruit is not just a snack at this time of year. It's the most natural time to eat it *in quantity*. At this time use fruit as a main course occasionally, with total comfort. You will lose weight if you need to, and give your body it's much-deserved summer housecleaning. Fruit is a natural cleanser. Most other foods (raw and steamed vegetables excluded) leave some toxic residues. But these important and refreshing fruit meals help remove those residues and rejuvenate you.

The following recipe can be tailored to whatever fruits are available or most enticing at a particular moment in time. This is a perfect luncheon entrée on a hot day.

12 (¼-inch) slices honeydew
36 cantaloupe balls
2 ripe peaches, plums, or nectarines, cut in 6 slices each
12 strawberries, stemmed and halved lengthwise
2 ripe figs, sliced
2 cups frozen honeydew chunks
2 cups frozen cantaloupe chunks

1. On 4 dinner plates, divide the fresh fruit in equal portions and arrange it attractively.

2. Process or blend the frozen melon separately until you have thick, smooth sherbets. If desired, swirl them together for a marbleized effect.

3. Top the fruit plates with 1 scoop each of cantaloupe and honeydew sherbet or a large scoop of the swirled topping. Serve immediately.

Serves 4.

Tips About Fruit Plates

1. If you are serving avocado, half a medium avocado per person is adequate. Brush with lemon to preserve color.

2. Nuts and seeds such as almonds, cashews, pecans, walnuts, sunflower seeds, or pumpkin seeds (all raw, of course!) can accompany any fruit plate, except ones containing avocado. You would not want to eat a concentrated fat like avocado (a *good* fat, remember!) with a concentrated protein like nuts. Fats actually inhibit the digestion of protein.

3. Any fruit plate can include celery and lettuce leaves.

Strawberry and Kiwi Flower Fruit Plate

15 minutes

This is a classic—a favorite blend of fruit flavors that I can't omit from any collection. Layering the fruit as "petals" of a large flower creates a striking and appetizing effect.

2 navel oranges, sliced into "wheels"
2 medium bananas, cut in ¼-inch-thick long diagonals
2 cups sliced strawberries
2 large kiwifruit, peeled and cut in lengthwise slices
½ cup orange juice or Strawberry-Banana Sauce (page 79)

1. Make a bed of orange "wheels" on 4 salad plates. Cover with "petals" of the banana diagonals.

2. Mound the sliced strawberries in the center, and trim with "leaves" of kiwi. Serve with sauce on the side.

Serves 4.

A Fruit Mosaic

20 minutes

Serve this elegant display of fruit purees as a first course. The brilliant colors, subtly blended where they come together, and their pure flavors will launch your meal in a most artistic and captivating way. Although it is so simple and easy to prepare, this dish has tremendous creative flourish.

4 kiwifruit
1 mango
1 papaya
2 to 3 Bartlett pears (approximately 1 pound)
2 tablespoons fresh lemon juice
16 strawberries for puree, plus 6 or 8 for garnish
Mint leaves
Strawberry flower (page 81)

1. Peel and quarter the kiwifruit, then puree in a blender or food processor, and chill in a bowl for 30 minutes or longer.

2. Peel the mango, slice it off the pit, and puree in a blender or food processor. Chill mango in a bowl for 30 minutes or longer.

3. Halve, seed, and peel the papaya; puree and chill as for mango.

4. Peel, quarter, and core the pears. Slice into a bowl and toss with lemon juice. Allow to sit for 10 minutes.

5. Hull, puree, and chill the strawberries. Set aside while you puree and chill the pears.

6. In a clockwise fashion starting with pear puree, then the strawberry, mango, kiwi, and papaya, spoon 2 tablespoons of each puree on large chilled dinner plates. Tap the plates lightly to spread the purees evenly. Swirl with a knife to create a mosaic. Garnish with mint leaves and a strawberry flower.

Serves 6 to 8.

WINTER FRUIT CEREALS FOR BREAKFAST

This is a way to prepare fruit in combination with nuts and seeds to arrive at a truly robust, filling, *uncooked* morning meal that rivals any cooked cereal you can eat. The difference is the nutritional quality. Your body works overtime to extract the usable nutrients that remain in processed, cooked cereals. With very little energy expenditure, fruit cereals reward you with abundant enzymes, vitamins, minerals, fatty acids, amino acids, and sugars—in short, everything you need!

The basic ingredients that go into fruit cereals are apples, bananas, nuts and seeds, almond milk or apple juice, and spices. You can mix in chunks of accent fruits like strawberries, peaches, mangos, blueberries, or pears, but since most of these are not in season when fruit cereals are at their best, they are optional accents rather than main ingredients.

Winter is the time for fruit cereals, just as summer is the time for all the other delectable fruit meals I have suggested. How lovely to have this hearty, all-fruit option when you crave a heavier, *full-of-life* meal. The natural fats in the nuts and coconut will give your body fuel to keep you warm.

Applenut Cereal

20 minutes

1 large banana, sliced
1 large apple, coarsely grated
¼ to ½ cup raw almonds, cashews, sesame seeds, sunflower seeds, or combination of nuts and seeds
Ground cinnamon to taste
Dash of grated nutmeg
1 teaspoon maple syrup (optional)
½ cup raisins or currants
Almond Milk to cover (page 60)

1. Combine the apple and banana in a medium bowl.
2. Coarsely grind the nuts and seeds in a food processor, blender, or nut and seed mill.
3. Sprinkle nuts and seeds over fruit. Add cinnamon, nutmeg, maple syrup (if using), and raisins or currants. Mix well.
4. Spoon into bowls and top with milk.

Serves 1 to 2.

Variation: Add some chunks of peeled Fuyu persimmon or pear to this nourishing breakfast.

Cocobanana Cereal

20 minutes

Here's a good fruit cereal for the whole family to enjoy. You can substitute apples for the pears.

4 crisp medium Bosc pears, peeled, cored, and sliced
4 ripe medium bananas, peeled and sliced
½ cup chopped dates or currants
2 teaspoons ground cinnamon
½ cup finely shredded coconut (optional)
½ cup Almond Milk (page 60)

1. Combine pears and banana in a medium bowl.
2. Add dates, cinnamon, and coconut.
3. Pour milk over fruit and mix well.

Serves 4.

Note: You can also spoon "dry" cereal into separate bowls and pass additional milk in a pitcher.

Fall Fruit Breakfast Pudding

10 minutes

This is a chewier pudding—a great "brisk morning" breakfast.

3 ripe bananas, peeled and sliced
3 tablespoons fresh orange juice
3 ripe pears, peeled, cored, and sliced
1 crisp apple, peeled, cored, and sliced
6 large dates, seeded and chopped
2 tablespoons raisins or currants
½ cup finely shredded coconut (optional)
3 Hychia persimmons (optional), cored and seeded
⅓ cup Almond Milk (page 60)

1. Combine the banana slices with the orange juice and toss to coat. Add the pear and apple slices.
2. Toss banana mixture with the dates, raisins, and coconut.
3. Add the persimmons and break up with a spoon. Add milk and mix well. As you stir, a thick pudding will "happen" where once there was a fruit salad.

Serves 6.

Fruinola

Granola is an acid-forming cooked grain that has its pros and cons. It's a lot better than Fruit Loops, but this cereal is even better than granola—at least in the morning, when your body is trying to cleanse and doesn't wish to be burdened with heavy food.

2 large, crisp apples, peeled and cored
1 tablespoon currants
¼ cup shredded coconut (optional)
¼ cup diced dried figs
¼ cup coarsely ground almonds
2 teaspoons maple syrup, (optional)
½ teaspoon ground cinnamon
¼ cup fresh apple juice

1. Place the apples and currants in a food processor and coarsely grind.
2. Combine the apple mixture with the coconut, figs, almonds, maple syrup, cinnamon, and apple juice. Mix well.

Serves 2.

Chewy Breakfast Pudding

5 minutes

One morning a four-year-old vegetarian cook named Kyra demanded a really chewy breakfast. This was the solution she helped create.

2 large dates, seeds removed
1 apple, peeled (if waxed) and cut in quarters, core removed
1 large frozen banana
Several sections of orange
3 large dates, diced into chewy bits

1. Place the first 4 ingredients in a blender and puree into a thick pudding.
2. Pour mixture into a tall glass or bowl and stir in dates. Eat with a spoon.

Serves 2 or 3.

ICIES

These are easy to make. All you need is frozen fruit. The flavors are many, and children love them. They stand on an equal footing with other frozen treats and are made easily in your food processor or blender. The procedure is simple:

1. Cut fruit into 1-inch chunks and freeze in airtight containers.
2. When ready to prepare an icy, simply puree the frozen fruit in a food processor or blender (with a little juice if necessary) until thick and creamy.

Practically any fruit you can freeze makes a wonderful icy. The following are some of our favorites:

cantaloupe
honeydew
strawberry
banana
peach
pineapple
papaya
apricot
tangerine
nectarine
persimmon
mango

Banana Icy

This is everyone's favorite, especially the toddler set. A little friend of mine named Alexandra had chronic severe earaches, but she loved yogurt and other dairy products. When her mom began replacing her milk with juices and her yogurt with Banana Icy, there were no more earaches for Alexandra!

Ripe bananas

Peel bananas and freeze them in an airtight container. Remove from freezer when frozen solid and blend in a food processor or blender with a little water or fresh orange juice.

CANDIES

To satisfy a sweet tooth and keep us energized, we developed these confections. We virtually lived on them during the day, with a salad at night, when we were on tour. They are so rich in vitamins, minerals, amino acids, and sugars that they calm the appestat for hours. These are great to have on hand when you're on the run. Keep them frozen or refrigerated in an airtight container.

Fruit Chewies

20 minutes

For those who have trouble digesting dried fruit and nuts simultaneously, replace the nuts with banana chips to maintain the crunch. Dehydrated banana is preferable to banana chips, which are fried.

1 cup mixed raw nuts and seeds, or dried banana or banana chips, approximately
8 chewy dates, seeds removed
½ cup Black Mission figs
1 cup raisins

1. Place the ingredients in a food processor and process until a big ball forms. If the mixture is too moist to form a ball, add more banana chips.
2. Roll mixture into balls, bars, or logs.

Yields 16 chewies.

Coconut-Date Balls

20 minutes

2 cups chewy dates, seeds removed
1 cup shredded coconut, approximately

1. Place dates and coconut in a food processor and process until a big ball forms. (Add additional coconut if the ball is slow in coming together. This means your dates are a bit moist for this recipe.)
2. Wet your hands and pinch off pieces from the big ball and roll them into small balls. Refrigerate or freeze.

Yields 12 balls.

Power Bars

40 minutes

If you have a dehydrater, you can dry the bananas for this recipe. Cut the bananas in thin slices and dehydrate them overnight.

¼ cup sesame seeds
¼ cup cashews
¼ cup peanuts
½ cup dates, seeds removed
1 cup dried bananas (or 1 cup currants)
½ cup Black Mission figs
1 cup raisins
1 cup shredded coconut
1/4 to 1/2 Cashew or Almond Milk (pages 63, 60), apple juice or water

1. Place sesame seeds, cashews, and peanuts in a food processor and chop to a fine or semifine meal, depending on how crunchy you like your candy.

2. Add dates, banana, figs, and raisins. Process, adding enough liquid through the top in small increments until a large ball of candy forms.

3. Place coconut in a pie plate. Roll pieces of "dough" into balls or form into bars and press each into the coconut to coat.

Yields 24 bars.

Note: Substitute any nuts or seeds you like. Also, substitute any dried fruit you prefer. For a simpler version, use only one type of nut and raisins. We give the idea and the method; the blend is up to you.

6

How to Replace Animal Products

ONE million people die every year from atherosclerosis—clogging of the arteries—which causes heart attacks, strokes, and other cardiovascular disease.[1] Every 32 seconds, 24 hours a day, someone dies of atherosclerosis. More deaths result from clogged arteries than all other causes combined.[2] And 98 percent of the children in our country already have at least one symptom of heart disease.[3]

This is not information usually found in a cookbook, but the truth is that this particular book was written because of this information. *Atherosclerosis is completely within our control.* Our leading medical and scientific authorities tell us that diets high in saturated fat and cholesterol produce atherosclerosis. To begin to take control, we need to know what foods provide all this saturated fat and cholesterol. Again, medical and scientific leaders are in no debate on this point: *The foods that contain saturated fat and cholesterol are animal products—all meat, chicken, fish, dairy, and eggs.* The more animal products you eat, the more likely you'll die prematurely from atherosclerosis. The more animal products you feed your children, the more likely they will be among the 98 percent who will have at least one symptom of heart disease.

In August 1988, Surgeon General C. Everett Koop made the reduction of animal products one of his national dietary guidelines in his "Report on Nutrition and Health." Only months later, the National Research Council strongly echoed his recommendations. The same conclusions had already been reached by the National Cancer Institute, the American Heart Association, and the World Health Organization. Although there is still a massive advertising campaign to sell animal products, the tide has turned. People are cutting back. Beef consumption alone has dropped from 94 pounds a year per person in 1976 to 70 pounds in 1988. That is very good news for our health and the health of our children.

This chapter tells you how to enjoy yourself tremendously without animal products. You will find that they can be replaced by foods higher in protein and calcium, devoid of cholesterol, and containing practically *no* saturated fat, yet they are *delicious.* In addition, pound for pound, they cost far less than animal-product counterparts.

[1]Surgeon General C. Everett Koop, "Report on Nutrition and Health", 1988, p. 4.
[2]Ibid.
[3]"The Dismal Truth About Teenage Health," *Reader's Digest,* March 1988.

IMPORTANT MESSAGE TO THE READER

In many of the recipes in this book, commonly used dairy products such as butter, cheese, milk, eggs, cream, and sour cream, which are high in cholesterol and saturated fat, have been replaced by vegetable oils, pure soy margarine, tofu, soy milk, egg replacer, and nut milks and creams. These zero cholesterol, low saturated fat replacements are substituted for dairy products in most recipes, measure for measure, and when more detailed procedures are required, they are consistently outlined.

In the event that you do not choose to use these replacements, or they are unavailable, you may use traditional low fat dairy products instead. My recipes have been designed to work equally well either with the more healthful replacement products or with dairy products.

NONDAIRY MILK AND CREAM

In Chapter 3, we acquainted you with some excellent replacements for milk. Using a simple blender, we turned almonds and water into frothy, creamy white milk. We did the same with sesame seeds, sunflower seeds, and even cashews. We then added strawberries, bananas, and other fruits and flavorings to make a sweet pink beverage, an eggnog, and a chocolate-milk "taste-alike." With the addition of frozen fruit, we offered a variety of delicious iced creams, pops, and milkshakes you have to experience to believe.

You can make nutritious milks easily and do not have to rely on dairy milk. These milks have the same creaminess with more *nutritional elements* (see table on page 95), less saturated fat, and *no* cholesterol. You can use this milk in every way that dairy milk is used: in beverages, baking, soups, and sauces.

Soymilk

I did not discuss soymilk in Chapter 3, because I wished to focus on the more flavorful nut and seed milks. These are easier and quicker to make than homemade soymilk, too. But soymilk is another nondairy milk product that can replace dairy milk in many recipes. For flavor and nutritional content, I prefer almond or sesame milk, but the advantage of soymilk is that you can buy it in vacuum-packed "boxes" in your supermarket. And it comes in plain, vanilla, chocolate, or carob flavors. For substitution in cooking, the plain is most useful. Flavored soymilks make good nondairy beverages. Perhaps you have never noticed soymilk where you shop. Since it does not need refrigeration until opened, it is not shelved in the dairy case. Most markets carry it, however.

Soymilk was developed in Japan after World War II, to feed hungry Japanese children. It is made from soybeans that have been soaked, finely ground with water, cooked, and strained. Commercial soymilks also contain barley, rice, oil, sweeteners, and, in some cases, the sweet flavorings just mentioned. I find it convenient to keep a few boxes of plain soymilk in my pantry, for those times when I need some nondairy milk "in a pinch." You can buy 1-quart or 8-ounce boxes; the smaller are handier, since frequently you only need a small quantity. The life of the milk is stamped on the box. Unopened, soymilk keeps for six months or longer; once opened, it keeps for about a week refrigerated.

Making Soymilk from Powdered Soymilk

10 minutes

Powdered soymilk is available at many natural foods stores and Asian markets. The flavor of the reconstituted is not as good as fresh soymilk, but the process is fast and easy. This milk is useful in baking.

To reconstitute the soymilk, combine ½ cup powdered soymilk with 1½ cups purified water in a medium saucepan. Whisk until well dissolved, then bring to a boil over high heat, stirring constantly. Reduce the heat to low and simmer for 3 minutes. You'll have 1½ cups of soymilk that can be served hot or cold.

NUTRITIONAL COMPARISON OF SOYMILK, TO DAIRY MILK, AND MOTHER'S MILK

	Soymilk	Dairy Milk	Mother's Milk
Water (grams)	88.6	88.6	88.6
Protein	4.4	2.9	1.4
Calories	52	59	62
Fat	2.5	3.3	3.1
Carbohydrates	3.8	4.5	7.2
Ash	0.62	0.7	0.20
Calcium (mg)	18.5	100	35
Sodium	2.5	36	15
Phosphorous	60.3	90	25
Iron	1.5	0.1	0.2
Thiamine (B_1)	0.04	0.04	0.02
Riboflavin (B_2)	0.02	0.15	0.03
Niacin	0.62	0.20	0.2

Source: *Standard Tables of Food Composition* [Japan]. Reprinted from William Shurtleff and Akiko Aoyagi, *The Book of Tofu* (Berkeley, California: Ten Speed Press, 1983).

Nondairy Cream

A thick cashew milk is a good substitute for cream. It contains practically no saturated fat and has zero cholesterol, but like dairy cream it should be used in moderation because it is *rich!* Treat Cashew Cream as a special-occasion food and use it in small amounts in place of dairy cream.

Cashew Cream

½ cup raw cashews or cashew pieces
1½ cups water
2 teaspoons maple syrup, or brown rice syrup

Combine cashews and water in a blender with the sweetener. Blend on high for 3 minutes or until you have a smooth cream. Add more water if cream is too thick.

Yields almost 2 cups.

Cashew Whipped Cream

Serve this delicacy on cold fresh-fruit pies, chilled pumpkin pie, or anything you feel "calls for a little whipped cream." It's easy to make and enthusiastically received. Definitely make it on Thanksgiving to have with Holiday Pumpkin Pie (page 355).

1 cup raw cashews or cashew pieces
1 cup water
1 to 1½ cups sunflower oil, approximately
4 tablespoons maple syrup
½ teaspoon vanilla extract (optional)
Pinch of salt

Blend cashews and water to form a thick cream. Slowly add the oil in a fine stream until cream thickens. Blend in maple syrup, vanilla, and salt. Chill and serve. (Cream will thicken substantially when chilled.)

Yields 2½ cups.

Sesame Tahini

Another cream substitute is sesame tahini. This is such a versatile food it deserves a section all its own.

Sesame tahini is a power food, a *miracle food.* Made from ground sesame seeds, it is highly nutritious. Sesame tahini is literally packed with amino acids, calcium, B vitamins, vitamin E, essential fatty acids, iron, manganese, phosphorus, potassium, sulfur, and zinc, yet it contains *no saturated fat* and *no cholesterol.* When the word really gets out about the nutritional value and versatility of this food, it will take its rightful place as a food staple in a hungry world.

Sesame tahini has a myriad of uses as a replacement for dairy cream, milk, eggs, butter, and cheese. It is available in two forms—raw or roasted—and obviously the raw is superior because its nutrients are intact rather than diminished by the roasting process. It is also available as an organic product, made from organic sesame seeds. Usually you will find it sold in 15-ounce jars in your natural foods store or in cans in your supermarket.

I now regularly use raw sesame tahini as a dairy replacement. Even though the amounts of dairy I had added were small, they still brought their unwanted saturated fat and cholesterol to my otherwise pure recipes. I find the substitution of tahini in every way *enhances* the finished product. In fact, the flavors are cleaner and more pleasing, and the dish is less greasy.

Over the last few years I have learned to use sesami tahini instead of cream in soups. It beautifully replaces mayonnaise or cheese in salad dressings. (In combination with minced vegetables, it becomes "Stedda" Tuna, page 110.) As Sesame Cream, it serves as a "mayonnaise" dressing on sandwiches, particularly those in pita bread. In baking and other processes requiring eggs, it is a binder replacement. You will find explicit directions for the successful use of sesame tahini throughout this book.

Note: The thicker sesame tahinis, which are preferable to the runnier ones, usually have a layer of oil on top when you open the jar. Since the objective is to reduce all fats, I pour this oil off rather than stirring it back into the tahini, as is sometimes directed. The product doesn't suffer in the least; it keeps just as well in this slightly drier form and is just as tasty.

Sesame Cream

5 minutes

This is not a sweet cream; it is savory. Use it in salad dressings and pita sandwiches to replace mayonnaise, on Tomburgers (page 187), in sauces where a little savory cream is needed as a thickener and as a binder. Make a batch and keep it in the refrigerator in a covered container. It will make itself useful!

1 garlic clove, pressed, or equal amount garlic powder (optional)
½ cup raw sesame tahini
¼ to ½ cup water, approximately
⅓ to ½ cup lemon juice, according to taste
1 teaspoon kelp powder or other salt-free seasoning (optional)

1. Place the garlic, tahini, and ¼ cup water in a blender container. Blend on high to turn into paste.

2. Add lemon juice, which will thin the paste. Add more water to thicken to desired consistency, then blend in desired seasonings.

Yields 1¼ to 1½ cups.

CHOLESTEROL-FREE MAYONNAISE

Although there are many excellent dairy-free mayonnaises on the market, if you wish to make a truly delicious one yourself, use raw almonds as the base instead of eggs. The finished product is thick, white, and incredibly good. Almonnaise is a cholesterol-free mayonnaise that reminds many of cream cheese. It can be used interchangeably with mayonnaise on sandwiches and in appetizers to contribute much to the sandwich that is more than just a condiment. Try it on Grandwiches (page 181), Goodwiches (page 175), Red Peppers and Almonnaise on Whole-Wheat Bagels (page 186), and all other sandwich suggestions in Chapter 8. Whisk some into your salad dressing for a special creaminess. Add herbs and use it as a dip (recipe to follow). Whisk a few tablespoons into lemon and water for a tangy white sauce for vegetables.

In 1988, I took my Almonnaise recipe and enriched it. The new version is superior in taste and keeping quality.

Enriched Almonnaise

25 minutes

½ cup raw almonds
½ to ¾ cup water or soymilk
2 rounded teaspoons soy powder (optional)
1 teaspoon nutritional yeast
Scant ¼ teaspoon garlic powder
¾ teaspoon salt-free seasoning or seasoned salt (kelp powder, ground rock salt, or substitute salt)
1 to 1¼ cups safflower or sunflower oil
3 tablespoons lemon juice
½ teaspoon apple cider vinegar

1. Cover almonds with boiling water and allow to cool slightly. Slip off the skins. Have all ingredients handy.

2. Place almonds in blender or food processor and grind to a fine powder. Add half the water or soymilk along with the soy powder, yeast, garlic powder, and seasoning. Blend well, then add the remaining water or soymilk to form a smooth cream.

3. With blender running on low, remove insert in top and drizzle in the oil in a thin stream until mixture is thick.

4. Keep blender running and add lemon juice and vinegar. Blend on low for 1 minute longer, to allow mixture to thicken to desired consistency. Refrigerate tightly sealed; this will keep 10 days to 2 weeks in the refrigerator.

Yields 1½ to 2 cups.

Note: Do not be discouraged if, on occasion, your Almonnaise does not thicken to your expectations. Homemade mayonnaise products are among the most sensitive to prepare, and sometimes they just don't respond. This recipe has been made successfully by many people, but once in a while it fails even for me. For every failure, however, I've had hundreds of successes that make it worth the small risk.

Herbed Almonnaise

This jazzed-up variation of Enriched Almonnaise makes a fantastic dip and is an absolute knockout on sandwiches (according to Harv). Use this herb mix or your own.

1 recipe Enriched Almonnaise
2 tablespoons poppy seeds
2 teaspoons dried chervil
2 teaspoons dried basil
2 teaspoons minced fresh chives or dried

At the end of blending the Almonnaise, add herbs and blend for 15 seconds more.

OTHER "BUTTERS"

There is more to spread on bread than butter, and considering that as little as 1 tablespoon of butter contains 35 mg of cholesterol and is 100 percent saturated fat, it seems worthwhile to investigate other options. People who like butter on vegetables will find that these substitutes work well on vegetables, too.

1. In Spain, toasted bread is brushed with a fine olive oil. The result is an inordinately good flavor that complements the bread. Olive oil is also delicious on vegetables. It substitutes well for butter even on baked potatoes (see Chapter 11).

2. Avocado is rich and buttery when mashed and spread on toast. It's a delicious butter substitute with zero cholesterol, the good fat your body uses, and substantial vitamins and minerals including vitamin E. As a dip for vegetables, such as artichokes or broccoli, you can make Avobutter (recipe follows).

3. Nut and seed butters are good alternatives to butter on bread, although since they are more concentrated, the result is far more filling (and for some people too heavy to be easily digested). I prefer nut butters as a dip for vegetables, but high-performance athletes tell me that some nut butters, particularly tahini, give them fuel for hours of exertion. That's an example of adaptation to satisfy individual needs! Peanut butter is the most commonly used nut butter, but nut and seed butters such as almond butter (not acid), sunflower seed butter, cashew butter, and tahini (sesame butter) are all excellent. Use them straight on bread, or dilute them with water and serve them as dips for raw or steamed vegetables.

Avobutter

Avocados are perfect for eating when still firm and yielding only slightly to the touch. Buy them hard, and usually overnight they will ripen to a perfect readiness. (Soft avocados have a less pleasing flavor because their oils are starting to turn rancid.) As soon as they begin to soften slightly, put them in your refrigerator, where they will continue to ripen, but more slowly.

1 medium avocado, halved, seeded, and flesh scooped into blender container (about 1 cup)
2 to 3 tablespoons lemon juice, according to taste
½ cup water, approximately
¼ to ½ teaspoon seasonings of your choice: kelp powder, salt-free seasoning, garlic powder, curry powder, or fresh ground pepper

Combine ingredients on medium-high in your blender. Liquefy to a smooth creaminess. (Add more water if you like your butter thinner.) Pour over vegetables or use as a dip.

Yields 1½ to 2 cups.

INSTEAD OF MEAT

I have always loved to cook! Even prior to 1975, before I became a vegetarian, I devoted the bulk of my creative time and energy to preparing meat-based dishes. For over a decade, I researched extensively the traditional and ethnic meat-based cuisines, and I loved preparing (and eating) the foods I made. But sometimes we find that our favorite activities are in disharmony with the needs of our body. In my case, my health had been so debilitated by all the animal products I was eating that I was forced to begin to cook with other ingredients. Although initially I missed the products I was accustomed to using and I frequently craved the foods I had been used to eating, I became increasingly excited about vegetarian cooking. As I began to feel the freedom and confidence that comes from giving my body what it thrives on, I dedicated myself to developing a new, more relevant vegetarian cuisine.

In those early days, when there was so much uncharted territory, I was thrilled with every discovery I made. Today again I find myself as excited as I was back in the early years, because now vegetarian cooking is expanding at a remarkable rate. With the new health and fitness awareness and the greater numbers of intelligent and creative people choosing healthier diets, new ideas and new foods are popping up so fast it's a challenge to keep up with the changes.

This atmosphere of change has had a dramatic effect in my kitchen. Recently I have had a breakthrough in developing exciting food products I call "Steddas," for "instead of." The base ingredient for these new foods is tofu, which is so flexible and adaptable that it can be whatever you want it to be and have it do just about everything animal products do—and more! Tofu has allowed me to redesign many of the traditional foods I used to make with animal products, in new, equally if not more delicious, yet far healthier ways.

Some of you might run for your hardcover edition of *Living Health* to reread what you thought we wrote about tofu. You're right! This is not what we said then! When the paperback *Fit for Life II: Living Health* came out, however, we were able to make a revised statement. The first edition reflected Harv's purist, natural hygiene view, which contends that the best in food must come from raw ingredients—and tofu definitely is not raw. The revised view was mine. (I am not very good at being a purist about anything but the need for eclecticism!) When Harv made his statement, I had not yet begun my tofu research; but by the time I made mine, I was deeply into a new experience with tofu and was excited about what I was finding.[1]

Harvey, for your information, has recently come around. Although he is still adamant about the benefits of living food, he also sees the culinary and nutritional rewards of tofu. As he dives into chunks of grilled "Stedda" Chicken Fillets (page 115) in his salad or grins with delight as he dips his celery into a tangy Cottage Tofu dip (page 105), he freely admits that—about tofu—he now has a much expanded point of view.

It is natural to rule out that which is unfamiliar—especially in today's kitchens, where time is often limited, and new ingredients are frequently too overwhelming to embrace. With that in mind, the final portion of this chapter is a minicourse in tofu preparation. You will find a broad spectrum of recipes ranging from "cheeses" and "eggs" as sandwich fillers and omelets to kebobs and mixed grills. All are included to give you a basic familiarity with tofu and a sense of confidence and expertise when you use it. In ensuing chapters, you will be given many more opportunities

[1]One of my most respected health advisors, Dr. Ralph Cinque, director of Hygeia Health Retreat in Yorktown, Texas, suggested that I eat tofu for my own health needs, and, as usual, he was absolutely right.

to take advantage of tofu. The goal is simple: that you begin to understand all that can be done with tofu, so it becomes a reliable ingredient in your kitchen.

Exactly What *Is* Tofu?

Tofu is a soft, white, cheeselike cake or block, sold packed in 1-pound containers in the refrigerator or produce section of virtually every supermarket in the country. Tofu contains soybeans, water, and a natural coagulant, and is made much as cheese is. Nutritionally, however, tofu is superior to cheese, and all other animal products for that matter. No other protein food exists so *inexpensively* (between 79¢ and $1.29 per pound), in such wide availability, and contains as much complete protein, calcium, vitamins, and minerals while being *so low* in calories, fat, and sodium and completely free of cholesterol and lactose. Just 1 cup of tofu supplies you with approximately:

50% of the RDA for protein
34% of the RDA for calcium
50% of the RDA for magnesium
30% of the RDA for iron
24% of the RDA for zinc
42% of the RDA for copper
24% of the RDA for phosphorus
16% of the RDA for folic acid
plus substantial amounts of B and B-complex vitamins, essential fatty acids, and other important nutrients.[1]

Tofu's nutritional credentials are truly impressive. Depending on its water content (there is more water in soft tofu and less in firm tofu), it contains between 8 and 17 percent complete and easily digestible protein. That's between 230 and 450 percent *more* than is found in whole milk but *without* the cholesterol and high saturated fat that milk contains. **In fact, numerous studies have shown that the soy protein in tofu will actually *lower* blood cholesterol, even if you are eating foods containing cholesterol along with it. When farmers want to reduce the amount of saturated fat and cholesterol in their livestock's meat, they feed them soybeans!**

Tofu is also high in *usable* calcium and can contain up to 43 percent calcium, which is more than the calcium contained in milk or eggs. Research has also shown that the calcium in tofu is more easily absorbed.

I wonder how many people remember all the publicity about fish oils several years ago and the highly touted ingredients they contain that prevent heart disease? **Those essential omega-3 fatty acids are also found in tofu but without the cholesterol that fish contains. In addition, most of the fat in tofu is polyunsaturated (while most animal fat is saturated); and unlike animal fats, the fat in tofu contains lecithin, a substance which is believed to help dissolve fat in the body.**

Many people have a difficult time digesting concentrated protein, a problem that evokes a direct-experience empathy from me. Although I didn't make the connection earlier, I later learned that eating meat, dairy, fish, chicken, and eggs as sources of protein were killing me. The pain I

[1]Information from *The Book of Tofu,* William Shurtleff and Akiko Aoyagi (Brookline, Mass.: Autumn Press, 1975) and USDA *Handbook 8–16.* Some variations due to rounding.

endured when I ate those foods was unbearable, and no antacid or digestive "remedy" ever gave me lasting relief. Now that I know what it means to live in a virtually pain-free state, it is incredible to me that I endured such intense suffering for so many years.

Tofu is the first high-protein food that my body has been able to digest with no problem whatsoever. In fact, I have discovered that tofu is often the first solid food given to infants in Japan, and I can understand why. Since tofu is 95 percent digestible, it is also highly recommended for the elderly who, past the age of sixty-five, have only about 15 percent of the digestive hydrochloric acid they had earlier.[1] Being free of lactose and low in calories, fat, and sodium, tofu is an ideal food for people who are lactose intolerant, trying to lose weight, or on low-sodium diets. It can also be prized by Americans for its high alkalinity, which mercifully offsets all the acid foods we consume. All animal products, by the way, are acidic, which is why so many antacids are advertised on television.

Culinary Utopia: A Dream Come True!

What is really exciting about tofu cooking is that there is so much you can do with it! When you put on your apron, you can work with the best of both worlds. You can make far more delicious, light, and nutritionally impeccable versions of old favorites. You'll find yourself wedding the old taste-tempting, waist-enlarging, pain-inducing, animal-based concepts with 100 percent irresistible, slenderizing, health-supporting vegetarian ingredients.

Tofu is rightfully called a culinary chameleon. Having such a bland nature of its own, it readily takes on the flavor of whatever is put close to it. That's what makes cooking with this food so much fun. You can keep on hand an entire wardrobe of flavorings to make tofu assume the character you desire.

When tofu first hit the American market several decades ago, it showed up mostly in Asian dress, tossed in vegetable stir-fries with soy sauce or tamari flavorings. But the recent expansion in vegetarian cooking has brought to light a multitude of other possibilities. With tofu you can make a cheesy lasagna or a traditional spaghetti bolognese that you'd swear contained meat! You can marinate and barbecue "Stedda" Chicken Fillets (page 115) using the same flavorings and techniques as meat preparation. You can use tofu in baking to make "cheesecake" and other light, dairy-free treats. In the American Vegetarian Kitchen, tofu turns into cottage "cheese," sour "cream," scrambled "eggs" and omelets, "huevos" rancheros, "matzo brie," "quiche," "egg" salad, burgers, fillet of "fish" sandwiches, and sauce meunières. In this book I call many of these foods "steddas," but everyone who eats them tells me they are not really *instead of* anything! They are fabulous, mouth-watering main events!

Buying and Storing Tofu

There are two basic types of tofu: Japanese, or silken, and Chinese. Silken tofu is finely textured and somewhat gelatinous. In highly refined and sophisticated Asian cooking it is an important

[1]Sara Shannon, *Diet for the Atomic Age* (Wayne, N.J.: Avery Publishing, 1987), p. 106.

ingredient, but for our purposes it is useful only in a few recipes. The more common Chinese tofu is the more versatile and it comes in two textures, soft (containing more water) and firm (containing less water). Both soft and firm Chinese tofu are coarse, less finely textured, and more compact and solid than silken tofu.

Since tofu is a perishable product, you will find it refrigerated in the produce or dairy cases of your supermarket or natural foods store. After you buy it, keep it refrigerated and use it by the expiration date stamped on the container. Keep it covered in fresh water, in a closed container in the refrigerator, for maximum freshness; even if you only use a chunk from a pound of tofu, cover the remainder with water and store it in a closed container.

Like some unpasteurized dairy products, tofu has a keeping quality of about a week and will stay freshest if its water is changed at least every other day. Signs of spoilage include sliminess, an "off" aroma, or a sour or slightly bitter taste. These admonitions aside, however, I do not find it overly perishable and these "signs" are rare. If it seems to require freshening, immerse it in boiling water or steam it for 2 to 3 minutes. Drain it and squeeze or wrap it to remove excess water.

Wrapping Tofu

Many tofu recipes, especially when it is used as a replacement for sour cream, cottage cheese, ricotta, or eggs, instruct you to use the tofu straight from the package. For "Stedda" meat, chicken, and fish, however, you may want to dehydrate the tofu slightly by drawing off some of the excess water. This is done by a simple process called *wrapping*:

1. Remove tofu from the container and discard water.
2. Cut the block in half lengthwise into two 1-inch-thick slabs or in 8 crosswise "fillets" approximately ½ inch thick.
3. Place the tofu slabs on a clean, dry kitchen towel. Wrap the towel firmly around them in several thicknesses and allow to rest for 30 minutes. (If the towel is thin, use two.)
4. Remove the tofu from the towel (which will now have absorbed much of the water from the tofu). Tofu is ready to use.

Freezing Tofu

When you want tofu to take on a chewy consistency, it can be frozen. Drain the tofu completely, cut it in quarters for better handling, and place it in a dated, airtight freezer container. When you are ready to use it (from one day to two to three months later), defrost it completely and squeeze the water out of it. (Since it now has a spongy consistency, it won't disintegrate when squeezed.) Crumble it or break it by hand into chickenlike chunks and marinate or use it as otherwise indicated in recipe. Defrosted tofu is particularly effective in stir-fried vegetable dishes, casseroles, and in Meatless Bolognese Spaghetti Sauce (page 280).

Marinating Tofu

Once tofu has been wrapped and excess water has been removed, you are ready for recipe preparation. One of the most common techniques is marinating. Several marinades are suggested in this and other chapters, or you can use a simple bottled marinade or sauce that you find pleasing. Pure and excellent sauces for marinating tofu abound, particularly in well-stocked natural foods stores. The key is to marinate the tofu long enough for it to absorb the flavors of the marinade. Wrapped tofu marinates most effectively because, having been dehydrated slightly, it rehydrates with the marinade.

Marinate the tofu for at least 30 minutes and up to two to three hours for best flavor. Place slabs, fillets, chunks, or matchsticks in a wide, shallow bowl or baking dish, so the marinade covers it evenly. Cover the container and set it in the refrigerator for the required length of time.

An important tip: a tofu marinade should *never* contain oil, because the oil will coat the tofu and prevent it from absorbing other flavorings. However, oil is needed when you grill or broil to prevent sticking. When you transfer marinated fillets or kebobs to the grill or broiler, add some oil to the remaining marinade and brush the tofu on all sides. It will brown and even get a little crusty, but it won't stick.

Mixing Tofu with Other Foods

Tofu contains such a large amount of water that it is an extremely light, digestible protein. However, to abide adamantly to food-combining principles, it is best added to or accompanied by salads and vegetable dishes. Those who need more flexibility in their diets will find that tofu mixes successfully and effortlessly with just about everything. Tofu is an alkaline food that helps neutralize acids other foods create, and it imposes precious little burden on the digestive tract, alone or in combination.

The mixing of animal proteins and starches creates problems for many people. Concentrated animal proteins and the saturated fats they contain place such a heavy burden on the digestive tract that the addition of a concentrated starch usually is the straw that breaks the camel's back. When you are crossing over into a pure vegetarian diet and are not consuming any animal products, combinations of certain plant proteins and starches generally are acceptable, particularly in the case of tofu.

How to Proceed

The general instructions I have just given on tofu preparation are basic procedures. All recipes involving tofu preparation repeat these simple procedures briefly as an additional guide.

You are now ready to proceed into the world of tofu "Steddas." Once these recipes become familiar, you'll probably keep a pound or two of tofu on hand routinely. Designate a tofu container in which you keep your tofu supply, and change the water every other day. You'll find yourself going for the "Steddas," instead of... *and life will take on a whole new glow!*

The recipes that follow give many ideas for tofu flavorings that you can easily make yourself. They also include some commercial products that are readily available. These products have helped make my own introduction to tofu carefree and convenient, and I recommend them for that reason.

"Stedda" Sour Cream

This recipe has the tang of sour cream and its creamy consistency, without the drawbacks. Use it every time you would use sour cream. Flavor it with chives, too.

5 to 6 ounces silken tofu
1 tablespoon soy oil
1 tablespoon nutritional yeast (optional)
2 tablespoons lemon juice
1 tablespoon tahini
2 teaspoons rice vinegar
1 teaspoon Umeboshi plum vinegar (optional)
Ground rock salt to taste (optional)

1. Steam tofu for 2 minutes.
2. Combine the ingredients in your blender container and blend on high for 1 minute.

"Stedda" Sour Cream and Onion Dip

½ cup "Stedda" Sour Cream
1 small garlic clove, pressed
½ cup minced green onions
½ cup Almonnaise (page 98) or dairy-free mayonnaise
1 teaspoon Worcestershire sauce

Place all ingredients in a food processor and process or combine by hand.

Yields 1½ cups.

Note: This dip improves in flavor if allowed to sit for a while. You can make it well in advance. It will keep for 1 to 2 days in the refrigerator.

Cottage Tofu or "Stedda" Feta

This substitute for cottage cheese can be used whenever you would use dairy cottage cheese. It is wonderful in salads, even replacing feta in Greek salads. Increase the amounts of the seasonings to suit your palate.

1 pound firm tofu
1 tablespoon soy oil (optional)
1 tablespoon apple cider vinegar
2 tablespoons lemon juice
2 tablespoons nutritional yeast (optional)
1½ tablespoons minced onion
1 tablespoon minced chives
2 teaspoons minced dill
½ teaspoon salt-free seasoning

Place half the tofu and the remaining ingredients in a blender and process to form a cream. Transfer to a bowl and set aside. Mash the remaining tofu with a fork, then mix it into the blended portion and combine well. Adjust seasonings to taste. Refrigerate, tightly covered, until ready to use.

Yields 2 cups.

"Stedda" Ricotta

This is excellent in Lasagna (page 278), Spanokopita (page 320), or any other recipe requiring ricotta.

1 pound firm tofu
⅓ cup olive oil
½ teaspoon ground nutmeg
½ teaspoon seasoned salt or ground rock salt

Place three-fourths of the tofu and the remaining ingredients in a blender. Blend until thick and smooth. Mash the remaining tofu into the blended mixture.

Yields 2½ to 3 cups.

Tofu "Cheese" and Olive Spread

40 minutes, 30 minutes of which is resting time

One of the most inspiring success stories coming out of a deep commitment to raise public awareness of the benefits of a vegetarian life-style is the *Vegetarian Times* story. Full of interesting menus and provocative articles, the magazine was started 17 years ago as a newsletter with three subscribers by a 21-year-old college student named Paul Obis. Today *Vegetarian Times* subscribers number in the hundreds of thousands and Paul Obis is its editor-in-chief.

This innovative tofu preparation is an example of the recipes you will find in each monthly issue.[1]

8 ounces soft tofu
1 tablespoon mellow miso (light)
1 tablespoon sesame tahini
4 tablespoons brown rice vinegar or lemon juice
1 small garlic clove, finely minced
Several springs fresh dill, finely chopped or ¼ cup each minced red onion and parsley
2 tablespoons chopped black or green olives

1. To freshen tofu, place in boiling water to cover. Turn off heat, cover, and let sit a few minutes; then immerse it in cold water briefly to cool. Remove tofu, wrap in cheesecloth or porous cotton, and gently squeeze out excess water.

2. Mash tofu thoroughly with miso and tahini. Gently mix in remaining ingredients. If time permits, let mixture rest, refrigerated, for 30 minutes or more to allow flavors to heighten.

Makes 1½ cups; 6 servings.

Note: Spread a generous layer of tofu-olive mixture on pita or whole-grain bread. Top with cucumber, lettuce or spinach, and sprouts. For a more elegant presentation, cut whole-grain bread into triangles and serve as tea sandwiches.

[1]*Vegetarian Times*, incorporating *Well-Being*, P.O. Box 570, Oak Park, Illinois 60630

"STEDDA" EGGS

So many people in recent years have given up eggs because their bodies can't take the sky-high doses of cholesterol. It's one of the first foods most doctors remove from a person's diet after a checkup, and rightly so. Of all animal products, eggs are the worst cholesterol offenders. One large egg yolk contains 252 mg of cholesterol, compared with 282 in a whole stick of butter or 152 in a cup of sour cream. Clearly, eggs are one of the foremost food contributors to heart disease. But for many people they are very hard to give up. Eggs are deeply ingrained in our food culture; scrambled eggs, fried egg sandwiches, and omelets are part of our culinary tradition.

Some people are not going to believe me when I say you can still enjoy those dishes. They're going to act as if I had just promised them the moon! But "the proof is in the pudding." In this case, the proof is in the "scrambler." Try for yourself what has been true for us and for loads of other people. You will realize, once again, that you can "have your cake and eat it, too."

Scramblers

5 minutes

There is a product on the market that you can add to soft or firm tofu that turns it into an egg look-alike. It is a dry seasoning called Tofu Scrambler Mix that disguises tofu as scrambled eggs. All who try it cheer at the discovery.

Scramblers are a brand-new fad that is sweeping the fitness scene. It has become the all-American substitute for eggs and their unwelcome cholesterol—the zero cholesterol solution.

1 pound soft or firm tofu
½ cup water
½ package Tofu Scrambler Mix

1. Crumble the tofu into a nonstick pan and cook, stirring over medium heat for 3 minutes.

2. Add water and scrambler mix, and stir, cooking for 2 minutes longer, until seasonings are evenly distributed and tofu is golden yellow.

Serves 3 to 4.

Note: Serve for supper with Oven-Roasted Potato Fries (page 247) and a big salad, or for brunch with French Toast (page 335).

Scrambled Tofu (Another Way)

10 minutes

If Tofu Scrambler Mix is not available, you can still make a delicious scrambled eggs substitute from tofu, using a simple blend of ingredients.

1 pound soft or firm tofu
2 teaspoons olive or sunflower oil
¼ teaspoon turmeric
¼ teaspoon curry powder
¼ teaspoon cumin
1 teaspoon onion powder
1 tablespoon nutritional yeast (optional)
Ground rock salt to taste (optional)
½ cup pureed tomato (made by liquefying one medium tomato with blender)
¼ cup minced scallions (optional)
Fresh ground pepper to taste

1. Crumble tofu into skillet. Add olive oil and begin sautéing, breaking up any large pieces of tofu with a fork. Add remaining ingredients and mix well.

2. Sauté tofu for 3 to 5 minutes, until mixture is light yellow in color and thoroughly heated. Tofu should be soft.

Serves 4.

Rancheros

30 minutes

1 pound soft or firm tofu, crumbled
2 tablespoons olive oil
½ packet Tofu Scrambler Mix
6 corn tortillas
1 small red onion, sliced
1 large garlic clove, minced
¼ cup minced fresh parsley or cilantro
3 large tomatoes, cut in wedges
1 (6-ounce) can fresh green chilies, chopped (optional)
¼ teaspoon ground cumin
Freshly ground pepper
9 avocado wedges, for garnish

1. Heat the crumbled tofu in a large nonstick skillet with 2 teaspoons olive oil, if desired, for 3 minutes, stirring continuously. Add scrambler mix and stir well to distribute seasonings evenly. Turn heat to low and cook tofu for 2 to 3 minutes longer.

2. While tofu is cooking, heat a separate smaller skillet on high for 1 to 2 minutes. Place tortillas, 1 at a time, in skillet and heat until soft and pliable, turning once or twice.

3. Place 2 tortillas on each of 3 plates and spoon one-third of the tofu mixture over the tortillas.

4. In the large pan, add the remaining olive oil, onion, and garlic and sauté over high heat, adding a little water if necessary to keep vegetables from scorching. Toss in parsley or cilantro, tomatoes, chilies, cumin, and pepper. Heat tomatoes slightly, but don't let them break up. Spoon sauce immediately over tofu and tortillas. Garnish with avocado.

Serves 3.

Scramblers with Fresh Shiitake Mushrooms

We love this with Potato-Lover's Salad (page 158).

1 tablespoon plus 2 teaspoons olive oil
½ pound fresh shiitake mushrooms, sliced
⅓ cup sliced green onions
1 pound soft or firm tofu
½ cup water
½ package Tofu Scrambler Mix
Black pepper to taste

1. Heat 1 tablespoon of olive oil in a skillet, and sauté mushrooms over medium-high heat until soft and glossy. Transfer to a serving dish and set aside.

2. Heat remaining olive oil in same skillet and sauté green onions until they begin to soften. Crumble the tofu into the skillet and cook, stirring and breaking up any large chunks, for 3 minutes.

3. Add the water and scrambler mix. Cook, stirring, for 2 minutes longer, or until green onions and seasonings are evenly distributed and tofu is golden yellow. Fold in mushrooms or place scrambler on a serving dish and spoon mushrooms over. Season with pepper, if desired.

Serves 3 to 4.

Variation: Substitute button mushrooms or rehydrated dried shiitake.

"Stedda" Matzo Brie

40 minutes

This traditional Jewish dish was devised to use up leftover matzo (a crackerlike unleavened bread) after the Passover holidays. The "Stedda" version uses up the matzo just as well and keeps everybody happy. *Le Chaim!* (To Life!)

2 whole-wheat matzos
1 cup plain soymilk, approximately
1 tablespoon sunflower oil
1 small onion, chopped
1 pound soft or firm tofu, crumbled
½ packet Tofu Scrambler Mix
Salt-free seasoning
Seasoned salt or freshly ground pepper

1. Break matzo into small pieces. Place in a shallow bowl and cover with soymilk. Soak for 15 to 30 minutes, until softened. Squeeze to extract as much milk as possible and set aside, reserving the milk.

2. Heat oil in a nonstick skillet and sauté onion, stirring until soft over medium heat. Add matzo and combine. Add tofu, mix well, and cook for 2 minutes.

3. Stir in reserved soymilk with additional soymilk or water to equal ½ cup. Add scrambler mix and mix well to distribute the ingredients. Season to taste with salt-free seasoning and freshly ground pepper. Serve with ketchup and a big salad.

Serves 3.

BURGERS AND OTHER SANDWICHES

Now we get into using "Steddas" in some of America's passion foods. With the appropriate fixings, you can relish some new-century burgers that are as slurpy, mouth-watering, and irresistible as their more "primitive" forerunners. In fact, they're so good and so good for you that they should go to the top of the list for all red-blooded, burger-loving, health-seeking Americans. Since these foods fall into our most popular genre, it's easy to embrace them. We can feel good about loving them and eating them, knowing that they are humane and ecologically sound versions of an American tradition.

"Stedda" Tuna

10 minutes

This is easy to make in a food processor in only 10 minutes, or a little longer by hand. Either way, it's well worth the effort. Use on a sandwich, on toast with thin cucumber slices and dill pickle, as a dip for raw vegetables or chips, or in a salad dressing. This food has sterling credentials. It is delicious, economical, nutritious, and has good keeping quality. Keep it on hand in a sealed container in the refrigerator.

1 celery stalk
1 large carrot, peeled
2 tablespoons minced onion
1 tablespoon minced green onion
½ cup chopped fresh parsley
¼ cup chopped fresh dill or 2 tablespoons dried
1 cup thick tahini (see Note)
⅓ cup lemon juice
2 tablespoons tamari
2 teaspoons kelp powder or ground rock salt to taste

1. In a food processor or by hand, chop celery, carrot, onion, and green onion, parsley, and dill until fine. Transfer to a medium bowl and set aside.

2. By hand or in food processor or blender, puree the tahini, lemon juice, and tamari with ½ cup boiling water.

3. Add tahini mixture to chopped vegetables. Thoroughly combine by briskly beating with a fork. Add a little water, if mixture is too thick, then add kelp powder.

Yields 2 cups.

Note: Thick tahini like peanut butter is preferable. If you can only get the watery variety, cut down on the water you add.

"Stedda" Egg Salad

10 minutes

Once you've tasted this, there will be no turning back. Serve with lettuce and tomato on toasted whole-grain English muffins, or as an accompaniment to a salad platter. Use as a dip for raw vegetables or chips.

8 ounces firm tofu
2 tablespoons minced celery
1 tablespoon minced green onion
½ teaspoon turmeric
¼ teaspoon curry powder
¼ teaspoon ground cumin
¼ teaspoon ground coriander
2 teaspoons nutritional yeast (optional)
½ teaspoon kelp powder or seasoned salt
2 to 3 tablespoons Almonnaise (page 98) or dairy-free mayonnaise
Freshly ground pepper (optional)

1. Crumble the tofu into a medium bowl. Add the celery and green onion.

2. Add turmeric, curry, cumin, coriander, yeast, kelp, Almonnaise, and pepper to taste. Mix well with a fork, mashing any large chunks of tofu so salad has uniform consistency.

Yields 1½ cups.

Happy "Chicken" Burgers

50 minutes

This is a wonderful recipe that can easily become a staple in any household.

1 cup firm tofu, wrapped for 10 minutes or longer
1 tablespoon olive oil
½ cup minced green onions
2 cups finely grated green cabbage
1 cup finely grated carrots
½ cup whole-wheat flour
¼ cup nutritional yeast (optional)
1½ tablespoons soy sauce
2 teaspoons baking powder
½ teaspoon poultry seasoning

1. Cut tofu in thin slices and wrap in several thickness of kitchen towel while you prepare other ingredients.

2. Heat oil in a skillet and add green onions. Sauté briefly, then add cabbage and carrot and sauté for 4 to 5 minutes, until soft. Set aside. Preheat oven to 350°F.

3. Cream the tofu in a food processor. Add the flour, yeast, soy sauce, baking powder, and poultry seasoning. Process until smooth. Add vegetables and pulse 3 times, just to combine and chop slightly. (This can also be done by hand.)

4. Spoon ⅓ cup of mixture in dollops onto an oiled baking sheet. Flatten to ¼- to ½-inch patties and shape in neat rounds. Bake for 15 minutes, then turn over and bake an additional 10 minutes.

5. Serve burgers on buns with Almonnaise, sliced tomato, sliced pickle, and sprouts. Or serve simply as pancakes with a sweet-and-sour sauce.

Serves 4.

"Stedda" Fish Fillets

35 minutes (after wrapping)

Once a week we used to go to a local natural foods restaurant where these were served on buns. Then we found out how easily we could make them ourselves. They're yummy on their own with lemon and tartar sauce, or great on a toasted whole-grain bun.

¾ pound firm tofu, cut in 4 (½-inch-thick) slices
1 cup fine bread or cracker crumbs
1 tablespoon nutritional yeast (optional)
¼ teaspoon garlic powder
¼ teaspoon onion powder
¼ teaspoon paprika
1 teaspoon powdered kelp or other salt-free seasoning
Olive oil

1. Place tofu slices on a clean kitchen towel and wrap towel around it several times. Allow to rest for 30 minutes. This step is optional.

2. Meanwhile, prepare breading mixture. In a pie plate or shallow bowl, combine crumbs, yeast, garlic and onion powder, paprika, and kelp. Mix thoroughly. Preheat oven to 350°F.

3. Brush sides and edges of tofu slices with olive oil. Dip into breading mixture and coat well. Place breaded slices on an oiled cookie sheet and bake for 20 minutes, until fillets are golden and crisp.

Serves 2 to 4.

"Stedda" Tartar Sauce

½ cup dairy-free mayonnaise or Enriched Almonnaise (page 98)
¼ cup grated dill or sweet pickle, according to taste
1 tablespoon lemon juice

Combine mayonnaise or Almonnaise with pickle and lemon juice and mix well.

Note: For the best fillet sandwich, brush whole-wheat buns with olive oil. Lightly toast buns, then spread bottom and top of each with a light coating of "Stedda" Tartar Sauce. Place one fish fillet on each of the four bun bottoms, add 1½ tablespoons tartar sauce, a tomato slice, and some alfalfa sprouts. Top with bun top.

Serves 4.

"STEDDA" MEAT MARINADES

When marinated, tofu can be treated as meat. You can cut it into fillets, marinate them, and then grill, broil, or pan-fry the fillets in the same way that many cuts of meat are prepared. Marinated tofu turns up as an important feature on a Mixed Grill Platter (page 115), threaded on skewers with vegetables (Kebobs, page 116), as sautéed chunks in many of your favorite salads ("Stedda" Chinese Chicken Salad, page 118), and last but not least, on sandwiches.

Whenever you marinate tofu, marinate plenty of it. You can grill or broil all of it and the cold leftovers can be used in sandwiches or salads. Here are some marinades. Each mixture is enough to marinate 1 pound of tofu:

All-Purpose Marinade I

2 teaspoons dry mustard
1/2 cup low-sodium soy sauce
1 teaspoon sorghum or cane molasses
2 tablespoons brown rice syrup or honey
Cayenne to taste (2 dashes are enough for us)
3 tablespoons minced onion or 1 teaspoon onion powder
2 garlic cloves, pressed, or 1 teaspoon garlic powder

All-Purpose Marinade II

1 cup rich vegetable stock
1 tablespoon Umeboshi plum vinegar or rice vinegar
2 teaspoons curry powder
2 teaspoons brown rice syrup (or honey)

"Chicken" Flavoring

2 heaping tablespoons powdered chicken-flavored vegetable broth
2 tablespoons hickory-smoked barbecue sauce
1 teaspoon rice vinegar
½ cup boiling water
2 tablespoons low-sodium soy sauce
¼ to ½ teaspoon salt-free seasoning, or pinches of paprika, rosemary, garlic powder, oregano, onion powder, basil, and parsley
Freshly ground pepper to taste

Barbecue-Style Marinade

2 teaspoons strong beefy-flavored vegetable broth
½ cup hot water
3 tablespoons hickory-smoked barbecue sauce
1 teaspoon Worcestershire sauce
¼ teaspoon onion powder
¼ teaspoon garlic powder
¼ teaspoon paprika
Pinches of savory, parsley, marjoram, basil, thyme, rosemary, and sage
½ cup coarsely chopped red onion

"Beefy" Marinade

¼ cup low-sodium soy sauce
½ teaspoon powdered vegetable broth, or 1 bouillon cube
½ cup water
2 teaspoons dry mustard
1 tablespoon sorghum molasses or honey
1 tablespoon brown rice syrup or honey
½ teaspoon garlic powder
1 teaspoon Spice Garden mushroom powder (optional)
½ teaspoon paprika

Sweet and Sour

½ cup green onion, minced
1 teaspoon garlic, minced
½ cup vegetable broth
2 tablespoons ketchup
¼ cup water
1 tablespoon low sodium soy sauce
¼ cup cilantro, minced (optional)
1 tablespoon rice vinegar
1 tablespoon honey or brown rice syrup
¼ teaspoon chili powder
Dash of cayenne pepper

"Stedda" Chicken Fillets

30 minutes for wrapping (optional)
30 minutes to 2 hours for marinating
15 to 20 minutes for grilling

This is one of my favorite tofu preparations. As part of the Mixed Grill Platter (see below) with lots of grilled vegetables, this makes an outstanding meal. Remember to add the oil to the marinade right before cooking to keep the fillets from sticking. (I also turn them several times, just to be sure.) Grill or broil the fillets about 4 inches from the heat source. Make plenty and keep them on hand in the refrigerator.

1 pound firm tofu
All-Purpose Marinade I (page 113) or "chicken" flavoring
2 tablespoons olive oil

1. Cut tofu crosswise into 8 slices. Place slices on a clean kitchen towel and wrap towel around it several times. Allow to rest for 30 minutes.

2. Add tofu slices to marinade and coat well on all sides. Place in refrigerator and marinate for 30 minutes to 2 hours.

3. Transfer marinated fillets to a plate. Add olive oil to marinade and brush fillets with it. Place fillets on a preheated grill or on rack in broiler pan and grill or broil 5 to 10 minutes on each side, brushing and turning fillets several times if you use a grill but only once in broiler.

Serves 4.

Mixed Grill Platter

30 minutes for wrapping (optional)
1 to 3 hours for marinating
15 minutes for grilling

1 pound firm tofu
All-purpose Marinade I or II (page 113), doubled
1 large red onion, cut in ⅓-inch slices
4 scallopini-cut zucchini or 1 large zucchini, cut in ¼- to ⅓-inch slices (if using large zucchini, slice on diagonal)
2 Japanese eggplant, cut in ¼- to ⅓-inch diagonal slices
2 large yellow squash, cut in ¼- to ⅓-inch diagonal slices
¼ cup olive oil

1. Cut tofu into 8 crosswise ½-inch-thick slices. Place on a clean kitchen towel and wrap towel around it several times. Allow to rest for 30 minutes.

2. Place tofu in a single layer in a large, shallow baking dish. Pour half the marinade over the tofu and turn slices to coat thoroughly. Place onion slices on top of tofu, then top with a little of the remaining marinade.

3. Place vegetables on top of onion and top with remaining marinade. Cover and refrigerate 1 to 3 hours.

4. Heat grill or broiler. Place vegetables and tofu on a rack 4 inches from the heat, in batches. Immediately combine olive oil with ½ cup of marinade and brush tofu and vegetables. Turn immediately to prevent sticking, then grill for 5 minutes or until lightly browned on one side. Brush again and turn, then grill until lightly browned on remaining side.

5. Transfer finished vegetables and tofu from grill to serving platter, and cook remaining tofu and vegetables, using same process.

Serves 4.

Variations: Asparagus, red and yellow pepper, and mushrooms can all be added to the platter, prepared in the same way.

Kebobs!

30 minutes for wrapping
1–3 hours for marinating
10 minutes for broiling

If you are using wooden skewers, soak them while you prepare the tofu and vegetables to prevent their burning. Serve the kebobs with Classic Green Salad (page 140) and Easy Broccoli Pilaf (page 300). Or make miniature kebobs as an appetizer.

1 pound firm tofu
2 large carrots, peeled and trimmed
2 medium red bell peppers
1 large red onion
12 mushrooms, trimmed
2 cups marinade of your choice
¼ cup olive oil

1. Cut tofu in lengthwise 1-inch slabs. Place slabs on a clean kitchen towel, wrap towel around them several times, and allow to rest for 30 minutes.

2. Cut carrots in ½-inch diagonal slices and steam for 15 minutes or until tender. Cut peppers and onion in ½-inch wedges.

3. Unwrap tofu and cut into 1-inch cubes. Place tofu and vegetables in a shallow baking dish. Add marinade and toss gently with a rubber spatula to coat thoroughly. Cover and refrigerate for 1 to 3 hours.

4. Thread marinated vegetables and tofu on skewers, always placing a slice of onion next to tofu cube for flavoring. Arrange kebobs on platter. Combine olive oil with ½ cup marinade and brush kebobs thoroughly.

5. Heat grill or broiler. Place kebobs on rack and cook, turning until lightly browned and brushing as frequently as you desire.

Serves 4.

Tofu Meunière

1 hour

Serve with Potatoes and Zucchini in Olive Oil (page 257) and Classic Green Salad (page 140).

1 pound firm tofu

Marinade

1 teaspoon crushed garlic
1 green onion, minced
3½ tablespoons lemon juice
2 tablespoons tamari, or 1 tablespoon tamari and 1 tablespoon teriyaki sauce
1 teaspoon dried rosemary
½ teaspoon kelp powder

Dredging Mixture

½ cup whole-wheat pastry flour
¼ teaspoon powdered kelp or ground rock salt and pepper

To Finish

2 to 3 tablespoons olive oil
Lemon juice
¼ cup minced fresh parsley, for garnish

1. Cut tofu in 8 uniform slices, ¼- to ½-inch thick. Place slices on a cloth towel and wrap in several thicknesses to extract moisture. Let sit, wrapped, for 30 minutes.

2. Combine the marinade ingredients with a whisk in large, shallow bowl or baking dish. Add tofu slices and marinate for several hours in the refrigerator.

3. Combine flour, kelp, and salt and pepper to taste in a shallow dish. Place tofu slices one at a time in the seasoned flour to coat.

4. Heat a large skillet with olive oil. Add tofu slices and sauté for 5 minutes on each side until golden brown. Transfer to a platter and season with lemon juice and garnish with minced parsley.

Serves 3 to 4.

Lemon "Stedda" Chicken

10 minutes

For a light, satisfying meal, serve this with Potato-Lover's Salad (page 158) and corn on the cob.

1 pound firm tofu
1 tablespoon olive oil
1 teaspoon pressed garlic
½ cup sliced green onions
1 tablespoon whole-wheat pastry flour
1 tablespoon nutritional yeast (optional)
½ teaspoon Umeboshi plum vinegar or brown rice vinegar
2 tablespoons teriyaki sauce or light soy sauce
1 tablespoon lemon juice

1. Cut tofu crosswise in ¼-inch slices, then cut slices in 1-inch segments.

2. Heat wok or large nonstick skillet and add oil and garlic. Add tofu immediately and stir-fry for 1 minute. Add green onions and stir-fry 1 minute longer.

3. Dust tofu and onion mixture with flour and yeast. Stir-fry for 2 minutes more, allowing tofu pieces to brown and crisp slightly. Add vinegar and teriyaki sauce, then stir-fry until completely absorbed. Add lemon juice and stir-fry 2 minutes longer.

Serves 4.

"Stedda" Chinese Chicken Salad

1 hour, 15 minutes

This is a great way to use marinated tofu chunks. You can sit down, eat a great big bowl of this heavenly salad and nothing else, feel full for 20 minutes, and then feel light and nourished, empty but fed, and—best of all—full of energy! This is an example of eating low on the food chain so that you can know what it feels to be high on life!

Serve with Sesame Eggplant (page 236) and Sweet Potato Biscuits (page 340).

Salad

1 pound firm tofu
"Chicken" Flavoring marinade (page 113)
2 tablespoons hickory-flavored barbecue sauce
½ cup safflower oil
1 cup rice sticks
1½ cups slivered mushrooms: shiitake, porcini, oyster, enoki, or button (optional)
2 tablespoons low-sodium soy sauce
2 bunches spinach
1 large sweet red pepper, chopped in ½-inch segments (1½ cups)
2 to 2½ cups English cucumber, julienned (page 212)

Dressing

2 tablespoons sesame seeds
1 tablespoon roasted sesame oil
1½ teaspoons low-sodium soy sauce
1½ tablespoons lemon juice
2 tablespoons teriyaki sauce
1 tablespoon rice vinegar
1 tablespoon pressed fresh ginger,* or 1 teaspoon powdered
2 teaspoons fresh crushed garlic

1. Cut tofu lengthwise so you have two 1-inch slabs. Place slabs on a clean kitchen towel and wrap in several thicknesses. Allow to rest for 30 minutes to draw out excess water.

2. Combine marinade and barbecue sauce. Heat safflower oil in a medium skillet, then drop 10 to 15 rice sticks at a time into hot oil. Sticks will puff up immediately and sizzle. Turn over until popping has ceased and immediately transfer to a dry towel to drain. Set aside.

3. Place tofu chunks in marinade. Toss gently so chunks are coated, then set aside for 30 minutes, turning once.

4. Sauté mushrooms in a medium skillet with the soy sauce until tender and soy sauce is absorbed. Set aside.

5. Chop spinach in fine pieces. Place in a large salad bowl with red pepper, cucumber, and mushrooms.

6. Prepare dressing by combining sesame seeds, sesame oil, and ½ teaspoon soy sauce in a small skillet. Toast seeds on low heat until slightly browned, about 5 minutes. Remove from heat and combine with remaining ingredients.

7. Pour marinating chunks of tofu and marinade into a large, dry skillet. Cook over medium-high heat until dry and slightly crusty on edges, stirring frequently and pouring off any excess liquid, about 10 to 15 minutes.

8. Add chunks and dressing to salad and toss well. Fold in rice sticks gently.

Serves 4.

*Use garlic press for pressing ginger.

7

How to Make Salads That Make *the Meal*

GIVEN a brand-new twist, salads will be the winning food, "the main event," the fuel for the next decade. The trend has already started, but mainly on a commercial basis. If you look at any of the popular, prepared foods sections in many supermarkets around the country, what will you find? A cornucopia of salads (where once there was a deli display) that entice the eyes and tempt the taste buds. Practically *anything* you might think of eating can now be found, cleverly incorporated into large platters of colorful, innovative, fully dressed salads.

It's no wonder salads are such a hit! They're versatile. They satisfy our desire for fresher, more nutritious food. They give us less of what we shouldn't eat and more of what now comes highly recommended. Since by their very nature they combine lots of light, living food with less more concentrated food, they digest easily and nourish more completely. Perhaps the most important key to their present success is that they are *absolutely delicious* and *never boring.* Also in their favor is the tendency to be "one-dish" meals, requiring only a plate or bowl and a fork, which means speedy, easy clean-up. They are also economical and keep for hours under refrigeration. Since most ethnic flavors can be expressed via salads, they have a wide palate appeal. Finally, they can be prepared in small quantities for one person or in huge vats for a crowd. Their popularity is well justified!

Of course, what we used to think of as salad and what we presently include under this label are practically unrelated entities. Remember when a salad was some Iceberg lettuce, a wedge of tomato, perhaps some sliced cucumber, and a little grated carrot all "dressed" with a bright orange liquid inexactly called "french dressing"? In the fifties, that's what most Americans called a salad. By the late sixties, we were adding some sunflower seeds, avocado, and sprouts. In the seventies, we branched into new varieties of lettuce, added beans, cheese, more sprouts, croutons, and wider range of dressings. But not until the late eighties did salads truly come into their own, featuring pasta, potatoes, or rice; chunks of meat, fish, chicken, or seafood; cheese; every possible vegetable; and exotics such as wild mushrooms, hearts of palm, and sun-dried tomatoes, with an infinite variety of dressings and sauces.

Main-Course Salads seem here to stay, and that's good news. However they are still most commonly found in take-home food cases, not as food prepared in the American kitchen. It is precisely in our own kitchens where Main-Course Salads should take command. They are too easy to make, and much less expensive when we make them ourselves. Main-Course Salads are one of the simplest, most creative vehicles for self-expression in the kitchen. As one-dish meals, they have been a dominant feature on the *Fit for Life* menu for over ten years. I assure you that the basic formula is as fundamental as 1, 2, 3. The background is nearly always the same. Only the accents change according to whim. Many delicious luncheons and dinners are in store when you make Main-Course Salads the focus of your meal.

The crown of the salad is, of course, the dressing, and nothing more brings out my dedication and determination. I hear the frequent lament, "I would eat so much more salad if I could only make a dressing I liked!" *You can!* Salad dressings are *easy!* It takes practically no skill at all to make a perfectly wonderful—no, a *fantastic* dressing. Can you uncap a bottle of olive oil? Can you squeeze the juice from a lemon? Can you insert a clove of garlic into a press and then press it? Can you sprinkle some seasonings into a bowl? Then you can make dressings! You can make dressings you and others will absolutely adore! Lots of them!

TWO-MINUTE DRESSINGS

There are two methods for making Two-Minute Dressings, and one does not replace the other. Both are valid techniques. They are also so easy there's no reason not to know both of them. The first is the bowl method.

BOWL-METHOD DRESSINGS

Basic Salad Dressing

Prepare this dressing directly into your salad bowl. All ingredients are measured into the bowl and then easily combined into a smooth, creamy dressing by beating with a whisk.

4 tablespoons extra-virgin olive oil (quality really counts!)
1½ tablespoons lemon juice
1 medium garlic clove, crushed (optional)
Seasoned salt, salt-free seasoning, or ground rock salt to taste (optional, and only for those whose palate requires it, in minute amounts)
Freshly ground pepper (optional)

Measure oil and lemon juice directly into salad bowl. Add crushed garlic, if desired, and seasonings to taste. Beat with whisk until smooth and creamy.

Yields enough for 2 to 3 large salads.

The Basic Salad Dressing is the framework for any other bowl dressing you wish to prepare. But there are some easy additions to this framework that enhance and even transform it, and they are certainly worth discovering. In all of the following addition suggestions, the equipment and procedure remain the same. Blend the ingredients into a cream directly in your salad bowl.

To the Basic Salad Dressing recipe, add one or more of the following, in any combination that suits you. (Specific combinations are to be found in the recipes to follow.) The list will give you a chance to modify your dressing according to your taste.

½ to 1 teaspoon Dijon-style mustard
1 teaspoon to 1 tablespoon dairy-free mayonnaise or Almonnaise (page 98)
1 teaspoon tahini plus 1 tablespoon water
Dash of Worcestershire sauce
1 teaspoon Umeboshi plum paste
1 to 2 teaspoons tamari or shoyu
1 teaspoon honey
1 to 2 teaspoons barbecue sauce
2 to 4 tablespoons Almond or Cashew Milk (page 60, 63)
1 teaspoon cashew butter or almond butter
1 teaspoon to 1 tablespoon "Stedda" Sour Cream (page 105)
1 tablespoon celery juice instead of salt
½ to 1 teaspoon dried herbs in any combination: basil, tarragon, chervil, oregano, savory, dill, thyme, chive, mint
1 tablespoon fresh herbs in any combination
½ to 1 teaspoon curry powder
Dash of cayenne
½ teaspoon paprika
¼ to ½ teaspoon dry mustard
1 teaspoon poppy seeds, or black or white sesame seeds
½ teaspoon kelp, dulse, or nori powder or flakes
1 tablespoon minced green onion or fresh parsley
2 tablespoons minced green or black olives

Dairy-Free Thousand Island Dressing

This all-time favorite (particularly among the younger set) is easily done in the salad bowl, but with a departure from the basic ingredients.

⅓ cup Almonnaise (page 98) or dairy-free mayonnaise
3 tablespoons honey-sweetened ketchup
2 teaspoons fresh lemon juice
¼ cup finely grated dill pickle

Measure Almonnaise, ketchup, and lemon juice into a large salad bowl. Add grated pickle. Combine with a whisk or hand blender.

Serves 2 to 3.

Fit for Life "House" Dressing

This is one of our favorite dressings. I use it on most of the salads I make because it just lends itself to so many different flavors. It is particularly delicious on a tender lettuce salad, lightly but thoroughly tossed. The tahini gives it a "cheesy" quality, as if you had added parmesan, but without the negative effects.

4 tablespoons extra-virgin olive oil
1½ tablespoons lemon juice
1 medium garlic clove, crushed
1 teaspoon tahini
1 tablespoon water
½ to 1 teaspoon Dijon-style mustard
Ground rock salt, seasoned salt, or salt-free seasoning to taste (optional)
Freshly ground pepper (optional)

Measure oil and lemon juice into salad bowl. Add garlic, tahini, water, and seasonings to taste. Beat with whisk until smooth and creamy.

Serves 2 to 3.

Real French Dressing

You can successfully add herbs to this dressing, but it stands on its own as one of the most popular dressings I make. It's simple, but people never grow tired of it. This is a personal version of the perfectly balanced, light salad dressings served all over France. American "french" dressing is anything but! Use your finest extra-virgin olive oil for this dressing; it will make a noticeable difference. This is a particularly appropriate dressing for tender greens.

4 tablespoons extra-virgin olive oil
1 medium garlic clove, pressed
1½ tablespoons lemon juice
¼ to ½ teaspoon Dijon-style mustard
Ground rock salt, seasoned salt, or salt-free seasoning to taste (optional; no salt is necessary because mustard contains salt)
Freshly ground pepper (optional)

Measure oil and garlic into salad bowl. Add lemon juice, mustard, and seasonings to taste. Whisk until dressing is light yellow and thick.

Serves 2 to 3.

Note: Especially with tender greens, avoid combining dressing with greens until right before serving. The salt component in the dressing will wilt the salad if it sits too long.

Mock Goat-Cheese Dressing

This is an excellent "cheesy" dressing, but surprise, surprise—no cheese!

- 6 tablespoons extra-virgin olive oil
- 2 to 3 tablespoons lemon juice
- 1 large garlic clove, pressed
- 2 teaspoons white or black sesame seeds or poppy seeds
- 2 tablespoons tahini
- 2 tablespoons dairy-free mayonnaise or Almonnaise (page 98)
- 4 to 6 tablespoons water, depending on how thick you like dressing
- Dash of Worcestershire sauce or Umeboshi plum vinegar (optional)
- Dash of cayenne
- Ground rock salt, seasoned salt, or salt-free seasoning (optional)
- Freshly ground pepper (optional)

Measure oil, lemon juice, garlic, sesame seeds, and tahini into salad bowl. Add mayonnaise, water, Worcestershire sauce, and seasonings to taste. Whisk until thick and creamy.

Serves 4 to 6.

Curried Mayonnaise Dressing

I used this dressing in *Fit for Life I* for the Curried Chicken Salad. I received so many letters raving about it. Try it on the new favorite, "Stedda" Chicken-Lover's Salad (page 157), for a real treat!

- 2 tablespoons extra-virgin olive oil
- 1 tablespoon fresh lemon juice
- 1 to 2 tablespoons eggless mayonnaise or Almonnaise
- 1 teaspoon honey
- ½ teaspoon curry powder
- ½ teaspoon dried basil, or 2 teaspoons minced fresh basil
- 1 teaspoon minced green onions
- ¼ teaspoon ground rock salt, or ½ teaspoon kelp powder
- Freshly ground black pepper

Measure oil, lemon juice, mayonnaise, and honey into a large salad bowl. Add curry powder, basil, green onions, rock salt, and pepper to taste. Whisk or hand blend until thick and creamy.

Serves 2.

Umeboshi Salad Dressing

The pickled paste from the Umeboshi plum, which is a Japanese vegetable—not a fruit—lends a salty, tangy flavor to this dressing. It is a particularly refreshing dressing in hot weather. Macrobiotic cuisine uses Umeboshi plum paste consistently for its alkaline properties. I use it occasionally, and in small amounts, because it is quite salty. You'll find it at many natural foods stores on the macrobiotic food shelves. Because it is salty it keeps indefinitely and does not need to be refrigerated.

2 tablespoons sesame or olive oil
1 teaspoon Umeboshi plum paste
½ teaspoon grated ginger
2 teaspoons lemon juice
1 tablespoon water
1 small tomato, peeled and chopped

Combine oil, plum paste, and ginger in a large salad bowl. Add lemon juice, water, and chopped tomato. Beat with a whisk or hand blend until well combined.

Serves 2.

Lime-Dill Dressing

Limes have a milder flavor than most lemons. You may need to use a little bit more lime juice if you substitute it for lemon juice. This is a refreshing dressing when fresh dill is in season.

¼ cup extra-virgin olive oil
2 tablespoons fresh lime juice
1 tablespoon fresh dill, snipped with scissors or minced
1 medium garlic clove, pressed
½ teaspoon Dijon-style mustard
Ground rock salt and freshly ground pepper to taste (optional)

Measure oil and lime juice directly into a large salad bowl. Add dill, garlic, mustard, and seasonings to taste. Beat with a whisk until thick and creamy.

Serves 3 to 4.

Chinese Salad Dressing

If you are making a salad that features lots of crisp Asian vegetables like bok choy, snow peas, mung bean sprouts, and Japanese cucumber, use this dressing with flavors from Asia.

⅓ cup light sesame oil or extra-virgin olive oil
1 large garlic clove, pressed
1 (1-inch chunk) fresh ginger, pressed, or ¼ teaspoon powdered
2 tablespoons tamari
Dash of cayenne
2 tablespoons fresh lemon or lime juice
2 teaspoons honey (optional)
1 teaspoon unhulled sesame seeds
1 tablespoon finely minced green onion (optional)

Measure oil, garlic, ginger, and tamari into a large salad bowl. Add cayenne, lemon juice, honey, sesame seeds, and green onion. Beat with whisk or hand blend until well combined.

Serves 4 to 6.

Garlic-Herb Dressing for a Crowd

Sometimes you want to make a huge salad for a potluck supper or picnic. You want it to be special, so a bottled dressing won't do. When I once made a Mediterranean Rice Salad (page 160) for forty people, I computed this dressing for that amount. It's nice to have on hand, just in case.

Normally this would be a bowl-method dressing, but not for this crowd. This one we do in the blender, which naturally leads me to the second method of preparing really delicious salad dressings.

4½ cups extra-virgin olive oil
¾ cup fresh lemon juice
10 medium garlic cloves or ¼ cup garlic powder
3 teaspoons paprika
2 teaspoons dried basil
2 teaspoons dried mint
2 teaspoons dried thyme
1 teaspoon dried oregano
1 teaspoon dried chervil
¼ cup seasoned salt

Measure half the ingredients in a blender and blend until smooth and creamy, taking care that garlic breaks down entirely. (You don't want people to receive a hunk of garlic in their mouth while enjoying your salad.) Measure the second half of the ingredients into the blender and repeat.

Serves 40.

Variations: (1) add 4 tablespoons of Dijon-style mustard for a tangier dressing (reduce the amount of seasoned salt by ¼); (2) add 4 tablespoons tahini and ½ cup water.

BLENDER-METHOD DRESSINGS

This is such an easy technique for making salad dressings! All the ingredients can be whipped in seconds with a hand blender. That's it! There's hardly a limit to what can be accomplished with this method. Here, I give you the combinations of ingredients that have worked for me.

The procedure is always the same. Measure the ingredients directly into the blender container. In only a few seconds of blending, your dressing will be a smooth, thick cream.

Note: If you wish to lower the oil content of any of these dressings, substitute for the oil indicated an equal amount of vegetable broth or carrot juice.

Kids' Preference Dressing

3 tablespoons dairy-free mayonnaise
¼ cup extra-virgin olive oil
2 tablespoons fresh lemon juice
1 medium garlic clove
Seasoned salt to taste

Yields ½ cup.

Blue Ribbon Seven-Herb Dressing

2 garlic cloves, crushed
½ cup olive oil
4 tablespoons fresh lemon juice
½ teaspoon dried basil
½ teaspoon dried chervil
¼ teaspoon dried thyme
¼ teaspoon dried oregano
½ teaspoon dried savory
¼ teaspoon ground coriander
⅛ teaspoon dried sage
Ground rock salt, seasoned salt, or salt-free seasoning to taste (optional)
2 teaspoons Dijon-style mustard
1 tablespoon dairy-free mayonnaise or Almonnaise (page 98)

Yields ¾ cup.

"Sour Cream" Garlic Dressing

¼ cup water
1 medium garlic clove
4 ounces soft tofu, preferably silken
¼ cup olive oil
3 tablespoons lemon juice
2 teaspoons rice vinegar
1 tablespoon poppy seeds
1 teaspoon dried dill
Seasoned salt or salt-free seasoning to taste (optional)

Yields 1½ cups.

Avo-Goddess Dressing

1 ripe avocado (medium to large)
1 medium cucumber, peeled and cut in chunks
2 teaspoons dried dill
Seasoned salt or salt-free seasoning to taste
1 tablespoon lime juice
2 tablespoons extra-virgin olive oil

Yields 1½ cups.

Tomato-Herb Dressing

1 large ripe tomato
1 tablespoon lemon juice
¼ cup extra-virgin olive oil
½ teaspoon dried tarragon, or 1½ teaspoons fresh
1 tablespoon fresh basil, or 1 teaspoon dried
Dash of Worcestershire sauce
¼ teaspoon dry mustard
Dash of cayenne
Salt-free seasoning to taste (optional)

Yields ¾ cup.

Lemon–Poppy Seed Dressing

1½ tablespoons poppy seeds
2½ tablespoons lemon juice
1 teaspoon honey or FruitSource
2 tablespoons dairy-free mayonnaise
½ teaspoon dry mustard
1½ tablespoons sunflower oil

Yields ½ cup.

Lemon Vinaigrette

½ cup extra-virgin olive oil
3 tablespoons lemon juice
1 tablespoon fresh thyme, or 1 teaspoon dried
1 tablespoon fresh dill
1 tablespoon fresh chives
Ground rock salt
Freshly ground pepper to taste (optional)

Yields ¾ cup.

Award-Winning Sesame Garlic Dressing

¼ cup olive oil
1 medium garlic clove
2 tablespoons lemon juice
1 heaping tablespoon tahini
2 tablespoons water
¼ teaspoon ground rock salt or salt-free seasoning
½ teaspoon dried oregano
½ teaspoon dried chervil
Freshly ground pepper to taste

Yields ½ cup.

"Cheesy" Dijon Dressing

¼ pound (4 ounces) firm tofu
¼ cup olive oil
1 medium garlic clove
1 small tomato
2 teaspoons low-sodium soy sauce
3 tablespoons water
½ teaspoon Dijon-style mustard
2¼ tablespoons rice vinegar
3 tablespoons lemon juice
1 tablespoon apple cider vinegar
1 (1-inch) chunk onion
1 tablespoon minced chives
1½ tablespoons fresh dill, or 2 teaspoons dried
¼ teaspoon ground rock salt (optional)

Yields 1½ cups.

Creamy Cucumber-Dill Dressing

2 tablespoons lemon juice
5 tablespoons extra-virgin olive oil
1 (4-inch) segment peeled cucumber
1 tablespoon dairy-free mayonnaise or Almonnaise (page 98)
⅛ to ¼ teaspoon dry mustard
2 tablespoons fresh dill, or 2 teaspoons dried
1 small garlic clove, or 1 small wedge red onion
Ground rock salt or salt-free seasoning to taste (optional)

Yields 1 cup.

Terrific Tamari Dressing

1 tablespoon extra-virgin olive oil
1 heaping tablespoon tahini
2 to 3 tablespoons purified water
1 tablespoon lime juice
1 (1-inch) chunk red onion
1 tablespoon tamari

Yields ½ cup.

Orange "French" Dressing

1 medium tomato
¼ cup dairy-free mayonnaise or Almonnaise (page 98)
¼ cup purified water
3 tablespoons olive oil
Garlic powder to taste
Seasoned salt or salt-free seasoning to taste (optional)

Yields 1 cup.

FAVORITE DIPS FOR VEGETABLE PLATES OR CHIPS

There is one more popular version of a salad dressing that I can't ignore, especially since we use this item so much as an appetizer. Dips are fun food. Who doesn't enjoy being close to a delicious dip surrounded by a colorful platter of sliced, full-of-life raw vegetables?

Linda's Delicious Hummus

My sister Linda is a hummus "nut," and she's also a busy lady, so I wasn't surprised when she developed the *fastest, best hummus* recipe. This is a highly nutritious dip for vegetables or chips or as a spread for sandwiches, prepared in only 10 minutes.

2 to 3 tablespoons water
Juice of 1 lemon (3 to 4 tablespoons)
1 medium garlic clove
¼ cup tahini
1 (17-ounce) jar garbanzo beans, drained

Measure olive oil and lemon juice in blender or food processor. Add garlic and tahini and blend until smooth. Add beans and blend until mixture is creamy.

Yields 2 cups.

Guacamole Calabasas

Everybody loves a good guacamole, and this is a zesty version that can be as mild or as spicy as your taste buds dictate, simply by adjusting the amounts of chili powder and cayenne. Use as a dip for raw vegetables, Crusty Roasteds Revisited (page 246), Oven-Roasted Potato Fries (page 247), or any good corn chip. Yum!

2 green onions, minced
1 large garlic clove, minced or pressed
1 large tomato, minced
1 tablespoon fresh lemon juice
½ cup minced fresh parsley
¼ cup minced cilantro
1 teaspoon ground cumin
½ teaspoon chili powder
Cayenne to taste
4 ripe avocados, peeled, seeded, and mashed (approximately 2 cups)
Ground rock salt or seasoned salt
Freshly ground pepper to taste

Chop all vegetables by hand or use a food processor, to process ingredients in the order given, using the steel blade.

Yields 3 to 4 cups.

Mock Guac

When avocados are not in season, this dip is a fine replacement for guacamole. Serve as a dip for crudités or chips, or spread a dollop on cucumber rounds as an appetizer, garnished with a slice of green or black olive.

1 (10-ounce) package frozen petite peas
1 tablespoon sunflower oil or soy margarine
1 tablespoon Almonnaise (page 98) or dairy-free mayonnaise
1 to 2 teaspoons ground cumin
½ teaspoon lemon juice
½ teaspoon sea salt (optional)
½ to 1 teaspoon ground coriander
Freshly ground pepper
1 to 2 tablespoons water (optional)

Steam peas in a vegetable steamer over boiling water until tender, approximately 5 minutes. Place hot peas in a food processor with oil or margarine, mayonnaise, and seasonings to taste. Process until smooth. Add water if a thinner consistency is desired.

Yields 2 cups.

Quick Guacamole

When there's no time for chopping and you want guacamole fast, this takes only 5 minutes. The oregano gives it a nice flavor.

2 ripe avocados, halved, seeded, and flesh scooped from skin
¼ to ½ teaspoon garlic powder
1½ to 2 tablespoons fresh lemon juice
½ teaspoon dried oregano
¼ to ½ teaspoon ground cumin (optional)
Freshly ground pepper to taste

Mash or blend the avocado until smooth. Add the remaining ingredients and mix well. Let the mixture stand for a few minutes. Chill, if desired.

Yields 1½ to 2 cups.

Baba Ganoush

This tahini eggplant dip is a deliciously savory mixture with a light, creamy consistency. I have served this dip to people who "don't care for eggplant or tahini" and watched with amusement as they gobbled it down!

1 medium eggplant (approximately 12 ounces)
¼ cup lemon juice
¼ cup tahini
1 to 2 garlic cloves, or garlic powder
Ground rock salt (optional)
1 tablespoon olive oil
¼ cup minced fresh parsley
Parsley sprigs

Preheat oven to 400°F. Pierce the eggplant in several places with a fork and place in a shallow baking dish. Cover loosely with a tent of foil and bake for 40 minutes or until tender and slightly imploded. Remove skin while it is still hot, and trim away ends if they have remained firm. Chop the flesh until fine or puree in a blender or food processor. Blend in most of the lemon juice and gradually add the tahini. Crush the garlic and add, beat well, then add remaining lemon juice and salt to taste, if desired. Beat in olive oil and minced parsley. Place in a shallow bowl and garnish with parsley sprigs.

Serves 4 to 6.

Note: If preparing ahead of time, store in a sealed container in refrigerator. Bring to room temperature before serving.

Bell Pepper Salsa

3 red bell peppers, chopped coarsely
1 green bell pepper, chopped coarsely
1 small green onion, chopped coarsely
3 plum tomatoes, quartered
3 tablespoons fresh lime juice or to taste
1 tablespoon olive oil
Freshly ground pepper

In a food processor, chop the peppers, onion, and tomato finely but do not let them liquefy. Transfer the mixture to a bowl, stir in the lime juice and the oil, and pepper to taste, and let salsa stand for 30 minutes.

Yields about 2 cups.

Salsa Verde

This can be used as a dip for chips, as a dressing, or as a sauce for enchiladas.

1 pound fresh tomatillos, peeled
1 medium onion
1 jalapeño or 2 serrano chilies
2 tablespoons minced cilantro
2 medium garlic cloves
½ teaspoon honey

Simmer tomatillos in water to cover for 3 minutes. Drain, then coarsely chop with all remaining ingredients in a food processor or blender. Just before serving, thin with water to saucelike consistency, if necessary.

Yields 2 cups.

HOW TO MAKE FRESH CORN CHIPS

Fresh corn tortillas
Safflower oil
Salt-free seasoning

Cut tortillas into strips and lay them out on a cookie sheet to dry for several hours. Heat ¼ inch oil in a skillet until a drop of water sizzles. Add the tortillas and fry until golden. Drain on paper towels and season to taste.

Classic Salsa (hot!)

When you make salsa with jalapeños, protect yourself with rubber gloves and take care not to get any juice near your eyes, nose, or mouth. Plus, clean your cutting board carefully afterward or other innocent foods could turn to fire! (It's not worth the trouble to me, and we don't like such hot foods anyway, since ulcers and destroyed taste buds are not our idea of a good time.) If you do like jalapeños, this Classic Salsa recipe is for you. It's one of the few truly hot recipes in this book, and I included it because I understand that some people really enjoy hot food. (A word to the wise, however; in Mexico, we find one of the highest ulcer rates in the world.)

2 cups peeled and chopped tomatoes
2 tablespoons minced cilantro
2 tablespoons minced red onion
1 teaspoon minced hot chilies
Dash of honey
Chili powder
Salt
Wine vinegar or lemon juice

Combine tomatoes, cilantro, onion, and hot pepper. Season to taste with honey, chili powder, salt, and wine vinegar.

Yields 2½ cups.

Easy Mild Salsa

If you're not into jalapeños, try this delicious salsa instead.

1½ cups chopped tomatoes (peeling is optional)
½ cup minced red onion
½ cup minced red bell pepper
½ cup minced green bell pepper
3 tablespoons minced cilantro (optional)
1 garlic clove, minced (optional)
3 tablespoons extra-virgin olive oil
Chili powder
Cayenne

Combine the tomatoes, onion, peppers, cilantro, and garlic in a medium bowl. Stir in oil, chili powder, and cayenne to taste.

Yields 2½ to 3 cups.

Tahina

Similar to Sesame Cream, this thick, garlicky tahini dip is great for chips or pita toasts as well as all varieties of vegetables. Although thick and pasty from the jar, tahini becomes white and milky as it is thinned with water. Lemon juice is the thickener.

1 cup tahini
1 to 2 teaspoons minced garlic
½ teaspoon salt
¾ to 1 cup water, approximately
⅓ to ½ cup lemon juice

Combine tahini, garlic, and salt in a blender or food processor, adding water and lemon juice as necessary to reach desired texture.

Yields 2½ cups.

Armenian Chilled Eggplant Dip

This is a delicious treat, especially on a hot day or as part of a buffet. The flavor is just exotic enough to bring a special diversity to any meal. Serve with chips and raw vegetables or in small bowls as a salad.

1 firm medium eggplant
1 medium green bell pepper
1 large garlic clove
1 cup water
1 large ripe tomato, peeled and finely chopped
1 tablespoon olive oil (optional)
1 teaspoon lemon or lime juice
Dash of salt or salt-free seasoning (optional)
Freshly ground pepper

Preheat the oven to 375°F. Pierce eggplant and pepper several times with a fork. Place in a shallow baking dish with the garlic. Add water to dish and bake vegetables until soft all over and quite deflated, about 1½ hours. Remove from oven, cool slightly, then peel both eggplant and pepper, discarding seeds from pepper.

Mash pulp of both vegetables (with the garlic) in a mixing bowl. Add tomato, oil, lemon or lime juice, and salt and pepper to taste. Mix well, mashing any large pieces of vegetable that might remain. Cover and chill for several hours.

Serves 6 to 8.

Kashuna Pâté

2 cups cashews
1 cup chopped cucumber
1 to 2 inner stalks of celery, leaves removed
½ medium carrot, peeled
1½ tablespoons powdered vegetable broth
⅛ teaspoon ground cumin
2 tablespoons tahini
1 tablespoon sesame seeds
⅓ cup chopped fresh dill
Dash of cayenne
Dash of chili powder

Grind cashews with cucumber in a food processor until pasty. Add remaining ingredients and puree until thick and smooth. Press into a lightly oiled shallow bowl or mold and refrigerate for several hours. Unmold and serve as a dip or spread on cucumber slices.

Serves 8 to 10.

Creamy Chive Dip

This tangy dip has a familiar flavor: it's "Stedda" sour cream and chives, but instead of saturated fat and cholesterol you get lots of protein (230 percent more than in whole milk!); more calcium than found in milk, eggs, or spinach in more usable form; omega-3 fatty acids which prevent heart disease; and lecithin which the body uses to dissolve fatty deposits. This is an easy recipe to whip up, and my recommendation is that you double it and spoon some into baked potatoes at your next meal.

5 to 6 ounces silken tofu, drained
1 tablespoon sunflower or a very mild extra-virgin olive oil
2 tablespoons lemon juice
¼ to ½ teaspoon kelp
2 teaspoons rice vinegar
¼ teaspoon ground rock salt (optional; if you leave it out, double the kelp)
2 tablespoons minced fresh chives

Combine all ingredients except chives in a blender and blend on high until creamy and smooth. Stir in chives.

Yields 1 cup.

SPROUTS: WHY EAT THEM?

When you eat a sprout, what you are actually eating is a tiny, easily digested plant at the peak of its nutritional value. This little plant is virtually brimming over with simple sugars, amino acids in complete protein form, fatty acids, vitamins (including, according to some experts, vitamin B_{12}), and easily assimilated minerals that are its very substance. Right up until the moment you eat a fresh, raw sprout, it is still growing and *increasing* in food value. All other plants steadily lose their food value after they are cut. Penny for penny (appropriate measure because sprouts are so relatively inexpensive), there is no food you can eat that gives you so much for your money.

If what you are looking for is a rich, nourishing food supply with an absence of pesticides, you'll find sprouts deliver! Look at them as a living "booster" food that literally boosts your immunity, maintains, repairs, and regenerates your body. See them as little nutritional powerhouses, and add them regularly and generously to your diet to accompany all the fresh fruits and vegetables you eat.

Buy Sprouts or Grow Them

Many natural foods stores and supermarkets now carry sprouts. To ensure the freshest, find out when they are delivered and buy them as close as possible to that date. Also, ask the produce manager if the supplier is sprouting from organic seeds, and request that the store use one that does, because many do. Avoid sprouts that look like they are losing their freshness, that are decomposing or turning dark at the root, or that are slightly wilted or sticky to the touch. Avoid sprouts with a rancid odor.

Sprouts are easy to grow at home. When you grow your own sprouts, you create a rewarding miniature garden in your kitchen, which is fulfilling for people not able to cultivate vegetable gardens outdoors. To grow sprouts all you need is a jar or tray, seeds, and water, and your living garden will grow for you even when it is snowing. Acquire a good text on the subject, such as Ann Wigmore's *The Sprouting Book*.[1]

Many pets will eat sprouts, which should be chopped up and mixed with their usual food. Begin with small amounts, since pets sometimes reject change in their foods. Sprouts fulfill dietary needs for them that food additives cannot even begin to handle.

[1]Ann Wigmore, *The Sprouting Book* (Wayne, N.J.: Avery Publishing, 1986).

AND NOW—SALADS!

If it's Life you are looking for in your food, this is another place to find it. The foods from which you make your salads are, for the most part, *full of life.* All the greens you enjoy—the lettuces and spinach, combined with the tomatoes, cucumber, celery, avocado, radishes, carrots and other raw vegetables—supply you with bioactive (bio = life, active = supporting) food. These life-supporting foods, coupled with sprouts, are your nutritional "money in the bank."

Now that you have your salad bowl and blended dressings, you can come up with the salads of your dreams. I have included a salad dressing recipe with each salad recipe so that you don't have to flip through the book constantly to locate appropriate ones. The salad section is divided into three parts:

1. Fast, fresh **Simple Salads** requiring 10 minutes or less to prepare

2. The **Main-Course Salads** that feature nontraditional additions

3. Cooked Salads that can be enjoyed on their own or combined with raw salads for a main-course salad creation. In all of these categories, but particularly the first and second, an important guideline applies:

> **For *Life,* plan your meal around your salad. Think about it first and then decide what will best complement it.**
>
> **Make your salad first. Then you'll have the most important food of the meal ready. Dressings can be added at the last minute on leafy salads to prevent wilting.**

For those seeking maximum success, high performance, and consistent health in the nineties, this section of the book will be one of the most, if not the most, actively used. To participate fully in the salad life-style, here are some tips:

1. When shopping, buy your produce *first,* because it is the most important food on your plate. If you are on a budget, make sure you maximize your ability to spend in the produce department by shopping there first and then minimize your expenditures in other parts of the market.

2. Remember that you can absolutely *live* on what you buy in the produce section.

3. Shop twice a week to ensure freshness. Most salad greens like the lettuces and spinach have an optimum 4- or 5-day refrigerator life. Keep them fresh by storing them in sealed plastic bags and washing them just prior to use. If you must wash a quantity in advance to save time, treat them gently to avoid bruising (which will hasten degeneration), dry them thoroughly, and store them in plastic bags in which you have placed a paper towel to absorb excess moisture.

4. To remove pesticides, wash lettuce and spinach by separating the leaves and soaking them in water.

5. Keep an abundance of fresh vegetables on hand *all the time,* so that you always have what you need for great salads. Stock your refrigerator with produce and use it at every meal. Consider everything else that you may purchase or store to be something that goes into or along with your salad.

A note about lettuce: All lettuces are not equal. Butter, Red Leaf, Boston, Bibb, or Limestone have been found to be the most digestible for people beginning to increase their salad intake. The slightly more fibrous varieties such as Salad Bowl or Romaine are pleasing to many people, but some find them a little difficult to digest. The standard head or Iceberg lettuce, being a hybrid, lacks some nutrients. If you like it, use it in combination with other lettuces. Bitter greens like chicory, endive, and radicchio with their strong flavor are unappealing to some palates. (Radicchio, however, can be mild; when it is, it is excellent in salads.) Watercress and arugula, which contain toxic mustard oil, should be used only in small quantities, because they are not popular with everyone.

Nutritionally, lettuce is a fine source of enzymes, amino acids, vitamins, and minerals. When people ask you, "What about protein?" tell them you get it from lettuce. They'll probably think you are kidding, but you couldn't be more correct! Remember, lettuce is 34% protein.

SIMPLE SALADS

Classic Green Salad

10 minutes

The simplest salad, and one of the best, is a beautiful fresh lettuce salad. It can only be really good, however, when your dressing is great and your lettuce is impeccably fresh. This simple lettuce salad is one of our favorite dinner items. As a team player when the main course is not a salad, this is a quick, complementary dish. I like to use this salad as an accompaniment to just about everything!

4 tablespoons extra-virgin olive oil
1½ tablespoons lemon juice
1 medium garlic clove, crushed (optional)
1 teaspoon Dijon-style mustard
Seasoned salt, salt-free seasoning, or ground rock salt (optional)
Freshly ground pepper (optional)
8 cups washed and dried Butter, Limestone, or Bibb lettuce pieces (or any fresh lettuce that is available)

1. Measure oil and lemon juice into a large salad bowl. Add garlic, mustard, and seasonings to taste. Whisk until smooth and creamy.

2. Break lettuce leaves into bite-size pieces, discarding heavy center ribs, directly into salad bowl with dressing. Toss gently and well.

Serves 3 to 4.

Variation: Use two-thirds lettuce and one-third fresh spinach leaves, or a combination of several varieties of lettuce.

A Salad You Can Live On

5 minutes

This simple salad is oil free and leaves you with a good, *clean* feeling. Highly recommended! Serve with "Stedda" Tuna (page 110), as a dip for cucumber and celery, or with Cottage Tofu (page 105) or Heavenly Carrot-Currant Salad (page 148).

3 to 4 cups Butter or Limestone lettuce pieces
2 cups spinach
1 tomato, cut in wedges
Several cucumber spears
Several celery stalks
Sprouts (alfalfa, sunflower, lentil, or other)
Juice of ½ small lemon

1. Thoroughly wash and spin-dry the lettuce and spinach. Break into bite-size pieces into a medium bowl.

2. Garnish with tomato wedges, cucumber spears, and sprouts. Squeeze lemon juice over all.

Serves 1.

Variations: (1) add ¼ cubed avocado; (2) sprinkle with 1 tablespoon ground sesame seeds or soaked sunflower seeds; (3) toss some lightly steamed vegies into salad; or (4) add grated carrot—or ¼ cup shelled pecans or almonds (forego avocado if adding nuts—too much fat!).

French Green Salad with Cottage Tofu

10 minutes

This new version of an old favorite is delicious. It's another trick to keep salads interesting and unusual, so your family and guests will continuously anticipate them enthusiastically.

3 tablespoons extra-virgin olive oil
1 tablespoon lemon juice
¼ teaspoon Dijon-style mustard
1 small garlic clove, pressed
Seasoned salt, ground rock salt, and freshly ground pepper (optional)
1 Butter lettuce
2 cups fresh spinach, stems removed
½ cup Cottage Tofu (page 105)

1. Measure first 5 ingredients directly into your salad bowl and whip until creamy with a whisk.

2. Add lettuce, broken into bite-size pieces and with heavy center rib removed. Coarsely chop the spinach and add it. Toss gently, then add Cottage Tofu and toss gently.

Serves 2.

Sprouted Lentil Salad

15 minutes

Lentils are so easy to sprout. Soak them in a sprouting jar for a few hours. Rinse and drain them well, set sprouting jar on its side in a dark place overnight; and in the morning, you will have crunchy, enzyme-packed, powerfully nutritious lentils. Rinse and drain them well in a colander and refrigerate in a sealed container until ready to use. They make a wonderful salad with lots of finely chopped vegetables.

Dressing

2 tablespoons extra-virgin olive oil
2 teaspoons lemon juice or to taste
¼ teaspoon ground cumin
¼ teaspoon curry powder
1 tablespoon minced fresh dill or 1 teaspoon dried (optional)
Freshly ground pepper to taste

Salad

2 cups lentil sprouts
¾ cup finely chopped tomato
½ cup finely chopped sunflower or alfalfa sprouts
1 teaspoon minced green onion
¼ cup minced fresh parsley
¼ cup minced celery
¼ cup minced red or yellow bell pepper (optional)

1. In a medium bowl, whisk the dressing ingredients.
2. Add lentil sprouts and the chopped vegetables. Toss well. Refrigerate until ready to serve.

Serves 3.

Blended Salad

5 minutes

Sometimes, in the middle of the day, you feel like having a quick salad but don't want to bother with dressing or even minimal prepping of vegetables. Or, you're so busy you don't even want to take the time to chew a salad! This is when a Blended Salad is really a lifesaver. Toss everything you want to have in your salad into your blender. If you're really hungry, toss in some almonds and sunflower or sesame seeds, and you've got a nutritious, "soupy salad" to eat with a spoon. Admittedly, this dish is not a "good looker," and I wouldn't recommend serving it to your finicky aunt from Omaha, but it sure does get the job done!

1 medium tomato
3-inch piece of cucumber, unpeeled or peeled, if waxed
1 small red or green bell pepper, seeds removed
2 cups lettuce pieces
1 large celery stalk
½ cup nuts or seeds (preferably soaked for a few hours or overnight)

1. Liquefy the tomato and cucumber in a blender. Add pepper and lettuce, using celery stalk to push leaves down while blender runs on medium. Liquefy celery.

2. Toss in nuts or seeds and coarsely chop so that your salad will have a little texture.

Serves 1 or 2.

French Green Salad with Basil Shiitake

20 minutes

In the winter, when good tomatoes are scarce and other salad vegetables tend to be inferior, we need a trick to keep salad interest high. This basil shiitake garnish dresses up a salad to the level of absolute elegance. Standard mushrooms, thinly sliced, can be substituted if neither dried nor fresh shiitake are available. You don't need many shiitake for this recipe; a few go a long way, so the cost is worthwhile, especially if you want a stellar salad to start your meal. Serve this salad as a first course, with hot bread.

1 large Butter lettuce
3 cups spinach leaves
4½ tablespoons extra-virgin olive oil
1½ tablespoons lemon juice
1 small garlic clove, pressed
½ teaspoon Dijon-style mustard
Seasoned salt (optional)
2 cups dried shiitake mushrooms (see Note), or 6 large fresh shiitake, stems removed and discarded, and caps thinly sliced
¼ cup fresh basil leaves, cut in slivers, or 1 teaspoon dried
Dash of sea salt (optional)

1. Wash and thoroughly dry the lettuce and spinach. In a large salad bowl, use a wire whisk to whip 4 tablespoons olive oil, lemon juice, garlic, mustard, and seasoned salt to taste until thick and yellow. Set aside.

2. Place remaining ½ tablespoon oil and shiitake in a skillet. Sauté, stirring to prevent scorching, then add any reserved shiitake soaking water as needed. Toss in basil and add salt, if desired. Sauté 1 minute.

3. Tear lettuce and spinach in bite-size pieces, into dressing in salad bowl, removing heavy center stalks from lettuce. Toss well. Serve on individual plates with a large spoonful of basil shiitake as a topping.

Serves 4 to 5.

Note: If using dried shiitake, soak in boiling water for 10 to 15 minutes. Drain, then squeeze water remaining in shiitake into a bowl, strain and reserve.

Antipasto, American Style

10 minutes

Salad

1 medium head lettuce
1½ cups green beans, cut in 1-inch segments
¾ cup prepared garbanzo beans, drained
⅓ cup black or green olives
1 cup chopped sunflower sprouts or spinach
1 medium tomato, cubed
¾ cup marinated artichoke hearts, drained and quartered
Several thin slices of red onion (optional)

Dressing

⅓ cup olive oil
2 to 3 tablespoons lemon juice, according to taste
1 teaspoon Dijon mustard
1 small or medium clove garlic, according to taste
Seasoned salt to taste
Fresh ground pepper to taste

1. Bring a quart of water to boil in a large saucepan. Add green beans and blanch until bright green and tender. Drain, shock under cold water, and set aside.

2. Break lettuce into bite-sized pieces. Add garbanzo beans, olives, sunflower sprouts or spinach, green beans, tomato, and artichoke hearts.

3. Prepare dressing: In container, cream oil, lemon, mustard, garlic, and seasonings with hand blender. Pour over salad. Toss thoroughly.

Serves 4.

Avocado, Jicama, and Grapefruit Salad

10 minutes

The avocado and grapefruit complement each other; the jicama adds a contrasting crispness. Digestively, the grapefruit, which is so low in sugar, works with the vegetables quite well. This is a beautiful salad to serve and to eat.

1 large or 2 small avocados
2 medium Ruby Red grapefruit
½ pound jicama
2 tablespoons walnut or flaxseed oil (optional)
1 tablespoon minced fresh parsley

1. Peel and seed the avocados and cut into wedges. Peel the grapefruit and cut into sections, reserving juice. Peel the jicama and cut into thin wedges the same length as the avocado slices.

2. On four separate plates, alternate slices of avocado, grapefruit, and jicama in a circle or fan.

3. Combine walnut oil, reserved grapefruit juice, and parsley in a small bowl. Drizzle over salads.

Serves 4.

Endive and Radicchio Salad

10 minutes

This is a perfect salad to accompany Italian entrées. The vinegar is very light; it is the tomatoes that supply the acidity for the dressing. No garlic—just a tiny bit of minced onion. Serve this salad first, especially if you are sensitive to mixing tomatoes or vinegar with starches that may be present in other dishes at the meal. Assemble the salad on individual plates and pour the dressing over each serving.

1 Belgian endive, trimmed
1 small bunch arugula
1 small radicchio
1 medium tomato, diced
1 to 2 teaspoons diced white onion
1 teaspoon minced fresh parsley
¼ cup olive oil
1 teaspoon lemon juice
½ teaspoon red wine vinegar
Salt and freshly ground pepper

1. Separate endive leaves and soak them for 5 minutes in salted ice water to remove bitterness. Drain and blot dry. Cut into 1-inch segments. Cut radicchio into bite-size segments. Remove stems from arugula and tear leaves into bite-size pieces. Arrange greens on individual plates.

2. Combine the diced tomato, onion, parsley, olive oil, lemon juice, vinegar, salt, and pepper to taste in a small bowl and mix briskly with a fork. Pour dressing over salads and pass pepper at table.

Serves 3 to 4.

Wilted Cabbage and Fresh Basil Salad

15 minutes

This is a New Wave slaw. Serve with Samosas (page 314).

1 small head green cabbage
¼ cup boiling water
2 tablespoons tahini
3 tablespoons lemon juice
1½ cups basil leaves

1. Cut cabbage into fine slivers. (See directions for Deli-Style Cole Slaw, page 151.) Add boiling water, let cool, then knead with your hands until cabbage breaks down and softens. Pour off water into a small bowl.

2. With a fork, mash tahini into cabbage water to dissolve lumps. Add lemon juice.

3. Coarsely chop the basil leaves, then add to cabbage. Pour tahini dressing over salad and mix thoroughly.

Serves 6 to 8.

Greek Salad 2000

20 minutes

For those *progressive* individuals who love Greek salads but no longer enjoy eating cheese.

Dressing

4 tablespoons extra-virgin olive oil
2 tablespoons fresh lemon juice or lime juice
⅓ teaspoon Dijon-style mustard
Dash of Worcestershire sauce
1 tablespoon Cottage Tofu or "Stedda" Ricotta
¼ medium tomato
3 tablespoons water
Herbamare or salt-free seasoning to taste
Freshly ground pepper to taste
4 large basil leaves or ½ teaspoon dried
1 tablespoon chopped red or white onion
½ teaspoon red wine vinegar

Salad

1 head Butter, Red Leaf, or Romaine lettuce
¼ bunch (approximately 2 cups) fresh spinach
1 cup arugula
⅓ cup Greek olives
⅓ cup "Stedda" Feta or Cottage Tofu (page 105)
Several thin rounds of red and yellow bell pepper
Several thin rounds of red onion (optional)

1. Blend dressing ingredients until smooth and creamy.

2. Break lettuce, spinach, and arugula into bite-size segments in a medium salad bowl. Add olives, feta, and pepper and onion rounds. Add dressing and toss well. *Serves 2 to 4.*

Kids' Favorite Salad

10 minutes

I have served this salad frequently to children of all ages, and it never fails to be a winner. Even those who declare they only want "a little bit," because they "don't usually like salad," end by gobbling it up and asking for more.

4 cups coarsely chopped Iceberg lettuce
1 medium tomato, cut in small cubes
½ cup chopped sunflower sprouts (which kids love)
½ medium avocado, cut in small cubes (¾ cup)
1 tablespoon extra-virgin olive oil
1 tablespoon lemon juice
1¼ tablespoons dairy-free mayonnaise or Almonnaise (page 98)
¼ teaspoon dulse flakes or seasoned salt
Dash of garlic powder

1. In a medium salad bowl, combine lettuce, tomato, sprouts, and avocado.

2. Add olive oil, lemon juice, mayonnaise, and seasonings. Toss well. *Serves 1 or 2.*

Tomatoes in Pesto

10 minutes

If you have pesto on hand, this is an excellent use. If you don't have it on hand, it's worth making for this recipe.

3 medium tomatoes, peeled and sliced
3 tablespoons pesto
3 tablespoons hot water
Freshly ground pepper

1. Submerge the tomatoes for 1 minute in boiling water. The skins will slide off easily. Set aside.

2. Mix the pesto with the hot water. Spread the mixture in a shallow serving dish.

3. Slice the tomatoes. Place on top of the pesto and then turn over gently with a fork so they are completely coated with pesto. Season with pepper to taste. Refrigerate until ready to serve.

Serves 4.

Spinach and Sun-Dried Tomato Salad

10 minutes

Sun-dried tomatoes can turn an ordinary salad into an elegant and exotic dish. You can buy them in packages in the supermarket (reasonably priced). If a brief rehydration step is necessary, follow the directions on the package. (Sun-dried tomatoes preserved in olive oil are still quite costly; the dried packaged variety work just as well.)

3 tablespoons extra-virgin olive oil
¾ to 1 tablespoons lemon juice
¼ teaspoon Dijon-style mustard, or 1 teaspoon dairy-free mayonnaise or Almonnaise (page 98)
6 cups fresh spinach, well washed and stems removed
¼ cup slivered sun-dried tomatoes
¼ to ½ cup Cottage Tofu or "Stedda" Ricotta (pages 105, 106)

1. Combine first 3 ingredients in a large salad bowl and beat with a whisk.

2. Thoroughly dry the spinach and break into bite-size pieces into a salad bowl. Toss in sun-dried tomatoes and "Stedda" Ricotta or Cottage Tofu. Toss well.

Serves 2.

Roma Tomatoes with Basil

10 minutes

This is a simple version of Tomatoes in Pesto, for when you don't have pesto on hand. Basil is such a pungent herb; its characteristic flavor highly complements tomatoes. Simply by tossing them with lots of finely slivered basil, you almost get the pesto flavor. This salad is great to fall back on when you want something special and don't have much time to create it.

8 ripe Roma tomatoes, peeled and thinly sliced
¼ to ½ cup slivered basil
2 tablespoons extra-virgin olive oil
2 teaspoons lemon juice
Ground rock salt
Freshly ground pepper to taste

1. Arrange tomato slices on individual plates or a small platter. Sprinkle with slivered basil.
2. Whip together dressing ingredients. Drizzle over tomatoes. Add additional pepper to taste.

Serves 3 to 4.

Heavenly Carrot-Currant Salad

10 minutes

With this salad around, you'll never crave carrot cake. If carrot cake were a Living food, this, in my opinion, is what it would be. Serve with English Cucumbers with Lime Juice and Mint (page 150) and warmed Easy Banana Bread (page 348).

¼ to ½ cup currants
½ cup water, heated to boiling, plus ¼ cup hot water
1 to 2 tablespoons tahini
2 teaspoons honey or brown rice syrup
1 tablespoon lemon juice
Dash of ground cinnamon (optional)
2 cups finely grated carrots

1. Soak currants in boiling water for 1 to several hours or overnight. Strain, reserving currant water; you will have from 2 tablespoons to ¼ cup.*

2. Place currant water, hot water, tahini, honey, lemon juice, and cinnamon in a blender and blend until creamy.

3. Place carrots and currants in a salad bowl. Pour dressing over and mix well.

Serves 1 to 4.

Variation: Add ¼ cup sprouted sunflower seeds and toss well.

*It is not necessary to soak currants. Simply add ½ cup water to dressing ingredients and increase sweetener to taste.

Romaine Lettuce and Spinach Salad with Nori and Avocado

10 minutes

The chewy, salty flavor of nori has come into its own via the sushi craze. I wonder how many sushi lovers have ever thought of putting nori in their salads to give them that "sushi" quality? Buy it in packages in the Asian section of your supermarket. It is reasonably priced and a little goes a long way.

Dressing

6 tablespoons extra-virgin olive oil
1½ to 2 tablespoons lemon juice
1 small garlic clove, crushed

Salad

1 Romaine lettuce, washed and thoroughly dried
2 cups spinach, washed, dried, with stems removed
1 large handful alfalfa sprouts
1 large handful sunflower seed or mung bean sprouts, coarsely chopped
5 sheets nori
1 medium avocado, peeled, seeded, and cubed

1. Measure dressing ingredients directly into a large salad bowl and beat together with a whisk until creamy.

2. Break lettuce into bite-size pieces, discarding heaviest center ribs. Coarsely chop spinach and add it to lettuce. Add sprouts.

3. Hold each piece of nori over a medium gas flame or electric burner set to high. Turn the nori quickly from side to side until it goes from black to bright green, a few seconds. Tear nori in 2-inch sections and add to greens. Toss well, then gently fold in avocado cubes.

Serves 4.

Note: Pretoasted nori is available in packages, but far more costly. Toasting is so easy, the additional expense is not worth it.

Variation: Substitute 1 cup thinly sliced cucumber for the avocado, for a lighter, equally delicious salad.

English Cucumbers with Lime Juice and Mint

5 minutes

You can use English or standard cucumbers for this refreshing "exercise in simplicity." Seed them to keep the salad from being watery. Mint aids digestion; take advantage of recipes that incorporate it.

2 English cucumbers, peeled, halved lengthwise, and seeded (6 to 7 cups)
Scant ¼ cup fresh lime juice
¼ cup minced fresh mint, or 2 tablespoons dried
Ground rock salt to taste (optional)

1. Use the thin slicing blade of a food processor or mandoline to cut cucumbers in thin crescents. Or slice them thinly by hand.

2. Transfer cucumbers to a medium bowl and mix in remaining ingredients. Refrigerate until ready to serve. The longer you can chill this salad, up to 1 hour, the better it will be, as the flavors blend.

Serves 6.

Shredded Carrots in Olive Oil

5 minutes

Some people don't care for a carrot-raisin salad because they don't like the raisins. For them, prepare a simple carrot salad like this one. Buy small to medium carrots for their sweeter flavor. Peel to remove the slightly bitter skin, and be sure to trim tip and 1 inch from top, since they are often bitter.

2 large carrots, peeled and trimmed
1 tablespoon extra-virgin olive, sunflower, or flaxseed oil
1½ teaspoon lemon juice
Pinch of salt

1. Finely grate the carrots and toss with oil.

2. Add lemon juice and salt, and mix well.

Serves 1 to 2.

Variation: Substitute dairy-free mayonnaise for the oil and lemon.

Mushroom-Fennel Salad

10 minutes

Fennel, which has been popular in Italy for decades, has finally come into its own as a vegetable in our country. Its refreshing, celerylike quality is enhanced by a mild anise, or licorice, flavor. Fennel seeds are chewed in India to aid digestion. It is an extremely alkaline vegetable like celery, and an appropriate addition to our overly acidic American diet. Serve this salad with Roma Tomatoes with Basil (page 148) and Mixed Grill Platter (page 115).

½ pound mushrooms, gently washed, stems removed
1 large bulb fennel, coarse outer stalks removed and end and leaves trimmed
¼ cup minced fresh dill
3 tablespoons olive oil
1 tablespoon lemon juice
1 tiny garlic clove, pressed
Freshly ground pepper (optional)

1. Cut mushrooms in ⅛-inch slices. Cut fennel across the bulb in ⅛-inch slices. Combine vegetables in a medium bowl and add dill.

2. Whip next 3 ingredients in a small bowl until thick and yellow. Pour over salad. Toss well, then season to taste with pepper.

Serves 3 to 4.

Variation: Add ¼ to ½ teaspoon Dijon-style mustard to dressing.

Deli-Style Cole Slaw

20 minutes

Seems like everyone loves cole slaw, especially as a summer picnic salad. I've been making it for years, and am constantly trying to perfect it. This latest version has that special "deli" cole slaw flavor. Cut the cabbage in your food processor and reduce the preparation time to 10 minutes! I like to cut cabbage by hand for cole slaw (instructions to follow), as a kitchen "meditation." Serve this cole slaw with Goodwiches (page 175) and Crusty Roasteds Revisited (page 246).

1 medium green cabbage, finely shredded
¼ cup boiling water
Ground rock salt to taste
2 tablespoons finely grated carrot
¼ cup minced fresh dill
1 teaspoon honey
½ cup dairy-free mayonnaise or Almonnaise (page 98)
3 tablespoons lemon juice
Freshly ground pepper to taste (optional)

1. Use the fine slicing blade to slice cabbage in food processor or by hand. To slice by hand, cut a 1-inch slice from the top of the cabbage (opposite end from the stem). Lay the slice flat on a cutting board, and with a very sharp chef's knife, cut the top into fine shreds. Then, holding the chef's knife in your cutting hand, hold remaining uncut cabbage in your free hand with cut side facing knife. Now begin cutting fine shreds off the cut face of the cabbage, turning the cabbage with your free hand to keep the cut surface flat. Keep cutting and turning until you are close to the core. Then begin cutting at a slight angle away from the core as you turn the cabbage, so you don't get shreds of the core.

2. Toss the shredded cabbage in a large bowl. Add the boiling water and salt, let cool, and then knead cabbage with both hands for 1 to 2 minutes to break it down slightly. Drain.

3. Add carrot to bowl along with dill. Drizzle honey over mixture, then add mayonnaise and lemon juice. Toss well and season with pepper. Refrigerate for hours, if possible, before serving.

Serves 6.

MAIN-COURSE SALADS

There is probably not another area of this book (nor another category of food) that allows for more creativity than Main-Course Salads. When taste *and* health are your dietary goals, you will find this exciting culinary concept offers both of these and much more. No other dish (with the exception of fruit salads) has as its constant background fresh, living food replete with all the enzymes, amino acids, vitamins, minerals, fatty acids, and carbohydrates in most usable form. In fact, the enzymes in the fresh vegetables of a main-course salad help break down whatever cooked food is added. This accounts for its unusual digestibility! These salads have several other important advantages and benefits, too.

1. Because they are essentially a high-water content food (containing more fresh vegetables than cooked food), they thoroughly support the *Fit for Life* principle that urges 70 percent of daily intake in the form of fresh living fruits and vegetables. They also support the guidelines from the surgeon general's "Report on Health and Nutrition" by using an increased measure of fresh vegetables rather than traditional cooked foods.

2. They are so quick and easy to prepare that, in most cases, they fit the Fix-it-Fast description, coming together as a complete meal in well under an hour.

3. They are highly economical.

4. They allow for individual expression of creativity at the same meal.

5. In most cases, Main-Course Salads are not a cold food in the traditional sense, since cooked ingredients, warm or at room temperature, are added. The hot food we eat destroys cells on our tongues and along the throat and esophagus as we swallow, but room-temperature or warm foods allow us to take our taste buds with us into our "seasoned years."

Main-Course Salads of Your Own Design

Amounts here are for salads for 4 people. The total raw background ingredients should equal *at least* 12 cups.

8 cups lettuce of your choice, cut or broken in smaller than usual pieces
2 cups spinach, watercress, or other green
1 to 2 cups sprouts, preferably nonconcentrated ones like alfalfa, clover, sunflower, radish, or buckwheat*
2 cups other raw vegetables of your choice, such as:
tomato cubes or slices
cucumber cubes, slices, or julienne (page 212)
shredded carrots or carrot matchsticks (page 212)
minced celery
cubed or sliced avocado
shredded red, green, or Chinese cabbage
sliced or minced onions
raw sliced mushrooms
sliced fennel
diced or strips of red, yellow, or green bell peppers

Your basic dressing includes:

6 tablespoons extra-virgin olive oil
2 tablespoons lemon or lime juice
¼ teaspoon pressed garlic or garlic powder
1½ teaspoons tahini, or ½ teaspoon Dijon-style mustard
2 tablespoons water, if using tahini
Ground rock salt, seasoned salt, or salt-free seasoning (optional)
Freshly ground pepper (optional)

Possible additions to a 12-cup salad for 4 persons include a total of 4 cups from the following:

Assorted Steamed Vegetables

artichoke hearts
asparagus
beets
broccoli
carrots
cauliflower
corn
peas
snow peas
string beans
sugar snap beans
yellow squash
zucchini

*Since you will be adding cooked, concentrated food to your salads, concentrated legume sprouts such as lentil, bean, or pea will make your salad too heavy. If you are only adding steamed vegetables, then you can add the concentrated sprouts.

Potatoes in Many Forms

(See "The All-American Potato," p. 245.)

broiled
riced (grated, after steaming)
roasted
sautéed
steamed

Pasta in Any Form

From macaroni to capelli, and everything in between. Even lasagna noodles can be cut in big chunks and thrown into your salad!

Other Grains

rice
couscous
barley
millet

"Stedda" Foods

(Or the actual animal products you are trying to minimize in your diet*)

cubes of "Stedda" Chicken Fillets (page 115)
cubes of Lemon "Stedda" Chicken (page 118)
cubes of Tofu Meunière (page 117)
dollops of Cottage Tofu (page 105)
cubes of sautéed tofu (see "Stedda" Mozzarella Salad, page 159)

Miscellaneous and Exotic Additions

artichoke hearts
beans of all kinds
corn or other chips
croutons or cubed bread
hearts of palm
olives
sautéed mushrooms
sea vegetables, particularly nori
sesame seeds, white or black
sun-dried tomatoes
sunflower seeds

The basic procedure is simple. Keep an assortment of lettuces, spinach, and other fresh vegetables on hand. All lettuces are good for a main-course salad, but they should be broken or chopped in smaller than usual segments so that they blend more easily with the other ingredients. Spinach can be chopped or sliced.

*The first main-course salad I created in 1976 was a beef-lover's salad. I had just become a vegetarian and when, on occasion, I craved beef too strongly (knowing that if I ate it in the traditional manner, it would make me feel terrible), I simply added a *little,* thinly sliced, to a big Living salad. All the Living food would help "usher" the beef through my body without drastic distress. The salad was the vehicle that helped break me of my beef addiction.

Decide what your salad theme will be. What additions do you wish to put in your salad? What do you crave? How can you work that into your salad? What does your body need to balance your day dietarily? Prepare the additions: slice, cube, shred, marinate, and so on. Then prepare the dressing right in the salad bowl. Add the greens and other optional raw vegetables to the bowl. Add the additions to the salad. Toss well to blend the flavors. Keep in mind that your finished product should not look like an ordinary salad. The additions should be highly visible and dominate the salad. If all you see is lettuce, there are not enough additions or you have not tossed adequately.

If you are making pasta, rice, potatoes, or couscous, make extra to have for future salads. Store these additions in closed containers in your refrigerator. Or, if you are steaming, baking, grilling, or broiling vegetables, prepare enough for your salads and refrigerate in closed containers. "Steddas" made ahead do salad duty, too.

"Stedda" Beef Salad

40 minutes

This really wonderful salad gives you the feeling you're eating barbecued meat, but it's just one of our "Stedda" tricks, out not to fool you but to satisfy you. Serve with a cream soup (page 191) and Potato Cakes (page 252).

Salad

1 pound firm tofu, cut in 12 thin crosswise slices and wrapped for at least 10 minutes
"Beefy" Marinade (page 114)
1 pound tender green beans, trimmed
8 cups Butter lettuce pieces
1 cup alfalfa or sunflower sprouts
1 Belgian endive, soaked in saltwater for 10 minutes, then sliced
2 cups spinach leaves
Freshly ground pepper to taste

Dressing

5 tablespoons extra-virgin olive oil
1½ tablespoons lemon juice
½ teaspoon Dijon-style mustard
1 small garlic clove, pressed

1. While tofu is drying in towel, put marinade in a shallow baking dish. Cut tofu into ¼-inch matchsticks and toss in marinade. Marinate for 20 minutes or longer while you prepare the rest of the salad.

2. Blanch green beans in boiling water for 3 minutes, or until bright green and tender. Cut into 1½-inch lengths and set aside.

3. Prepare dressing by measuring 4 tablespoons olive oil, lemon juice, mustard, and garlic directly into a large bowl and beating to combine with a whisk or hand blender.

4. Finely shred the lettuce and add to bowl. Add sprouts and endive. Finely chop spinach and add.

5. Place tofu and marinade in a skillet and sauté with remaining tablespoon oil over medium-high heat for 8 to 10 minutes, or until tofu is brown and slightly crisp at edges. Toss tofu directly into salad. Add green beans and pepper to taste. Toss well and serve. *Serves 3 to 4.*

Nifty Salad with Peas and Shiitake Mushrooms

25 minutes

This was inspired by the house salad at the Nifty Café in Santa Fe.

Salad

4 cups frozen peas
1 tablespoon safflower oil
¼ cup sliced green onions
¼ teaspoon minced garlic
1 cup cubed tofu (optional)
½ teaspoon ground cumin
1 cup sliced shiitake mushrooms
1 tablespoon minced fresh basil, or ½ teaspoon dried
½ finely sliced cucumber
6 cups Butter lettuce pieces
3 cups Salad Bowl lettuce pieces
1 medium tomato, cut in 12 segments

Dressing

½ cup olive oil
¼ cup water
⅛ to ¼ cup lemon juice
3 large garlic cloves
1 teaspoon honey
⅓ cup dairy-free mayonnaise
⅓ cup fresh basil leaves
Salt
Freshly ground pepper to taste

1. Steam peas until tender and set aside.

2. Heat wok. Add oil, green onions, and garlic. Stir-fry for 10 seconds, then add tofu and stir-fry for 1 minute. Add cumin and continue stir-frying 2 minutes longer, or until tofu cubes are slightly crispy. Add shiitake slices to wok and stir-fry until tender, 3 to 4 minutes, adding a little purified water as necessary to keep vegetables and tofu from scorching.

3. Mix peas into stir-fried vegetables. Stir in basil and cucumber.

4. Prepare dressing by combining ingredients in a blender and blending until creamy.

5. Assemble salad. Arrange mound of greens on 3 salad plates. Spoon pea mixture over greens and drizzle with dressing. Garnish with 4 tomato segments on each plate.

Serves 3.

"Stedda" Chicken-Lover's Salad

25 minutes

Dressing

4 tablespoons olive oil
1½ tablespoons lemon juice
3 teaspoons Almonnaise (page 98) or dairy-free mayonnaise
¼ teaspoon curry powder
⅛ teaspoon dry mustard
1 medium garlic clove, crushed
2 tablespoons water
½ teaspoon kelp (optional)
Ground rock salt to taste
Freshly ground pepper to taste

Salad

4 "Stedda" Chicken Fillets, grilled or broiled (page 115)
6 cups Butter lettuce pieces
3 cups spinach, stems removed
¼ cup carrot julienne (page 212)
½ cup alfalfa sprouts
½ cup diced tomato (1 medium)
2 cups steamed asparagus, cut in 1-inch diagonals (optional)

1. Prepare dressing by combining ingredients in your salad bowl and whisking until thick and creamy.

2. Cut "Stedda" Chicken Fillets in ½-inch cubes and set aside. Coarsely shred the lettuce and coarsely chop spinach. Cut wisps of carrot with a lemon zester or carrot peeler.

3. Combine lettuce, spinach, diced fillets, carrot, alfalfa sprouts, tomato, and asparagus in bowl with dressing. Toss well. Adjust seasonings.

Serves 3.

Potato-Lover's Salad

30 minutes

The original recipe for this salad is twelve years old, and it clearly demonstrates the necessity for updating cooking techniques. I used to sauté the potatoes in butter, which is clearly not necessary. The cubed potatoes broiled in a little olive oil with garlic are far superior, and this simple change removed all cholesterol and all but a trace of saturated fat from the recipe. Serve this on individual dinner plates with a bowl of Old-Fashioned Cream of Celery Soup (page 198) and Red Pepper Party Sandwiches (page 185).

Salad

3 cups red potatoes, cut in ½- to 1-inch cubes and steamed 10 to 15 minutes or until just tender
1 tablespoon olive oil
¼ teaspoon minced garlic, or ¼ teaspoon garlic powder
6 cups Butter lettuce, in ¼-inch slivers
2 cups Romaine, Salad Bowl or Iceberg lettuce, in ¼-inch slivers
2 cups coarsely chopped spinach
1 cup alfalfa sprouts
1 cup coarsely chopped sunflower sprouts
½ cup finely slivered red cabbage or finely chopped tomato
3 cups thin broccoli florets, steamed until bright green and just tender, about 3 to 4 minutes

Dressing

4 tablespoons extra-virgin olive oil
2 tablespoons dairy-free mayonnaise or Almonnaise (page 98)
1 medium garlic clove, pressed
1½ tablespoons lemon juice
½ teaspoon Dijon-style mustard (optional)
½ teaspoon kelp powder or other salt-free seasoning
¼ teaspoon dried thyme
Freshly ground pepper to taste (optional)

1. Toss potatoes in olive oil and garlic and spread in a single layer on a cookie sheet. Place in preheated broiler and broil 4 inches from heat for 5 minutes, turning once, or until potatoes are crusty and golden.

2. Prepare dressing in a large salad bowl. Measure ingredients directly into bowl and beat until creamy with a whisk.

3. Add greens, sprouts, and cabbage to bowl. Toss in potatoes and steamed broccoli. Toss very well.

Serves 4.

Variation: Add 1 cup sliced onion rings to potatoes and toss together in the olive oil and garlic. Spread onion rings, halved or quartered, on cookie sheet with potatoes and broil as indicated. Toss both into the salad.

"Stedda" Mozzarella Salad

15 minutes

The Italians have a traditional tomato and cheese salad that you now see in many take-home salad displays, but it is high in saturated fat and cholesterol. This version is equally satisfying but totally free of cholesterol and extremely low in saturated fat. The delicious flavors are still there, and it's a substantially lighter, healthier dish. It's excellent with Basic Lemon Broccoli (page 226) or Cream of Asparagus and Fennel Soup (page 197). We find this to be an impeccable supper on a hot summer day, with chilled rather than hot soup. Cooling and nourishing!

8 ounces firm tofu, cut in ½-inch slices, wrapping optional
1 teaspoon ground kelp or ground rock salt to taste
1 tablespoon plus 1 teaspoon extra-virgin olive oil
2 tablespoons minced green onion
2 ripe large tomatoes, peeled and cubed
2 tablespoons minced fresh basil, or 1 teaspoon dried
4 cups Butter or Limestone lettuce, in ½-inch shreds
2 teaspoons lemon juice
Freshly ground pepper to taste

1. Cut tofu into ½-inch cubes. Season with kelp or salt. Heat 1 teaspoon of the olive oil with the green onion in a nonstick skillet. Add tofu cubes. Sauté, tossing cubes in the oil, until they are just slightly browned, approximately 3 minutes.

2. Toss tomato with basil and remaining olive oil.

3. Shred lettuce into a medium salad bowl. Toss tofu cubes and green onion with tomatoes, then pour tomato-tofu mixture into the bowl with lettuce. Add lemon juice and pepper, and toss well.

Serves 2.

Mediterranean Rice Salad

30 to 60 minutes, depending on rice

This is another classic main-course salad that I have been making for over a decade. I used to add pimento-stuffed green olives, but more recently have substituted slivers of sun-dried tomatoes. This is easy to make in large quantities for entertaining.

Salad

1 cup white or brown basmati or long-grain brown rice
2 to 2½ cups water, depending on rice
1 teaspoon sunflower oil
1 tablespoon olive oil
2 to 3 cups sliced zucchini
1 teaspoon dried basil
1 teaspoon dried oregano
8 cups Butter or Red Leaf lettuce, in ¼-inch slivers
4 cups coarsely chopped spinach, or 2 cups arugula and 2 cups spinach
1 cup alfalfa or sunflower sprouts
⅓ cup slivered sun-dried tomatoes, or ½ cup sliced pimento-stuffed green olives
¼ cup chopped fresh basil, or 2 tablespoons chopped fresh mint (optional)
Ground rock salt to taste (optional)

Dressing

½ cup extra-virgin olive oil
3 tablespoons fresh lemon juice
1 large garlic clove, pressed
½ to 1 teaspoon honey (optional)
½ teaspoon dried chervil
¼ teaspoon dried mint
½ teaspoon dried thyme
⅛ teaspoon dried tarragon
½ teaspoon Dijon-style mustard
½ teaspoon ground rock salt or salt-free seasoning
Freshly ground black pepper to taste

1. Place rice in a medium saucepan. If using basmati rice, add 2 cups of water and 1 teaspoon sunflower oil. If using brown rice, add 2¼ cups of water and 1 teaspoon sunflower oil. Bring to a boil, stir once, cover, and simmer for 20 minutes for white basmati rice and 40 minutes for brown rice. Remove basmati rice from heat and fluff with fork; do not lift cover of brown rice for an additional 10 minutes, but do remove from heat.

2. While rice is cooking, heat olive oil in a large skillet or wok. Add zucchini, basil, and oregano and sauté, stirring frequently (add 1 to 2 tablespoons water to prevent scorching) over medium-high heat for 5 to 7 minutes, or until zucchini is just tender; do not overcook or it will fall apart in the salad.

3. Measure dressing ingredients into hand blender container and blend until creamy.

4. Add slivered and chopped greens to salad bowl with dressing. Add rice and zucchini and toss well. Fold in sprouts, sun-dried tomatoes and fresh herbs. Adjust seasonings. You may need a dash more salt, since no salt was added to the rice during cooking.

Serves 4.

Pasta and Corn Salad

25 minutes

Crunchy corn and pasta are a wonderful and unusual combination.

Salad

8 cups butter lettuce
2 cups spinach
1 bunch (approximately 2 cups) arugula or watercress, if arugula is not available
5 ears corn
2 cups asparagus, preferably grilled
1 cup sliced pimiento-stuffed olives
8 ounces pasta (jinenjo soba, whole-wheat, or vegetable pasta)

Dressing

4 tablespoons olive oil
2 tablespoons Cottage Tofu (see page 105)
½ medium tomato, chopped
1 small clove garlic
4 tablespoons water
Several dashes Worcestershire sauce or ½ teaspoon red wine vinegar
3 tablespoons fresh lemon juice
½ teaspoon Dijon mustard
Herbamare to taste
6 large leaves fresh basil (approximately ¼ cup chopped) or 1 tablespoon dried basil

1. Cook your choice of pasta according to package directions for al dente. Drain and rinse well in cold water to prevent clumping.

2. Steam corn for 10 minutes and cut from cob.

3. Measure dressing ingredients into hand blender container. Blend until creamy and set aside.

4. Blanch asparagus for 4 minutes or, if you have a grill, you can brush them with olive oil and grill till slightly crispy on the outside. (See page 221 for Grilled Asparagus.) Asparagus can also be stir-fried rather than blanched or grilled. (See page 222.)

5. Break lettuce into bite-sized pieces. Break arugula and spinach into smaller pieces. Add corn, asparagus, and olives to lettuce. Cut or break pasta into 3″ lengths and add to salad. Add dressing and toss well.

Serves 4.

Easy Tostada

35 to 40 minutes

You can use a commercial salsa for this salad (one that has no sugar or preservatives), or you can make your own very easily. Substituting vegetables for the beans makes this a light, California-style Mexican meal. It's great for a summer picnic with Tomburgers (page 187).

Vegetables

1 cup frozen petite peas
1 cup fresh corn, cut from the cob
1 cup diced carrots
1 cup diced string beans

Salsa

1½ cups chopped tomatoes (peeling is optional)
½ cup minced red onion
½ cup minced red bell pepper
½ cup minced green bell pepper
3 tablespoons minced cilantro
1 garlic clove, minced (optional)
3 tablespoons extra-virgin olive oil
Chili powder and cayenne to taste

Guacamole

1 large avocado
2 teaspoons lemon juice
½ teaspoon ground cumin
¼ teaspoon dried oregano

Salad

8 cups shredded Iceberg lettuce
4 cups shredded Romaine lettuce
Corn chips
Olives, for garnish

1. Place peas, corn, carrots, and beans in a steamer over boiling water and steam until tender.

2. Prepare salsa by chopping and mincing all the vegetables and combining them in a medium bowl. Add olive oil, chili powder, and cayenne and mix well.

3. Prepare guacamole by mashing avocado in a bowl and mixing in other ingredients.

4. Place shredded lettuces in a large salad bowl. Add steamed vegetables and ¾ cup of salsa. Toss well.

5. To serve, transfer salad to 4 large plates and surround each serving with a ring of corn chips. Spoon a dollop of guacamole on top of each tostada, then garnish with olives. Pass remaining salsa to be drizzled over tostadas, if desired.

Serves 4.

Easy Bean Tostada

30 minutes

This beany cousin of the Easy Tostada on page 162 borrows the same salsa dressing and guacamole, but beans replace the vegetables.

Salsa

1½ cups chopped tomatoes (peeling is optional)
½ cup minced red onion
½ cup minced red bell pepper
½ cup minced green bell pepper
3 tablespoons minced cilantro (optional)
1 garlic clove, minced
3 tablespoons extra-virgin olive oil
Chili powder and cayenne to taste

Guacamole

1 large avocado
2 teaspoons lemon juice
½ teaspoon ground cumin
¼ teaspoon dried oregano

Tostada

4 cups shredded Iceberg lettuce
4 cups shredded Romaine lettuce
1 cup corn, cut from cob and steamed with ¼ cup minced green onions
1 cup alfalfa sprouts
¼ cup finely grated carrot
1 cup cubed tomato
1½ cups refried pinto beans, heated
3 corn tortillas, heated on a dry skillet until soft
Olives, for garnish

1. Prepare salsa by combining the chopped and minced ingredients. Stir in the olive oil and seasonings.

2. Prepare guacamole by mashing the avocado in a bowl and mixing in the other ingredients.

3. Place the shredded lettuces in a large salad bowl. Add the corn mixture, alfalfa sprouts, carrot, and tomato. Add ¾ cup of the salsa and toss well.

4. Place hot tortillas on 3 large salad plates. Top with refried beans and equal portions of salad. Top with guacamole. Drizzle extra salsa over the top and garnish with olives. *¡Olé!*

Serves 3.

California Primavera Salad

20 to 25 minutes

½ pound any pasta—macaroni, rotelle, shells, fettuccine, soba, udon, or a combination
1 firm avocado, halved, peeled, seeded, and cut in ½-inch dice
2 medium tomatoes, peeled and cut in ½-inch dice
¼ cup diced celery
1 red bell pepper, seeded and diced
1 cup peeled, seeded, and diced cucumber
2 tablespoons extra-virgin olive oil
¼ cup minced fresh basil or 1 tablespoon dried
1 tablespoon minced red onion (optional)
1 tablespoon olive oil
4 cups tender lettuce (Butter, Red Leaf, Bibb), in ¼-inch shreds
2 cups coarsely chopped spinach and arugula
Ground rock salt to taste
Freshly ground pepper to taste

1. Cook pasta according to package directions. While cooking, place diced and minced vegetables in a large salad bowl. Add the extra-virgin olive oil and seasonings and allow to marinate.

2. Drain pasta and toss in 1 tablespoon olive oil. Add shredded greens to marinating vegetables in salad bowl, then add pasta and toss well. Adjust seasonings.

Serves 2.

Exotic Mushrooms and Vegetables in a Salad

40 minutes

An elegant salad as a first course for entertaining. Use baby vegetables if they are available.

Salad

¼ pound fresh oyster mushrooms
¼ pound fresh shiitake mushrooms
1 tablespoon extra-virgin olive oil
2 tablespoons minced red onion
1 package enoki mushrooms, ends trimmed
2 tablespoons minced fresh parsley
½ pound thin asparagus, ends trimmed
6 cups Butter or Limestone lettuce pieces
1 cup boiled, peeled, and cubed or julienned beets (leave baby beets whole)
Cherry tomatoes, halved

Dressing

4 tablespoons extra-virgin olive oil
1 tablespoon plus 1 teaspoon lemon juice
¼ teaspoon Dijon-style mustard
1 tiny garlic clove, pressed

1. Rinse mushrooms gently. Cut large oyster mushrooms in half; slice shiitake, removing and discarding stems. Heat oil in a skillet with the minced onion. Cook for 2 minutes over medium heat, stirring to prevent scorching, then add oyster and shiitake mushrooms and sauté until soft and juicy, about 4 minutes. Add enoki mushrooms and sauté less than 1 minute. Add parsley and set aside.

2. Place asparagus in boiling water and blanch for 2 minutes, or until bright green. Drain and shock by dipping in ice water. Set aside.

3. Measure dressing ingredients into a medium bowl. Beat with a whisk until creamy. Remove 1½ tablespoons of dressing and set aside. Break lettuce into bite-size pieces directly into remaining dressing and toss gently.

4. Divide salad into 2 equal portions on dinner plates. Divide mushrooms, beets, and asparagus between plates and arrange on lettuce. Garnish with cherry tomato halves. Drizzle salads with remaining dressing.

Serves 2.

Spring Garden Vegetable Salad

30 minutes

If you like, serve this with Spanokopita (page 320).

Salad

4 cups chopped Iceberg or Salad Bowl lettuce
4 cups chopped Butter lettuce
½ cup chopped tomato
½ cup black olives
½ cup alfalfa sprouts
½ cup sunflower sprouts
1 cup thin broccoli florets, steamed
1 cup small cauliflower florets, steamed
1 cup cubed zucchini, sautéed
1 cup cubed yellow squash, sautéed
1 cup snow peas, blanched and halved
1 cup petit peas, steamed

Dressing

5 tablespoons extra-virgin olive oil
2½ tablespoons lemon juice
2 tablespoons dairy-free mayonnaise or Almonnaise (page 98)
½ teaspoon Dijon-style mustard
Dash of Worcestershire sauce
2 tablespoons water
1 teaspoon minced onion

1. Place lettuce in a large salad bowl.

2. Measure dressing ingredients into hand blender container and blend until creamy.

3. Add tomato, olives, and sprouts to lettuce. Toss in cooked vegetables. Add dressing and toss well.

Serves 4.

Julienned Cucumbers and Chard with Fennel

30 minutes

Although this salad contains no lettuce, it seems to work well as a main-course salad. It's light and refreshing, and yet flavorful and interesting enough to be the focus of your meal. Accompany it with West Indian Sweet Potato Soup (page 195) for a great combination. For a relaxing meditation after a hectic day, julienne the cucumbers by hand.

Salad

2 teaspoons olive oil
8 to 10 medium mushrooms, stems removed
2 to 3 tablespoons minced green onion
3 cups coarsely chopped green chard
3 large hothouse cucumbers, julienned (do not peel) (page 212)
½ red bell pepper, cut in small triangles (½ cup)
½ cup finely chopped fennel or dill leaves

Dressing

1 tablespoon Dijon-style mustard
2 tablespoons olive oil
Juice of 1 lemon
Seasoned salt to taste
¼ cup finely minced green onion

1. Heat olive oil, mushrooms, and green onion in a medium skillet. Sauté until mushrooms are just soft.

2. Steam chard and toss with cucumber and red pepper. Add mushrooms and sprinkle with fennel.

3. In a separate small bowl, combine mustard, oil, lemon juice, seasoned salt, and green onion. Mix well, then pour over salad and toss well.

Serves 4 to 6.

Variation: Combine with Lemon "Stedda" Chicken (page 118) and toss well for a hearty salad.

COOKED SALADS

These are not salads in the traditional sense, because they contain few, if any, greens and raw vegetables. I include them here because they complement simple salads and can easily be turned into Main-Course Salads by adding them to a green salad. All are wonderful on a buffet table.

Marinated Paintbox Vegetables

30 minutes

This crunchy and colorful salad of raw and lightly steamed vegetables is appealing on its own, or it can be tossed with lots of greens for a beautiful effect. Use whatever vegetables you have on hand, but choose a nice "palette" of colors. Remember, the body gets its first nourishment from what it *sees.*

Marinade

⅓ cup olive oil
4 tablespoons lemon juice
¼ cup chopped fresh parsley
2 medium garlic cloves, minced
2 teaspoons Dijon-style mustard or tahini
½ teaspoon honey (optional)
½ teaspoon dried basil
Pinch of dried tarragon
Pinch of dried thyme
Salt and freshly ground pepper to taste

Vegetables

6 cups of 4 to 5 of the following:

Raw

cucumbers, cherry tomatoes, radishes, celery, carrots, red or green bell peppers

Cooked

steamed broccoli, cauliflower, green beans, carrots, butternut squash, zucchini, yellow squash, asparagus, snow peas, garbanzo or kidney beans

1. Combine the marinade ingredients in a blender until smooth.

2. Prepare vegetables and combine in a medium bowl. Pour dressing over vegetables. Toss gently, then cover and chill for 2 or more hours.

Serves 4 to 6.

Dilled Pea Salad

15 minutes

Adding the mayonnaise to the salad while the peas are hot results in a glazed effect when the salad is chilled.

1 small red onion
1 tablespoon olive oil
1 to 2 tablespoons water
4 cups frozen petite peas
¼ teaspoon dried sage
¼ teaspoon dried thyme
1 teaspoon honey or 2 teaspoons brown rice syrup
3 tablespoons dairy-free mayonnaise or Herbed Almonnaise (page 98)
3 tablespoons chopped fresh dill or 1 tablespoon dried
Ground rock salt to taste (optional)
Freshly ground pepper

1. Chop red onion to pea-size dice. Heat the olive oil with the onion in a heavy skillet with a lid. Cook, adding 1 to 2 tablespoons water, until onion softens.

2. Add peas to skillet and mix well. Add dried herbs and sweetener. Cover and steam 5 to 7 minutes, or until peas are tender.

3. Stir in mayonnaise, dill, salt, and pepper to taste.

Serves 6.

Mushroom Ratatouille

7 minutes

This is a lovely salad that can be added to a green salad, used as a topping on Scramblers (page 108), tossed with pasta, or served on crackers or cucumber rounds as an appetizer. Eaten hot or cold it is delicious, and couldn't be easier.

2 tablespoons olive oil
1 teaspoon dried thyme
1 teaspoon dried oregano
½ cup finely chopped red onion
1 pound mushrooms, ends trimmed, caps thinly sliced
1 large fresh or canned tomato, peeled and chopped (1 cup)
Ground rock salt
Freshly ground black pepper

1. Heat the oil, spices, and onion in a skillet. Add mushrooms and sauté until natural juices form.

2. Add chopped tomatoes and salt and pepper to taste.

Serves 3.

Tofu Salad

15 minutes

A lovely lady who cooks for her children in a most caring manner sent this recipe for us to try. We all thought it was quite good. Include it on a salad plate or roll in a Goodwich (page 175) for "finger-licking" goodness!

½ cup finely chopped onion
1 tablespoon olive oil
1 pound firm tofu, finely chopped or mashed
½ cup sweet pickle relish
1 cup finely chopped celery
⅓ to ½ cup dairy-free mayonnaise
1 tablespoon brown mustard

1. Heat onion and oil in a nonstick skillet and sauté until soft over medium heat. Add tofu and sauté, stirring, for 3 minutes.

2. Combine cooked tofu mixture with the relish, celery, mayonnaise, and mustard. Serve at room temperature or chill until ready to use.

Serves 4 to 6.

Fit for Life Corn Salad

20 minutes

Here's an updated version of one of the most popular recipes from *Fit for Life I.* It's indispensable picnic fare. And for a summer feast, serve Vegetable Lasagna (page 278), Corn Salad, julienned carrots, Potato Burek (page 312), and a Classic Green Salad (page 140).

1 tablespoon olive oil
1½ cups diced red onion
1½ cups diced red bell pepper
1½ cups diced green bell pepper
1½ teaspoons curry powder
½ teaspoon dried oregano
½ teaspoon turmeric
4 to 6 cups cooked corn (if using fresh corn, boil for 3 to 5 minutes until just tender, cool briefly, and cut from cob)
½ cup sliced pimiento-stuffed olives
⅓ cup Almonnaise (page 98) or dairy-free mayonnaise
Ground rock salt
Freshly ground pepper (optional)
2 tablespoons chopped cilantro (optional)

1. Heat oil in a large skillet. Add onion and sauté for 2 minutes, stirring frequently. Add red and green peppers and sauté, stirring frequently, for 2 minutes more. Add curry powder, oregano, and turmeric and sauté briefly.

2. Combine corn and sautéed vegetables in a large bowl. Stir in olives. Add Almonnaise or mayonnaise, salt and pepper to taste, and cilantro. Stir well. Refrigerate until serving.

Serves 6.

Linda's Tabouli

1 hour for soaking
10 minutes for assembly

Tabouli is made from bulgur wheat, a favorite delicacy of Genghis Khan. It's not surprising, since this hulled, precooked grain made from crushed wheat berries originated in ancient Turkey. Bulgur is available in varied gradations, from fine to coarse, and in different colors, the darker of which are preferable since they probably still contain some of the bran. Tabouli is the classic bulgur salad, and it is fast and easy, lovely served in summertime with other salads.

2 cups bulgur wheat
4 cups water
3 medium tomatoes, peeled, cored, and chopped
1 cup minced fresh parsley
¼ cup minced fresh mint
¼ cup extra-virgin olive oil, or more to taste
Juice of 1 lemon

1. Soak bulgur in water for 1 hour. Drain well.
2. Add remaining ingredients. Mix well.

Serves 6 to 8.

Note: If you are not going to use the entire amount at one sitting, cut the recipe. Leftover bulgur acquires the same slightly fermented flavor that you notice in a tomato sandwich that has sat for too long. The tomato ferments the wheat.

Warm Lima Bean Salad

20 minutes

If you love lima beans, you'll adore this salad. It's a special way to have them.

1½ (10-ounce) packages frozen Fordhook or baby lima beans
3 tablespoons plus 2 teaspoons olive oil, or 2 teaspoons vegetable broth or water for sautéing
¼ cup diced red onion
¼ cup diced red bell pepper
Scant 1 tablespoon lemon juice
½ teaspoon Dijon-style mustard
Pinch of dried tarragon
Pinch of dried thyme
Freshly ground pepper

1. Place the frozen limas in a steamer over boiling water and steam for 12 to 15 minutes, or until they are tender but not mushy.

2. Heat 2 teaspoons of oil in a nonstick skillet with the onion and pepper. Sauté, stirring frequently, over medium heat, adding 1 to 2 tablespoons water to keep the vegetables from scorching, until they are soft.

3. In a medium bowl, whisk together the remaining 3 tablespoons of olive oil, lemon juice, mustard, tarragon, thyme, and pepper to taste. Add the warm lima beans and the sautéed vegetables and mix well.

Serves 4 to 6.

Broccoli-Orzo Salad

20 minutes

Orzo looks like rice but feels like pasta in your mouth; actually it is a rice-shaped pasta. It's a nice change of pace for pasta lovers. If you want to jazz up this salad, add a few tablespoons of pesto! For a party buffet, serve this with Spanokopita (page 320) or Mixed Grill Platter (page 115), Potato Cakes (page 252), French Green Salad with Cottage Tofu (page 141), and Corn on the Cob (page 233).

Dressing

2 tablespoons olive oil
1 teaspoon lemon juice
1 teaspoon balsamic vinegar (optional)
1 medium garlic clove, pressed, or 1 teaspoon garlic powder
Freshly ground pepper
¼ cup slivered fresh basil or 2 teaspoons dried

Salad

3 cups steamed broccoli florets
8 ounces orzo, cooked al dente and drained
2 large tomatoes, peeled and chopped, or ½ cup slivered sun-dried tomatoes
2 green onions, minced
¼ cup minced fresh parsley
¼ cup chopped black olives

1. In a small bowl, measure dressing ingredients and combine.

2. In a large bowl, combine broccoli, orzo, tomatoes, green onions, parsley, and olives. Add dressing and adjust seasonings to taste. Refrigerate or serve at room temperature.

Serves 4.

Variation: Substitute couscous or several "flavors" of vegetable linguine, broken into 1-inch segments like confetti.

Green Beans, Red Onions, and Jicama

30 minutes

Jicama is a brown-skinned, root vegetable that has long been prized by Mexican, Latin American, and Asian cooks. It is rather unappealing looking on the outside, but once the thick skin is cut or peeled back, there is a white, crisp, thirst-quenching vegetable that adds its texture willingly to many vegetable dishes and salads. Jicama is well presented when it is julienned. Do this by hand with a mandoline, or in your food processor.

1 pound thin green beans
1 cup thinly sliced red onion
5 tablespoons plus 2 teaspoons olive oil
½ teaspoon roasted sesame oil
2 teaspoons rice vinegar
½ teaspoon honey
2 tablespoons low-sodium soy sauce
2 tablespoons lemon juice
½ teaspoon ground ginger
1½ cups julienned jicama (page 212)
2 tablespoons black or white sesame seeds
Freshly ground pepper

1. Trim ends from green beans, and cut in half crosswise. Blanch in boiling water for 4 minutes or until al dente. Drain, shock in cold water, drain again, and pat dry.

2. Thinly slice the onion, then sauté briefly in 2 teaspoons olive oil. (Or, if you like raw onion, leave raw and set aside.)

3. Measure remaining olive oil and next 6 ingredients in a large bowl. Combine with a whisk. Add green beans, onion, and jicama. Toss well, then sprinkle with sesame seeds and pepper to taste. Refrigerate for 30 minutes before serving.

Serves 6.

Cold Rice and Spinach Salad

15 minutes

2 teaspoons plus 2 tablespoons olive oil
½ cup diced red onion
4 cups chopped fresh spinach
2 teaspoons lemon juice
2 teaspoons Umeboshi plum paste or rice vinegar
2 tablespoons low-sodium soy sauce
4 cups cooked brown rice
1 tablespoon minced green onions (optional)

1. Heat 2 teaspoons olive oil in a skillet. Add onion and sauté until soft. (Add a few teaspoons of water to prevent browning.) Add spinach and braise until soft. Set aside.

2. In large bowl, combine remaining 2 tablespoons olive oil, lemon juice, plum paste, and soy sauce. Stir in rice and spinach. Add green onions, if desired.

Serves 4.

How Much Should You Eat?

Average "unstretched" stomachs hold 4 to 6 cups of food, depending on the size of the individual. When you eat, there should be some room left in the stomach so that the food can mix and turn. Therefore, you should stop eating *before* your stomach is packed, when 3 to 5 cups of food have been eaten.

Food quantities of 3 to 5 cups seem like tiny amounts if you have consistently overeaten and have stretched your stomach. Don't panic! Use the measurements as a guide, and begin cutting back to more rational amounts gradually, allowing your stomach to slowly shrink back to normal.

For years, Dr. Roy Walford of UCLA, one of the world's eminent gerontologists, has been demonstrating on laboratory animals that rationally restricted food intake *doubles* their life span. It also increases their energy, and diminishes drastically their incidence of cancer, cataracts, kidney disease, and heart ailments. Dr. Walford applies these findings to human longevity: "If you are talking about extending maximum life span, there must be a reduction in caloric intake. The stronger immunity system that will result from the restricted diet will mean... a significant delay in afflictions that hit the elderly, such as senility and arthritis. People will be productive longer...."

We can benefit from Dr. Walford's findings. We can learn, over the long term, to eat well but *less*. The process unfolds as you learn not to fill your stomach to maximum. In leaving some room for movement, you will experience a lighter, more energetic feeling after eating. You will work, sleep, and relate better with that energy. Stuffing yourself places a burden on your entire body that can make you grouchy after eating. It can also cause irritability and depression, because on a subconscious level overeaters know that they have abused themselves with food.

Overeating robs energy from every other aspect of your life, and it forces you to work a lot harder to keep fit. The willpower you exercise in eating just the right amount of food at every meal will bolster your feeling of power over yourself and your life, and that will spill over into other areas, where you find yourself suddenly excelling in unexpected ways.

One final note. Any food if overeaten *will do you harm.* That means that even the most luscious and nutritious choice—for example, watermelon—will result in lost energy and a tummy full of spoilage to be processed out.

8

What Should I Put in a Sandwich?

SINCE *Fit for Life* was published, one of the most frequently asked questions has been, "What should I put in a sandwich?" This concern is more widespread now than ever before. Former Surgeon General Koop's "Report on Nutrition and Health" has made people newly aware that so much of what they put in their sandwiches is unnecessarily high in saturated fat and cholesterol. Eggs, cheese, chicken, beef, pork, tuna, turkey, and the like are all way up there (see pages 6–7). It is obvious that new sandwich ideas are long overdue.

Sandwiches have been in the *Fit for Life* kitchen for years. When kids are around, this is certainly one of the most popular foods. We have found that many foods you'd never think would qualify actually make first-rate sandwiches. They're easy and economical. And in addition to being highly digestible and energizing, they taste great!

THE GOODWICH PRINCIPLE

We briefly discussed this concept in *Fit for Life;* and just when I think that everybody's got it down, I hear that someone *just discovered* Goodwiches and is ecstatically living on them. You bet they are! Goodwiches are practically a life-support system.

The Goodwich is actually an edible plate. Whatever your heart desires goes in layers on a soft, hot whole-wheat tortilla or chapati, which is then rolled burrito-style and eaten end to end. Goodwiches store marvelously and are convenient to have on hand. You can make a batch of six to eight quickly and keep them in your refrigerator. They have a two- to four-day shelf life, depending on the filling; however, I find that unless I make a dozen at a time, they never last that long. For one person, there is probably no more convenient food. Just heat your tortilla and put salad and vegetables on it, then roll and eat—a whole meal in a few minutes.

In addition, Goodwiches give you the enjoyment of eating bread without eating a lot of it.

Tortillas are light compared to two slices of bread or a bun. If you think I'm implying that these are a weight-loss food, you are right. In addition, Goodwiches are very economical. Practically anything can go into a Goodwich, which will be apparent when you turn these pages and see the items we use. After you know the basic procedure, you can refer to specific recipes for successful ones and then begin to develop your own.

How to Make a Goodwich

You'll need the following equipment:

1 medium nonstick skillet
a vegetable steamer
assorted graters, knives, colander
a spreader or spatula
plastic wrap for storage

The ingredients for 6 Goodwiches are:

6 whole-wheat tortillas
6 to 8 cups assorted steamed vegetables, raw vegetables, salads, cooked salads, or "Steddas" of your choice
Condiments, such as Almonnaise, dairy-free mayonnaise, barbecue sauce, mustard, olive oil, Thousand Island dressing, tartar sauce, soy sauce, and the like
Trimmings—sliced pickles, sautéed onions, chopped olives, sprouts, slivered sun-dried tomatoes, strips of roasted red bell pepper

Prepare the steamed vegetables, cooked salads, or "Steddas." Vegetables should be cut in long, thin segments so they will roll well. Also prepare the raw salad or sliced or shredded raw vegetables. Select and prepare the trimmings and assemble the condiments. Now, here's the procedure for assembling a Goodwich (see illustrations on page 177):

1. Have your filling ingredients ready.

2. Heat a nonstick skillet over medium-high heat. Drop 1 whole-wheat tortilla or chapati on the hot, dry skillet. Cook for 15 seconds, rotating the tortilla in a circular fashion with your fingers to prevent sticking. Flip the tortilla over and heat in the same way on the second side for 10 to 15 seconds, until it begins to puff slightly.

3. Place the hot tortilla on your work surface. Spread tortilla generously with condiment(s) of your choice.

4. In center of tortilla, place a line, end to end, of your desired filling ingredients and trimmings.

5. Tuck lower half of tortilla around filling and roll tightly, like a burrito or crepe. Eat immediately while still warm, or wrap tightly in plastic and store in refrigerator. Goodwiches are great warm or cold.

HOW TO ASSEMBLE A GOODWICH

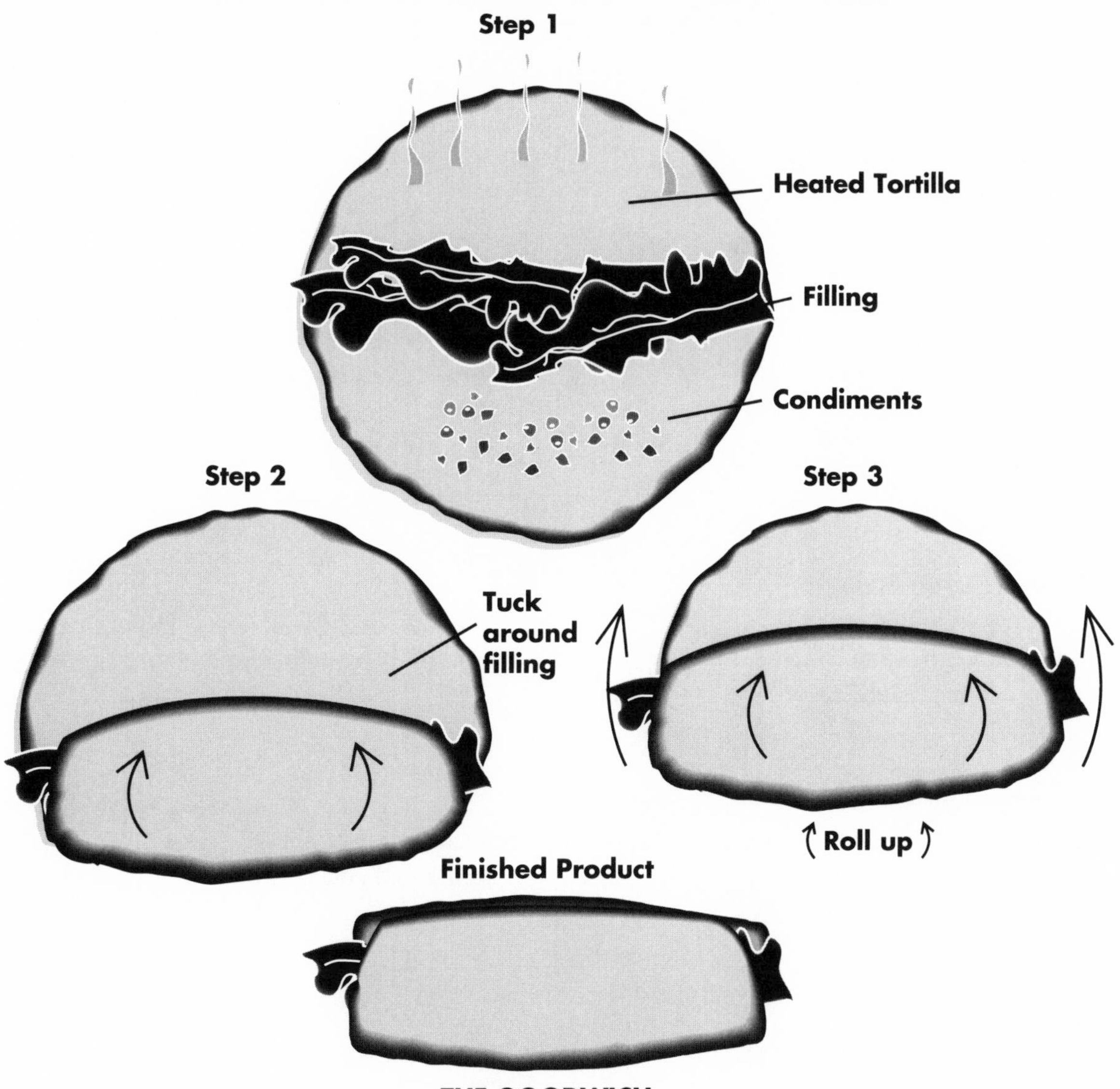

What to Put in a Goodwich

Raw Vegetables

avocado
cucumber
finely shredded carrot
finely shredded red or green cabbage
shredded lettuce and spinach
sprouts
tomato (only if eating Goodwich immediately. Stored, tomato will ferment the tortilla)

Steamed Vegetables

asparagus
broccoli
carrot
cauliflower
spinach or other greens

Sautéed Vegetables

eggplant
mushrooms
onions
peppers
zucchini

Simple Salads

Main-Course Salads

Cooked Salads

"Steddas"

Condiments and Trimmings

Almonnaise (page 98)
barbecue sauce
ketchup
mayonnaise
mustard
soy sauce
tartar sauce
Thousand Island dressing
chopped olives
roasted red bell peppers
sliced dill pickles
sun-dried tomatoes
sweet pickle relish

Miscellaneous

rice
vegetables

Great Goodwiches We've Known

On the Run—Sliced tomato, cucumber spears, and avocado slices with Almonnaise (page 98) or mayonnaise and alfalfa sprouts. Clean and delicious!

Hot Broccoli—Steamed broccoli, Almonnaise (page 98) or mayonnaise, and alfalfa sprouts with some salt-free seasoning. Simple, but so-o-o good. Add sautéed mushrooms for a change of pace.

New York Goodwich—Almonnaise (page 98) or mayonnaise, hot broccoli and cauliflower, shredded carrot and red cabbage, dill pickle spears, onions sautéed in barbecue sauce, and shredded lettuce. Very popular.

L.A. Goodwich—Everything that the New York Goodwich has but hold the onions and substitute avocado and sprouts. A winner!

Burritto Muy Bueño—Refried beans, salsa, shredded lettuce, "Stedda" Sour Cream (page 105), and avocado. Filling! Boys love it!

"Stedda" Beef in a Goodwich—"Stedda" Beef Salad (page 155) with Almonnaise (page 98) or mayonnaise. Divine!

Chinese "Stedda" Chicken—"Stedda" Chinese Chicken Salad (page 118) with Almonnaise (page 98) or egg-free mayonnaise. Exotic!

"Stedda" Chickwich—Strips of grilled "Stedda" Chicken Fillets (page 115) or Lemon "Stedda" Chicken (page 118), Almonnaise (page 98) or mayonnaise, Dijon-style mustard, sliced tomato, chopped lettuce and spinach, and alfalfa sprouts. Heavenly!

Brown Rice and Vegies—Steamed brown rice mixed with shredded carrot, blanched snow peas, minced green onions, mung bean sprouts, shredded cabbage, and low-sodium tamari. Hearty!

"Stedda" Tuna—Mayonnaise or Almonnaise (page 98), "Stedda" Tuna (page 110), thin cucumber slices, sliced tomato, and sprouts. Yum!

About Tomatoes on Sandwiches

Many people love tomatoes on sandwiches, and tomatoes on sandwiches (or Goodwiches) that will be eaten immediately are not a problem. (Unless you suffer from digestive problems, in which case you might want to avoid the acid-starch combination that results from tomatoes and bread and can aggravate digestive disorders.) Tomatoes on sandwiches that sit for hours (or on Goodwiches that you store in the refrigerator) *can,* however, be a problem. When fresh tomatoes are close to bread or other starches, fermentation begins. The tomato and the bread literally begin to *spoil* each other. If you are not going to eat your sandwich immediately I suggest you leave the tomato off, or pack it separately to be added later.

OTHER SANDWICHES AND FILLINGS

We introduced the super "Stedda" burgers and sandwiches in the How to Replace Animal Products chapter. They are, undoubtedly, some of the best sandwiches you could possibly eat. They do everything for you that burgers used to do, yet they leave you feeling high and energetic. Just in case you've forgotten about them, we list them here:

"Stedda" Egg on a Muffin—With dairy-free mayonnaise or Almonnaise (page 98), sliced tomato, and sprouts on an English muffin.

"Stedda" Tuna on Toast—With dairy-free mayonnaise or Almonnaise, thinly sliced cucumber, kelp powder, lemon juice, tomato, and alfalfa sprouts.

"Stedda" Chicken—On toasted whole-wheat bun with dairy-free mayonnaise or Almonnaise, Dijon-style mustard, dill pickle, tomato, shredded carrot, and alfalfa sprouts.

"Stedda" Fish Fillet on a Bun—With tartar sauce, sliced tomato, and alfalfa sprouts.

I used to love fried eggs with ketchup and alfalfa sprouts or lettuce on toast. When I ate one (especially on whole-grain toast with the alfalfa sprouts), I thought I was doing something good for myself. Back then, eggs were considered good sources of protein and calcium—the "Perfect Food," remember?

Here's what is true about eggs:

- Eggs are one of the leading sources of saturated fat and cholesterol in the United States.
- In one carefully conducted double-blind study, it was shown that only 1 egg a day for 3 weeks raised blood cholesterol by 12 percent.[1]
- When your blood cholesterol rises by 12 percent, your risk of heart attack increases by 24 percent.
- Even if your blood cholesterol is "normal," your risk of dying from a disease caused by clogged arteries is over 50 percent.
- If you do not eat saturated fat and cholesterol, your risk of dying from a disease caused by clogged arteries is 5 percent.

Now taste my recipe for the "I Used to Love a Fried Egg" Sandwich.

[1]F. Sacks, "Ingestion of Egg Raises Plasma Low Density Lypoproteins in Free-Living Subjects," *Lancet,* 1 (1984), p. 647.

"I Used to Love a Fried Egg" Sandwich

8 minutes

2 ¼-inch slices firm tofu
1 scant tablespoon nutritional yeast or mustard
Salt and fresh pepper (optional)
1 teaspoon olive oil
2 slices whole-grain bread, lightly toasted
Dairy-free mayonnaise or Almonnaise (page 98), ketchup, mustard
Alfalfa sprouts or lettuce
Several thin slices of tomato (optional)

1. Dip the tofu slices in the nutritional yeast to coat, or brush lightly with mustard. Season to taste with salt and pepper.

2. Heat oil in a skillet. Add tofu slices and sauté over medium-high heat for 3 minutes on each side, turning once.

3. Assemble sandwich using bread, mayonnaise or other spread, tofu, sprouts or lettuce, and tomato.

Yields 1 sandwich.

The Grandwich

5 minutes

I know a young vegetarian boy whose life absolutely works, and this sandwich is one of the reasons. He depends on it when he's got that "I'm starved!" feeling; as far as he's concerned, no one makes it better than he does. Eat this with soup and some tortilla chips. What a lunch!

2 slices whole-grain bread, lightly toasted
Almonnaise (page 98) or dairy-free mayonnaise
¼ to ½ avocado, mashed or sliced
4 thin tomato slices
Sunflower or alfalfa sprouts

1. Toast bread lightly and spread with Almonnaise. Mash avocado on one slice of bread.

2. Top with tomato slices, sprouts, and second slice of bread. Cut in half, diagonally.

Serves 1.

Cucumber Sandwich That Works

5 minutes

A comfortable-to-eat, appetizing cucumber sandwich begins with paper-thin cucumber slices. Choose cucumbers that are small and not too seedy or watery for your sandwiches. It is not necessary to peel them first unless you have a waxed cucumber.

2 slices lightly toasted whole-grain bread
Dairy-free mayonnaise, Almonnaise (page 98), and/or mustard to taste
⅓ cup paper-thin cucumber slices
Alfalfa, sunflower, or radish sprouts; or watercress or several tender slices of Butter lettuce
Thin tomato slices (optional)

1. Spread toast with condiment of your choice.
2. Add neat lines and layers of cucumbers, sprouts or lettuce, and tomato, if desired.

Serves 1.

Open-Face Curried Cauliflower Sandwich

15 minutes

People can't believe it's cauliflower! Serve it on crackers for appetizers, too, or exclude the bread and make the curried cauliflower part of a salad plate. As a sandwich, serve with traditional Ukrainian Cabbage Soup (page 201) or Full of Life Vegetable Soup (page 195) and Broiled Yam Chips (page 263).

1 small cauliflower, steamed until soft
2 teaspoons lemon juice
½ teaspoon powdered kelp or seasoned salt
½ teaspoon curry powder
¼ teaspoon dried oregano
¼ teaspoon ground coriander
⅛ to ¼ teaspoon dry mustard
¼ to ½ cup Almonnaise (page 98) or dairy-free mayonnaise
4 slices whole-grain bread, lightly toasted
4 thin slices of large tomato
Several sprigs of watercress
Black sesame seeds

1. Mash the cauliflower, then add the lemon juice, seasonings, mustard, and Almonnaise. Mix thoroughly.

2. Spread cauliflower mixture neatly on each slice of toast. Top each with a slice of tomato. Cut each slice diagonally, and tuck small sprigs of watercress under the tomatoes for garnish. Sprinkle lightly with sesame seeds.

Serves 2 to 3.

Variation: Chop ¼ cup watercress and mix into cauliflower mixture. Use as a stuffing for warmed pita pockets with shredded carrot, shredded lettuce, and chopped tomato. Or use as a stuffing for artichokes.

Sushi "Alive"

25 minutes

This is a winner. The first time I made it, I tested it on an eight-year-old American boy, a thirty-year-old Frenchman, and a forty-two-year-old Nicaraguan lady. They all loved it!

¼ cup sesame seeds
½ cup raw cashews
¾ cup lentil sprouts
1 medium carrot
½ small green bell pepper
1 (4-inch) celery stalk
2 tablespoons olive oil
1 leaf Chinese cabbage
2 teaspoons tamari
8 sheets toasted nori
1 large tomato, halved and thinly sliced
Alfalfa and sunflower seed sprouts

1. Place the sesame seeds, cashews, and lentil sprouts in a food processor and process until thick and mealy. Add the carrot, pepper, and celery and process until smooth. Add the olive oil, cabbage, and tamari and process until the cabbage is chopped but not liquefied. (The cabbage should add some texture to the mixture.)

2. Spread approximately ½ cup filling on the lower half of a sheet of nori. Add a line of sliced tomatoes and sprouts. Roll and eat immediately or wrap in plastic wrap and store until ready to use. (As the sushi sits, the nori becomes less crunchy.)

Serves 8.

Genevieve's Mushroom Burgers

10 minutes

A reader named Genevieve sent me this recipe in 1987. Thank you, Genevieve!

2 teaspoons olive oil
2 large mushrooms, sliced
Juice of fresh lemon
2 teaspoons dairy-free mayonnaise, Almonnaise (page 98), or Dijon-style mustard
Lettuce
Tomato slices
Onion rings (optional)
1 tablespoon alfalfa sprouts
3 thin slices cucumber
1 slice of green bell pepper
1 large whole-wheat roll

1. Heat olive oil in skillet and sauté mushrooms for 3 minutes until tender. Sprinkle with lemon.

2. Place all ingredients on lightly toasted roll, and munch!

Serves 1.

Yogi-Child's Peanut Butter–Carrot Sandwich

5 minutes

I call this "Yogi-Child's" because only the *flexible* child will consider it. But of course there are more and more flexible children out there, thanks to the good work of their parents. So, try this nontraditional peanut butter and bread combination, more easily digested with the raw-vegetable "helpers."

2 slices whole-wheat or other whole-grain bread, lightly toasted
Good-quality unsalted peanut butter
¼ to ⅓ cup shredded carrots (taste-test to be sure they are sweet)
Lettuce or alfalfa sprouts

1. Spread both pieces of bread with peanut butter. Add carrots and lettuce or sprouts.
2. Close it up and bag it for the lunchbox or serve immediately.

Serves 1.

Roasted Red Peppers

4 large red bell peppers

Place peppers on a baking sheet in preheated 400°F oven, turning frequently until skin blisters on all sides. Remove peppers from oven and place in paper bag. Close tightly. Allow to sit for 20 minutes while the skins "sweat off." Peel loose skins from peppers, remove seeds and ribs and discard. Cut peppers in strips of desired thickness. Use plain or marinated.

The Incredible Red Pepper

(And How to Use It on a Sandwich)

Red peppers, when roasted, turn into the most amazing sandwich filler. They are easy to roast, and no matter how I serve them, people always wolf them down. Some say, "I've never eaten a red pepper before in my life!" Others comment, "Gee, and I don't usually *like* red peppers!" Both comments are made as they reach for seconds, thirds, and even fourths. Red peppers can be roasted in the oven or on a grill, but since ovens are more accessible than grills, I give that technique. Once roasted, use them immediately or marinate for storage in refrigerator for up to 4 weeks. Since they keep so well, and can be used so well, it pays to roast a lot.

Marinade for Roasted Red Peppers

2 garlic cloves, cut in thin slivers
1/2 teaspoon kelp powder (optional) or ground rock salt to taste
4 tablespoons extra-virgin olive oil
4 large red bell peppers, roasted

Combine marinade ingredients in medium bowl. Add roasted red pepper strips and marinate 1 hour before using or store in refrigerator in tightly sealed container until ready to use.

Linda's Marinated Red Pepper Sandwich

5 minutes

2 slices whole-grain bread, lightly toasted
Dairy-free mayonnaise or Almonnaise (page 98)
Marinated roasted red peppers
Grated carrots
Thinly sliced cucumbers
Dijon-style mustard

1. Spread bread generously with condiments.
2. Add remaining ingredients.

Serves 1.

Red Pepper Party Sandwiches

15 minutes

This is another way to use roasted red peppers that is easy, and bound to be a tremendous hit! I love to serve these at parties. People make such a fuss over them. They are also wonderful at high tea.

12 small dinner rolls, preferably whole-wheat, ideally onion flavored
Extra-thick Almonnaise (page 98)
2 to 3 large roasted red peppers
Watercress sprigs

1. Cut rolls carefully in half (so they will look pretty, as well as taste divine) and place on a cookie sheet, open for toasting. Toast in a 450°F for 5 minutes, taking care not to char them.

2. Remove rolls from oven and spread both halves with Almonnaise. Place a slice of red pepper, cut exactly to fit the lower half of each roll. Top with small sprigs of watercress and the top half of the roll.

Serves 5 to 6.

Variation: Cucumber slices may be substituted for the peppers.

Red Peppers and Almonnaise on Whole-Wheat Bagels

10 minutes

Earlier in the book, I described Almonnaise as a cross between mayonnaise and cream cheese. This is where that cream-cheese quality really becomes apparent, especially if you have made a nice, thick batch.

4 whole-wheat bagels, halved and lightly toasted
Extra-thick Almonnaise (page 98)
Plain or marinated roasted red peppers

1. Lightly toast bagels, then spread with Almonnaise.
2. Add neatly cut slices of red peppers.

Serves 4 to 6.

Spicy Tofu Tacos

15 minutes

Spoon this delicious filling onto soft corn tortillas or into crispy taco shells, top with avocado, tomato, sprouts, shredded lettuce, and salsa. Makes a great weekend lunch.

1 small onion, diced
1 small red pepper, diced
1 tablespoon olive oil, or water for sautéing
1 teaspoon paprika
1 tablespoon cumin
1 teaspoon chili powder
4 to 6 tablespoons water
1 pound firm tofu (frozen and defrosted or fresh)
2 tablespoons ketchup
2 tablespoons hickory barbecue sauce (a spicy sauce works well)
Ground rock salt to taste (optional)
6 to 8 corn tortillas or taco shells

1. Sauté onion and red pepper with olive oil in large skillet, adding paprika, cumin, and chili powder as vegetables begin to soften. Add water and stir well to allow vegetables to cook through.
2. Crumble tofu into skillet. (If you are using frozen and defrosted tofu, be sure to squeeze out all the excess water.) Add ketchup and barbecue sauce and stir well. Sauté for 5 minutes. Season to taste with salt, if desired.

Serves 3 to 4.

Tomburgers

20 minutes

I've talked about these in other books, but I include them here, because I just don't want anybody to miss them. This is what we serve at July 4th picnics, when those beautiful beefsteak tomatoes are in season and nobody wants anything too heavy because it's so hot! Tomburgers have everything we want to eat, and couldn't be juicier. Fresh whole-wheat burger buns are important. Serve with Mediterranean Rice Salad (page 160), Crusty Roasteds Revisited (page 246), Grilled Asparagus (page 221), and Corn on the Cob with "Stedda" Butter Sauce (page 233) for a winning July 4th Picnic.

6 whole-wheat burger buns, lightly toasted
Almonnaise (page 98) or dairy-free mayonnaise
Guacamole Calabasas or Quick Guacamole (pages 132 and 133)
6 (¾-inch) slices of beefsteak tomatoes
Barbecued onions (see Note)
Alfalfa sprouts
Sliced dill pickle

1. Spread toasted buns with Almonnaise. Place 1 tablespoon of guacamole on bottom of each bun.

2. Add tomato slice, onions, sprouts, and pickle. Cover with top half of bun.

Serves 6.

Note: Barbecued onions are easy:

2 large red onions, halved and thinly sliced
½ to 1 cup hickory-flavored barbecued sauce

Place onions and barbecue sauce in a large nonstick skillet and sauté over medium heat until onions are soft and coated with sauce. Add a little water, if necessary, to keep mixture from scorching. Stir frequently.

Yields enough for 12 Tomburgers.

Hummus in Pita

10 minutes

3 whole-wheat pita pockets
1 cup hummus (page 131)
Chopped tomato
Shredded lettuce
Alfalfa Sprouts
Slivers of dill pickle
Tahina (page 136)

1. Warm the pita pockets. Slice off a 1-inch strip from each top.

2. Spread ⅓ cup of hummus inside each pita, then stuff pita with tomato, lettuce, sprouts, and pickle. Spread generously with Tahina. These are drippy and good.

Serves 3.

Variation: Add several tablespoons of Lebanese Green Beans (page 238) to pockets with salad ingredients.

9

Soups Make the World Go 'Round!

I *COULD* sing you a song, set to the familiar tune, about soups. Soups, like cookies or muffins, are a loving food. They fill a house with "I love you, I care about you" aromas and energy. In our busy lives, homemade soups may have lost some footing, but with a few new ideas on how to make them *quickly* while keeping them delicious, perhaps we can return them to their rightful position.

Soups cost only a little but fill the tummy. They can be light or hearty, brothy or creamy, depending on the time you have and the weather; and they usually rely on basic, readily available ingredients. Nearly every culture has its basic soups, from which we can borrow ideas, ingredients, and techniques. Our soups, of course, are made without meat or dairy products. In this chapter you'll find stocks and broths based on vegetables and wonderful cream soups without a drop of cream. And in thirty minutes, using one simple technique, you will be able to make at least a dozen different soups!

Salad and soup make a high-energy meal. Pair a main course salad and a thirty-minute cream soup, and you'll be rarin' to go when you finish. Yet the food is so good, your taste buds will feel they've been to a party.

Remember, if the non-dairy replacements for dairy products used in these recipes are not available or you do not choose to use them, you may use traditional low fat dairy products instead with successful results.

SEASONINGS FOR SOUPS

Most people these days make an effort to avoid the harmful knee-jerk addition of salt to foods requiring flavor enhancement. They are looking for alternatives that will have the same effect but will be either devoid of salt or lower in salt content. There are many salt substitutes available in the supermarkets and natural foods stores to help you do this; some seasonings containing less salt can also be quite effective. In cooking soups, I have particularly found one seasoning to be of unusual interest: miso.

Miso is a rich, thick paste used in Japan for flavoring a wide variety of dishes. It has traditionally been produced by the Japanese since the seventeenth century by a process of natural fermentation that transforms soybeans, brown rice, or barley into many types of miso; each region in Japan has its own particular variety.

Miso is a staple ingredient in Japanese and macrobiotic cooking. Given its salty nature, it replaces salt in any food; despite its salt content, it is widely considered to be highly nutritious and possesses unusual health-supporting properties. It provides essential amino acids, and is said to supply vitamin B_{12}. It contains other B-complex vitamins, calcium, and iron. Miso is a highly alkaline food, which helps neutralize acids in the bloodstream. It also contains beneficial lactobacillus microorganisms that help maintain intestinal flora that contribute to our ability to resist disease.[1]

What I find most interesting about miso, however—and why I am amenable to using it, particularly in soups—is information I have uncovered on its radioprotective properties. Radioprotective foods have the ability to eliminate radioactive elements from the body and protect it against radioactive onslaught. Given that the average living environment is more or less saturated with radioactive elements, from television screens, computers, microwave ovens, radar, radio and television transmission towers, security systems, automatic door openers, and even digital clocks, foods considered to be radioprotective are worthy of interest. Miso contains zybicolin, a binding agent, identified in 1972, that binds with radioactive and other toxic elements in the body and removes them. Research in Japan on miso's effects on the body supports this theory.[2] The Japanese, who have survived nuclear attack, are so enthusiastic about miso and its beneficial effects that, in addition to adding it to many foods, people often drink a cup of hot miso broth instead of coffee or tea in the morning which, unlike these popular morning beverages, alkalizes rather than acidifies their blood and energizes them throughout the day. (See Chapter 3.)

All of this having been said, you would not wish to use an ingredient, no matter how beneficial, if it did not enhance the flavor of your food. I find the flavor of miso, used sparingly, to be far more pleasing than that achieved through the addition of seasoned salts. It is smoother, more soothing, and delicate, but of definite high quality.

All of these positive attributes, however, are true only in the case of *unpasteurized* miso, since heat destroys the fragile nutrients it contains. Unfortunately, much of the miso we see in our country is pasteurized. But in many natural foods stores and Japanese markets, you can buy high-quality, aged, unpasteurized miso in 1-pound tubs or plastic packages.[3] Unpasteurized miso will be either light (yellow or white) or dark (red). The light contains a smaller proportion of soybeans to barley or brown rice. Higher in simple sugars, B vitamins, and lactic acid, it is less salty and sweeter, too. Added to soups or other dishes, such as mashed potatoes, it will have a slightly creamy effect. As such, light miso is an excellent substitute for dairy. Dark miso is high in soybean content and is saltier. It is very high in amino acids and fatty acids. Added to legumes, in the form of soups, casseroles, or loaves, it is an excellent seasoning. For dishes you boil, add it at the end to preserve its nutritional integrity.

Miso is a delicious, but *very concentrated* flavoring that must be used in moderation. A recommended daily intake is between ½ and 1 teaspoon per person per day. If you use it in proper amounts as a seasoning, as indicated in these recipes, you will consume it properly.

Another soup seasoning is chicken-flavored vegetable broth. There's no chicken here, but the chicken flavor is an amazing facsimile of the real thing! Dissolved in water, the seasoning creates a "chicken" stock that is extremely useful in soup preparation.

[1]Sara Shannon, *Diet for the Atomic Age* (Wayne, N.J.: Avery Press, 1987), p. 147.
[2]Shannon, *Diet,* pp. 146–48.
[3]Packages should be kept refrigerated and, once opened, should be placed in a tightly closed container before refrigerating.

DAIRY-FREE CREAM SOUPS

You can make impeccable cream soups in just 30 minutes, from almost any vegetable you have on hand. These soups are outstanding in their simplicity. Their flavors are uncomplicated and true because each vegetable's own flavor is the essential ingredient. Of course, the freshness and quality of the vegetable you use certainly influences the quality of soup, but even vegetables that are less than perfectly fresh make very good cream soups.

Master this simple procedure, then the options for variations are practically without limit. You'll be able to make excellent cream soups from broccoli, asparagus, potato, summer squash, winter squash, pumpkin, yam, onion, leek, cabbage, cauliflower, spinach, carrot, celery—the list goes on and on! And none will require more than 9 basic ingredients, 6 basic steps, and 30 minutes' time.

You'll need the following basic equipment:

tea kettle
1 2- to 4-quart soup pot with lid
1 chef's knife
measuring cups
1 large stainless-steel, Melanine, or glass bowl that can take heat
1 blender (a hand blender definitely saves time and clean-up)

Basic Cream Soup

Try this with cauliflower, broccoli, asparagus, and any other vegetables that you favor. The results will be stupendous with a minimum of time and effort.

1 medium onion
1 medium celery stalk
1 medium garlic clove
1 tablespoon olive oil
4 cups chopped vegetable, in ½- to 1-inch pieces
5 cups water
2 tablespoons light miso or 2 vegetable bouillon
1½ tablespoons tahini
Freshly ground pepper (optional)

1. Bring water to a boil in a tea kettle. Coarsely chop the onion and celery. Thinly slice the garlic.

2. In a soup pot, heat oil, onion, garlic, and celery. Cook and stir 1 minute over medium heat, then add vegetable. Continue cooking and stirring 1 minute longer.

3. Add boiling water and bring back to a boil over high heat. Stir briefly and reduce heat to medium. Cover and cook 8 minutes. Lift cover, stir in miso, and continue cooking and stirring for another 2 minutes, until miso is dissolved and vegetables are tender. (At this point, you may puree soup directly in the pot with a hand blender, liquefying a small amount of soup with the tahini in a separate bowl and returning it to the pot. Or, follow steps 4 through 6.

4. Pour soup into a bowl to cool. Remove ½ cup of broth from soup and stir remaining soup to cool it. While soup is cooling, place tahini and ½ cup broth in a blender. Blend to a smooth cream. Set aside.

5. Place three-fourths of soup in blender and liquefy to a cream. Pour into original soup pot. Place remaining one-quarter of unblended soup in blender. Pulse-blend for 2 to 3 seconds, allowing mixture to remain lumpy and textured. Pour it into creamed portion in the original soup pot.

6. Place soup over medium heat and stir in tahini mixture. Gently reheat soup, taking care not to let it boil and stirring frequently. Add pepper to taste.

Serves 4 to 5.

Variations:

(1) if you don't have light miso, substitute 2 vegetable bouillon cubes, 2 tablespoons powdered vegetable broth, or 5 cups of homemade stock;

(2) creamed soups can be served hot or cold. If serving cold, skip the reheating.

(3) add ½ teaspoon dried thyme, basil, or marjoram to the sautéing vegetables for fuller flavor;

(4) add 1 tablespoon nutritional yeast to the soup pot when you add the water.

Note: After the tahini mixture has been added to the cream soup, boiling will make the tahini itself thicken and the soup will be too thick. Take care to reheat GENTLY, *not to boil!*

OTHER SOUPS

There is a whole world of other soups to explore: traditional Japanese miso soups that take less than 10 minutes to make, quick and easy "full-of-life" vegetable soups, icy gazpacho, and more.

Herbed Vegetable Stock

1 hour

If a homemade vegetable stock is what you're after, this one will serve almost any purpose. Remember, a stock can only be as good as the vegetables that go into it.

1 onion
2 zucchini
4 large garlic cloves
2 carrots
3 celery stalks
1 potato
leek greens
chard stems if available
mushroom stems
1 bunch parsley
1 sprig thyme or ½ teaspoon dried
1 bay leaf
1 sprig summer savory or ½ teaspoon dried
4 peppercorns
8 cups cold water

1. Coarse chop all the vegetable ingredients (except the garlic) in ½- to 1-inch chunks. Place in soup pot with herbs and seasonings.

2. Cover with cold water, bring to a boil, then cover and simmer over medium low heat for 45 minutes.

3. Strain.

Yields 8 cups stock.

Variation: For richer stock, saute vegetables first in 2 tablespoons olive oil.

Miso Soup with Ginger and Green Vegetables

10 minutes

Here's a miso soup with vegetables and a hint of ginger. It will keep you feeling soothed and smoothed, and not the least bit hungry. The reason this soup is so helpful is that miso is alkaline. Alkaline foods neutralize acids from "big city living."

6 cups water
2 cups thin broccoli florets
1 cup tofu cubes, in ½-inch pieces
1 cup snow peas
1 cup coarsely chopped watercress
1 (½-inch) slice fresh ginger, pressed in garlic press (1 teaspoon)
3 tablespoons soy miso

1. Bring water to a boil. Add broccoli and tofu, and return to a boil. Simmer 2 minutes, then add snow peas, watercress, and ginger.

2. Remove ¼ cup of water from soup. Dissolve miso in it, then add to soup, stir well, and simmer 2 minutes. Remove from heat. Vegetables should be bright green and al dente.

Serves 3 to 4.

If you have a low energy day, here's a good menu:

a.m.—Simple fruit salad and fresh juice
lunch—Blended Salad (page 142)
4 p.m.—Handful of dried figs and peppermint tea or juice
dinner—THIS SOUP
before retiring—Plate of orange wedges or a banana

Easy Miso Soup with Vegetables and Tofu

10 minutes

This makes a great lunch or serves as a light accompaniment to salad on an "I'd better eat lightly" day. Do not boil the miso, but rather add it to the soup at the end of the cooking time and simmer for only 1 or 2 minutes longer.

4 cups water
2 green onions, minced
3 large leaves green chard, chopped (2 cups)
2 ears corn, kernels cut from cob (2 cups)
4 ounces soft or firm tofu, cut in ½-inch cubes
2 tablespoons soy miso

1. Heat water to a boil. Add vegetables and tofu. Cook 5 minutes.

2. Remove ¼ cup water and dissolve the miso in it. Add miso water to soup, lower heat, and cook, stirring, for 1 or 2 minutes longer. Stir before serving, since good-quality misos tend to separate slightly.

Serves 3 to 4.

Summer Bisque

25 minutes

Here's a tangy cold bisque of cauliflower and red chard. Remove the stems of the chard to preserve the pale "greenness" of the soup.

2 tablespoons olive oil
6 cups small cauliflower florets
1 cup chopped white onion
½ cup chopped celery
2 teaspoons garlic
6 cups chopped red chard, loosely packed (stems and heavy center rib removed)
6 cups boiling water
2 tablespoons light miso or chicken-flavored vegetable broth
1 tablespoon tahini
½ cup water
Freshly ground pepper
1 tablespoon lemon juice

1. Heat oil, cauliflower, onion, celery, and garlic in a medium soup pot. Sauté briefly, then add chard and cook, stirring, until it begins to wilt.

2. Add boiling water, return to a boil, cover, and simmer 15 minutes. Remove from heat. Add miso and stir to dissolve. Dissolve tahini in ½ cup water, then add to soup and mix well.

3. Use a hand blender or food processor to blend soup to a textured puree. Add pepper to taste and lemon juice. Chill until ready to serve.

Serves 6.

Variation: Green chard, spinach, or sorrell can be substituted for the red chard.

Full of Life Vegetable Soup

15 minutes

This is a marvelous soup at any time, but especially when someone is feeling a little out-of-sorts and wants "something warm and soothing" for dinner.

1 small onion
2 green onions
2 celery stalks
2 carrots
1 zucchini
1 garlic clove, pressed
2 green chard leaves or kale
2 cups broccoli florets
1 tablespoon olive oil
6 cups water
2 vegetable bouillon cubes or 2 tablespoons powdered vegetable broth
½ cup minced fresh parsley

1. Cut vegetables in ½-inch dice, except for chard and broccoli; coarsely chop chard and cut broccoli into thin florets.

2. In a large pot, sauté onion, green onions, celery, carrots, zucchini, and garlic in oil. Add water and bouillon cube and bring to a boil. Simmer, covered, for 5 minutes.

3. Add chard and broccoli to pot. Return to a boil and simmer, covered, for another 5 minutes.

4. Stir in parsley. Cover and remove pot from heat for 2 minutes. Uncover and serve.

Serves 3 to 4.

West Indian Sweet Potato Soup

35 minutes

Great for kids, this potato soup has an appealing texture and a real "island" flavor. A moderately thick soup, good in a mug! It freezes well.

8 cups water
1 vegetable bouillon cube
2 medium carrots, peeled and diced
1 medium onion, finely chopped
2 large Garnett red sweet potatoes, peeled and cut into ½-inch cubes
3 to 4 garlic cloves, minced
3 celery stalks, finely chopped
2 tablespoons brown rice miso (dark) or 2 vegetable bouillon cubes
Freshly ground pepper to taste

1. Heat water and bouillon cube in a large soup pot. Add carrots, onion, potatoes, garlic, and celery. Bring to a boil and simmer until potatoes are very soft, approximately 15 to 20 minutes.

2. Remove one-fourth of soup and set aside. Liquefy the remaining three-fourths of the soup to a cream with a hand blender or food processor. Pulse-blend the remaining soup to chop only. Combine creamed and coarse-chopped mixtures. Stir in miso and reheat, stirring occasionally for 5 minutes.

Serves 8.

Easy Corn Chowder

40 minutes

This is an example of a creamy soup that contains absolutely no dairy—not even a dairy substitute. The secret is in the stirring!

1 tablespoon olive oil
2 cups diced white onions
1½ cups diced celery
½ cup diced carrot
¾ cup diced bell pepper (red, green, or yellow)
4 cups peeled and cubed potatoes (½-inch cubes or smaller)
¼ teaspoon ground sage
8 cups water (or water to cover vegetables by ½ inch)
2 tablespoons light miso or powdered vegetable broth
3 cups fresh or frozen corn kernels
3 tablespoons minced green onion

1. Measure oil into a large soup pot. Add onions, celery, carrot, and pepper and sauté until vegetables begin to soften, 3 to 4 minutes. Add potatoes and sage. Mix well and sauté an additional 3 minutes.

2. Add water, bring to a boil, cover, and simmer over medium-low heat for 10 to 15 minutes, or until potatoes are tender but not mushy.

3. Remove ½ cup of broth and dissolve miso in it. Add to soup and mix well. Cook soup an additional minute, stirring continuously.

4. Remove one-third of soup with lots of vegetables in it and set aside. Blend remaining two-thirds of the soup until smooth with hand blender or food processor. Stir in reserved soup, corn, and green onion.

5. Bring soup to a low boil, stirring frequently, and simmer for 10 minutes on low heat, continuing to stir so soup does not stick to the bottom.

Serves 8.

Green Pea Soup with Cashew Cream

35 minutes

1 cup diced celery
1½ cups finely chopped white onions
1 tablespoon olive oil
4 cups shredded Romaine lettuce
1 tablespoon honey
6 cups purified water
½ teaspoon dried thyme
½ teaspoon dried basil
1 tablespoon light miso or 1 vegetable bouillon cube
4 cups frozen petite peas
2 tablespoons raw cashews
Ground rock salt (optional)
Freshly ground pepper

1. In a large soup pot, sauté celery and onions in olive oil over medium heat for 3 minutes, stirring frequently. Add lettuce and braise for 2 minutes, until it is limp, stirring constantly. Add honey, water, thyme, basil, and bouillon.

2. Bring soup to a boil, then stir in peas. Return to a boil, cover, and simmer until peas are very tender, approximately 10 minutes. Stir in miso and cook for an additional 1 minute, allowing miso to dissolve. Cool slightly.

3. Remove 1 cup of broth from soup. Place in blender with cashews and blend on high until you have a thick, smooth cream. Set aside.

4. Strain soup and reserve 1½ cups of vegetables. Blend the remaining soup until smooth, using a hand blender or food processor. Add reserved vegetables and pulse once or twice to slightly chop.

5. Combine the blended soup and Cashew Cream. Season to taste with salt and pepper. Reheat, but do not boil. Serve warm or chilled.

Serves 6.

Cream of Asparagus and Fennel Soup

40 minutes

A lovely chilled summer soup. Delicious warm in the winter, too.

1 tablespoon olive oil
1 medium onion, chopped
½ cup sliced green onions
1 small potato, peeled and cubed (optional)
2 pounds asparagus, trimmed and cut into 1-inch segments
1 bulb fennel, leaves and root end trimmed, coarsely chopped
7 cups water
1 tablespoon powdered vegetable broth, or 1 vegetable bouillon cube
1 tablespoon light miso (optional)
1 tablespoon fresh tarragon, or ¼ teaspoon dried
1½ tablespoons chopped fresh basil or ½ teaspoon dried
¼ to ½ cup Cashew Cream (1 heaping tablespoon raw cashews liquefied in ½ cup water)

1. Heat oil with onion and green onions in a large soup pot. Add potato, asparagus, and fennel, then sauté briefly, stirring constantly. Add water, bouillon, miso, and herbs. Mix well and bring to a boil. Cover and reduce heat to medium. Simmer 20 minutes or until vegetables are tender. Prepare Cashew Cream in blender.

2. Cool soup slightly, then liquefy with a hand blender or food processor until smooth and creamy. Stir in Cashew Cream. Adjust seasoning and reheat but do not boil.

Serves 6.

Old-Fashioned Cream of Celery Soup

30 minutes

We all ate it out of cans for so long that practically no one has ever experienced a *fresh* cream of celery soup. But once you've made this, you'll know the difference. This is a crowd-pleaser, since most people love celery.

1 cup finely chopped onion
2 tablespoons olive oil
2 tablespoons whole-wheat pastry flour
5½ cups water
⅓ cup soymilk
4 cups diced celery
2 cups peeled and diced potatoes
3 tablespoons light miso or chicken-flavored vegetable broth
½ teaspoon garlic powder
Fresh pepper

1. In a medium soup pot, heat onion with oil and sauté for 2 minutes, stirring. Add flour and stir well. Slowly add 2 cups water, stirring to avoid lumping. Bring to a boil and stir until thick and smooth.

2. Combine the soymilk and remaining water. Add to soup pot and bring to a boil. Add celery and potatoes, return soup to a boil, and simmer 15 minutes or until celery is very tender.

3. Remove ½ cup of broth from soup. Dissolve miso in it, then return to soup pot and stir well for an additional minute. Cool briefly.

4. Puree half of the vegetables from the soup with a hand blender or food processor, taking as much potato as possible to be pureed. (You don't want too many chunks of potato, since this is cream of *celery* soup.) Return puree to soup and stir well. Add pepper to taste.

Serves 6.

"Feeling Great" Bowl o' Noodles

10 minutes

Noodle soup is one of those remarkable comfort foods that just about everyone adores. Serve this straight from the wok, with whole-grain toast and a big Classic Green Salad (page 140). I like to use a chicken-flavored vegetable broth for this recipe.

1 teaspoon vegetable oil
½ teaspoon roasted sesame oil
1 cup sliced shiitake or button mushrooms
8 ounces precooked linguine, fettuccini, or brown rice udon
4 cups boiling vegetable stock
4 ounces soft or firm tofu, cut in ½-inch cubes
6 cups coarsely chopped green chard, or spinach
2 tablespoons low-sodium soy sauce

1. Heat oils in a wok. Add mushrooms and stir-fry for 1 minute. Add noodles and stir-fry 1 minute to heat through.

2. Add boiling vegetable stock, tofu, and chard. Bring to a boil and simmer 2 minutes to cook chard and tofu. Stir in soy sauce.

Serves 4 to 6.

Curried Pea and Lettuce Soup

30 minutes

A slight departure from the dairy-free cream soups, this recipe relies not only on the flavor of the peas but also the welcome spicy additions. It's a tangy, flavorful soup that serves beautifully warm or chilled. The lemon zest or mint leaf garnishes make it elegant.

3 tablespoons olive oil or water for sautéing
1 large onion, finely chopped
1 medium garlic clove, minced
2 teaspoons curry powder
¾ teaspoon turmeric
½ teaspoon ground coriander
¼ teaspoon ground cumin
1 tablespoon whole-wheat pastry flour
1 head Butter lettuce, shredded (about 4 cups)
2 tablespoons lemon juice (reserve peel for garnish)
2 teaspoons honey
2½ cups fresh or frozen peas
5 cups chicken-flavored vegetable broth or other rich vegetable stock
1½ tablespoons tahini
Freshly ground pepper
Mint leaves and lemon zest, for garnish

1. In a medium saucepan, heat oil, onion, and garlic over medium heat. Stir often and allow to soften, but do not brown. Add curry powder, turmeric, coriander, and cumin and cook, stirring, for 15 seconds. Stir in flour and blend well.

2. Add lettuce, lemon juice, sweetener, and peas. Mix well. Remove from heat and gradually stir in stock. Return to heat and bring to a boil over high heat, stirring constantly. Cover, reduce heat to low, and simmer 8 to 10 minutes or until peas are tender. Cool briefly.

3. Remove ½ cup of broth and add tahini, blending mixture to a cream. Set aside. Use a hand blender or food processor to blend remaining soup until creamy. Return to soup pot, add tahini mixture, and reheat, but do not boil, stirring constantly. Add pepper to taste.

4. Cut tiny threads of lemon peel from reserved lemon peel with a zester. Serve warm or chilled, garnished with lemon zest and a few small mint leaves.

Serves 4 to 5.

Vegetable Rice Soup

5 minutes

All you need is leftover rice and some fresh vegetables and you've got a great lunch. It's for busy moms.

3 cups water
2 teaspoons chicken-flavored vegetable broth
1 carrot, peeled and sliced thin on the diagonal
2 ears corn, kernels cut from cobs, or 1½ cups frozen corn
1½ cups coarsely chopped chard or cabbage
2 teaspoons soy miso or 1 vegetable bouillon cube
1 cup cooked white basmati or brown rice

1. Bring water and broth to a boil. Add carrot and corn, and cook at a low boil for 3 minutes.

2. Add chard or cabbage and miso. Stir well to dissolve miso, then cook at a low boil 2 minutes longer.

3. Stir in rice and serve.

Serves 2.

Winter Garden Soup

50 minutes

What makes this pure vegetable soup hearty and delicious is the caramelized onions.

1 tablespoon olive oil
2 large garlic cloves, minced
1 large white onion, quartered and sliced
1 large leek, halved, sliced, and soaked to remove sand
2 cups peeled, quartered, and diced carrots
2 cups thinly sliced celery
1½ cups cubed yam or butternut squash
2 cups sliced zucchini
2 cups fresh or frozen corn kernels
2 cups coarsely chopped cabbage
½ teaspoon dried thyme
¼ teaspoon dried sage
½ teaspoon dried oregano
8 cups vegetable stock, or 8 cups water and 3 vegetable bouillon cubes
Ground rock salt (optional)
Freshly ground pepper
1 tablespoon lemon juice

1. Heat oil in soup pot. Add garlic, onion, and leek and cook over medium heat, stirring, until brown and caramelized.

2. Add carrots, celery, yam, zucchini, corn, and cabbage, stirring and cooking briefly after each addition.

3. Add herbs and stock. Bring to a boil, then cover and simmer for 25 minutes.

4. Add salt and pepper to taste, then stir in lemon juice.

Serves 6.

Traditional Ukrainian Cabbage Soup

30 minutes

The sweet-and-sour flavor of this soup is complemented by Potatoes and Zucchini in Olive Oil (page 257) and a simple salad. No need to add salt; the miso supplies enough. Fresh chopped tomatoes are added at the end when the cooking is completed.

2 tablespoons olive oil
2 cups sliced leeks
1 medium red onion, sliced
2 carrots, halved and cut in ⅛-inch rounds
1 medium green cabbage, coarsely chopped (7 to 8 cups)
1 teaspoon dried thyme
7 cups boiling water
1 tablespoon powdered chicken-flavored vegetable broth (optional)
1 heaping tablespoon light miso or 1 vegetable bouillon cube
3 tablespoons lemon juice
1 tablespoon honey
2 medium tomatoes, peeled and chopped (2 cups)
Freshly ground pepper

1. Heat oil, leeks, and onion in a soup pot. Sauté, stirring for 2 minutes or until vegetables begin to soften. Add carrots and cabbage, and continue sautéing over medium heat until cabbage begins to wilt. Add thyme and stir well.

2. Add boiling water and broth to water. Stir well. Cover and bring to a boil and simmer over medium heat for 10 minutes. Remove cover and stir in miso, lemon juice, and honey. Simmer for 3 or 4 minutes longer, then stir in tomatoes. Add ground black pepper to taste.

Serves 6.

Traditional American Vegetable Soup

1 hour, 10 minutes

Many of us were raised on the canned version of this traditional soup. This is my healthful version of a national favorite. Cut all vegetables in ¼-inch diced pieces.

1 tablespoon olive oil
1 teaspoon minced garlic
2 cups diced onion
½ teaspoon thyme
2 cups diced carrots
2 cups diced celery
2 cups corn (fresh or frozen)
2 cups diced potatoes
1½ cups diced green beans
1½ cups petite peas
1½ cups diced cabbage
8 cups water
2 tablespoons powdered vegetable broth or 3 vegetable bouillon cubes
1 heaping tablespoon soy miso
1 tablespoon tomato paste
Freshly ground pepper to taste

1. Heat oil with garlic, onion, and thyme and sauté until onion begins to soften, approximately 2 minutes.

2. Add carrots, celery, corn, potato, green beans, peas, and cabbage. Sauté for 2 minutes, stirring frequently.

3. Add water and bring to a boil. Stir in powdered vegetable broth, miso, and tomato paste. Cover and bring to a boil. Simmer for 35 to 40 minutes. Adjust seasoning.

Serves 6.

East Indian Chard and Shallot Soup

45 minutes

This is an elegant soup, adapted from *The Greens Cook Book* recipe for Spinach Soup with Indian Spices. It is perfect for entertaining and has a truly delicate flavor.

5 tablespoons extra-virgin olive oil
6 shallots, chopped (approximately 1 cup)
1 large garlic clove, chopped
3 tablespoons basmati rice
1 teaspoon cumin seeds, or 1½ teaspoons ground cumin
¼ teaspoon grated nutmeg
6 to 7 cups Indian Vegetable Stock (recipe follows) or vegetable stock of choice
1 bunch fresh green chard leaves, stems removed, and chopped (about 6 cups)
1 tablespoon light miso
½ cup Cashew Cream (1 heaping tablespoon raw cashews liquefied in ½ cup water)
1 to 2 tablespoons lemon juice
Freshly ground pepper
1 slice whole-grain bread, cut into ½-inch cubes (crusts trimmed)

1. Heat 3 tablespoons of the oil and the shallots, garlic, and rice in a large soup pot. If using cumin seeds, use an electric spice or coffee grinder to grind the seeds to a fine powder. Add the cumin powder and the nutmeg to the pot. Cook, stirring frequently, for 5 minutes, then add 1½ cups Indian or vegetable stock, cover, bring to a boil, and simmer over low heat for 10 minutes.

2. Add the chard to the pot. When pieces have begun to cook down, add the remaining stock. Bring to a boil, cover, and simmer 5 minutes.

3. Remove ½ cup of stock from the soup, add miso, and dissolve. Return miso mixture to soup and simmer, stirring for 1 minute.

4. While soup is cooling, prepare Cashew Cream in blender. Use a hand blender or food processor to blend slightly cooled soup to a smooth puree. Stir in the Cashew Cream, lemon juice, and pepper to taste. Reheat gently, but do not boil.

5. Sauté the bread cubes in the remaining 2 tablespoons oil until just crisp. Serve the soup, garnished with the croutons.

Serves 6.

Indian Vegetable Stock

50 minutes

Use this exotic stock for curries or curried soups. Its wonderful flavor will greatly enhance whatever you cook in that genre. The Indian spices can be found at Indian markets, gourmet food shops, or in the herb and spice section of many natural foods stores. They are an important part of any spice collection.

2 carrots, peeled
1 large or 2 medium zucchini
1 celery stalk
1 white onion, peeled
1 medium potato
Several sprigs of parsley
2 large garlic cloves
2 tablespoons sesame or olive oil
2 teaspoons coriander seeds
1 teaspoon cumin seeds
¼ teaspoon cardamom seeds
8 cups purified water
3 whole cloves
Small piece of cinnamon stick or a pinch of ground cinnamon

1. Cut all the vegetables into ½ to 1-inch pieces and chop the garlic. Heat the oil and garlic in the stockpot. Add the seeds and sauté briefly.

2. Add the chopped vegetables, parsley, cloves, and cinnamon to the pan and sauté, stirring frequently, over medium heat for 10 minutes. Add the water, bring to a boil, and simmer over medium-low heat for 25 to 30 minutes. Strain and use for soups. Or, if you wish to use in curries or stews, simmer for 30 minutes longer uncovered to reduce and strengthen flavor.

Yields 6 to 7 cups.

Summer Gazpacho

15 minutes

The warm-weather months are the time for gazpacho, when fresh tomatoes are at their best. The longer this soup sits, the more the flavors are enhanced—even overnight, if possible. For a light summer lunch, serve the gazpacho with "Stedda" Tuna on toast (page 110) and Dilled Pea Salad (page 168).

1½ pounds ripe plum tomatoes, peeled (6 cups)
½ green bell pepper, seeded and cored
1 red bell pepper, seeded and cored
3 green onions
4 pickling cucumbers, peeled
2 tablespoons extra-virgin olive oil
Lemon juice to taste (up to 3 tablespoons)
Kelp powder or other salt-free seasoning

1. Place one-third of the tomatoes in a food processor or blender and puree. Add green pepper and ½ red pepper and puree. Add green onions and 3 cucumbers and puree again. Pour mixture into a bowl.

2. Use a food processor to coarsely chop the remaining vegetables and add to pureed mixture. Stir in olive oil, lemon juice, and kelp to taste. Chill.

Serves 4 to 6.

Traditional Indian Dal

1 hour

Mung dal is a split mung bean available at Indian markets and some natural foods stores. Asafetida is a pungent powder Indians use to replace onions and garlic; it leaves no residual odor on the breath. Kari leaves are an Indian herb. The green chili looks like an elongated green pepper and has a mild flavor; it is available in supermarkets.

1 cup mung dal, cleaned and washed
7 to 8 cups purified water
Ground rock salt (optional)
1 teaspoon ground coriander
1½ teaspoons turmeric
1 teaspoon minced fresh ginger
1 teaspoon safflower or sunflower oil
½ to 1 teaspoon ground cumin, or ½ teaspoon cumin seeds
Pinch of asafetida (the tiniest of pinches; this seasoning is strong!)
1 green chili, minced
Several kari leaves, crushed (optional)
1 tablespoon minced cilantro
2 to 3 tablespoons fresh lemon or lime juice
1 small tomato, chopped

1. Bring mung dal and water to a boil and simmer 20 to 25 minutes. Add salt to taste, coriander, turmeric, and ginger and continue simmering.

2. Heat oil in a small frying pan. Add cumin, asafetida, chili, and kari leaves. Fry several minutes, until chili softens, and then add to soup.

3. Continue simmering soup 20 minutes longer. Add cilantro and lemon juice. Just before serving, stir in chopped tomato.

Serves 8.

Lentil Soup with Elbow Macaroni

1 hour, 30 minutes

4 tablespoons olive oil
2 garlic cloves, minced
1 large red onion, finely chopped
1 bay leaf
1 large celery stalk, finely chopped
1 medium carrot, finely chopped
1½ cups brown or green lentils, washed and cleaned
3 sprigs fresh thyme, or ¼ teaspoon dried
½ cup minced fresh parsley
14 cups water
6 fresh plum tomatoes, peeled, seeded, chopped, and juice squeezed out and reserved; or 1 (16-ounce) can plum tomatoes, seeds squeezed out, tomatoes chopped, and juice reserved (optional)
½ cup elbow macaroni or other similar pasta
2 tablespoons soy miso (optional)
Ground rock salt
Fresh ground pepper

1. Heat oil with garlic and red onion in a soup pot. Add bay leaf, celery, and carrot and sauté briefly. Add lentils, mixing well. Add thyme and parsley and mix in. Cook on medium heat until vegetables begin to soften slightly, then add water, juice from tomatoes, and chopped tomatoes. Bring to a boil, cover, and simmer for 45 minutes.

2. Stir in pasta and miso. Return to a boil and simmer, uncovered, for 30 minutes longer, or until pasta is tender. Add extra water to thin the soup, if necessary; then season with salt and pepper to taste.

Serves 6.

Success with Soups Made from Beans and Other Legumes

1. Bean soups cook for a long time, but they actually require very little of your time. They generally take less than 30 minutes to assemble, and then, with a minimal amount of stirring on your part, do the rest on their own. Make them when you have a day at home and are busy with other activities, so you can leave for a moment now and then to stir your soup.

2. Always cook bean soups in a heavy pot (enamel or heatproof glass). If your soup pot is too thin, the beans will tend to stick. Always stir when you bring the soup to a boil and then simmer on low heat.

3. Usually, legumes such as lentils, split peas, and the smaller beans, such as adzuki, baby limas, or navy beans do not require soaking. They soften during the 2- to 4-hour cooking time required. (Lentils cook to perfection in an hour or less.) Soaking is required for larger beans or if indicated for a specific recipe. If you have neglected to soak the beans overnight, you can always use the quick-soak method (page 291).

4. Make large quantities of bean soups because they store or freeze so well (with the exception of those made with lentils) and are wonderful to come home to when you've had a busy day. Just make a salad while you are heating them and you have a meal. To defrost, transfer frozen soup from freezer to refrigerator the day before you wish to use it.

5. Bean soups can be difficult to digest. Place a strip of kombu in the pot and cook the soup for a long time.

6. Soups from beans and other legumes are highly nutritious and economical. In addition to a great taste treat and the feeling of satisfaction during and after eating them, they give you plenty of important nutrients. Check the Nutrition Chart (page 365) and see how many times legumes are listed.

Hearty Split Pea Soup with Beans and Barley

3 hours

This is an easy, old-fashioned recipe for the kind of cold-weather soup we all loved to eat at Grandma's house. It takes less than half an hour to prepare and then cooks on its own for the rest of the time, with only an occasional stirring. Don't be afraid to make this large amount. It freezes beautifully!

14 cups water
2 cups diced onions
1½ cups diced carrots
2 cups diced celery
2 cups chopped lettuce or cabbage
⅔ cup minced fresh parsley
4 green onions, thinly sliced
2 garlic cloves, minced
1 medium zucchini, quartered and sliced (optional)
⅓ cup green split peas
⅓ cup yellow split peas
2½ tablespoons barley
2 tablespoons baby lima beans or other tiny white beans
3 tablespoons ajuki beans
1 tablespoon powdered vegetable broth
Seasoned salt or any salt-free seasoning
Freshly ground pepper

1. Bring water to a boil in a large soup pot. Add the ingredients in the order given, except for the salt and pepper, which can be added at the end of the cooking time.

2. Return soup to a boil, skimming off any foam or scum that comes to the surface with a large spoon. (Repeat this skimming process several times in the first half-hour of cooking, until no more scum forms.) Cover and reduce heat to medium-low.

3. Simmer soup for 2½ hours, stirring periodically to ensure that the barley isn't sticking. At end of cooking time, adjust seasonings to taste.

Serves 6 to 8.

Classic Black Bean Soup

3 hours, 30 minutes

Make this soup on a cool day and simmer it for hours to bring the beans to a nice soft consistency. Although the quick-soak method will work for this recipe, it is preferable to soak the beans overnight to cut the cooking time by at least an hour.

1¾ cups black beans, measured dry, and then soaked overnight
12 cups water
2 teaspoons olive oil or water for sautéing
1½ cups onion, diced
2 teaspoons minced garlic
½ cup green onion, diced
¾ cup carrot, diced
¾ cup red pepper, diced
2 teaspoons ground sage
1 bay leaf
1 teaspoon ground rock salt or salt-free seasoning
2 teaspoons powdered vegetable broth or 1 vegetable bouillon
Freshly ground pepper to taste

1. Discard soaking water from beans. Beans will have swollen to much more than 1¾ cups, so do not remeasure the soaked beans.

2. In large, heavy bottomed soup pot, heat olive oil or water and onion, garlic, green onion, carrot, and red pepper. Add sage and bay leaf and sauté for several minutes or until onions begin to wilt. Add soaked and drained beans and fresh water. Bring to a boil and skim off any scum that may form on the top.

3. Reduce cooking temperature to low, cover soup and allow to cook for 3 hours, stirring occasionally and taking care that heat is low enough so that beans do not stick.

4. At end of cooking time, uncover and allow soup to continue cooking as you stir in salt, if desired, powdered vegetable broth and fresh pepper to taste. Discard bay leaf. Use hand blender to puree soup to desired consistency, breaking down only about half the beans, or transfer half the soup to a blender, puree, and return to soup pot. Adjust seasonings.

Serves 6 to 8.

10

Eat Your Vegetables—and Enjoy *Them!*

THROUGHOUT history, up until the early years of this century, people used to eat large quantities of heavy food, sometimes more than 7,000 calories a day, to maintain their strength and, in some cases, just to keep warm. Fatty meats, heavy sauces, loads of butter, plenty of stews, grains, and sweets were regularly consumed. Twelve-hour days on the farm, milking, harvesting, and bailing by hand, scrubbing floors and washing clothes by hand, constructing roads and buildings essentially by hand—these kinds of activities and a lack of central heating, air-conditioning, elevators, automobiles, television, and other modern conveniences made it easy to expend the heavy food intake.

Today, at the end of the twentieth century, it is obvious that human dietary needs have changed dramatically. The average office worker burns less than 85 calories an hour, less than 2,000 calories a day, unless exercise is an integral part of the daily schedule. The rich and fatty foods we once needed to generate warmth now only make us fat and lethargic. Few of our daily activities require personal body strength. The majority in our population lives a sedentary life.

It is obvious that the era that lies ahead requires a totally different eating pattern. Fundamental influences are at work that will soon succeed in completely revolutionizing national eating habits. For many of us, this revolution has already taken place, and we find in our contemporary eating habits that we are totally divorced from the past.

New eating patterns require new basic materials. Meats and dairy, heavy starches, and refined sweets can no longer play a major role; they are inappropriate foods for a sedentary society. On the other hand, foods once pushed aside or served as mere accompaniments to a heavy meal can be principal players. None fits this category better than vegetables!

THE VENERABLE VEGETABLE

In Asian and Middle Eastern cooking, vegetables have always been prized as highly as meats. Historically in American cooking they have been relegated to a subordinate position as soggy, overcooked side dishes dutifully eaten rather than relished. It took the health revolution, with its emphasis on nutrition, *nouvelle cuisine* and its focus on simplicity, and most recently California cuisine, which features all the beautiful vegetables grown in that state to create national interest in vegetables as bona fide *food*. Now, all over this country, vegetables are enthusiastically presented in a myriad of new and exciting culinary creations. As main and complementary ingredients in restaurants and in home kitchens, vegetables are beginning to hold central position.

In truth, vegetables, like fruit, are among the perfect foods for this era. They give us everything we look for in our food: easily digestible amino acids, essential fatty acids, complex carbohydrates, fiber, calcium, iron, magnesium, phosphorus, potassium, sodium, trace minerals, and vitamins A, B, B-complex, C, E, and folic acid. Yet they do so without giving us unwanted cholesterol or saturated fat! In fact, vegetables give us practically everything we need to be beautifully healthy, but they will never slow us down or make us feel heavy. There is no other food you can eat that will give you a wider range of nutrients and yet be so available, versatile, and economical. As benign and complete sources of nutrition, vegetables are the appropriate food for this age.

Freshness

When it comes to vegetables, there is no overstating the virtue of freshness. They are more tender, juicy, and full of flavor when freshly picked.

A vegetable remains alive for some time after harvest. Leafy vegetables retain their life for a few days, while potatoes last for several months. In broader terms, most vegetables stay fresh from three days to a week, with root vegetables having a longer storage life. Remember, however, that all plants begin to *lose nutrients and flavor* the moment they are removed from the ground. Therefore, your proximity to where they are grown and the distribution in your area determine the quality of your vegetables.

"To everything there is a season." This phrase from Ecclesiastes is particularly true of vegetables. Whatever the season brings is the wisest choice. The vegetables of the season are the freshest, most ideal for our bodies at that point in the year. So you will find the light, watery vegetables—the summer squashes, tomatoes, eggplants, peppers, cucumbers, and corn—in lovely abundance during the warm, summer months. Potatoes, winter squashes, artichokes, carrots, broccoli, and cauliflower are cooler-weather crops that are more highly suited to our needs during those seasons. All vegetables come at a time when they are most in harmony with what the body requires.

With modern ease of distribution and the dominance of agribusinesses, we see farming techniques that no longer respect the law of seasons. This large-scale production ensures year-round vegetables, but with certain liabilities. Most vegetable varieties are grown more for size and sturdy structure to withstand mechanization and long-distance shipping than for flavor. The land is farmed intensively, on a year-round basis to ensure maximum yields and profits—a practice which requires using undesirable chemical pesticides, fertilizers, and crop-boosters. Even with all the produce availability, it is still better to shop for vegetables that are in season. Price, quality, and flavor will all be better if you do. For example, you may be able to get corn on the cob all year round, but it will be considerably more expensive during most of the year and a better buy during the summer. Flavor and texture will be incomparably better in season.

Stand-Ins

Stand-ins are how I view most frozen or canned vegetables. Sometimes you need them, or have to rely on them, but you know they are stand-ins at best. Before freezing, most vegetables are blanched (briefly boiled) to stop all enzymic activity, so flavors and colors will be constant. This process in effect terminates the life of the vegetable. It damages the texture, alters the flavor, and destroys most nutritional components. None of these effects justifies convenience; they are only to be endured if there is no alternative. Remember, fresh is *always* better.

It is best to view canned vegetables as foods already prepared, with no kinship whatsoever to fresh. Canned vegetables are cooked—frequently overcooked—in their containers. In flavor, texture, and nutritional value, they can't compete with fresh. Irrelevant and outdated for this vibrant, "Life-conscious" era, they belong to a past of soggy, overcooked vegetables.

Broadening the Principles

In previous books, I have cautioned against the acidic result of cooking tomatoes, spinach, and fruit, always in the context of a broader diet including at least some animal products. Animal products, it should be understood, cause the most acid in our bodies. In the context of a pure vegetarian diet, I occasionally offer dishes that include cooked tomatoes, spinach, or cooked fruit for the sake of variety and for people who enjoy these foods. Personally, I have found that, without the greater concentrations of acid that animal products produce, the smaller amounts of acid from plant sources can be tolerated by most people.

Remember that the principles of good eating are tools rather than rules. If your experience is that acid-producing foods upset your metabolic balance, avoid recipes that involve cooking tomatoes, spinach, or fruit.

BASIC TECHNIQUES

The following pages present a minicourse in vegetable-cooking techniques. From easy to easy is how I like to describe them. The first section describes the processes of steaming, boiling, blanching, sautéing, stir-frying, braising, stewing, baking, broiling, and grilling. Each is a one-, two-, or three-step process deliberately simplified so that you can have at your fingertips plenty of practical tips for vegetable cookery. And following the minicourse is a large collection of vegetable recipes, some of which are purposefully basic so that you begin to explore the realm of creativity that vegetable cooking offers. You also can take advantage of the simple, pristine flavors and attributes of the easiest and quickest vegetable preparations.

Steaming

This is possibly the best way of preserving the nutrients in vegetables. There is, however, a rule that should always be observed: Keep the cooking time short. You can shorten the cooking time by cutting dense vegetables such as carrots in thin pieces. (Soft vegetables such as zucchini become soggy when steamed, so it is preferable to sauté them.)

You can tell by their color when steamed vegetables, particularly the green ones, are ready. When the color is bright, test them with the tip of a sharp knife. They will pierce readily if done.

When vegetables are ready, immediately uncover the pot and remove to stop the cooking process. Never leave them sitting in the steaming pot with the lid on, even if the heat has been turned off, because they will continue to cook. Since every vegetable requires a different steaming time, it is best to steam them separately or add faster-steaming vegetables after slower ones have partially steamed. You can steam vegetables and hold them cold as a preliminary step to many final preparations. They can, for example, be sautéed in a little oil with seasonings right before serving.

Equipment

covered pot, large enough to hold a vegetable steamer tray
vegetable steamer tray

Ingredients

the vegetable or vegetables of your choice,
cut in small pieces if dense, larger if soft

How to Julienne a Vegetable

1. Cut 1/8" slices from vegetable. If it is a long vegetable, such as a carrot, cut slices on the diagonal.

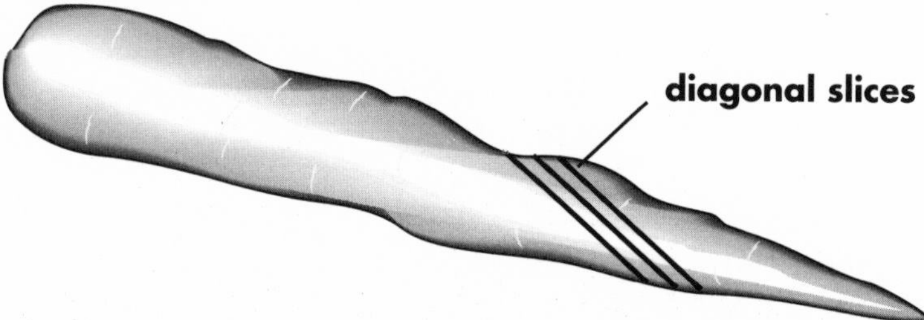

2. Place diagonal slices or thin rounds on a cutting board in small stacks. Cut matchstick slivers.

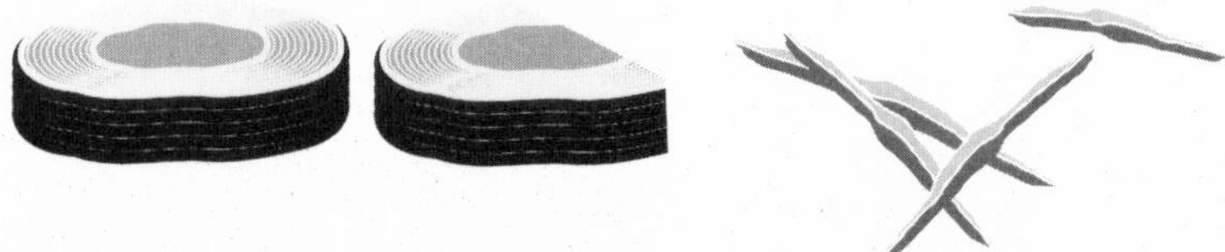

This is an excellent technique for cutting raw carrots, cucumbers, celery root, and zucchini.

Procedure

1. Place steamer tray in bottom of pot. Add water up to ½ inch below tray. Always make sure water level is below the steamer tray. Otherwise, when the water boils, it will bubble above the tray and vegetables will become soggy from contact with it. Bring water to a boil, then add vegetables and steam over a gently rolling boil until bright in color and tender when pierced with sharp knife.

2. Immediately remove vegetables from steaming pot. Spread on platter to cool.

Note: If you have allowed your vegetables to steam too long, immediately transfer them to a cookie sheet and place in freezer for 3 or 4 minutes. This maximizes whatever crispness remains.

Boiling and Blanching

The difference between boiling and blanching is only length of time. In boiling, you allow the vegetable to become completely tender. In blanching (or parboiling) you cook them only long enough to tenderize them slightly in preparation for other cooking steps. Blanching usually takes only 1 to 3 minutes.

As a preliminary cooking step, blanch:

asparagus
carrots
celery
celery root
fennel
green beans
snow peas

Certain vegetables, such as beets and green beans, respond best to boiling rather than steaming, because they absorb water to become tender. But since boiling leaches out the water-soluble nutrients, dulls color and sweetness, and makes vegetables soggy, it should be used minimally. It is best to rely on steaming, and even presteaming, whenever possible. Certain vegetables, such as artichokes and broccoli, should never be boiled because they lose so much flavor.

To time a boiling vegetable, bring water to a boil, add the vegetable, and then wait until water comes to a boil before you *begin timing*. Use a large quantity of water so that the vegetable is immersed and can cook as fast as possible. Do not cover the pot; leaving vegetables uncovered helps preserve their natural color. And like steaming vegetables, watch boiling vegetables carefully to prevent overcooking.

Equipment

a large pot to hold plenty of water

Ingredients

vegetable of your choice, whole for boiling or whole, sliced, or julienned for blanching

Procedure

1. Bring plenty of water to a boil in a large pot.

2. Add vegetables and boil, uncovered, until tender when pierced with the tip of a sharp knife. Drain and pat dry.

Sautéing

This technique is similar to pan-frying, but it takes less time and uses less oil. The chief piece of equipment is a skillet, preferably with a nonstick surface. Vegetables are cooked briefly and actively (sauté means "jump"), in a small amount of oil. In many cases, broth or water may be substituted for the oil. Vegetables are cut in small pieces so they cook in a short time and remain crisp. The pan is moved vigorously over the heat. Vegetables that take a long time to cook, such as carrots or green beans, should be blanched before sautéing. Always dry vegetables before sautéing in oil to prevent splatters. A vegetable that is coated or breaded needs to be turned less frequently than uncoated vegetables, which need to be kept briskly moving (by stirring or shaking the pan). Vegetables may be sautéed alone or in combination. Start with those that take longer, then add quick-cooking ones. Do not preheat oil in pan first, but rather add vegetables first, then add oil to minimize the amount of heating the oil undergoes.

Equipment

nonstick skillet or wok
wooden or plastic spatula

Ingredients

vegetables of your choice, cut in slices, julienned, or rough chopped
1 to 2 tablespoons olive oil, water, or vegetable broth
seasonings of your choice, for example:
- bread crumbs
- lemon juice
- minced fresh parsley
- minced onions
- minced garlic
- dried or fresh herbs
- freshly ground pepper
- diced tomato
- white or black sesame seeds
- rich vegetable stock or low-sodium tamari

Procedure

1. Cut vegetables in ⅛-inch slices. Place in hot skillet with a small amount of oil or vegetable broth.

2. Sauté over medium-high heat, keeping vegetables moving briskly while they cook. When they are bright-colored and just tender, if desired add seasonings. Sauté 1 minute longer, then serve.

Note: To prevent scorching, add a few teaspoons of water or broth to vegetables as you stir them.

Stir-Frying

In ancient China, it was customary for peasants to spend many isolated months during the planting, growing and harvesting seasons away from their villages. They lived in huts in the vast plains of fields, where fuel was scarce and had to be brought from great distances. To conserve their limited fuel supply, a cooking technique evolved that called for maximum preparation and minimum cooking time. Thus, stir-frying, the cooking of thin fragments of food in a few moments, as a cooking procedure was designed to conserve energy.[1]

This is Asian-style sautéing, always done in a wok. High heat and brief cooking are the foremost qualities of this technique, and the result is a tender crispness with lots of bright color in the vegetables. You can stir-fry practically any vegetable. Many can be stir-fried fresh, such as onions, green onions, very thinly cut broccoli, zucchini, chard, spinach, peas, peppers, cabbage, bok choy, mung bean sprouts, and mushrooms. Others, such as green beans, thick asparagus, carrots, snow peas, fennel and thicker cuts of broccoli cook better if they have been blanched or lightly steamed first. There are many variations to stir-frying in terms of main ingredients and glazes. You will find examples in individual recipes.

Cutting your vegetables in a "roll-cut" will give you better stir-fries. The advantage is that roll-cutting enlarges the cut surface of the vegetable and thus allows it to cook faster and more evenly. Roll-cutting works especially well for long, thin vegetables, and creates a particularly attractive dish. To roll-cut, place vegetable on a cutting board and hold with your free hand. Make a diagonal cut, rotate the vegetable with your free hand one-third around, and make another diagonal cut. Turn vegetable one-third and make another diagonal cut; continue rotating one-third and cutting until entire vegetable is cut in diamond or gemlike segments (see drawing). Roll-cutting works especially well for carrots, asparagus, zucchini, green onions, and green beans.

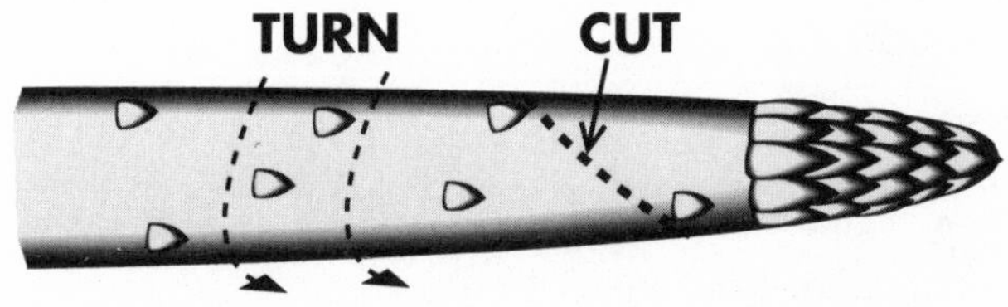

Equipment

wok, nonstick or carbon steel are best
flat, narrow wooden spatula for tossing
garlic press
measuring spoons and cup
several small bowls to hold various ingredients

[1]Reay Tannahill, *Food in History* (New York: Stein and Day, 1981), p. 145.

Ingredients

Vegetables

1 tablespoon safflower or sunflower oil
½ teaspoon minced garlic combined in a small bowl with ½ tablespoon additional oil
4 cups of one vegetable or a combination of vegetables, cut in small uniform pieces for quick cooking

Basic Glaze

½ cup rich vegetable stock
1 to 2 tablespoons low-sodium soy sauce or tamari
2 teaspoons arrowroot or kuzu dissolved in ¼ cup cold water plus 1 teaspoon safflower oil

Procedure

1. Assemble all ingredients near wok. Preheat wok.

2. Pour a tablespoonful of oil into the heated wok and swirl to coat sides. Add garlic and remaining oil and immediately toss in vegetables. Stir-fry for 3 to 5 minutes, or until vegetables are almost tender and bright colored.

3. To glaze vegetables, add stock and tamari. Stir-fry briefly, then add arrowroot mixture. Bring to a boil and bubble briefly to thicken sauce, then transfer vegetables and sauce to serving dish immediately.

Note: Safflower or sunflower oil are commonly used in stir-frying because they are relatively stable at high temperatures. Adding a small amount of oil to the thickener helps keep it from forming lumps in the sauce.

Braising and Stewing

These methods may sound complicated, but they're not. Vegetables are cooked in a medium oven, in liquid, slowly so their flavors mingle. The liquid becomes the sauce, and the braised and stewed vegetables are usually not crisp, but are tender and soft instead.

The difference between braising and stewing is not so much technique but ingredients and time required for cooking. Braising usually consists of one vegetable, a stew incorporates many. Both contain some liquid, although at times a stew cooks in its own juices without any liquid added. This always requires, however, that some watery vegetable be added.

Both braises and stews usually contain flavorings and seasonings, such as garlic and herbs, or they can be cooked on a bed of finely chopped vegetables, such as carrot, onion, and celery, called a *mirepoix*. Braises can be main courses or part of a main-course vegetable plate, but generally they are side dishes. Stews are filling enough to stand on their own as a main course. If a thick sauce is desired, flour can be added in the early stages of stewing or, as a final step in braising, the vegetables can temporarily be removed from the cooking liquid, which is then reduced to a thick sauce by rapid boiling. For a stew that combines long-cooking vegetables with those that cook more quickly, begin with the former and add the latter only when others have begun to soften. If you wish to braise a tough or fibrous vegetable like celery, blanch it first. For stews, however, all cooking is done during the cooking process, which will be as long as necessary for the vegetables to become tender.

Equipment

a heavy skillet or shallow stovetop casserole
measuring cup and spoons
wooden cooking spoon
slotted spoon or tongs

Ingredients

olive oil
complementary seasonings, such as:
  minced garlic
  chopped onions
  chopped celery
  chopped carrots
braising vegetable of choice, whole if small, or sliced or chopped if large
stock or water to half-cover vegetables
fresh or dried herbs
whole-wheat pastry flour (optional)
lemon juice
sweetener such as brown rice syrup or honey
chopped fresh parsley or chives (optional)

Procedure for Braising

1. Preheat oven to 375°F. Place oil in pan. Add seasonings to oil and saute, stirring over medium heat for 3 minutes.

2. Add vegetable and herbs, and saute, stirring, for 1 to 2 minutes. Add stock or water, bring to a boil, and place, tightly covered, in oven. At end of cooking time, when vegetables are tender (approximately 20 minutes), if desired, thicken sauce, by transferring vegetables to serving dish, bringing liquid to a boil, and boiling rapidly to reduce. Stir in a little lemon juice and pour sauce over vegetables, or return vegetables to liquid in pot and mix to thoroughly coat them. Sprinkle with parsley or chives, if desired.

Procedure for Stewing

To stew vegetables, use same procedure as for braising, with the following changes:

1. Begin cooking denser vegetables like carrots, potatoes, celery, artichoke bottoms, turnips, mushrooms, and onions first. Sauté complementary seasonings and vegetables in a little flour to thicken gravy.

2. Add lighter, more watery vegetables when first vegetables are becoming tender.

3. Allow vegetables to stew in their own juices or add ⅓- to ½-cup liquid for every 1 cup vegetables. (**Note:** Include some watery vegetables in your selection if not adding any cooking liquid.)

4. Cook, covered, over very low heat or bake in 375°F oven.

Baking

Baking is an ideal technique for many vegetables, such as potatoes, winter squashes, eggplant, onions, garlic, and beets. The easiest baking procedure is simply to cook the vegetable whole, in its skin. Sometimes, as with onions, a little water must be added to the pan to keep juices from burning. Baking times will range from 1 hour for smaller squashes and eggplant to several hours for beets. Baking temperatures range from 375° to 425°F.

Many vegetables that are too thin-skinned to bake whole can be sliced; drizzled with olive oil; seasoned with onion, garlic, or dried herbs; covered with oiled parchment (instead of foil); and baked until tender. To make gratins, which are baked dishes, you cube or slice the vegetables, toss them with flour or bread crumbs, or cover with Cashew Milk, and drizzle them with oil and seasonings. Then bake them, uncovered, until tender. If you use flour or bread crumbs, you will have flavorful, tender vegetables under a crusty top. If you bake in Cashew Milk, your vegetables will be tender and coated with a creamy sauce.

Artichokes, eggplants, and cabbages or other leafy vegetables can be stuffed and baked. This is done in a heavy covered casserole or baking dish covered with oiled parchment. Usually a liquid, broth or water, is added to keep them from drying out. Since there are a number of ways vegetables can be baked, follow the specific procedures for each recipe in this section.

Broiling and Grilling

Whether broiling or grilling, handle the vegetables in the same way. First, brush them with oil to prevent sticking or drying out. Or marinate the vegetables before broiling or grilling. Broiled or grilled vegetables must be sliced fairly thin to expose as much surface as possible which allows them to cook quickly. Fibrous vegetables such as leeks or celery, or dense ones such as carrots or asparagus, should be blanched before broiling or grilling, then brushed several times with oil while cooking. Soft, watery vegetables such as eggplant or summer squash need only be brushed with oil or marinade once on each side.

Sometimes you will want to cut vegetables into small pieces and broil them in an ovenproof dish. This will work beautifully as long as you first coat them well with oil and toss them frequently. Broil at 550°F; if the vegetables begin to char, increase the distance from the heat. Do not lower the temperature.

When grilling, use a moderate, rather than hot flame. Ideally, vegetables should be tender and only slightly browned. When there is no time for a marinade, brush with olive oil mixed with a clove of crushed garlic. Precook carrots, winter squashes, fennel, and other dense vegetables before broiling. Precooking asparagus is optional, but if the stalks are very thick, parboil them, otherwise they may overcook on the outside and undercook in the center. Summer squashes, eggplant, mushrooms, onions, and peppers can all be grilled fresh. A delicious variation is to broil skewers of small chunks of marinated vegetables.

Equipment

grill or broiling pan with rack
small bowl or measuring cup
brush
spatula or tongs

Ingredients

olive oil
pressed garlic
vegetables of your choice, cut in ¼-inch-thick slices

Procedure

1. Preheat broiler for 10 minutes or prepare grill and allow coals to burn down to a moderately hot flame. Combine oil and garlic in a small bowl.

2. Place vegetables on rack, brush with oil, turn, and brush with oil on second side. Grill, turning and brushing, until both sides are lightly browned and vegetables are tender.

SAUCES FOR VEGETABLES

Before getting down to actual vegetable recipes, here are some sauces that you'll find useful in a variety of ways.

Avocado Butter

Use as a dip or sauce for steamed artichokes, broccoli, Brussels sprouts, carrots, and other vegetables.

1 ripe avocado, chopped
½ to 1 cup purified water, depending on water in avocado
1 to 2 tablespoons lemon

Puree ingredients with hand blender or food processor. Chill until ready to use.

Yields 2 cups.

Variation: Substitute lime juice for lemon. Add several leaves of fresh basil during blending.

Onion Sauce

As a butter-free dip for artichokes or a sauce for other vegetables, particularly broccoli, this is an easy winner. It adds that special element to simple vegetables that make people think you've been in the kitchen all day (even though this takes only 10 minutes to prepare).

2 teaspoons olive oil
1 medium white onion, thinly sliced (1 cup packed)
¼ teaspoon ground thyme
1 cup purified water
4 teaspoons powdered vegetable broth or soy miso, or 1 vegetable bouillon cube
2 tablespoons olive oil

Heat oil and onion in a skillet. Add thyme and sauté, stirring for 3 to 4 minutes, until onion begins to brown. Add water and powdered vegetable broth, miso, or bouillon cube. Bring to a boil and simmer 3 to 4 minutes over high heat to reduce liquid by one-fourth. Puree the onion mixture with a hand blender until it becomes a thick, smooth sauce. Add oil and blend briefly to combine.

Yields 1¼ cups.

Oil-Free Herb Sauce

Use this sauce instead of butter or oil on cooked vegetables.

1½ cups vegetable stock
1 sprig fresh thyme, or ¼ teaspoon dried
1 small piece bay leaf
1 garlic clove
½ teaspoon lemon juice

Place stock, thyme, bay leaf, and garlic in a saucepan. Boil to reduce by half. Add lemon juice and pour over vegetables or use as a dip for artichokes.

Yields ¾ cup.

Note: To reheat cold artichokes, place in baking dish, pour this sauce over artichokes, cover loosely with foil, and bake for 20 minutes at 375°F.

Tomato-Mayo Sauce

Serve this with steamed vegetables or as a dressing for a mixed vegetable salad.

½ cup dairy-free mayonnaise or Almonnaise (page 98)
1 large, ripe tomato, peeled, seeded, and chopped
4 tablespoons Dijon-style mustard
2 tablespoons chopped onion

Place ingredients in blender container and blend until smooth. Chill until serving time.

Yields 1 cup.

VEGETABLES FROM A TO Z

Flavorful Steamed Artichokes

50 minutes

Artichokes are great when you want something filling but prefer to stay with vegetables. They take a while to eat, are fun to eat, and are one of the best salad accompaniments. When they give them a chance, kids tend to fall in love with artichokes. At a recent dinner party for seven 8- to 11-year-old boys, the enthusiastically received menu also included Kids' Favorite Salad (page 146), Corn on the Cob (page 233), and New Shepherd's Pie (page 310). The artichokes were the winning item!

4 artichokes
1 bay leaf
Several slices of lemon
6 peppercorns
1 garlic clove

1. Wash artichokes by holding them, leaves pointing up, under the faucet. Hit them on the counter *hard,* leaves down, so they will open and be easier to clean and will steam through to the heart. (Although it is customary to trim the leaves, artichokes lose some flavor when you do.)

2. Put water in steaming pot. Add bay leaf, lemon slices, peppercorns, and garlic. Place steamer tray over water. Bring water to a boil. Place artichokes on tray with leaves *down* and stems *up,* so that water will not accumulate at base, resulting in soggy artichokes.

3. Steam over medium heat for 30 to 45 minutes, depending on size. The artichokes are ready when an inner leaf can be removed easily.

Serves 4.

Grilled or Broiled Asparagus

7 to 10 minutes

These are a special treat, served whole as part of a vegetable plate or as a side dish, or cut into segments and added to a main-course salad. Allow them to crisp ever so slightly for added texture and flavor.

2 tablespoons olive oil
½ teaspoon pressed garlic
1 pound thin asparagus, trimmed

1. Preheat oven to broil or heat grill to medium.

2. Combine oil and garlic in a small bowl.

3. Place asparagus on grill or broiler rack, and brush with garlic-flavored oil. Grill for 4 to 5 minutes, brushing and turning, then remove when outer layer begins to crisp.

Serves 3 to 4.

Variation: Add 2 tablespoons barbecue sauce to olive oil–garlic mixture.

Asparagus Bolognese

25 minutes

For a Fix-it-Fast menu, serve this with Simple Lo Mein (page 272) and Classic Green Salad (page 140).

2 pounds medium asparagus, trimmed
¼ cup minced red or green onion
3 tablespoons minced fresh basil
3 tablespoons fresh lemon juice
2 tablespoons extra-virgin olive oil
3 medium tomatoes, peeled, seeded, and diced
Salt and freshly ground pepper
1 tablespoon snipped fresh chives

1. In a large pot of boiling, salted water, cook asparagus for 3 minutes or until bright green and barely tender. Remove with tongs to a bowl of ice water to cool. Drain, pat dry, and arrange on a serving platter with the tips facing in the same direction.

2. In a medium bowl, whisk together onion, basil, lemon juice, and oil. When well combined, stir in tomatoes and season to taste with salt and pepper. Spoon over asparagus. Garnish with chives. Serve at room temperature.

Serves 5.

Asparagus with Tofu

45 minutes

This is a great Chinese dish when asparagus is in season. Accompany it with Chinese Cucumber Pasta (page 274), Classic Green Salad (page 140), or Deli-Style Cole Slaw (page 151).

2 teaspoons minced or pressed fresh ginger
1 tablespoon mirin
3 tablespoons dark soy sauce or tamari
½ teaspoon roasted sesame oil
8 ounces firm tofu, sliced into thin strips
1 teaspoon arrowroot, or 1½ teaspoons cornstarch
2 tablespoons safflower oil
½ to 1 teaspoon minced garlic
1 pound asparagus, roll-cut into 2-inch segments

1. Combine ginger, mirin, soy sauce, and sesame oil in a small bowl and mix well. Toss tofu strips in sauce and marinate for 30 minutes to several hours.

2. Drain tofu and reserve sauce. Add enough cold water to marinade to equal ⅓ cup. Dissolve arrowroot in this mixture.

3. Heat wok over high heat. Add 1 tablespoon oil and coat well. Combine garlic with additional 1 tablespoon of oil and add to wok. Add tofu and stir-fry briefly, about 4-5 minutes. Remove from wok.

4. Add remaining oil to wok, then stir-fry asparagus over medium heat until bright green and heated through. Return tofu to the wok and add sauce. Increase heat to high and cook until sauce thickens. Serve immediately. *Serves 4 to 6.*

Variation: Substitute blanched broccoli for asparagus.

Beets and Turnips on a Bed of Greens

30 minutes

1 bunch beets and greens
1 bunch baby turnips and greens
1 tablespoon lemon juice
1 tablespoon olive oil

1. Wash beets and greens thoroughly and gently to avoid breaking skin. Trim greens from beets, leaving 1 to 2 inches of stem. Do not trim root end of beets. Place beets in water to cover and boil 20 to 30 minutes, depending on size, until tender when pierced with the tip of a sharp knife.

2. While beets are cooking, wash turnips and greens. In a separate saucepan, cook turnips as for beets but allow only 10 minutes for baby turnips, 20 to 30 minutes for large turnips.

3. While beets and turnips are cooking, coarsely chop reserved stems and greens. Place stems in steamer over boiling water for 3 minutes, add greens, and steam 2 minutes longer. Transfer greens and stems to serving dish.

4. Rinse beets and turnips under cold water. Slip off skins. Leave turnips whole. Cut beets in slices and then cut slices in julienne or julienne in food processor. Arrange turnips and beets on the bed of greens. Drizzle with lemon juice and oil. *Serves 2.*

Variation: Marinate beets and turnips in Real French Dressing (page 124) for several minutes before arranging on greens; omit lemon and oil from above recipe.

Lemon Beets

25 to 30 minutes

Use this as a side dish with Main-Course Salads.

2 pounds beets without greens (approximately 6 medium beets—leave root and 2 inches of stem intact)
1 tablespoon lemon juice

1. Scrub beets and boil in plenty of water for 30 minutes or until tender when pierced with a sharp knife.

2. Shock beets under cold water and cool slightly. Peel and coarsely grate by hand or julienne in food processor. Toss with lemon juice. *Serves 4 to 6 as a side dish.*

Variation: Add 2 teaspoons brown rice vinegar to lemon juice for a tangier flavor.

Steamed Beet Greens and Chard

12 minutes

These iron-rich greens cook in a jiffy, in their own juices.

1 bunch red chard
1 bunch beet greens
1 tablespoon lemon juice

1. Wash and coarsely chop greens. Place in a covered pan over low heat and cook for about 10 minutes, stirring once or twice.

2. Sprinkle with lemon juice and toss.

Serves 2 to 4.

Beet, Carrot, and Cauliflower Mosaic

2 hours

For a beautiful first course, instead of soup, combine several vegetable purees adjacently on a platter. Each vegetable stands on its own as well, for a pureed side dish.

1 bunch celery, cut in 2-inch pieces, strings removed
4 large beets, scrubbed and trimmed (leaving roots and 2 inches of stem attached)
2 large carrots, cut into ½-inch pieces
1 small cauliflower, trimmed into florets
Freshly ground white pepper
Ground rock salt

1. In a large saucepan, cover celery with 2 inches of cold water. Bring the water to a boil, and simmer the celery, covered partially, for 15 to 20 minutes or until tender. Drain and puree in a food processor. Season to taste. Pour into a bowl and chill, covered, for at least 1 hour.

2. In a large saucepan, cover the beets with 2 inches of cold water, then bring the water to a boil. Simmer the beets, covered, for 45 to 55 minutes, or until tender when pierced. Drain the beets, peel, and trim. Puree in food processor. Season to taste. Pour into a bowl, cover, and chill for at least 1 hour.

3. In a large saucepan, cover the carrots with 2 inches of cold water. Bring the water to a boil, then simmer the carrots, covered partially, for about 15 minutes or until they are tender. Drain and puree. Season to taste. Pour into a bowl, cover, and chill for at least 1 hour.

4. In a large saucepan of boiling water, cook the cauliflower, partially covered, for 10 minutes or until tender. Drain and puree. Season to taste. Pour into a bowl, cover, and chill for at least 1 hour.

5. Thin the purees slightly with water, if necessary, to make them the same consistency. Then put about 1½ tablespoons of each puree on large, chilled serving plates. Work clockwise, beginning with celery, then cauliflower, beet, and carrot. Tap the plates lightly and the purees will spread out. To achieve a design, swirl with a fork.

Serves 6 to 8.

Braised Belgian Endive

25 minutes

Belgian endive is grown in the dark, with sand heaped around it to keep it white. Sunlight activates the chlorophyll, which turns it green. When you buy endive, look for ones that are yellow-white. This is a tangy dish. When you serve rich entrees, use it as an accompaniment that cleanses the palate.

2 to 3 tablespoons olive oil
6 Belgian endive, cut in half lengthwise
2 to 3 cups water or vegetable stock
3 tablespoons lemon juice

1. Preheat oven to 375°F. Heat oil in a large skillet. Add endive and brown on both sides.

2. Add water or stock to come halfway up endive. Add lemon juice, cover, and place in oven for 20 minutes, or until most of liquid is absorbed and endive is tender.

Serves 6.

Braised Bok Choy

15 minutes

1 tablespoon safflower oil
2 teaspoons minced garlic
1 large carrot, cut in scant ¼-inch diagonals (optional)
1 teaspoon minced fresh ginger
1 cup sliced leek or green onion, cut in ½-inch diagonals
1 medium bok choy, cut in ½-inch diagonals, leaves coarsely chopped
1 cup rich vegetable stock
1 tablespoon tamari

1. Preheat oven to 375°F. Heat a large oven-proof skillet. Add oil, garlic, and carrot and sauté for 1 minute, until carrot begins to brown.

2. Add ginger and leek, and sauté for 1 minute

3. Add bok choy and sauté until slightly limp, a few seconds. Add stock and tamari to skillet and bring to a boil.

4. Cover and place skillet in oven for 15 minutes. When done, simmer for 2 minutes longer on stove to reduce sauce, if necessary.

Serves 4.

Basic Lemon Broccoli

8 minutes

This is *so* basic, and so versatile; it complements many more complicated dishes.

1 bunch broccoli, cut in florets
1 tablespoon fresh lemon juice
2 teaspoons olive oil

1. Steam broccoli until bright green and al dente, approximately 5 minutes.
2. Place broccoli in serving dish and drizzle with lemon juice and oil. Serve warm or cold.

Serves 3 to 4.

Broccoli and Bowties

20 minutes

So easy and so good!

½ pound bowtie noodles
2 bunches broccoli, stems removed, coarsely chopped
1 to 2 tablespoons extra-virgin olive oil
Ground rock salt (optional)

1. Prepare noodles according to package directions.
2. Steam broccoli for 5 minutes or until just tender and bright green.
3. Combine hot noodles, broccoli, olive oil, and seasoning to taste. Toss well.

Serves 4.

Broccoli d'Italia

10 minutes

1 tablespoon olive oil
1 garlic clove, crushed
1 bunch broccoli, cut in thin florets, 2 inches long
⅔ cup vegetable stock
3 tablespoons lemon juice
Ground rock salt

1. Heat wok, then add olive oil and garlic. Sizzle garlic for 2 to 3 seconds, and toss in broccoli. Stir-fry broccoli in garlic oil for 2 minutes.
2. Add ⅓ cup stock, toss well, cover, and steam for 2 minutes.
3. Remove cover, toss broccoli again, and add ⅓ cup more stock. Cover and steam again for 1 minute.
4. Uncover and sprinkle with lemon juice and salt to taste. Toss well, then test for tenderness. Place in serving dish immediately to stop cooking.

Serves 4.

Brussels Sprouts à la Ritz

25 minutes

12 medium Brussels sprouts
1 tablespoon olive oil
1 tablespoon lemon juice
1 teaspoon Worcestershire sauce

1. Trim sprouts of stems and coarse outer leaves. Steam for 15 minutes, or until tender when pierced with a sharp knife. Remove from steamer and set aside.

2. Heat olive oil in a medium saucepan or skillet. Toss sprouts in oil, then add lemon juice and Worcestershire sauce. Toss again.

Serves 2 to 3.

Steamed Cabbage in Wedges

5 minutes

Steamed cabbage has a pleasing, zesty flavor. Cutting it in wedges helps it hold together and look more attractive on the platter. This couldn't be easier; just steam and drizzle with fresh lemon or grapefruit juice and a few drops of olive oil. Or, pass the Oil-Free Herb Sauce (page 220).

1 medium green cabbage, cut in quarters or sixths
Lemon juice, olive oil, or sauce of choosing

1. Place cabbage in a vegetable steamer over boiling water. Cover and steam for 4 to 5 minutes. Cabbage should have a bright green color.

2. Remove from steamer with tongs and drizzle with lemon juice, oil, or sauce. Serve immediately.

Serves 4 to 6.

Cabbage and Lima Beans with Garlic

30 minutes

½ to 1 teaspoon minced garlic
2 tablespoons olive oil or water for sautéing
1 teaspoon curry powder (optional)
½ teaspoon minced ginger (optional)
½ small green cabbage, coarsely shredded
1 (10-ounce) package frozen Fordhook lima beans
1½ to 2 cups water
1 teaspoon light miso (optional)

1. Heat garlic and oil in a large saucepan or skillet with lid. Sauté briefly, stirring. Add curry and sauté 1 minute, stirring. Add ginger and cabbage, and mix well. Add lima beans and stir to combine thoroughly with cabbage.

2. Bring water to a boil in a separate, small saucepan. Stir in miso and simmer 1 minute, until dissolved. Pour over cabbage and lima mixture, bring to a boil, cover, and cook over very low heat, stirring frequently, for 20 minutes, or until limas are tender.

3. Remove vegetables to serving dish with a slotted spoon. Bring liquid to a boil in pot and boil to reduce by half. Pour over vegetables.

Serves 4.

Chinese Cabbage with Caraway and Thyme

4 minutes

2 teaspoons safflower oil
½ teaspoon caraway seeds
1 small Chinese cabbage, cut in 1-inch slices
½ teaspoon dried thyme
1 tablespoon lemon juice
Dash of kelp or ground rock salt

1. In a skillet or wok, heat oil and caraway seeds until seeds begin to sizzle.

2. Add cabbage and thyme, and stir-fry over medium heat for 2 to 3 minutes, until cabbage wilts. Add lemon juice and kelp.

Serves 2 to 3.

Savoy Cabbage and Petit Peas with Tomato and Basil

15 minutes

The lacy savoy cabbage makes a beautiful effect in this dish, but standard white cabbage can be substituted with excellent results.

1 tablespoon olive oil
1 medium savoy cabbage, coarsely chopped
¼ teaspoon minced garlic
1½ cups chopped spinach or green chard
1 medium tomato, peeled and diced, and its juice
1 box frozen petite peas
2 teaspoons fresh basil, minced, or ½ teaspoon dried
Fresh ground pepper to taste (optional)
Ground rock salt to taste

1. Briefly heat olive oil in a large nonstick skillet or wok. Add cabbage and garlic and sauté over medium heat for 3 to 4 minutes, stirring constantly, until cabbage begins to wilt.

2. Add chard, tomato (and its juice), and peas to cabbage mixture. Stir in basil. Sauté for 2 minutes, stirring constantly, cover and steam over medium low heat for 2 additional minutes, until peas are tender and greens are still bright in color. Add seasonings to taste.

Serves 4 to 6.

Carrots Vichy

25–30 minutes

Serve these caramelized carrots with Baked Rice (page 296), Italian-Style Zucchini (page 242), and Classic Green Salad (page 140).

4 large carrots, peeled
1 tablespoon olive oil
1 heaping tablespoon maple syrup
Ground rock salt to taste
Freshly ground pepper (optional)

1. Slice carrots into ⅛-inch-thick diagonals.

2. Heat oil in skillet. Add carrots and sauté, stirring continuously. Add sweetener and purified water to cover. Bring to a boil over high heat and cook, uncovered, until water is absorbed and carrots are slightly sticky and caramelized, stirring occasionally.

3. Just before end of cooking, add seasonings to taste.

Serves 3.

Variations:

(1) add ½ teaspoon minced fresh ginger when almost all the water has been absorbed;
(2) add ½ teaspoon dried thyme when you add sweetener.

Sweet Carrots au Naturelle

1 hour, 30 minutes

Similar to Carrots Vichy but with a totally different effect, this old favorite is in a new and improved version, with olive oil replacing butter. Whenever I serve this, someone inevitably remarks, "I *never* in my wildest dreams thought carrots could taste like *this*!"

1 pound carrots (approximately 6 to 7 medium), peeled
1 to 2 tablespoons olive oil
3 tablespoons chopped fresh basil or 1 tablespoon dried
Ground rock salt
Freshly ground pepper
2 tablespoons maple syrup

1. Using food processor or by hand, cut carrots into fine julienne. (See page 212 for hand cutting techniques.) Preheat oven to 375°F.

2. Place carrots in a heavy earthenware casserole with a cover. Toss with oil, sprinkle with basil and salt and pepper to taste, and drizzle with maple syrup. Bake, covered, stirring occasionally, for 1 hour or until carrots are tender.

Serves 8.

Baked Carrots au Gratin

1 hour, 15 minutes

Rich and go-o-ood, so creamy but with no cholesterol! It's a favorite.

5 extra-large carrots, in ⅛-inch slices (approximately 5 cups)
⅓ cup cashew pieces blended with 1½ cups water
1½ tablespoons olive oil
½ to 1 teaspoon sweet Hungarian paprika

1. Preheat oven to 375°F.

2. Place carrots in a small casserole and add cashew milk. Drizzle with olive oil and sprinkle generously with paprika.

3. Place casserole in oven and bake, uncovered, for 1 hour. Stir 2 or 3 times during cooking, adding additional paprika each time.

Serves 4.

Puree of Carrot with Potato

20 minutes

A great salad accompaniment!

2 small white potatoes, peeled
3 medium carrots
1 teaspoon powdered vegetable broth
1½ cups water

1. Peel potatoes and carrots. Cut into 1-inch segments and boil in vegetable broth and water until tender.

2. Mash or puree with hand blender or in food processor until smooth, using broth as necessary to achieve pureed consistency.

Serves 3.

Curried Cauliflower and Green Chard

20 minutes

Serve with Indian Dal (page 204), rice, and Classic Green Salad (page 140).

2 teaspoons sesame oil
2 teaspoons black mustard seeds
1½ teaspoons curry powder
½ teaspoon turmeric
½ teaspoon ground coriander
¼ teaspoon ground cumin
¼ teaspoon ground ginger
½ cup sliced green onions
1 medium cauliflower, cut in triangles (½-inch florets)
¼ cup water
¼ cup shredded coconut blended with 1 cup water
2 cups chopped green chard
1½ tablespoons lemon juice

1. Heat oil in a heavy skillet with a lid. Add mustard seeds and spices, and sizzle over medium-high heat briefly, until seeds begin to pop. Immediately add green onions and sauté, stirring for 1 minute.

2. Stir in cauliflower and mix well to coat with spices. Cook briefly, then add water and coconut cream. Mix well. Cover and simmer 7 minutes or until cauliflower is tender.

3. Stir in chard and lemon juice. Steam, covered, for 3 minutes or until chard is limp.

Serves 4.

Braised Celery with Garlic-Crumb Topping

1 hour, 20 minutes

This technique can be used with many vegetables. The celery must be boiled first, because it is so fibrous, but after that the dish "cooks itself" in the oven. The result looks like you put in a lot of effort, but you know the truth!

Celery

5 cups water
3 cups diced celery, in ¾-inch pieces

Herb Sauce

2 cups water
2 large garlic cloves
Assorted herbs—sprigs of dried thyme, chervil, rosemary, oregano, and 1 bay leaf, or ¼ teaspoon each herb
2 teaspoons light miso

Garlic Crumb Topping

1 cup whole-wheat bread crumbs
1 teaspoon pressed garlic
¼ cup minced fresh parsley
2 tablespoons olive oil

1. Bring water to a boil in a medium saucepan. Add celery and boil 15 minutes. Preheat oven to 325°F.

2. Meanwhile, prepare herb sauce. Bring water to a boil in a small saucepan and add garlic and herbs. Cover and boil for 10 minutes. Stir miso into herb sauce then simmer, stirring, for 1 minute.

3. For topping, combine bread crumbs, garlic, and parsley. Oil a shallow baking dish. Drain the celery and put into dish. Pour herb sauce over and top with crumbs. Drizzle with olive oil, then place in oven and bake for 1 hour or until topping is crisp and liquid is absorbed.

Serves 4.

Fresh Chard in a Light Chinese Glaze

15 minutes

2 bunches fresh chard, red or green or both
1 tablespoon safflower oil
1 garlic clove, pressed
1 1-inch chunk fresh ginger, pressed
1 cup vegetable stock
1 tablespoon low-sodium soy sauce
1 tablespoon mirin, or 1 teaspoon honey
1 tablespoon brown rice vinegar
½ teaspoon roasted sesame oil
2 teaspoons arrowroot dissolved in ¼ cup cold water and 1 teaspoon safflower oil
Dash of sesame seeds (optional)

1. Trim chard stems and coarsely chop stems and leaves, or use only leaves for this dish.

2. Measure safflower oil into a small bowl and, with garlic press, press garlic and ginger into it. Set near wok.

3. Combine stock, soy sauce, mirin, vinegar, and sesame oil in a small bowl and set near wok.

4. Heat wok. Add oil-garlic-ginger mixture and immediately add chard. Toss chard to heat through, coat with oil, and wilt over medium heat. When slightly wilted, add stock mixture and bring to a boil, stirring continuously until chard is tender but still bright in color.

5. Add thickener and allow sauce to bubble and thicken. Pour into serving dish and serve immediately, sprinkled with a light dusting of sesame seeds for garnish.

Serves 4.

Swiss Chard and Tomatoes

20 minutes

Chard is an easy vegetable to grow in any sunny plot. It grows from seed and in my garden "volunteers" to come back every year. I use green chard for this recipe, and cook it very lightly. I always nibble at the raw stems. They are so full of good, natural salts the body craves.

1 tablespoon olive oil
¼ cup minced fresh chives, or ½ teaspoon pressed garlic
1 medium onion, chopped
16 leaves fresh green chard, washed and coarsely chopped (including stems)
2 medium tomatoes, peeled and chopped

1. Heat oil in a wok. If you are using garlic, add it to the oil; if using chives, add them at the end. Add onion and stir-fry for 2 minutes until transparent. Add chard to hot oil and stir-fry for 1 minute.

2. Cover the wok and steam chard over medium-low heat in its own juices until just wilted. Stir in chives and remove from heat. Stir in fresh tomatoes. Mix well.

Serves 3 to 4.

Corn on the Cob with "Stedda" Butter Sauce

7 minutes

Some people think that if they can't put butter on their corn, there's no sense having it. You can please and surprise them with this piquant, slightly spicy sauce. They'll look at corn on the cob with a whole new attitude after this meal.

½ teaspoon pressed garlic, or ½ teaspoon garlic powder
¼ teaspoon ground cumin
¼ teaspoon paprika
Dash of cayenne
Dash of chili powder
2 tablespoons extra-virgin olive oil
6 ears fresh or frozen corn

1. Combine spices and garlic with olive oil.

2. Bring plenty of water to a boil in a large pot. Add corn and return to a boil, then boil 3 minutes (or steam for 5 minutes). Remove corn from water or steamer basket and brush with sauce.

Serves 3 to 6.

Mexican-Style Corn

20 minutes

For a Fix-it-Fast meal, serve this with "Stedda" Chicken-Lover's Salad (page 157) and Braised Bok Choy (page 225).

2 (10-ounce) boxes frozen corn or 8 ears fresh corn, kernels cut from cob
2 teaspoons safflower oil
¼ cup diced red onion
¼ cup diced green bell pepper
¼ cup diced red bell pepper
4 sliced green olives
¼ to ½ teaspoon ground cumin
¼ teaspoon dried oregano

1. Place corn in vegetable steamer over boiling water and steam until tender, about 5 to 10 minutes.

2. While corn steams, heat oil and onion in a skillet. Add bell peppers and sliced olives, and sauté 3 minutes, or until vegetables begin to soften. Add cumin and oregano, and stir-fry for 1 minute.

3. Add steamed corn and mix well.

Serves 4.

Savory Succotash

40 minutes

I like to make a big pot of this on Friday, so there will be some leftover for weekend lunches with salads. However, my family loves this meal so much that sometimes there are no leftovers. Use fresh corn cut from the cob, if you can get it. Otherwise, substitute frozen and add the corn when you add the peas. This is a filling main course. All you need is a green vegetable and a salad to round out the meal. For Fix-it-Fast options, try West Indian Sweet Potato Soup (page 195), Classic Green Salad (page 140), or Spicy Zucchini Bread (page 349).

½ tablespoon olive oil
½ tablespoon safflower oil
¾ cup diced onion
½ cup diced celery
3 tablespoons unbleached all-purpose flour or whole-wheat pastry flour
4 large carrots, diced (3 cups)
2 (10-ounce) boxes frozen Fordhook or baby lima beans
3 cups fresh or frozen corn kernels
3 cups chicken-flavored vegetable broth, heated to boiling
2 teaspoons dried thyme
1 teaspoon dried sage
3½ cups frozen petite peas
¼ teaspoon garlic powder
Ground rock salt or seasoning of your choice
Freshly ground pepper

1. Heat butter and oil in a large pot with onion and celery. Sauté over medium-high heat, stirring frequently, for 3 minutes. Stir in flour and carrots, and mix well to combine. Add frozen lima beans and corn, boiling stock, thyme, and sage. Mix well.

2. Bring mixture to a boil over high heat, cover, and simmer over medium heat for 20 minutes, stirring occasionally. Lower heat slightly if vegetables on the bottom begin to stick.

3. Stir in peas, garlic powder, salt, and pepper. Return to a boil over high heat; cover and simmer once again over medium heat for 10 more minutes. Adjust seasonings to taste.

Serves 8.

Sweet and Sour Eggplant

15 minutes

This recipe is accomplished most quickly by using Japanese eggplants, which are less likely to be bitter. Standard eggplants are best salted to leach out the bitter juices, but this requires an extra 20 to 30 minutes. Either way, the dish is easy.

4 medium Japanese eggplants, or 1 medium standard eggplant
1 tablespoon safflower oil
1 large garlic clove, minced
1 bunch green onion, cut in 1-inch lengths
½ cup chicken-flavored vegetable broth
2 tablespoons ketchup or tomato sauce
¼ cup water
1 tablespoon low-sodium soy sauce
1 tablespoon rice vinegar
2 teaspoons honey
2 teaspoons arrowroot dissolved in 4 tablespoons cold water
¼ cup minced cilantro

1. Cut unpeeled eggplant in ½-inch cubes. (If using standard eggplant, sprinkle cubes with salt, place in a large colander, let sit for 20 minutes, rinse, and pat dry.) Assemble remaining ingredients close to wok.

2. Heat wok over medium-high heat. Add oil, garlic, and green onions. Stir-fry 1 minute, then add eggplant and stir-fry for 2 minutes.

3. Add broth to wok, lower heat to medium, toss vegetables for 30 seconds, cover, and steam for 4 minutes. While vegetables are steaming, combine ketchup, water, soy sauce, vinegar, and FruitSource in a small bowl.

4. Uncover wok. Raise heat to medium-high, and stir-fry for 1 to 2 additional minutes, until eggplant is tender. Add sweet-and-sour mixture and toss well to coat. Stir in arrowroot mixture and allow sauce to thicken. Turn out into a warm serving bowl. Garnish with cilantro.

Serves 4.

Easy Stuffed Eggplant

1 standard eggplant, or 4 medium Japanese eggplants
1 tablespoon olive oil
1 small onion, diced
1/2 cup chopped fresh Italian parsley
2 medium cloves garlic, minced
1/2 pound mushrooms, chopped
1/2 cup whole-grain bread crumbs
1 teaspoon allspice (optional)
1/4 cup barbecue sauce
Ground rock salt to taste
Freshly ground pepper to taste

1. Preheat oven to 350° F. Halve the eggplant lengthwise and scoop out pulp. Chop it finely.

2. Sauté eggplant in oil with onion, parsley, garlic, and mushrooms. Add bread crumbs and seasonings. Stir in barbecue sauce.

3. Stuff the mixture into reserved shells. Bake 15 minutes. Spoon mixture from shells to serve.

Serves 4.

Note: A little water in baking dish will prevent sticking.

Sesame Eggplant

1 hour, 20 minutes

Here's a light, flavorful eggplant dish with an interesting twist for those who love this vegetable.

1 standard eggplant, or 4 small Japanese eggplants, peeled
2 tablespoons low-sodium soy sauce or tamari
1 teaspoon minced fresh ginger, or 1/4 teaspoon powdered
1 tablespoon olive oil
2 tablespoons minced fresh parsley
2 teaspoons lemon juice
2 teaspoons sesame seeds

1. Cut the eggplant into thick 1/2-inch slices and marinate for about 1 hour in the soy sauce or tamari.

2. Place the ginger in a heavy skillet. Add the oil and eggplant, and brown it, turning several times, adding water, rather than additional oil, as needed, to keep eggplant moist.

3. When tender, sprinkle eggplant with parsley, lemon juice, and sesame seeds.

Serves 4.

Linda's Ratatouille Santa Fe

2 hours

My younger sister Linda is such an inspired vegetarian cook that I love to share the recipes she sends me. Both of us have been strongly influenced by our Mom to view time in the kitchen as critical to the health and happiness of our families. Since our teenage years, whenever we are together, we always seem to end up in the kitchen, exchanging ideas and creating "feasts."

1 pound zucchini
1 pound Japanese or standard eggplant
Salt
¼ to ⅓ cup olive oil
3½ cups sliced onions
3 large garlic cloves, pressed into 2 teaspoons olive oil
1 cup sliced green bell peppers
3 cups peeled, seeded, and chopped tomatoes
Freshly ground pepper
¼ to 1 teaspoon dried thyme

1. Cut zucchini into thin rounds; you should have 4 cups. Cut eggplant into thin rounds, again to have 4 cups. Salt the eggplant lightly (if using standard eggplant) and drain for 20 minutes on paper towels. Rinse and pat dry. Preheat oven to 350°F.

2. In a large skillet, heat one-third of the olive oil with the zucchini and sauté until lightly browned; remove to paper towels and drain. Repeat with another third of oil and the eggplant. Finally do the process one last time with the remaining oil, onions, garlic, and pepper, but do not drain these last vegetables.

3. Transfer onion mixture, zucchini, and eggplant to a 3-quart enamel or glass casserole at least 2 inches deep. Fold tomatoes into other vegetables. Cover casserole with a lid, and bake for 30 to 45 minutes. Several times while the casserole is baking, uncover and suck up juices from the bottom with a bulb baster, then drizzle them over the top. Casserole is ready when juices are thick and syrupy. Serve hot, warm, or cold.

Serves 6 to 8.

Braised Fennel

35 minutes

The sweet flavor of fennel is complemented by the savory garlic. This is a lovely item for a vegetable plate of braised, grilled, and steamed vegetables.

2 large fennel bulbs
2 medium garlic cloves, minced
1 tablespoon olive oil
1 cup vegetable stock
Freshly ground pepper

1. Preheat oven to 375°F. Trim ends of fennel and cut away stems below leaves. Remove tough outer ribs. Halve, core, and thinly slice lengthwise (or crosswise, if you prefer).

2. Heat garlic and oil in a skillet for 1 minute over medium heat. Toss in fennel and sauté, stirring frequently for 3 minutes, allowing fennel to brown slightly.

3. Pour stock into skillet and bring to a boil. Pour over fennel. Bake in oven, uncovered, for 25 to 30 minutes. Season to taste with fresh ground pepper.

Serves 4.

Green Beans, Italian Style

10 minutes

When really good green beans are available, this is the best and easiest way to serve them.

1 pound tender young green beans
Ground rock salt
2 teaspoons lemon juice
2 tablespoons extra-virgin olive oil

1. Bring lots of water to a boil in a large pot. Trim ends of beans and cut or break them in half.

2. Add a pinch of ground rock salt to water and add beans. Cook at a rolling boil for 3 minutes or until bright green and tender. Drain and place in a large bowl of ice water. Drain and pat dry.

3. Place green beans in a bowl. Sprinkle with lemon juice and toss well. Add olive oil and toss again to thoroughly coat beans with oil. Serve chilled or at room temperature.

Serves 4 to 6.

Lebanese Green Beans

1 hour, 10 minutes

This is a particularly good recipe for mature beans, which tend to be a little tough.

1 teaspoon to 1 tablespoon olive oil
1 large onion, sliced or diced
2 pounds green beans, trimmed and cut in 2-inch segments
½ teaspoon ground cumin
Freshly ground pepper
1 vegetable bouillon cube
2 teaspoons sesame seeds
Lemon juice to taste

1. Heat the oil and onion in a heavy skillet with a lid. Sauté, stirring frequently, until onion is soft and slightly browned. Add the green beans and water to cover. Mix well. Stir in the cumin, pepper, and bouillon cube. Cover and cook 1 hour, stirring frequently.

2. When the beans are very tender and the onion has dissolved into a brown gravy, sprinkle with sesame seeds and serve hot or cold, with a squeeze of lemon.

Serves 4.

Wilted Lettuce

5 minutes

Use the heavy outer leaves of head lettuce, or any type of lettuce you may have. It's a wonderful side dish. Serve with Easy Seven-Vegetable Stew (page 258) and cole slaw.

3 tablespoons water
6 cups coarsely chopped lettuce leaves
2 teaspoons olive oil
½ teaspoon salt
Squeeze of lemon (optional)

1. Bring water to a boil in a saucepan or skillet. Add lettuce and toss well.
2. As lettuce wilts, add oil and salt. Sprinkle with lemon juice and toss well.

Serves 3.

Baked Mushrooms

25 minutes

A great topping for baked potatoes.

1 pound button mushrooms, sliced
2 tablespoons olive oil
1 to 3 large garlic cloves, pressed or sliced
Freshly ground pepper
¼ cup minced fresh parsley

1. Preheat oven to 450°F. Place ingredients in a casserole with a lid.

2. Cover casserole and bake, stirring once. When mushrooms are bubbling in their own juices, turn oven down to 350°F and bake for an additional 10 minutes or until tender and most of the juices are absorbed.

Serves 3 to 4.

Stuffed Mushrooms

25 minutes

8 large stuffing mushrooms, stems removed and finely chopped
2 tablespoons olive oil or vegetable broth for sautéing
1 large garlic clove, crushed
3 tablespoons whole-wheat bread crumbs
¼ teaspoon dried basil
1 teaspoon lemon juice
Freshly ground pepper

1. Preheat oven to 375°F. Sauté mushroom stems in oil or vegetable broth in a nonstick skillet. Add garlic and bread crumbs, and additional olive oil, if necessary. Stir in basil and sauté briefly.

2. Fill mushroom caps with stuffing. Cover with parchment and bake for 20 minutes or until tender. Sprinkle with lemon juice and freshly ground pepper to taste.

Serves 4.

Parsnips in Parsley

18 minutes

8 medium parsnips, peeled, trimmed, and quartered lengthwise
2 tablespoons olive oil
¼ cup minced fresh parsley

1. Place parsnips in a skillet with water to cover. Bring to a boil, then simmer, covered, for 15 minutes or until tender. Drain.

2. Add olive oil and parsley to skillet and then add parsnips. Heat and toss to coat.

Serves 4 to 6.

Petite Peas with Thyme and Garlic

10 minutes

This is a quick way to make peas elegant.

1 tablespoon olive oil
1 large garlic clove, minced
1 (16-ounce) bag frozen petite peas
½ teaspoon dried thyme
2 cups chopped Butter or Romaine lettuce
Seasoned salt
Freshly ground pepper

1. Heat oil, garlic, and peas in a skillet. Add thyme and lettuce.

2. Mix well, then cover and steam over low heat for 5 minutes. Peas should be bright but tender and lettuce should be wilted. Add seasoned salt and pepper to taste.

Serves 6.

Skillet Peas and Rosemary

20 minutes

½ cup red onion, diced
1 tablespoon olive oil
2 cups fresh spinach, chopped
3 cups frozen petite peas
¼ cup diced tomato
½ teaspoon rosemary, tied in cheesecloth
Ground rock salt to taste
Freshly ground pepper to taste

1. Heat onion in skillet with oil until tender. Add spinach and peas and sauté briefly.

2. Add tomato and rosemary bundle and continue sautéing until spinach is wilted and peas are tender, approximately 3 minutes. Season to taste. Remove rosemary bundle.

Serves 4.

Easy Rapini alla Romana

10 minutes

Rapini (or broccoli rabe or rape) is a leafy Italian broccoli with tiny florets and a distinctive sharp flavor. Since rapini is so strong in flavor, it can take lots of garlic without being overwhelmed. This dish will really please Italian food buffs and garlic enthusiasts.

2 bunches (approximately 2 pounds) rapini
2 tablespoons olive oil
2 teaspoons minced garlic
3 tablespoons fresh lemon juice
Ground rock salt
Freshly ground pepper

1. Trim the fibrous ends from rapini stems so you use only the crisp tender part of the stalks.

2. Blanch the rapini in a vegetable steamer over boiling water for 2 minutes. Remove with tongs to a large bowl of ice water. Pat dry and set aside.

3. In a heavy skillet, heat olive oil and garlic. Cook garlic for approximately 1 minute, then add rapini, tossing gently to coat with oil. Cook for 3 minutes, or until leaves are wilted and stems are tender.

4. Sprinkle rapini with lemon juice, and season to taste with salt and pepper.

Serves 6.

Baked Acorn Squash

1 hour

2 acorn squash
1 tablespoon FruitSource, date sugar, or maple syrup
½ cup fresh orange juice
Ground cinnamon and nutmeg
1½ cups water

1. Preheat oven to 375°F. Wash the squash and cut in half crosswise. Scrape out seeds, cut bottoms level, taking care not to cut a hole in cavity. Arrange in a shallow baking dish.

2. Place ½ tablespoon sweetener in each squash. Add 2 tablespoons orange juice to each and sprinkle with cinnamon and nutmeg.

3. Pour water down the side of the baking dish to cover the bottom. Cover loosely with foil lined with parchment and bake for 45 minutes to 1 hour, or until squash are tender enough to mash in skins.

Serves 4.

Easy Winter Squash au Gratin

2 hours, 40 minutes

Use Hubbard, Butternut, or any other dense winter squash for this easy and delightful gratin. Pop it into a slow oven and let it bake! No effort at all, yet it seems so elegant.

3 cups peeled and cubed winter squash
½ teaspoon minced garlic
¼ cup minced fresh parsley
3 tablespoons whole-wheat pastry flour
2 tablespoons olive oil
Freshly ground pepper (optional)

1. Preheat oven to 325°F. Place squash in a medium bowl and toss with garlic and parsley. Add flour and mix well to thoroughly coat cubes.

2. Oil a small, shallow baking dish. Pour squash mixture into dish and drizzle with oil. Bake 2½ hours, or until crusty on top and soft underneath. Squash should still hold its cubed shape.

Serves 2 to 3.

Note: This dish makes a great topping for Easy Seven-Vegetable Stew (page 258). Simply spoon the stew into bowls and place some squash au gratin on top. Couldn't be easier, but it tastes like you worked all day.

Italian-Style Zucchini

25 minutes

2 large or 4 small zucchini
1 to 2 teaspoons minced garlic
2 tablespoons olive oil
2 teaspoons dried basil
2 teaspoons dried oregano
1 teaspoon paprika
Freshly ground pepper

1. Use a food processor or mandoline to cut zucchini into thin ⅛-inch lengthwise strips.

2. Combine garlic with olive oil in a small bowl, then add half of mixture to a large nonstick skillet with half the zucchini. Season with half the herbs and paprika, and sauté over medium-high heat, turning with tongs until zucchini is bright green and al dente. Remove from skillet and set aside.

3. Repeat process with remaining ingredients. Transfer zucchini to a serving dish and season to taste with pepper.

Serves 4.

Skillet-Steamed Zucchini, Carrots, and Chard in Tahini-Umeboshi Sauce

A food processor makes this dish a breeze, although the vegetables can be grated by hand as well. Serve this warm or cold, as a delicious sauce for spinach linguine, or at room temperature on a lettuce salad with sliced tomato.

1 small Maui onion, peeled
1 teaspoon olive oil
1 large or 4 small zucchini
¾ cup water
2 medium carrots
4 large chard leaves, stems removed
2 tablespoons tahini
1 teaspoon Umeboshi plum paste
2 tablespoons lemon juice

1. Thinly slice the onion. Heat skillet and coat with oil. Add onion and sauté, adding a few tablespoons of water so onion does not burn.

2. Cut zucchini and carrots into medium julienne. Add to onion and continue sautéing, adding water as needed to allow vegetables to cook through.

3. Coarsely chop chard. Add to skillet and toss all vegetables well to combine.

4. With the steel knife in food processor, or using a hand blender, combine tahini, ¼ cup water, plum paste, and lemon juice. Pour over vegetables and continue cooking vegetables in sauce, mixing well, for 5 minutes.

Serves 3.

Easy Zucchini and Vegetables in a Skillet

25 minutes

This is a dynamic method of cooking any combination of vegetables you prefer. The flavors blend deliciously. The results seem quite elaborate.

2 to 3 tablespoons olive oil
1 medium onion, sliced
1 medium clove garlic, minced
1 teaspoon thyme
¼ teaspoon oregano
1 to 1½ cups water or vegetable broth
2 cups small broccoli florets
1½ cups small cauliflower florets
3 cups coarsely chopped cabbage
2 cups thinly sliced zucchini
1 large tomato, peeled and coarsely chopped (including juice)
2 tablespoons fresh minced basil (optional)
Freshly ground pepper to taste

1. Heat half the olive oil in a large nonstick skillet. Add the onion, garlic, thyme, and oregano and sauté over medium high heat, stirring frequently for 2 minutes, adding a few tablespoons of water or broth to prevent scorching.

2. Add the broccoli and cauliflower florets to the skillet and continue sautéing, stirring constantly, adding water or broth in ¼-cup increments as needed to keep the vegetables moist and allow them to cook through. Sauté until vegetables turn bright color, approximately 3 minutes.

3. Stir in the cabbage, zucchini, chopped tomato with its juice, and remaining olive oil. Continue sautéing the vegetables, stirring constantly. Add fresh basil and water or broth, if needed, to keep the vegetables moist. Sauté an additional 5 minutes until all vegetables are tender. Season to taste with freshly ground pepper.

Serves 4–6.

11

The All-American Potato

POTATOES are one of America's national foods. In fact, in only a few places in the world do people rely as much as we do on the potato as an accompaniment to practically anything and everything else that is eaten.

Nutritionally potatoes, to borrow Harvey's words, are "right on the money." This food is a perfect example of the complex carbohydrates we are told to eat by all our scientific leaders. They're fuel food—food our bodies crave to burn—as their sugars break down and enter our bloodstreams slowly, giving us the constant energy we need for life's daily trials. They supply us with vitamins (B_1, B_2, B_3, and C), iron, folic acid, calcium, potassium, and phosphorus. Scientists agree that our protein needs range from 2 to 11 percent. And potatoes are 11 percent protein!

Thick-skinned Russets are the common baking potatoes. Higher in starch, Russets are best in sautéed preparations and also make excellent mashed, roasted, broiled, and grilled potato dishes. Flavorful new potatoes (red-skinned) steam or boil to perfection, or roast and bake to creaminess. They are excellent in potato salads because they hold their shape and do not break down. Thin white-skinned new potatoes are usually boiled or steamed, but they can also be baked and roasted. I find these to be an all-purpose potato. New on the market are Yellow Finns, a golden-fleshed variety that are slightly sweet and very moist. Bake, roast, boil and mash them; they are unusually creamy and delicious. And don't forget yams and sweet potatoes. Bake, steam, candy, and roast them; cube and add them to soups; turn them into whipped purees or cold, sweet pies.

An especially stellar attribute of the potato is that it contains not one drop—not even a millidrop—of saturated fat or cholesterol. So let's stop saturating the potato with fat and serving it with globs of cholesterol! Let's revamp the french fry and export it back to our good friends in France with a brand-new healthful twist!

Now that you know they are a protein-providing food, feel comfortable treating potatoes as legitimate *main* courses rather than side dishes.

New American Fries

12 minutes

Here's a new version of our national food. You'll notice that we keep the fries but throw out the oil! Introducing New American Fries for the New American Attitude that rejects clogged arteries as a national characteristic!

2 large Russet potatoes, peeled or unpeeled
1 tablespoon olive oil
Condiments of your choice, such as ketchup

1. Preheat the broiler.

2. Cut potatoes in thin french-fry cut (3/8 inch), using a food processor or mandoline. Brush a large cookie sheet with oil.

3. Place potatoes on sheet in 1 layer and brush with oil. Place cookie sheet on a rack 6 inches from heat. Broil potatoes for 7 minutes, turn potatoes, and broil for an additional 3 to 5 minutes, depending on how golden and crisp you like your fries.

4. Transfer potatoes from cookie sheet to platter with a spatula. Serve immediately, with ketchup, if desired.

Serves 2 to 3.

Crusty Roasteds Revisited

15 minutes

These are New American Fries in a potato-chip shape, and are they ever well received! At a recent meeting with fast-food industry executives, we brought Crusty Roasteds to the table first, by accident, instead of with the main course. It took less than three minutes to get the rest of the food to the table, but in that time the plate of Crusty Roasteds was completely emptied. It was amusing—and not surprising. Serve with New York Goodwich (page 179) and Deli-Style Cole Slaw (page 151).

2 medium Russet potatoes, unpeeled
1 tablespoon olive or safflower oil
½ teaspoon pressed garlic
Seasoned salt

1. Preheat the broiler.

2. Slice potatoes in 1/8-inch slices. Brush a cookie sheet with 1 teaspoon of oil. Mix remaining oil with garlic in a bowl. Arrange potato slices on cookie sheet, then brush with garlic-oil mixture. Sprinkle with seasoned salt to taste.

3. Place cookie sheet under broiler about 4 inches from heat. Broil potatoes until crusty, approximately 7 minutes. Remove from cookie sheet with spatula.

Serves 2 to 3.

Oven-Roasted Potato Fries

1 hour 45 minutes

We received more mail about Crusty Roasteds from *Fit for Life* than any other recipe. These rival them as all-time great potatoes—crisp and chewy on the outside, soft on the inside. Pass the ketchup!

6 large red-skinned, White, or Russet potatoes
Dashes of assorted seasonings:
  seasoned salts
  herbs such as thyme and rosemary
  paprika
  ground rock salt
  freshly ground pepper
4 tablespoons olive oil
½ cup minced chives (optional)

1. Preheat the oven to 425°F. Cut the potatoes lengthwise into fingers. (Cut in half first, then cut each half in 5 or 6 fingerlike wedges.)

2. Arrange potatoes in large, heavy baking dish and season according to taste.

3. Pour oil over potatoes and mix well. Cover dish with foil and bake 45 minutes. Uncover, mix well, and bake additional 45 minutes, turning once. Sprinkle with chives before serving.

Serves 6.

Easy Oven-Baked Hash Browns

1 hour

This is a perfect dish for those days when you have no time to prepare dinner, and it's another good reason to keep cooked potatoes on hand.

6 large red-skinned potatoes, steamed, peeled and thinly sliced
1 small onion, thinly sliced
2 large cloves garlic, minced
4 tablespoons olive oil
Ground rock salt and freshly ground pepper to taste
Paprika to taste
1 tablespoon minced parsley
1 tablespoon soy margarine, cut into bits (optional)

1. Preheat the oven to 450°F. Place potatoes in lightly oiled baking dish. Add onion, garlic, olive oil, and salt and pepper. Toss well. Dust lightly with paprika and parsley. Dot with margarine.

2. Bake 15 minutes. Turn with a spatula. Lower heat to 350°F and bake 30 minutes to an hour longer. Potatoes can remain in warm (300°F) oven for up to two hours or until you are ready to eat.

Serves 3 to 4.

Carrot Hash Browns

40 minutes

We received so many raves about these from *Fit for Life* that we include them here.

3 tablespoons safflower oil
½ small white onion, finely grated
3 carrots, peeled and finely grated
3 Russet potatoes, scrubbed and finely grated
Ground rock salt (optional)

1. Heat oil and onion in a nonstick skillet. Add carrots and potatoes, then seasoning. Sauté until browned on one side. Flip over and sauté on second side until browned.

2. Break potato cake apart with a wooden or plastic spatula into small chunks or serve in wedges, cut from the round.

Serves 3.

Perfect Mashed Potatoes

20 to 25 minutes

4 cups peeled White or Russet potatoes, cut in quarters
1 bay leaf
1 celery stalk
8 peppercorns
1 large handful parsley
1 large garlic clove, peeled
2 tablespoons light miso
2 tablespoons soymilk (optional)
1 tablespoon olive or sunflower oil
Freshly ground pepper to taste

1. Place potatoes in a large pot and cover with water. Add bay leaf, celery, peppercorns, parsley, and garlic. Bring to a boil and simmer, covered, for 10 to 15 minutes or until tender. Do not overcook or potatoes will be mushy.

2. With a slotted spoon, transfer potatoes from pot to a large bowl, taking care to leave peppercorns behind. Reserve potato water. Combine ¼ cup potato water with miso and mix well to dissolve.

3. Mash potatoes, adding miso mixture, additional potato water as necessary, soymilk if desired, oil, and pepper. Whip well. Serve immediately or transfer to a casserole and keep warm in 300°F oven (for 30 minutes or less) until ready to serve.

Serves 2.

Gravies for Mashed Potatoes

People like gravy on their mashed potatoes, so here are some recipes.

Easiest Gravy

3 tablespoons olive oil
3 tablespoons whole-wheat flour
2 tablespoons powdered vegetable broth, or 2 vegetable bouillon cubes
3 cups potato water or plain water

Heat oil in a large skillet. (A skillet is preferable to a saucepan because gravy distributed over a larger heated area thickens faster.) Whisk in flour and powdered vegetable broth. (If using bouillon cubes, add liquid first and then add cubes.) Add potato water or plain water slowly, stirring with a whisk over medium-high heat, until gravy thickens to desired consistency.

Yields 3 cups

Browned Onion Gravy with Tarragon

If you have homemade vegetable stock, to substitute for the commercial bouillon, this gravy is even better.

1 tablespoon olive oil
1 large white onion, sliced
1 1/2 cups water
2 teaspoons powdered vegetable broth, or 1 vegetable bouillon cube
1/4 teaspoon dried tarragon
1/8 teaspoon dried sage
Dash of nutmeg
1/4 teaspoon dried chervil

Heat oil in a large skillet over high heat. Add sliced onion and sauté, stirring frequently, until onion is browned and caramelized, about 15 minutes. Add water and powdered broth, tarragon, sage, nutmeg, and chervil. Bring to a boil, lower heat to medium, and simmer gravy until reduced.

Yields 3/4 cup

Rich Brown Gravy

Serve this over French Vegetable Mélange (page 307) or as an exotic accompaniment to a platter of steamed vegetables.

1/4 cup olive oil
1 cup mirepoix, consisting of:
  1/3 cup diced carrot
  1/3 cup small diced onion
  1/3 cup diced celery heart
  1/2 small bay leaf
  1/4 teaspoon dried thyme
1/4 cup whole-wheat pastry flour
5 black or white peppercorns
1/4 cup coarsely chopped fresh parsley
4 cups water
2 vegetable bouillon cubes, or 2 scant tablespoons powdered vegetable broth
Sea salt
Freshly ground pepper

Heat the oil in a heavy saucepan. Add the mirepoix and sauté until it begins to brown. Add the flour and stir until brown. Add the peppercorns and the parsley. Stir well and add the water and bouillon cubes. Simmer for about 2 hours stirring occasionally. Sauce should be the consistency of whipping cream. Strain.

Yields approximately 2 cups.

Note: 4 cups of rich vegetable stock can be substituted for the water and bouillon cubes.

Creamy Mushroom-Onion Gravy

This creamy gravy is just as good as Grandma's, and really adds the right touch to mashed potatoes. You might also try this over grains for a very hearty meal.

1½ tablespoons olive oil
1 onion, diced (1½ cups)
1 small glove garlic, minced
1 cup sliced mushrooms
1 tablespoon whole-wheat pastry flour
3 tablespoons nutritional yeast (optional)
1½ cups mashed potato broth
1½ tablespoons strong powdered vegetable broth or 2 vegetable bouillion cubes.

Heat oil in a medium skillet. Add onion and garlic and sauté until soft, about 3 to 4 minutes. Add mushrooms and sauté 2 to 3 minutes longer, stirring occasionally. Stir in flour and yeast. Slowly add potato broth, stirring with a whisk to dissolve lumps until smooth. Add gravy mix and continue to stir. Allow gravy to simmer and thicken over medium heat for 5 minutes. (Stir in a little more potato broth if gravy gets too thick.)

Yields 1¼ cups.

Note: To prevent a skin from forming on the surface of gravy that is prepared in advance, simply press the waxed paper onto the surface of the gravy. When ready to serve, remove the waxed paper and gently reheat the gravy.

French Potato Pancake

1 hour

A large potato pancake that is cut like a pie and served in wedges.

6 to 8 medium White Rose or white-skinned or Russet potatoes, peeled
Ground rock salt to taste
3 tablespoons olive oil

1. Coarsely grate the potatoes. Wash and drain them several times, spread them on a towel, and roll in the towel to dry them. Sprinkle with salt.

2. Heat 2 tablespoons of oil in a nonstick skillet. Add potatoes and pat down with a spatula to form a neat pancake. Cover pancake and cook over medium heat for 20 minutes.

3. Lift cover horizontally, so that condensed water doesn't drip back into skillet. Dry cover. Place a large platter or pizza pan on the skillet and invert. Pancake will slip onto platter, cooked side up.

4. Add remaining oil to skillet and slide pancake back into skillet, cooked side up.

5. Pat down and cook for 20 minutes, uncovered.

6. Slide pancake onto platter and cut into wedges to serve. *Serves 4.*

Potato Cake

1 hour, 20 minutes

A smaller, much thinner version of the French Potato Pancake, these are served as an appetizer, with salads or soups, or as an enhancement to many meals.

6 medium baking potatoes, peeled and coarsely grated
Olive oil as needed
Ground rock salt
Freshly ground pepper

1. Use grated potato immediately or cover it with cold water to prevent oxidizing. Drain and thoroughly squeeze water from potato by rolling it in a towel. Place potato in a bowl. Season to taste with salt and pepper.

2. Heat an 8-inch nonstick skillet. Add a small amount of olive oil and approximately one-third of the seasoned grated potato. Use a wooden or rubber spatula to press the potato down into skillet so pancake will be thin, and keep edges pressed in. (Lacy edges brown too quickly.) Cook over medium-high heat, continously pressing down with spatula so inner layers of potato are close to heat and can cook through.

3. When first side is evenly browned, flip the cake and add a little more olive oil around edges. Cook second side in same fashion, continously pressing down with spatula and keeping edges neat. Turn out on plate, allow to cool slightly, and cut in 6 wedges. *Serves 6 to 8.*

Note: These thin pancakes can be prepared hours in advance and reheated in a hot oven just before serving.

Potatoes Anna

1 hour, 15 minutes

This is a beautiful dish and it is very easy to prepare.

8 new or Yellow Finn potatoes at least 2 inches in diameter, peeled, thinly sliced, and dried in a towel
5 tablespoons olive oil
Ground rock salt
Freshly ground pepper

1. Preheat oven to 375°F. Heat an ovenproof skillet and add 1 tablespoon olive oil.

2. Immediately begin placing potato slices in pan, overlapping them slightly, beginning around the edge of pan in a flower petal arrangement until bottom of pan is covered. Drizzle with scant 1 tablespoon oil and season with salt and pepper to taste.

3. With skillet on medium heat, repeat step 2 until you have 3 or 4 layers of potatoes and all slices are used up.

4. Place in oven and bake 1 hour. Potatoes should pierce easily with a sharp knife and have lightly browned edges. Invert onto a platter, cut in quarters, and serve.

Serves 4.

For Quick Solutions

Always bake more potatoes than you'll need for your meal. Cold baked potatoes can be used for so many quick and delicious meals. Their hearty baked flavor adds something special to any dish. Remember, too, that large new potatoes bake fantastically well, not just Russets. And cold yams are best!

1. Slice them thin, arrange slices on an oiled cookie sheet, brush with garlic and olive oil, add a little of your favorite seasoning, and broil for a few minutes.
2. Cube and toss in salads.
3. Peel, cube, and toss in broth with other vegetables. In 15 minutes, you have a hearty soup.
4. At lunch, serve cold sliced baked potato with sliced avocado. A dash of seasoned salt and a big salad rounds it out. What a great meal!
5. Add mashed cold yams to muffin or biscuit batters.
6. Toss cold yam slices in at the end of a vegetable stir-fry.
7. Add cold cubed yams to soup. They'll dissolve and make a healthy sweet broth.

Fried Hash Bakes

15 minutes

Baked potatoes make the best fried potatoes. When you are baking potatoes, bake a few extra, cool them completely, and keep them in the refrigerator (for up to a week), wrapped in plastic or stored in an airtight container.

2 large baked potatoes
2 tablespoons olive oil
Ground rock salt
Freshly ground pepper (optional)

1. Slice or coarsely chop potatoes, skins and all.

2. In a nonstick pan, sauté potatoes in oil and seasonings to taste until slightly crisp and golden.

Serves 4.

Variation: For a lighter but equally flavorful dish, you can peel the potatoes before sautéing them.

Curried Potato Salad

30 minutes

This is a bright yellow, spicy potato salad that wins raves of approval. It's great for picnics or as a substitute for the broiled potatoes in the Potato-Lover's Salad (page 158).

2 tablespoons olive oil
½ teaspoon black mustard seeds
⅓ teaspoon cumin seeds (optional)
½ teaspoon turmeric
½ cup diced carrot, blanched for 3 minutes
½ cup chopped onion, or ½ cup minced green onions
5 cups steamed, peeled, and cubed potatoes
½ teaspoon ground cumin
½ teaspoon ground coriander
Ground rock salt (optional)
¼ teaspoon cayenne or to taste
1 tablespoon lemon or lime juice
2 tablespoons minced cilantro or fresh parsley

1. Heat the oil in a heavy saucepan. Add the mustard seeds, cook until they just begin to pop, and quickly add the cumin seeds, turmeric, diced carrot, and onion. Sauté the onion for 3 minutes, stirring frequently, over medium heat until soft.

2. Add the potatoes and sauté for 2 minutes, stirring continuously. Stir in the ground cumin, coriander, and cayenne and salt to taste. Mix well. Cover and cook for 5 minutes over low heat.

3. Remove lid; add the lemon juice and cilantro or parsley. Serve hot or at room temperature.

Serves 6.

Roasted Potato Skins with Creamy Chive Dip or Tahina

30 minutes

Here's something that disappears the minute you put it out. With this new and improved version, they'll be diving in like never before! You can't make enough of these.

4 large baking potatoes, scrubbed and dried
1 tablespoon olive or sunflower oil
Salt-free seasoning
Creamy Chive Dip (page 137) or Tahina (page 136)

1. Preheat oven to 450°F. Use a paring knife to peel the skin from the potatoes end to end into ¾-inch wide strips. Remove a thin layer of the potato flesh with each strip. Place the peeled potatoes in a bowl of water and reserve for another use.

2. Generously oil a cookie sheet and arrange the potato strips, skin side up, in one layer. Bake for 15 to 20 minutes, or until strips are crisp and golden. Toss the potato skins with the seasoning and transfer to racks to cool. (Skins may be prepared a day in advance and reheated at 450°F for 5 minutes.) Serve with choice of dips.

Serves 4.

Deli-Style Potato Salad

15 minutes

8 cups cooked potatoes, peeled and thinly sliced
⅓ cup minced celery
2 tablespoons minced green onion
4 ounces silken tofu
1 tablespoon nutritional yeast
1 tablespoon Tofu Scrambler
½ cup dairy-free mayonnaise
1 teaspoon yellow mustard
½ teaspoon dry mustard
Ground rock salt
Freshly ground pepper

1. Combine potatoes with celery and onion in large mixing bowl.

2. In smaller bowl, mash tofu with yeast and Scrambler. Add mayonnaise and mustards. Mix well.

3. Add tofu mixture to potato mixture and mix thoroughly. Season to taste. Refrigerate until ready to serve.

Yields 9 cups.

Picnic Barbecued Baked Potatoes

5 to 10 minutes

There's something about the flavor of a baked potato grilled over coals. These are even more heavenly, dipped in guacamole, Herbed Almonnaise (page 98), or ketchup!

3 large cold baked potatoes
3 tablespoons olive oil
1 large garlic clove

1. Cut potatoes into ¼-inch slices. Mix oil and garlic in a small bowl.

2. Place potatoes on grill over medium coals. Brush with garlic oil and immediately turn. Brush second side with oil. Grill potatoes for 3 to 4 minutes on each side until nicely browned, brushing with oil when necessary.

Serves 3.

Stuffed Idahos with Curry

1 hour, 25 minutes

2 large Idaho potatoes
½ cup water
1 to 2 teaspoons olive oil
1 medium onion, quartered and sliced
¼ teaspoon ground cumin
¼ teaspoon curry powder, or more to taste
1½ tablespoons nutritional yeast (optional)
1 tablespoon light miso
2 teaspoons tahini
Sweet Hungarian paprika

1. Preheat oven to 400°F. Wash potatoes and pierce them gently in a few places with a fork to allow steam to release and prevent skins from bursting. Bake for 1 hour and 15 minutes, or until perfectly soft throughout.

2. While potatoes are baking, heat oil, 2 tablespoons water, and onion in a medium skillet. Sauté 2 minutes, then add cumin and curry and sauté 1 minute. Add yeast and sauté an additional minute. Stir in remaining water, miso, and tahini. Bring to a boil, stirring, to dissolve all seasonings, then set aside.

3. Remove potatoes from oven and cool slightly. Roll on a work surface with the flat of your hand to loosen pulp. Slice open lengthwise and scoop pulp into a mixing bowl, taking care not to break skins. Preheat broiler.

4. Add onion mixture to potato in bowl. Mash and combine with a hand blender or potato masher. Spoon filling into potato skins, dust with paprika, and broil for 5 minutes or until crusty on top.

Serves 2.

Potato Boats

30 minutes

Here's another popular version of an American potato dish. Stuffed baked potatoes—absolutely and deliciously dairyless.

2 large Idaho or Russet potatoes, baked and cooled slightly
½ pound winter squash (Banana squash, Butternut, or Hubbard)
2 to 3 tablespoons olive or sunflower oil
¼ to ½ teaspoon ground cumin
Ground rock salt or salt-free seasoning
Freshly ground pepper
Sweet Hungarian paprika

1. While potatoes are cooling, cut skin from squash and cut squash into small cubes; you should have ¾ to 1 cup. Place in a vegetable steamer and steam over medium heat until very soft. Preheat broiler.

2. Cut potatoes in half lengthwise and gently scrape pulp from skin, taking care not to tear skin. Combine squash, potato pulp, all but 2 teaspoons olive oil, cumin, and salt and pepper to taste with a potato masher or food processor until you have a creamy puree.

3. Fill potato skins with potato-squash mixture. Brush with reserved oil and dust with paprika. Place under broiler for 10 minutes or until lightly browned.

Serves 2 to 4.

Potatoes and Zucchini in Olive Oil

30 minutes

This is a refreshing, light potato dish, perfect for hot-weather dining. Serve warm or at room temperature. This dish is a perfect example of the simplest ideas often being the most profound.

6 red-skinned potatoes
4 small zucchini, cut into ¼-inch slices
2 tablespoons extra-virgin olive oil
2 teaspoons lemon juice
Ground rock salt or seasoned salt
Freshly ground pepper

1. Steam potatoes until tender, approximately 25 minutes. Cool slightly, then quarter and cut into ¼-inch slices.

2. Steam zucchini until bright green and just tender, about 5 minutes. Allow to cool.

3. Combine zucchini slices and potato slices in a medium bowl. Toss gently with olive oil, lemon juice, and seasonings to taste.

Serves 3 to 4.

Bubble and Squeak

40 minutes

This family favorite is adapted from a traditional English dish that we ate for the first time at an excellent restaurant in London called Langens. It is a great way to use leftover steamed potatoes. This recipe works best when potatoes have been chilled for several hours. They then grate more easily without losing texture and becoming mushy.

10 to 12 medium potatoes, steamed until just tender and peeled
4 tablespoons olive oil
1 small onion, coarsely grated
½ medium green cabbage coarsely grated or sliced in ¼-inch strips, (approximately 4 cups)
3 to 4 tablespoons water
Salt-free seasoning
Freshly ground pepper

1. Grate potatoes on a coarse grater. Place 2 tablespoons oil in a nonstick skillet at least 10 inches across. Heat with onion and sauté over medium heat until soft.

2. Add cabbage and continue sautéing, adding 3 or 4 tablespoons water to keep cabbage from scorching, until cabbage turns bright green and soft. Add potatoes and salt and pepper to taste. Mix thoroughly.

3. With a spatula, press mixture evenly into pan to form a flat cake. Cook over medium heat until the bottom of the cake is browned and crispy, approximately 15 minutes.

4. Cover pan with a flat platter or pizza pan, and invert skillet to remove cake. Add remaining 2 tablespoons oil and coat entire skillet evenly. Slide potato cake carefully back into skillet and press down to brown second side. Cook until surface of cake is crispy and inside is soft. Slide onto serving platter and cut into pie-shaped wedges.

Serves 4 to 6.

Easy Seven-Vegetable Stew

1 hour

1 tablespoon olive oil
1½ cups diced onions
½ to 1 teaspoon minced garlic
1 cup celery, diced in 1-inch pieces
1 teaspoon dried thyme
3 tablespoons whole-wheat pastry flour
2 cups carrot rounds, in ½-inch pieces
3 cups potato cubes, in 1-inch pieces
1 white onion, quartered and cut in eighths
3 cups water, approximately
1 bay leaf
Ground rock salt
Freshly ground pepper
1½ cups zucchini rounds, in ½-inch pieces
1 cup frozen peas
2 cups coarsely chopped green cabbage

1. Preheat oven to 325°F. Heat oil with diced onions, garlic, and celery in a heavy casserole.

Sauté 5 minutes, stirring frequently. Add thyme and flour, and sauté, stirring, until mixture is well coated with oil.

2. Stir in carrots, potatoes, and onion quarters and mix well. Add water, bring to a boil, and add bay leaf and salt and pepper to taste. Cover and place in oven. Set timer for 30 minutes.

3. Remove stew from oven. Stir in zucchini, peas, and cabbage. Add a little additional water, if necessary. Replace cover and return to oven for 20 minutes. Remove from oven and adjust seasonings. Remove bay leaf.

Serves 4 to 6.

Note: This stew can be prepared in advance and reheated right before serving. It keeps and freezes beautifully.

Variation: Omit zucchini and substitute 2 cups steamed broccoli. Add broccoli 10 minutes before stew has finished cooking and do not replace lid. (Without lid, broccoli will remain a lovely bright green and stew will be absolutely beautiful.)

Curried Potatoes in Tomato Gravy

45 minutes

This aromatic potato dish is adapted from a traditional Indian preparation called *alu ki-sabzi.* It's a great party dish with savories and salads. All the spices are available from Indian markets, and many are sold in supermarkets. The harder-to-find items are optional.

¼ cup sesame oil
1 teaspoon cumin seed (optional)
1 teaspoon dried kari leaves (optional), or 1 bay leaf
3 teaspoons ground coriander
1½ teaspoons ground cumin
¼ teaspoon paprika
½ teaspoon turmeric
Ground rock salt
6 medium tomatoes, peeled and pureed or finely chopped, or 1 (17-ounce) can plum tomatoes without the juice
1 bunch cilantro, finely chopped
9 to 10 white medium potatoes, peeled and diced
4 cups water or vegetable stock
2 teaspoons lime juice

1. Heat oil in a heavy stovetop casserole (a LeCreuset or Corning Visions pot with lid or a pressure cooker). Stir in cumin seed and kari leaves, coriander, cumin, paprika, turmeric, and salt. Add the tomatoes and cilantro, and cook until liquid evaporates.

2. Add potatoes and sauté 5 minutes. Add water and bring to a boil, mixing well. Cover and cook over medium heat for 20 minutes, or until potatoes are tender.

3. Lift cover and cook another 5 to 10 minutes over low heat, stirring occasionally to mash a few of the potatoes to thicken the gravy. Stir in lime juice and adjust seasonings.

Serves 8.

Note: This dish can be made in advance and stored in the refrigerator for several days.

Family Casserole

1 hour, 10 minutes

For less than $5, you can feed a family of five with this delicious casserole. It requires some basic preparation steps, yet your family will feel they are eating something that took all day to prepare. Serve the casserole with the Simple Gravy. The flavorful potato water is important; you use it to mash the potatoes and as a stock for the gravy. Allow the mashed potato crust to brown nicely in the oven.

Mashed Potato Crust

5 medium to large Russet potatoes, peeled
1 garlic clove
1 celery stalk
1 bunch parsley
8 peppercorns
1 medium onion
1 bay leaf
1 tablespoon light miso
1 tablespoon olive oil
Paprika

Filling

1 tablespoon olive oil
¾ cup diced red onion
1 garlic clove, minced (1 teaspoon)
½ pound mushrooms, sliced (optional)
1 pound firm tofu, wrapped or frozen and defrosted
4 tablespoons hickory-flavored barbecue sauce
1 tablespoon nutritional yeast (optional)
1 tablespoon instant gravy mix or other strong powdered broth
1 teaspoon dried thyme
1 teaspoon paprika
1 tablespoon tamari
1 cup frozen or fresh corn
1 cup chopped spinach or green chard

Simple Gravy

2 tablespoons olive oil
2 tablespoons whole-wheat pastry flour
2 teaspoons nutritional yeast (optional)
1 tablespoon instant gravy mix, or 1 vegetable bouillon cube
2½ cups reserved potato water

1. Peel and quarter potatoes. Place in a medium or large pot with water to cover. Add garlic, celery, parsley, peppercorns, onion, and bay leaf. Bring to a boil, cover, and simmer over medium-low heat for 15 to 20 minutes or until very tender.

2. While potatoes are cooking, prepare filling. Heat 1 tablespoon oil, onion, and garlic in a large skillet. Sauté for 1 minute over medium heat, then add mushrooms and sauté for 2 minutes. Crumble tofu in chunks into skillet and sauté briefly, mixing well. Stir in barbecue sauce, yeast, gravy mix, thyme, paprika, and tamari. Mix well and sauté, stirring frequently, for 10 minutes over medium heat. Preheat oven to 400°F.

3. Transfer potatoes from water to a large bowl, reserving potato stock. Add miso, oil, and ¾ to 1 cup potato stock to potatoes, in ¼- to ⅓-cup increments, mashing as you add the stock. Add only enough water to moisten potatoes adequately. Do not overmoisten.

4. Add corn and spinach to filling and mix well. Pour filling into an oiled, shallow ovenproof casserole. Pat down with back of a large spoon. Spread potato crust evenly over filling, smoothing top with a spoon or spatula. Dust evenly with paprika. Bake for 30 to 40 minutes, or until crust is golden.

5. While casserole bakes, prepare gravy. Heat oil in a large skillet. Add flour and yeast, and stir with a whisk over medium heat to form a paste. Slowly stir in 2½ cups of reserved potato water, whisking as you stir to allow gravy to thicken. Stir in instant gravy mix and continue whisking until gravy is thick and smooth; add additional potato water, if necessary.

6. Serve casserole with crust on the bottom and filling on top. Spoon gravy over top.

Serves 5.

Vegetable Tsimmis with Potato Dumplings

1 hour, 20 minutes

This is an old family recipe, passed down from my Grandma Ida. When she made it, it contained beef. This is my vegetarian version. "Tsimmis" means stew.

Stew

1 medium onion, finely chopped
2 tablespoons olive oil
1 large onion, sliced
2 celery stalks, cut in chunks
1 bunch carrots, grated
1 bunch carrots, cut in large chunks
4 sweet potatoes or yams, peeled and cut in chunks
2 tablespoons flour
2 vegetable bouillon cubes
6 cups water, heated to boiling
3 large zucchini, cut in chunks
¼ cup fresh parsley, minced
1 tablespoon fresh dill (optional)

Dumplings

4 medium potatoes, peeled and grated
2 tablespoons soy powder or egg replacer for 2 eggs
3 tablespoons whole-wheat pastry flour
1 tablespoon safflower oil
Ground rock salt to taste
Freshly ground pepper to taste

1. In a heavy ovenproof pot, combine oil, onions, and celery and sauté until limp. Add the grated and chunked carrots and the sweet potatoes. Add flour and coat well.

2. Combine bouillon cubes with boiling water to create vegetable broth and add the broth to vegetable pot. Cover and bring to a boil. Simmer 10 minutes, while you peel and grate the potatoes for the dumplings. Before assembling dumplings, add zucchini chunks to stew. Add parsley and dill.

3. Preheat oven to 375°F. Combine dumpling ingredients; mixture should be thick. Drop in large spoonfuls on top of bubbling vegetable stew, then bake, covered, for 30 minutes. Uncover and bake 10 minutes more.

Serves 8.

Christmas Casserole of Whipped Yams and Winter Squash

45 minutes

2 large acorn squash, halved and baked for 45 minutes to an hour or until tender
2 large or 4 medium yams, baked
1 tablespoon FruitSource, date sugar, or maple syrup
½ cup fresh orange juice
Ground cinnamon and grated nutmeg

1. Preheat oven to 350°F. Scoop squash from skin of squash. Place in a large mixing bowl or food processor. Remove yam flesh from skin and add to squash. Whip or mash together, incorporating sweetener and orange juice.

2. Place mixture in casserole and dust with cinnamon and nutmeg to taste. Bake for 20 to 30 minutes.

Serves 8.

Easy Stewed Yams and Zucchini

30 minutes

1 tablespoon olive oil
1 medium onion, chopped
1 celery stalk or 1 parsley root, peeled and chopped
3 medium carrots, peeled and cut in ½-inch rounds
1 White Rose or Russet potato, peeled and grated (can be already cooked) (optional)
1 large yam, peeled and cut in 1-inch dice
2 cups water
¼ cup chopped fresh parsley
1 vegetable bouillon cube
2 large zucchini, quartered and cut in 1-inch dice
Salt-free seasoning
Freshly ground pepper

1. In a heavy heatproof casserole or saucepan, heat oil with onion and celery or parsley root. Sauté for 2 to 3 minutes.

2. Add potato, carrots, and yam. Mix well. Add water, parsley, and bouillon cube. Cover and cook 10 minutes.

3. Add zucchini and seasonings to taste. Cover and cook until zucchini is tender but still bright green, and sauce is thick, about 10 minutes more.

Serves 4.

Broiled Yam Chips

15 minutes

2 medium yams, cut in ⅛-inch slices
2 tablespoons sunflower oil
Salt-free seasoning (optional)

1. Lightly oil 2 cookie sheets. Arrange yam slices on the cookie sheets with slices side by side, not overlapping.

2. Brush slices with oil. Sprinkle lightly with seasoning, if desired. Broil close to the heat for 10 minutes or until lightly browned.

Serves 4.

Candied Yams

1 hour

2 pounds small yams
2 tablespoons maple syrup
1 tablespoon sorghum molasses
1 tablespoon sunflower oil
Ground cinnamon

1. Peel yams and cut into 2-inch chunks. Steam for 20 minutes or until tender. Preheat oven to 375°F.

2. Drain and arrange yam chunks in a shallow casserole. Drizzle maple syrup, sorghum molasses, and sunflower oil over yams. Dust with cinnamon.

3. Bake for 35 to 40 minutes, turning yams once or twice to allow for even browning.

Serves 4.

12

Pasta—East Meets West

THE history of pasta is as tangled as the strands on a plate of tagliatelle. There are theories that it came to the West with Marco Polo, from his expedition to China in the thirteenth century. But pasta scholars are hardly in agreement on its Chinese origins. Some point to substantial evidence of its far earlier existence in the Mediterranean region. Etruscan murals dating back to 400 BC show floured tables and the simple tools used to make homemade pasta. Prior to Marco Polo's report, in 1298, that Chinese natives were eating "lasagna," a Genoese notary in 1278 recorded a chest of macaroni among the items of a soldier's estate.

The probability, of course, is that pasta existed in both China and Italy well before the voyage of Marco Polo, and that both cultures developed their noodle cuisines independently. Today, many wonderful pastas reflect these two paths of evolution. From Italy we get spaghetti, linguine, fusilli, rotelle, lasagna, fettuccine, macaroni, vermicelli, tagliatelle, penne, rigatoni, and the like. Rice sticks (*maifun*), bean threads or cellophane noodles, wontons, udon, soba, ramen, and somen all come from Asia. Since in our country we have dishes from both East and West, there is probably no place on Earth with greater pasta options!

A GOOD THING?

Certainly the range of pasta choices we can make is great. After all, pasta is a complex carbohydrate—the celebrity food in this age of fitness and health consciousness. How wonderful that there are so many varieties.

But there's a slight reservation when we look past size and shape to ingredients. All complex carbohydrates, after all, are not equal. Whole-grain pastas are far more beneficial than the more commonly used ones made from refined semolina (a flour derived from the endosperm of durum wheat), because their fiber is intact and retains more of the original nutrients.

"But I've had whole-wheat pasta," you moan, "and it's just like eating wet cardboard!" I know what you mean. Our palates are used to white-flour pastas, and it takes time to recognize that whole-grain pastas are *different,* not inferior. I have found that certain whole-grain pastas are equal in texture and actually superior in flavor to refined. In particular, Asian pastas are highly successful. They usually are a combination of wheat and buckwheat, wheat and brown rice, soy or sesame flours, and frequently are enhanced with a Chinese herb called mugwort or *jinenjo,* a wild mountain yam. Soba and udon are truly delicious and excellent replacements for practically any refined pasta. In the natural foods industry, too, pastas from newly marketed grains such as quinoa or lupini flour (made from lupin) are high in fiber, protein, calcium, vitamins, and minerals and have excellent flavor and texture. Worth mentioning too are wheat and Jerusalem-artichoke pastas, which have excellent flavor and texture and somewhat enhanced nutritional content.

FIX-IT-FAST PASTA

Pasta cooks quickly and combines naturally with vegetables and salads, making it a great choice for Fix-it-Fast menus. The Fix-it-Fast pasta dish involves preparing an easy sauce or vegetable mixture in a large pot, skillet, or wok, to which you then add your cooked pasta, hot or cold. For example, you sauté garlic and onions, then add fresh or canned tomatoes, basil, oregano, parsley, and your pasta. Or, you sauté or steam a blend of your favorite vegetables, add herbs of your choice and olive oil for a quick primavera. Chop fresh tomato, cucumber, peppers, avocado, and cilantro; toss them with olive oil for a tempting Pasta Mexicana. For a spicy Szechwan or milder Cantonese pasta, prepare vegetables in the wok with Asian sauces; toss the cooked soba or udon directly in the wok with the sauce and heat through. You can also do curried pasta, stroganoffs, or practically any other sauce with pasta. And remember the main-course salad principle. When all you feel like making is your salad, toss your pasta directly into it; that's by far one of the best ways to enjoy pasta.

Angel Hair Pasta with Fresh Tomato Sauce

10 minutes

Serve this pasta with Flavorful Steamed Artichokes (page 221) with Avocado Butter (page 219) and French Green Salad with Cottage Tofu (page 141).

8 ounces angel hair pasta
3 large, ripe beefsteak or 8 Italian plum tomatoes, peeled, seeded, and cut into ½-inch dice
1 large garlic clove, minced (2 teaspoons)
¼ cup chopped fresh basil, or 2 teaspoons dried
¼ to ½ teaspoon salt
Freshly ground pepper
2 tablespoons extra-virgin olive oil

1. Prepare pasta according to package directions. While pasta is cooking, begin preparing sauce.

2. Combine tomatoes, garlic, basil, salt, pepper to taste, and olive oil. Mix well.

3. Add half the sauce to piping hot pasta, mix, and then top pasta with remaining sauce.

Serves 2.

Note: If you have time, allow the sauce to sit for 30 minutes to 1 hour before you prepare the pasta.

Linguine with Traditional Sauce of Fresh Tomatoes

20 minutes

For many people, the acidity of a cooked tomato sauce is uncomfortable. This recipe uses a traditional method first, then has chopped fresh tomatoes added at the end. The result is delicious and delightful.

½ pound brown rice udon, linguine, or other pasta
1 medium garlic clove
1 small onion
1 small carrot
1 small celery stalk
2 tablespoons olive oil
1 vegetable bouillon cube
1 teaspoon dried basil or ¼ cup chopped fresh
¼ cup minced fresh parsley
¼ cup water
6 medium tomatoes
Freshly ground pepper (optional)

1. Prepare pasta according to package directions. While pasta cooks, prepare sauce. Using a food processor, mince the garlic, then finely chop the onion, carrot, and celery.

2. Place vegetables in a heavy saucepan with oil. Sauté until vegetables begin to soften, stirring frequently, then add bouillon, basil, parsley, and water. Cover and simmer over medium heat for 5 minutes or until vegetables are tender. Set aside.

3. Plunge tomatoes in boiling water for 30 seconds. Peel and coarsely chop by hand or pulse 2 or 3 times in a food processor so pieces of tomato hold their shape. Stir fresh tomatoes into cooked vegetables. Adjust seasonings, then combine with hot pasta. *Serves 2.*

Fettuccine with Zucchini Sauce and Fresh Tomatoes

20 minutes

Zucchini and pasta complement each other. Add some tomatoes and basil, and this is really pasta Italiana!

½ pound fettuccine or other pasta
2 tablespoons olive oil
2 tablespoons water
4 small zucchini, quartered and cut in ⅛-inch slices
¼ teaspoon dried oregano (optional)
2 medium tomatoes, peeled and cubed
2 tablespoons minced fresh basil, or 1 teaspoon dried
Ground rock salt
Freshly ground pepper

1. Prepare fettuccine according to package directions. While pasta cooks, prepare sauce. Place oil and zucchini in a medium skillet. Sauté over medium-high heat, adding water as necessary to prevent scorching. Toss and stir zucchini for 3 minutes, adding oregano as you cook. When zucchini are bright green, remove from heat and set aside.

2. Place pasta in a large bowl. Add zucchini, chopped tomatoes, fresh basil, and seasonings to taste. Toss well. *Serves 2.*

Spaghetti with Quick and Easy Cooked Tomato Sauce

20 minutes

¾ pound artichoke spaghetti or other pasta
1 tablespoon olive oil
¾ cup chopped onions
⅓ cup chopped celery
⅓ cup chopped carrot
½ teaspoon minced garlic
6 large tomatoes, peeled and chopped, or 1 (28-ounce) can peeled Italian tomatoes, drained and chopped
¼ teaspoon dried oregano
½ teaspoon dried basil
Ground rock salt
Freshly ground pepper
1 tablespoon tomato paste (optional)

1. Prepare pasta according to package directions. While pasta cooks, prepare sauce. Heat oil in a medium saucepan with onions, celery, carrot, and garlic. Sauté over medium heat for 3 minutes, stirring frequently.

2. Add tomatoes to vegetables along with oregano, basil, and salt and pepper to taste. Stir in tomato paste, cover, and simmer over low heat until tomatoes break down and sauce is chunky, but fairly uniform in consistency, approximately 10 minutes. Stir once or twice during cooking period.

3. Pour sauce over hot spaghetti.

Serves 3.

Variation: For a smoother, more uniform sauce, simmer for 40 to 50 minutes, stirring occasionally.

Linguine with Asparagus

20 minutes

Asparagus and pasta love each other. This recipe is so easy, yet the dish is so elegant.

½ pound linguine or brown rice udon
1 pound asparagus
3 tablespoons olive oil
2 tablespoons minced shallots
1 cup sliced mushrooms
1 tablespoon tahini dissolved in ¼ cup water
Freshly ground pepper (optional)
Pinch of tarragon

1. Prepare pasta according to package directions. While pasta cooks, break woody ends from asparagus. Roll-cut in 1-inch diagonals, leaving tips whole. Blanch asparagus for 2 minutes or, if they are thin, proceed with next step, using them raw.

2. Heat 3 tablespoons oil and shallots in a large skillet. Sauté until shallots are soft, then add asparagus and cook until bright green and tender-crisp, approximately 5 minutes, shaking pan over heat. Add mushrooms and sauté 2 minutes, shaking pan continuously.

3. Add linguine to skillet with remaining tablespoon oil and tahini mixture. Mix well. Adjust seasonings.

Serves 2.

Thin Spaghetti with Curried Courgettes and Green Onions

20 minutes

Courgettes are baby zucchini, often with beautiful yellow-orange blossoms attached which are edible. They are available at some supermarkets in the special vegetable section, and they can also be easily grown in your garden. We plant zucchini seeds in the spring and harvest courgettes all summer. This vegetable is really special, and it adds tremendously to pasta. The subtle hint of curry makes this a truly wonderful pasta dish. If courgettes are not available, substitute yellow squash.

1 pound thin artichoke spaghetti or other light-colored spaghetti
3 tablespoons olive oil
1 teaspoon curry powder
¼ teaspoon turmeric (optional)
¼ teaspoon ground coriander (optional)
¾ cup chopped green onions, including greens
1 pound courgettes, coarsely chopped (approximately 4 cups)
2 tablespoons minced cilantro (optional)
1 teaspoon lime juice
Ground rock salt (optional)

1. Prepare pasta according to package directions. While pasta cooks, prepare sauce. Heat 2 tablespoons olive oil in a large skillet. Add curry powder, turmeric, and coriander and sizzle briefly in the oil, stirring continuously.

2. Add green onions and sauté over medium heat until onions begin to soften. Toss in courgettes and sauté, stirring continuously, until vegetables turn bright, approximately 5 minutes. Stir in minced cilantro and lime juice.

3. Place pasta in a large serving bowl. Add remaining tablespoon oil and the vegetable curry. Mix well. Adjust seasonings. *Serves 4.*

Escarole "Soup"

35 minutes

Serve this with crusty bread and "Stedda" Chicken-Lover's Salad (page 157).

1 tablespoon olive oil
1 small onion, sliced
1 head escarole, coarsely chopped (or other green)
4 cups chicken-flavored vegetable broth or any strong vegetable stock
2 ounces vermicelli, broken in 1½-inch lengths
Ground rock salt
Freshly ground pepper

1. In a large saucepan, heat oil and onion. Sauté 3 minutes, or until soft.

2. Add escarole and sauté 1 minute.

3. Add stock, bring to a boil, and simmer over medium-low heat, covered, for 15 minutes.

4. Uncover, return to a boil, add vermicelli, and simmer, uncovered, for 15 more minutes. Add salt and pepper to taste. *Serves 2 to 3.*

Shells with Easy Pesto and Peas

25 minutes

So many people love pesto but do not realize how easy it is to make. Make this in the summer, when the fresh basil is in season. Accompanied by a fresh tomato salad, this dish makes a wonderful summer meal.

1/2 pound shells
2 medium garlic cloves, or more to taste
4 cups fresh basil leaves
4 tablespoons pine nuts
½ cup extra-virgin olive oil
2 cups shelled peas
Ground rock salt to taste

1. Prepare pasta according to package directions. While pasta cooks, prepare pesto. With blade running in food processor, drop garlic in through opening and mince. Add basil leaves and process until finely chopped. Add pine nuts and process until finely chopped. Drizzle in olive oil in a fine stream until a thick paste forms.

2. Place peas in a vegetable steamer and steam for 4 to 5 minutes, or until bright green and tender.

3. Remove ½ cup of pasta water from pasta pot before draining pasta. Combine pasta water and ¼ cup pesto. Heat briefly but do not boil.

4. Place pasta in a large bowl. Add peas and pour pesto over top. Toss well.

Serves 2.

Note: To store remaining pesto, place it in a jar and cover top with a thin layer of olive oil to prevent browning of basil leaves. Cover with a tight-fitting lid. Pesto will keep for weeks refrigerated.

Mixed Pastas in Mushroom-Onion Sauce

20 minutes

This recipe includes a little trick for getting some whole-grain pasta into regular pasta lovers. Cook a pound of fettuccine *and* half a pound of whole-grain spaghetti. Mix the two after cooking; the whole-grain pasta tends to disappear in the sauce. Serve this with Traditional Ukrainian Cabbage Soup (page 201), Baked Acorn Squash (page 241), and Classic Green Salad (page 140).

1 pound fettucine
½ pound jinenjo soba or other whole-grain spaghetti
1 tablespoon olive oil
1 large garlic clove, minced
1 large or 2 medium white onions, sliced ¼-inch thick
1 pound large mushrooms, stems trimmed, with half chopped and half thinly sliced
1½ cups strong vegetable stock
½ teaspoon mirin or white cooking sherry
½ cup chopped fresh Italian parsley
Ground rock salt
Freshly ground pepper

1. Cook pastas separately, according to package directions for al dente. Drain, rinse thoroughly under cold water to prevent sticking, and set aside.

2. Heat oil, garlic, and onion in a large, nonstick skillet. Sauté, stirring frequently, over medium heat, until onion softens. Stir in chopped mushrooms and continue cooking and stirring for several minutes, adding 1 cup stock as you stir. Add sliced mushrooms and sauté until soft.

3. Add remaining stock, mirin, parsley, and salt and pepper to taste. Continue cooking until sauce is thick and a rich brown color, approximately 3 to 5 minutes.

4. Stir in pastas and mix well. Heat thoroughly over low heat, stirring constantly to prevent sticking. Adjust seasonings.

Serves 4.

Wild Mushrooms and Fettuccine with Garlic, Oil, and Parsley

45 minutes

We have my Mom to thank for this superb recipe. It requires a little forethought, since the Italian mushrooms have to be soaked until soft, but once that is accomplished, the preparation time is minimal. Here's a menu suggestion: Cream of Asparagus and Fennel Soup (page 197), Wild Mushrooms and Fettuccine with Garlic, Oil, and Parsley, Classic Green Salad (page 140), Tomatoes in Pesto (in summer; page 147) or Baked Carrots au Gratin (winter; page 230).

½ ounce dried Italian mushrooms (porcini)
½ pound fresh mushrooms
½ pound fresh shiitake mushrooms, stems removed
1 pound plain fettuccine, spinach fettuccine, or other pasta
¼ cup extra-virgin olive oil
2 teaspoons minced garlic
3 tablespoons minced fresh parsley
Ground rock salt
Freshly ground pepper

1. Soak dried Italian mushrooms in warm water to cover for 30 minutes or until soft.

2. Thinly slice fresh mushrooms. You should have about 6 cups. Set aside.

3. Prepare pasta according to package directions.

4. Drain Italian mushrooms. Strain soaking liquid through cheesecloth or a very fine sieve to remove sediment. Chop Italian mushrooms until semifine, then combine liquid and chopped Italian mushrooms in a medium saucepan. Bring to a boil and simmer until all the liquid has evaporated.

5. Heat oil with garlic in a skillet. Sauté briefly, then add parsley and fresh mushrooms. Cook 1 minute. Add cooked Italian mushrooms and salt and pepper to taste, and cook until liquid has evaporated. Combine with fettuccine and mix well.

Serves 4.

Note: If fresh shiitake are not available, substitute dried. Soak them briefly and then proceed with instructions as if they were fresh.

Keep Cold Pasta on Hand

It is useful to have cold pasta on hand, particularly if you like Asian pasta dishes. Usually, the preparation is done in a wok, and cold pasta is heated along with the vegetables. To shorten the cooking time and conserve energy (yours and the environment's), cook extra pasta to have on hand for stir-fries or to toss into soups and salads. Rinse it well in cold water after cooking, so strands won't stick together. Store cold pasta in a covered container in the refrigerator. It will stay fresh for at least three days.

Simple Lo Mein

12 minutes

Use a whole-grain Asian pasta, like buckwheat or jinenjo soba, and enjoy this simple pasta dish with vegetables in place of rice.

½ pound thin Asian noodles, cooked according to package directions
4 tablespoons safflower oil, approximately
¼ cup rich vegetable stock
1 tablespoon low-sodium soy sauce or tamari
½ teaspoon fresh ginger, pressed, or ¼ teaspoon ground (optional)
½ teaspoon garlic, pressed (optional)
3 green onions, roll-cut in 1-inch lengths
2 to 3 large bok choy, chard, or spinach leaves, coarsely shredded

1. Prepare noodles according to package directions, or use cold noodles prepared in advance. When noodles are ready, toss with 1 tablespoon oil and set next to wok.

2. Combine stock and soy sauce and set next to wok. Combine ginger and garlic in 1 tablespoon oil and set next to wok along with onions and bok choy.

3. Heat wok over high heat. Add 1 tablespoon oil to wok and swirl to coat on the sides. Add ginger-garlic mixture and green onions. Stir-fry until fragrant and onions turn a bright green, then add bok choy and stir until just wilted. Transfer vegetables to a warm serving plate and reserve.

4. Wipe wok with a paper towel. Add remaining tablespoon oil and swirl to coat sides of wok. Reduce heat to medium and add cooked noodles. Heat without stirring, for 1 minute, then begin to stir gently, adding a little more oil if needed to prevent sticking. Add stock mixture and stir well.

5. Return vegetables to the pan and toss well. Turn heat to high and continue cooking and stirring until liquid is nearly absorbed. Transfer to warm serving platter.

Serves 2.

Variation: Add 1 cup small tofu cubes along with bok choy.

Vegetable Lo Mein

35 minutes

½ pound brown rice udon or other Asian noodle
2 tablespoons safflower oil
¼ cup roll-cut green onions, in irregular diagonals
½ teaspoon pressed garlic
1 cup roll-cut zucchini, in irregular ½-inch gems
½ cup matchstick carrots
3 cups long, thin broccoli florets
½ cup dried shiitake mushrooms, soaked for 20 minutes (optional)
3 cups coarsely chopped cabbage
2 tablespoons low-sodium soy sauce
2 tablespoons tamari
1 tablespoon light miso (barley or brown rice)
½ teaspoon roasted sesame oil
Freshly ground pepper

1. Cook pasta according to package directions or use cold noodles you have on hand. Toss with 1 tablespoon safflower oil and set near wok.

2. Set onion, garlic, and zucchini near wok. Steam carrots and broccoli for 3 minutes each. Set near wok. Drain and slice shiitake, straining broth. Combine ½ cup broth, soy sauce, tamari, miso, and sesame oil in a bowl and set near wok.

3. Heat wok over high heat. Add 1 tablespoon safflower oil and swirl to coat sides. Add green onion and garlic and stir-fry until fragrant and bright green. Add zucchini and shiitake, and stir-fry for 3 minutes, tossing continuously and adding a few drops of broth–soy sauce mixture to keep vegetables moist.

4. Add cabbage to wok and stir-fry 1 minute, tossing continuously. Add broccoli and carrots and stir-fry 1 to 2 minutes, until all vegetables are brightly colored and lightly cooked. Turn out onto work platter.

5. Add remaining broth–soy sauce mixture to wok and bring to a boil, stirring to reduce and thicken slightly. Boil for 1 minute, stirring continuously.

6. Add pasta to sauce and heat through for 1 minute, mixing gently. Return vegetables to wok and combine gently with noodles. Cook for 1 minute. Season with pepper to taste. Turn out onto serving platter or serve directly from wok.

Serves 4.

Chinese Cucumber Pasta

15 minutes

The special quality of this simple dish comes from the fresh cucumber slivers that combine so refreshingly with the pasta. It's a nice accompaniment to Tomburgers (page 187) or as a picnic entry. Serve it warm or cold.

½ pound brown rice udon or other flat pasta
3 cups long, thin broccoli florets
¼ cup low-sodium soy sauce or tamari
1 tablespoon sesame oil
1 teaspoon roasted sesame oil
2 teaspoons sesame seeds
3 cups slivered hothouse cucumbers
1 tablespoon chopped green onions

1. Prepare pasta according to package directions or use cold pasta you have on hand.
2. Steam broccoli until bright green and just tender. Combine soy sauce, oils, and sesame seeds in a bowl.
3. Combine cucumber, broccoli, and pasta in a large, shallow serving bowl. Add sauce and chopped green onions, mix well, and adjust seasonings.

Serves 3.

Pasta Mexicana

15 minutes

½ pound mugwort soba or any thin, green spaghetti
1½ cups cubed tomatoes
1 cup cucumber matchsticks
1 medium avocado, peeled, seeded, and thinly sliced crosswise
1 cup Salsa (pages 134, 135) or prepared salsa
1 tablespoon extra-virgin olive oil
½ teaspoon dried oregano
¼ teaspoon ground cumin
¼ teaspoon chili powder
Cayenne to taste
¼ to ½ cup minced cilantro

1. Prepare pasta according to package directions. Rinse under cold water and set into large, shallow serving bowl.
2. Add tomatoes, cucumber, and avocado to serving bowl.
3. Combine salsa, oil, oregano, cumin, chili powder, and cayenne to taste. Mix well, then pour over pasta. Add cilantro and toss gently to distribute vegetables evenly.

Serves 3 to 4.

Buckwheat Soba, Oyster Mushrooms, and Asparagus

30 minutes

Grilled oyster mushrooms give this Asian pasta dish a unique touch. Commercial mushrooms or shiitake can be substituted for the oyster mushrooms.

Pasta

½ pound buckwheat soba, cooked al dente, drained, and rinsed under cold water
½ pound fresh oyster mushrooms
1 tablespoon olive oil
1 tablespoon safflower oil
½ teaspoon minced garlic
3 cups roll-cut asparagus
2 to 3 cups chopped fresh spinach
2 cups julienned hothouse cucumber
2 cups mung bean sprouts
1 tablespoon wine vinegar (optional)
Freshly ground pepper

Sauce

¼ cup teriyaki or low-sodium soy sauce
½ teaspoon powdered vegetable broth
1 teaspoon roasted sesame oil
2 tablespoons brown rice vinegar

1. Place pasta in a large, shallow serving bowl or platter and set aside. Brush mushrooms with olive oil and grill or broil until slightly browned on the edges, turning once. Set aside.

2. Combine sauce ingredients in a small bowl and set near wok with asparagus.

3. Heat wok. Add garlic to safflower oil and mix well. Pour into wok and immediately add asparagus. Stir-fry for 3 to 4 minutes over high heat, adding a few teaspoons of sauce to keep asparagus from scorching until asparagus are tender and bright green. Pour remaining sauce over asparagus. Cook briefly, then add to pasta, using a spatula to scrape out remaining sauce.

4. Add spinach, cucumbers, and sprouts to pasta and asparagus. Toss thoroughly, adding tablespoon of vinegar, if desired. Gently fold in oyster mushrooms. Season with pepper to taste.

Serves 4.

Pasta Primavera

25 minutes

Who doesn't enjoy a pasta primavera? The sun-dried tomatoes add a nice touch to this quick, delicious version.

1 cup fresh or frozen peas
1 pound fresh asparagus, trimmed and cut in 1-inch lengths
1 cup thin green beans, trimmed and cut in 2-inch lengths
1 cup sliced carrots, in thin diagonals
3 tablespoons olive oil
½ pound spaghettini
¼ cup sun-dried tomatoes or diced red bell pepper
2 tablespoons snipped fresh basil or chives
4 tablespoons minced fresh parsley
1 cup Romaine leaves, thinly slivered
Freshly ground pepper

1. Bring a large pot of water to a boil. Blanch the peas, asparagus, green beans, and carrots for 1 to 3 minutes each, until tender-crisp. Remove to colander with slotted spoon, shock under cold water, pat dry, and set aside.

2. Return water to a boil and add 1 tablespoon olive oil. Add pasta and cook until al dente.

3. While pasta is cooking, heat remaining olive oil in a large skillet. Add blanched vegetables (and red pepper, if using), and sauté 1 minute, preserving bright color of vegetables. Stir in sun-dried tomatoes.

4. Drain pasta and transfer to large serving bowl. Toss immediately with vegetables, basil, parsley, and Romaine. Season to taste.

Serves 3 to 4.

Mushroom Stroganoff

25 minutes

Serve this with Broccoli d'Italia (page 226) and Classic Green Salad (page 140).

1 tablespoon olive oil
1 medium onion, chopped (1½ cups)
½ teaspoon minced garlic
½ pound mushrooms, thinly sliced (approximately 4 cups)
3 tablespoons lemon juice
½ teaspoon dried tarragon
½ teaspoon sweet Hungarian paprika
1 cup vegetable broth or water
2 tablespoons tahini
Freshly ground pepper
1 small tomato, peeled, seeded, and diced (optional)
8 ounces artichoke noodles, cooked and drained
2 tablespoons minced fresh parsley

1. Heat the oil in a nonstick skillet with the onion and garlic until soft. Add mushrooms and continue sautéing and stirring until mushrooms soften. Add lemon juice, tarragon, and paprika, and mix well.

2. Blend vegetable broth and tahini. Pour over mushroom mixture and mix well. Remove from heat. Season to taste with pepper.

3. Stir in tomato and spoon mixture over hot noodles. Garnish with parsley.

Serves 2.

OTHER PASTA DISHES

Mild Szechwan Noodles in Peanut Sauce

45 minutes

Pasta

1 cup slivered carrots
½ cup bean sprouts, blanched
½ pound thin asparagus, roll-cut
1 pound cooked thin pasta, rinsed well under cold water (a thin buckwheat soba is great)
½ cup slivered green onion
1 cup slivered hothouse cucumber

Sauce

1 teaspoon minced garlic
1 teaspoon minced fresh ginger
1 tablespoon minced green onion
6 tablespoons smooth or chunky peanut butter
2 tablespoons tamari or low-sodium soy sauce
1 tablespoon mirin, or 2 teaspoons honey
1 tablespoon spicy barbecue sauce
1 tablespoon roasted sesame oil
1 teaspoon dry mustard
½ teaspoon salt
⅓ cup vegetable stock

1. Blanch carrots and bean sprouts each for 1 minute. Drain immediately and pat dry with paper towel. Blanch asparagus until bright green and crisp, about 3 minutes.

2. Prepare sauce by combining ingredients in a bowl with a hand blender or whisk.

3. Combine noodles, green onion, cucumber, carrots, asparagus, and sprouts in a serving dish. Add sauce, toss well, and serve at room temperature.

Serves 4.

Vegetable Lasagna

1½ to 2 hours

This lasagna works with so many dishes, but a particularly nice party menu includes Sweet Carrots au Naturelle (page 229), Dilled Pea Salad (page 168), French Green Salad with Basil Shiitake (page 143), and Potato Burek (page 312).

Noodles

1 (10-ounce) box lasagna noodles, preferably artichoke lasagna
1 teaspoon olive oil

Tofu Ricotta

1 pound firm tofu
2 tablespoons extra-virgin olive oil
Ground rock salt to taste
¼ teaspoon freshly grated nutmeg, or ½ teaspoon ground

Vegetable Filling

2 garlic cloves, crushed in 4 tablespoons olive oil
1 large, 2 medium, or 4 small zucchini, cut in ⅛-inch-thick lengthwise slices (approximately 3 cups)
1½ teaspoons dried basil
1½ teaspoons dried oregano
½ teaspoon sweet Hungarian paprika
Ground rock salt
Freshly ground pepper
3 cups mushrooms, stems removed, caps thinly sliced
1 (10-ounce) box frozen chopped spinach

To Assemble

Olive oil
¾ cup prepared tomato sauce (pages 266, 268, 280)
Dried basil
Dried oregano
Sweet Hungarian paprika
Ground rock salt
Freshly ground pepper

1. Prepare lasagna noodles. Bring water to a boil in a large pot, add pasta and olive oil, return to a boil, and simmer, stirring once or twice to prevent sticking. Cook for time indicated on package for al dente consistency. Drain, rinse thoroughly under cold water, and lay out on clean towels. Cover with a towel to prevent drying.

2. Prepare ricotta. Crumble three-fourths of the the tofu (12 ounces) in a food processor or blender. Add oil, salt, and nutmeg. Process only until mixture is slightly lumpy. Finely crumble remaining tofu into mixture and set aside.

3. Using 1 tablespoon of the garlic oil for each batch, cook zucchini in a single layer, in several batches, in a large skillet. Sprinkle each batch of zucchini generously with basil, oregano, paprika, salt, and pepper. If the slices are thin enough, you will not need to turn them. Sauté until bright green and tender-crisp. Remove from skillet and set aside.

4. Add remaining 1 tablespoon garlic oil to skillet. Toss in mushrooms and sauté until tender and slightly brown on edges. Remove from skillet and set aside.

5. Steam spinach until defrosted. Squeeze to remove excess water and set aside.

6. Preheat oven to 350°F. Lightly brush a shallow 9 × 13-inch baking dish with olive oil. Place a scant ladle of tomato sauce in dish and spread over bottom. Put a layer of 3 noodles on top of sauce. Cover with a thick masking of ricotta. Top with layers of zucchini, mushrooms, spinach, and salt and pepper to taste. Repeat layers of tomato sauce, pasta, ricotta, zucchini, mushrooms, spinach, and seasonings twice more, reserving 3 lasagna noodles, ½ to ¾ cup ricotta, and 2 tablespoons tomato sauce for final layer.

7. End with a final pasta layer, a masking of ricotta, and a thin brushing of tomato sauce. Dust with basil, oregano, and paprika. Cover with foil lined with parchment (see Note). Bake 45 minutes, then cool a few minutes before cutting. Serve hot.

Serves 8.

Note: Parchment prevents leaching of aluminum into the food. (See page 33.)

Vermicelli with Eggplant Sauce

45 minutes to 1 hour

1 pound vermicelli or spaghettini
2 pounds eggplant (2 medium), unpeeled, cut in ⅜-inch dice
1¼ teaspoons salt
¼ cup olive oil
2 bell peppers, yellow or red, diced
1½ teaspoons minced garlic
2 pounds tomatoes (5 large), peeled, seeded, and chopped, or 1 can (35-ounce) peeled Italian tomatoes, drained and chopped
10 Calamata or other brine-cured olives, coarsely chopped

1. Prepare pasta according to package directions. Drain and keep warm.

2. Salt eggplant cubes and let sit for 15 to 30 minutes in a colander. Rinse under cold water and blot dry with paper towel.

3. Combine eggplant and oil in a large skillet with a lid. Cook over medium-high heat, stirring occasionally, until eggplant begins to soften. Reduce heat to medium-low, cover, and cook 10 to 12 minutes.

4. Add garlic, peppers, and tomato to skillet. Mix well and cook uncovered for 7 minutes. Stir in olives and cook 2 to 3 minutes longer. If smoother texture is desired, puree half the sauce in a food processor. Serve over prepared vermicelli.

Serves 6 to 8.

SAUCES FOR PASTA

Sometimes you just want a sauce that you can pour over the pasta of your choice. You may like to keep them on hand, frozen, for those days when all you have is ten minutes to make a salad and cook some pasta. The following are recipes for sauces that you can prepare in advance and heat up in a few minutes to add to your pasta. Some sauces in the previous recipes fall into this category: Fresh Tomato Sauce (page 266), Quick and Easy Cooked Tomato Sauce (page 268), Eggplant Sauce (page 279), Peanut Sauce (page 277), and Easy Pesto (page 270) can be kept on hand and quickly added to hot pasta.

Meatless Bolognese Spaghetti Sauce

Many people love the classic meat, sausage, and tomato sauce that has been traditional in this country for decades, but they don't love all the saturated fat and cholesterol it contains. When you eat *this* sauce, you will not believe it contains no meat. It looks, smells, and tastes just like your old favorite, but it has no cholesterol, very little saturated fat, and more calcium, usable protein, and iron than meat sauce. And it's economical, too! Use this sauce on pasta and in lasagna; spread a little on pizza if you want a "meatier" pizza.

This excellent sauce is enhanced when it is made with frozen firm tofu. To freeze tofu, drain it, cut it in 2 to 4 slices, place in a container with a tight-fitting lid, and freeze overnight. Thaw and squeeze out as much water as possible before using.

12 ounces firm tofu, frozen and defrosted
2 tablespoons olive oil
4 large garlic cloves, minced (1 heaping tablespoon)
2 cups finely chopped white onions
½ cup diced carrots
2 tablespoons tomato paste
1 (14-ounce) can plum tomatoes, chopped
1 (14-ounce) can tomato sauce
Dash of cayenne
1 teaspoon paprika
1 teaspoon dried basil
1 teaspoon dried oregano
½ cup minced fresh Italian parsley
Ground rock salt
Freshly ground pepper

1. Place the tofu in a food processor and process to the consistency of ground beef.

2. Heat the oil with the garlic, onions, and carrots in a heavy saucepan. Sauté, stirring, for 2 minutes, then add the tofu and tomato paste. Sauté, stirring, for 2 minutes and then add the tomatoes, tomato sauce, cayenne, paprika, basil, oregano, parsley, and salt and pepper to taste. Cover and simmer 1 hour, stirring occasionally.

Yields 8 cups.

Variation: Add 3 cups sliced mushrooms to sautéing vegetables and tofu before adding tomatoes and tomato sauce. Sauté 3 minutes.

Lentil Bolognese

1 hour

A heavy sauce—best in winter.

2¾ cups water plus additional 1 cup if necessary
1 cup brown or green lentils
2 tablespoons olive oil
1 onion, finely chopped (1¼ cups)
2 garlic cloves, crushed (2 teaspoons or more, according to taste)
1 carrot, finely chopped (¾ cup)
1 celery stalk, finely chopped (¾ cup)
1 (28-ounce) can tomatoes, drained and chopped
½ to 1 teaspoon dried oregano
Ground rock salt
Freshly ground pepper

1. Bring water to a boil in a large pot. Stir in the lentils and simmer, covered, for about 40 minutes, or until liquid is absorbed and lentils are soft.

2. In a medium saucepan, heat the oil. Add onion, garlic, carrot, and celery. Cook over low heat, stirring occasionally, until soft. Stir in tomatoes and oregano. Season with salt and pepper to taste. Cover and simmer gently for 5 minutes.

3. Add the cooked lentils and cook, stirring occasionally, until well combined and heated through.

Yields 4 cups.

Sesame Sauce

5 minutes

Here's an uncooked sauce that you can add to hot or cold pasta. It's especially good when you also add some matchstick cucumbers or other vegetables at the same time.

½ cup lightly toasted sesame seeds
1 teaspoon minced garlic
½ teaspoon minced fresh ginger (pass through garlic press)
6 tablespoons olive or sesame oil
1 teaspoon toasted sesame oil
1 to 2 tablespoons mirin (optional)
⅛ teaspoon red pepper flakes
6 tablespoons low-sodium soy sauce
1 tablespoon powdered vegetable broth
½ cup water

1. Lightly toast sesame seeds for 1 minute in hot nonstick skillet.

2. Place all ingredients in a blender or food processor in order given and process after every 3 additions. Process entire mixture until thick.

Yields 1½ cups.

Dairy-Free "Cheese" Sauce for Any Pasta

10 to 15 minutes

½ cup minced green onions
2 tablespoons olive oil or water for sautéing
1 tablespoon whole-wheat pastry flour
3 tablespoons nutritional yeast
1½ to 2 cups water
2 tablespoons sesame tahini
2 teaspoons "chicken"-flavored vegetable broth or light miso
½ cup soymilk
Fresh ground pepper to taste
Ground rock salt

1. Heat green onions and olive oil in a medium skillet and sauté for 3 minutes. Add flour and stir well to dissolve. Add nutritional yeast and slowly add water, whisking to combine ingredients into a smooth sauce. Stir in tahini and vegetable broth.

2. Whisking continuously, allow sauce to cook over medium high heat until it begins to bubble. Whisk in soymilk. Cook sauce for 2 minutes, whisking continuously, until it is thick and bubbly. Season with fresh ground pepper and ground rock salt, if desired.

Yields 1½ to 2 cups of sauce, enough for one pound of pasta.

Variation: For a delicious addition, stir 2 cups of cooked corn into finished sauce and pour over 1 pound of thin green pasta.

13

Foods for the Planet

LET'S BEGIN WITH WHOLE GRAINS

The story of civilization can be traced to the cultivation of grains. Throughout history, grains have been humanity's staff of life, and their attributes are uniquely suited to our survival needs. High in complex carbohydrates, low in fat, with ample quantities of protein, vitamins, and minerals, grains contain practically every nutrient required by our bodies.

Most of the world's populations rely more heavily on grains than on any other food. In Asia, they make up over 70 percent of an individual's daily diet, with 1 billion Chinese eating a pound of rice every day. Although in the United States nearly two-thirds of the arable land is used to grow grains, a full 90 percent of that grain is fed to livestock. In fact, in spite of all the attention given to the need for complex carbohydrates in our diet, grains still make up only 30 percent of an average American's diet. This figure is perhaps half of what it was only a century ago, when 60 percent of the American diet was composed of grains. (As our grain consumption has gone down, our disease ratios have gone up!) Unfortunately, today the small percentage of grains eaten by Americans are, for the most part, predominantly refined.

How a Whole Grain Differs from a Refined One

A whole grain has three parts, which are housed in an inedible hull. The heart of the grain is the *endosperm,* composed primarily of starch and protein, which serves to nourish the seedling before it sprouts leaves. Surrounding the endosperm is the *germ*—the embryo of the seed—which sprouts into a new plant. The germ is rich in nutrients, containing protein, unsaturated fats, carbohydrates, and B-complex vitamins, vitamin E, and minerals, specifically iron. The third part is the *bran*—several layers of protective coating that surround the endosperm and germ. It is in the bran that the greatest concentration of fiber is found; bran also provides B vitamins and minerals such as phosphorus and potassium. Although indigestible to humans, bran's important role is to pull along the other components of the whole grain, thus facilitating their passage through the digestive tract.

When you eat a whole grain from which the inedible hull has been removed, your body gets the benefit of all that grain has to offer. All the protein, complex carbohydrates, unsaturated fats, fiber, B and B-complex vitamins, vitamin E, iron, phosphorus, potassium, and other nutrients present can be used by your body in the whole form in which they naturally occur. From such whole food your body is able to build healthy blood, bone, and tissue; fulfill its energy demands; and maintain itself without a drain on nutrient or energy reserves.

On the other hand, when nutritious whole grains are refined for commercial use, that is not the case. In the refining process, the nutrient-laden germ and the fiber-rich bran are *both* removed. What is left is simply the endosperm, with its starch and protein components. Stripped away are all the vitamins, minerals, fiber, unsaturated fats, and most of the valuable proteins and complex carbohydrates. (Think of refined grains as similar to buying lunch in a Styrofoam container, throwing out the contents, and making a meal of the container. It's almost that unreasonable an act.)

One advantage of this stripping process is increased shelf life (the Styrofoam container lasts a lot longer than its contents would, too), but this is gained at a nutritional cost that cannot be overstated. The illustration below graphically makes clear the extent of the loss.

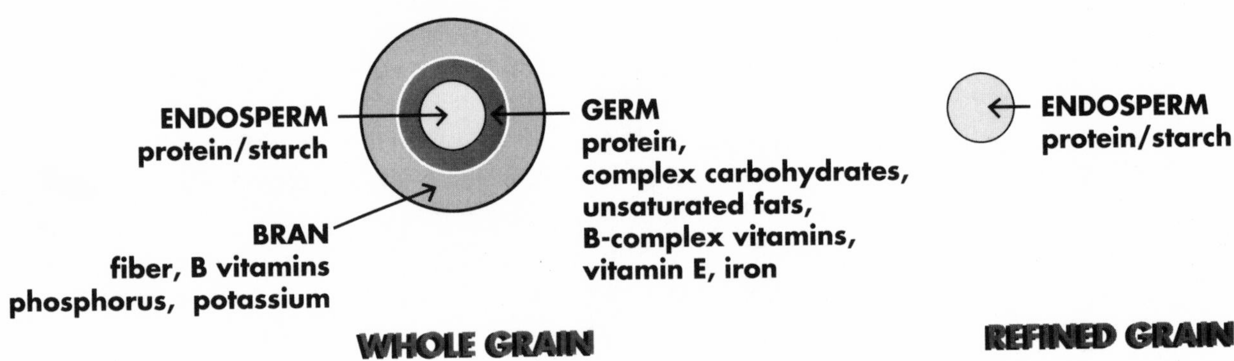

When refined grains are enriched, a handful of the lost nutrients are put back, but they are no longer in the synergistic design that Nature created. Many of the original nutrients are *not* restored, moreover, and there is no way to put back the important fiber that is lost. In addition, the starchy grain, stripped of most of its complex carbohydrates and other nutrients, requires *more* body energy to process than it releases, usurps *more* nutrients than it provides, and thus, drains the body's energy and nutrient reserves.

On the brighter side, the current trend in the United States indicates a slow evolution toward whole grains. You need only visit a natural foods supermarket, where awareness is at its peak, to see that whole-grain products, in bulk and in packages, are among the largest selling items. The manufacturers of supermarket food are working to fulfill the demand for whole grains in their products, too. In this chapter I offer simple preparation techniques that can bring more whole grains into your kitchen. Later, you will find a fundamental whole-grain preparation technique and a collection of some of our favorite grain recipes. But first . . .

LET'S TALK ABOUT LEGUMES

"Legume" is a broad term used to cover a category of whole foods, of which beans are a part. Frequently, the word "bean" is used interchangeably with "legume," which is confusing because some legumes are not thought of as beans. For example, split peas, lentils, and black-eyed peas are also legumes. I use the term "bean" when talking about beans and the term "legume" when discussing the broad category.

Specifically, legumes include:

green and yellow split peas
brown (or green) and red lentils
black-eyed peas
small, oval black beans
tiny, white navy beans
Mexican pinto beans
fava beans
Asian red azuki beans
baby and Fordhook lima beans
Indian mung beans
chick peas (garbanzo beans)
large, white Great Northern beans
red kidney beans
soybeans

Legumes have erroneously been considered fattening, when in reality they contain negligible amounts of fat; they are filling, rather than fattening. In fact, eaten moderately with lots of vegetables, legumes are an excellent weight-loss and weight-maintenance food. The popularity of ethnic food has begun to put them in a more favorable light. Spicy Indian dals and curries, Middle Eastern falafel, Mexican burritos—all these rely on legumes and have demonstrated to the American consumer the delicious taste and versatility of this food.

At low cost, legumes provide a bounty of nutritional benefits. Containing only a trace of polyunsaturated fat, which is beneficial in its whole-food context, they are one of the best sources of cholesterol-lowering fiber. Legumes have a fiber content almost as high as bran in cereals. They are also excellent sources of complex carbohydrates, high-quality protein, vitamin A, B-complex vitamins, and minerals, including iron, calcium, phosphorus, and potassium.

Legumes are a whole food found in abundance in supermarkets. They are also available in bulk in most natural foods markets. But as with any other whole food, selection is important. Color and shape indicate quality. For instance, white beans should be white, not stained with gray, uniform in shape, and smooth, not wrinkled or pitted. Less than 2 percent should be split or open at the seam, indicating rough handling or too rapid drying. If you bite a bean and it doesn't crack open but only dents, it was not sufficiently dried. In general, look for well-shaped, vibrantly colored legumes. Buy them where the turnover is good, since the older they are, the longer they will take to cook.

Legumes can be stored for up to a year. Keep them on hand in airtight glass jars in your pantry. After cooking, legumes also freeze well (with the exception of lentils), which justifies making a large quantity. Most versatile for freezing are the hearty legume soups, which are so welcome with a salad on a cold winter day.

But Aren't They Difficult to Digest?

Yes and no! This seeming problem can easily be a nonproblem if you pay attention to several factors. It is true that some people feel a measure of discomfort after a meal containing legumes.

The discomfort comes from their complex sugars (oligosaccharides), which arrive intact in the large intestine and are not easily broken down by enzymes. Studies show that regular, rather than occasional, consumption of legumes minimizes this problem, as the intestinal enzymes gradually adjust.

There are other variables that can alleviate a digestion problem, because it is really not the legume, but what we do with it that is the cause. Some legumes are far easier to digest than others, and I always emphasize these in my cooking. The smaller varieties, which do not require soaking and which cook the fastest, such as split peas and lentils, are digested most easily.

There are several tricks to enhance the digestibility of problematic beans when you cook them:

1. Be sure they are cooked until they are soft throughout. Remember that this particular food is unique in its large amounts of both protein and starch. Since the body is taxed digestively when proteins and starches are both present in high ratios, adequate cooking is imperative to ensure that these nutrients are in their most easily digestible form. Undercooked beans are not very tasty, anyway.

2. Discard the original soaking water. From a nutritional standpoint, it is preferable to cook beans in their soaking water, since some nutrients from the beans leach into it during the soaking process. However, some oligosaccharides (complex sugars) will be removed if you discard the soaking water and cook in fresh water.

3. The herb savory can be added to the beanpot to enhance digestibility. A small potato, added at the beginning of the cooking cycle and discarded at the end, will have the same effect.

4. Adding kombu to beans helps soften them so they will digest more easily.

5. Do not salt beans prior to or during cooking. This toughens their skins and makes them less digestible. If you are planning to add salt, do it at the end of cooking.

6. Since legumes are such a concentrated food, eat only small amounts. It is a mistake to eat as much of a bean dish as you would a salad (unless you are planning some mighty hard labor). Even in cultures where legumes are staples, they are not eaten in huge quantities at any one meal. In addition, combine beans with light foods rather than heavy ones. They already place an ample digestive burden on the body, so no fair asking it to do more. For maximum comfort and digestibility, I have found that beans and vegetables are the best combination.

How Best to Use Legumes

In a healthful vegetarian diet, legumes can play a supportive, but somewhat secondary role. Their lengthy cooking time and the necessary presoaking, which many of them require, make them less practical for busy people. In addition to their above-mentioned digestibility, the most versatile of the legumes are split peas and lentils, which make excellent soups in a relatively short time. And they don't require soaking. Other legumes, particularly the large beans which require lengthy cooking, are now available in jars (or less desirable cans). Although this is a less economical way to go, it is more practical. In natural foods stores you will find excellent prepared organic beans in jars, which can be kept on hand and used in soups, hummus, refried beans, bean dips, stews, chilies, and salads. But when the spirit moves you and you have the time, a large pot of beans, bubbling away on your stove, will fill your house with a wonderful, homey aroma that you can never get from prepared beans. Once prepared, some can be frozen for later use.

Remember that tofu (the miracle base for all the "Stedda" recipes) is a form of soybean, and it is probably one of the most digestible foods on earth. It contains everything the soybean contains but the fiber, and since it comes from legumes, it deserves to be mentioned here.

No More Confusion

The recent realization that the body builds proteins from its storehouse of amino acids (the amino acid pool) has laid to rest the mistaken theory that we have to combine plant proteins in order to get complete protein at every meal. Unfortunately the public still believes this. Many people still feel that it is necessary to complement beans with grains to supply a complete protein for the body. Dr. Nathan Pritikin called this "one of the most misleading [ideas] in the last few years, because everybody now thinks food balancing is essential. [It] gives the impression that vegetable proteins don't have significant percentages of amino acids."[1]

This misconception confused people and caused them to be uncomfortable because they were eating too much food—and that made it very hard for them to digest beans! The originator of the theory has come to the rescue. Frances Moore Lappe, author of *Diet for a Small Planet,* first presented the theory in the late sixties, but, in her revised 1981 edition, she went out of her way to emphasize that her protein combining idea was unwarranted. She said, "In combating the myth that meat is the only way to get high-quality protein, I reinforced another myth. I gave the impression that in order to get enough high quality protein without meat, considerable care was needed in choosing foods."[2] The focus on combining beans with grains to satisfy protein needs also gave people the impression that they could not look to plant foods *outside* these two categories (grains and beans) for protein, specifically to fruits and vegetables. We have seen in the chart on page 396 that protein is, in fact, available in most, if not *all,* foods from the plant kingdom.

Thankfully, what is now known to be true is that vegetable proteins, in whatever combination, can more than satisfy our protein needs, and can do so without providing the inherently harmful fats and cholesterol that animal products contain.

HOW TO COOK WHOLE GRAINS

All whole grains are cooked in the same basic way, combined with water or vegetable broth that allows them to swell, soften, and transform into food for our bodies. There is no skill necessary in the cooking of whole grains. They are amazingly easy to prepare. The cooking time and the amount of liquid required for each grain varies, but otherwise the technique is nearly always the same.

You'll need the following equipment:

colander
measuring cup
heavy saucepan or skillet with lid

[1]Nathan Pritikin, "Vegetarian Times," 43, p. 22.
[2]Frances Moore Lappé, *Diet for a Small Planet* (New York, NY: Ballantine, 1982), p. 162.

The ingredients for 2½ to 3 cups or 2 servings are:

1 cup whole grain of your choice
Appropriate amount of liquid (water or vegetable stock) for 1 cup of grain (see table on page 289)
1 to 2 teaspoons vegetable oil

1. Measure the grain into a fine colander and rinse it thoroughly.
2. Bring liquid to a boil in a saucepan. Add grain and oil, return to a boil, cover, and simmer over low heat until liquid is absorbed. Avoid stirring during the cooking time, which will make the grain mushy.

Variation (optional): Some grains have a nuttier flavor if toasted before cooking. Toast in a dry nonstick skillet or one to which 1 tablespoon of olive oil has been added. Stir the grain continuously while toasting over moderate heat until aromatic, then add boiling water and cook as above.

Specific Grains

Amaranth—A tiny, round seed, half the size of millet. Amaranth is an ancient grain of the Aztecs. Of all the grains, it has the highest protein content and is so powerful nutritionally that the National Academy of Sciences has cited it as one of the world's most promising foods. Since amaranth is still grown as a specialty crop, however, it is not widely available and is most often seen as a component of cereals or cookies. It should be widely grown, since it is a hardy crop, resistant to both drought and cold. The grain itself cooks to a cereal-like consistency and is best used as a sweetened cereal or in savory casseroles. Available from mail-order sources.

Barley—The most ancient cultivated grain. It is a hardy staple crop in any climate. Barley's mild flavor and chewy texture make it an excellent addition to soups and other grain dishes, a good substitute for rice, and an innovative salad ingredient. Pearl barley is more highly refined; most of its bran and germ have been removed. Scotch barley is more nutritious; being slightly less refined, it retains more of the germ and bran. Barley has been shown to lower blood cholesterol.

Buckwheat Groats (kasha)—An ancient food, first cultivated in China and later in Eastern Europe; it is still widely used in both areas. High in protein and minerals, it is one of the best grain sources of calcium. It has a strong flavor, which makes it an excellent substitute for brown rice, and is especially delicious with browned onions and sautéed mushrooms.

Popcorn—Grown specifically as a snack food, first cultivated by the Incas. It is low in calories and fat (unless you add fat), and very high in fiber. The preferable cooking method is in a hot-air popper that requires no oil; ⅓ cup of unpopped corn make 8 cups of popped corn.

Millet—A staple food in ancient India, Egypt, and China before rice. It is also renowned as a staple food of the long-living Hunzas of the Himalayas. Millet is the only grain that is not acid in the body and, as such, is well recommended. It has high-quality protein; is rich in iron, potassium, and calcium; and is very digestible. Use as a sweetened cereal, in stews and casseroles, as a substitute for rice, and as a stuffing for vegetables.

Oats—Cultivated since the early Christian era. Oats are an ideal crop for cold-weather cul-

COOKING TIMES AND SPECIFIC DIRECTIONS FOR WHOLE GRAINS

Grain *(1 cup)*	Water *(in cups)*	Time *(minutes)*	Directions
amaranth	2½–3	20–25	• bring to a boil, simmer, uncovered, over low heat
barley			• bring to a boil, simmer, covered, over low heat
Scotch	3–3½	50–55	
pearl	2½–3	40–45	
buckwheat groats (kasha)	2	15–20	• toast first, add boiling water, simmer, covered, over *very* low heat
millet	2½	35–40	• toast first, add boiling water, simmer, covered, over *very* low heat
oats			
whole	3–4	45–60	• soak overnight, simmer until tender in boiling water
steel–cut	4	40–45	
rolled	1½	10	• stir into boiling water, remove from heat, and let stand
popcorn	(see page 288)		
quinoa	2	15	• bring to a boil, stock adds flavor, simmer, covered, over *very* low heat
rice			
long–grain	1½	55	• stir measured rice into boiling water, return to a boil, cover and simmer over *very* low heat
short–grain	1½	55	
brown basmati	2¼	35–40	
white basmati	1¾	15	
sweet rice	1½	35–40	
wild rice	3½	55–60	• soak and drain, bring to a boil, simmer until grains pop, and drain
wheat			
whole berries	3½–4	55–60	• soak overnight, add boiling water, cover and simmer over low heat
bulgur (pre–cooked)	2	15–20	• pour boiling water over and let stand 30 minutes
cracked wheat (raw)	3	35–40	• toast first, add boiling water, cover and simmer over low heat
couscous (pre–cooked)	2	15	• add to boiling water and stir and simmer for 2 minutes, cover, remove from heat and allow to sit for 10–15 minutes. (Can be toasted first.)

tivation. Of the common grains, oats are highest in protein, second only to amaranth and quinoa. They are rich in calcium, iron, and phosphorus. Containing a higher proportion of fat than most other grains, they have the reputation of a warming food, appropriate for cold climates. (Fat helps the body store heat and energy.) Whole oats retain the beneficial bran and germ. Use in baking, as a cereal, added to other grains for chewiness, and sprouted. Steel-cut oats are the whole oat sliced into small pieces; are best used in cereals. Rolled oats are steamed and rolled flat; instant oats are pre-cooked. Both retain the nutrients of whole oats.

Quinoa—Like amaranth, an ancient Andean grain. It thrives at high altitudes in poor soil, and is presently under cultivation in Colorado. Quinoa is available both as a grain and as flour, although it is still relatively expensive since it is harvested by hand. It is smaller than millet, but in cooking puffs up to four times its dry volume, so relatively speaking you get plenty of grain for your money. Like amaranth, quinoa has the highest amount of high-quality protein of all the grains, and it is also rich in calcium, phosphorus, and iron. It has a mild nutty flavor that is improved by toasting, a fluffy texture, and cooks quickly. Substitute quinoa for bulgur, rice, and couscous. Use it as a stuffing; it is also good in casseroles and salads.

Rice—The staple grain of half the world's population, with its origins in India. It is a recent grain in Western cuisine, dating only from about the seventeenth century. Worldwide, white rice is more heavily consumed than brown rice, but brown rice is nutritionally far superior. In North America, organic brown rice is now widely available, and it is of the finest quality and flavor. High in fiber, low in fat, moderate in protein, rice when refined loses two-thirds of its vitamins, two-thirds of its fiber, 20 percent of its protein, and half its minerals. A shift in Asia from brown rice to white rice caused nutritional deficiency diseases until the Asians began to enrich their white rice. Brown basmati rice originated in India and is now grown in California. White basmati has a popular, nutty flavor and appealing texture, but it is refined.

Wheat—Currently the world's most widely cultivated grain crop; dates back thousands of years in Chinese and Egyptian records. More wheat is produced in the United States than anywhere else in the world, but what we consume is mostly in refined form. Refined wheat, stripped of its bran and germ, loses as much as 80 percent of its vitamins and minerals and 93 percent of its fiber! The protein content remains high, since wheat protein is concentrated in the endosperm. Enriched wheat has only a few vitamins returned to it, so it nowhere near approximates whole wheat. Wheat berries are not frequently eaten as a grain food, but they are good for sprouting, in soups, salads, casseroles, and baking. For unrefined bulgur, wheat berries are parboiled, then dried and cracked, retaining the nutritional value of the whole-wheat berries. Use bulgur instead of rice in pilafs, casseroles, as a stuffing, and in bread doughs. Couscous is made from refined durum wheat, using only the endosperm, which is steamed, dried, and cracked. It has a pleasant light texture and pastalike flavor, but its nutritional benefits are not much greater than those of refined pasta. Use couscous in place of rice, mixed with vegetables, and in salads. Cracked wheat is like bulgur, but it takes longer to cook and has a stickier texture. It retains the nutritional benefits of wheat berries.

Wild rice is not a rice at all, nor is it a grain, but rather it is the seed of an aquatic grass. However, it is cooked and used like a grain. Wild rice is native to North American freshwater lakes and rivers. It is expensive because of its relative scarcity. It mixes well with regular rice and it is never refined. It is rich in nutrients, high in high-quality protein, and vitamins, minerals, and fiber; and it is low in fat. Wild rice is frequently featured in pilafs with other grains and is delicious added to creamed soups.

HOW TO COOK LEGUMES

Legumes—specifically beans—take a long time to cook but not much effort. With a few exceptions, all must be soaked prior to cooking, which greatly reduces cooking time. The only legumes that need no soaking are split peas, mung beans, black-eyed peas, and lentils. The secret with beans is to plan ahead. If you decide to include them in a meal but fail to allow time for soaking and adequate cooking, they will not be a successful addition. Beans cannot be rushed. In fact, if you try to rush them by boiling them rapidly instead of allowing them to simmer slowly, their skins will burst and you will spoil them.

There are two soaking methods for beans:

Long Soak Method

Place beans on a tray and check them for any stray stones and other impurities. Then rinse them well in a colander. Place them in a large pot and cover with 3½ to 4 cups of water for every cup of beans. Cover and refrigerate to prevent possible spoilage until the next day. When you are ready to prepare the beans, drain and rinse them and then add additional water. No specific amount is required. Just be sure that there is plenty for them to simmer in. A rule of thumb is to add at least double the volume of beans.

Quick-Soak Method

If you forget to soak beans overnight, you can still make them using this 1-hour soaking method. I find that the beans do not hydrate as well, and therefore cooking time is still quite lengthy, however it is a good emergency technique.

Rinse and sort beans as above. Place in cooking pot with 3½ to 4 cups water to 1 cup of beans. Bring water to a rolling boil and immediately remove beans from the heat, allowing them to stand, covered, for 1 hour. Cook as described below; see also chart on page 289.

Cooking Procedure for all Beans That Require Soaking

You'll need the following equipment:

tray
measuring cup
colander
large heavy pot with lid

1. Measure beans onto tray in a single layer so you can spot and remove any tiny stones or other impurities. Place in a colander and rinse well.

2. Soak according to one of the two methods given.

3. Discard soaking water and add fresh water to pot so that you have twice as much water as beans.

4. Bring to a boil, cover, and simmer over medium-low heat until tender, from 45 minutes to 3 hours. Remember to cook beans slowly, rather than under rapid boil, which breaks their skins. Slow simmering allows for the best flavor to develop and ensures an even texture. To test for doneness, press a bean between your thumb and forefinger; if it yields to pressure evenly, it is done.

Additions to Your Bean Pot

Beans cook well in plain water, but there are additions that will enhance their flavor, texture, and aroma. There are also additions that should not be made, because they will interfere with a successful result.

To improve flavor add bay leaf, garlic, and chopped onion.

To improve digestibility, add savory. Add a 4-inch strip of kombu also to soften the beans and make them more digestible.

Do not add salt until the very end because it hardens the beans and lengthens the cooking time. Tomatoes will have the same effect. Never add baking soda (often recommended to shorten the cooking time and make beans more digestible), because it destroys nutrients.

HANDY BEAN CHART

Bean	Pre-Soak	Cooking Time	Comments and Complementary Seasonings
adjukis	yes	1 hr	Asian origins, highly digestible, more flavorful than kidney beans. Good in chili. Soy sauce, ginger, miso, garlic.
black beans	yes	1–2 hrs.	Also called turtle beans. Latin American, Mediterranean, and Asian. Strong flavor, takes well to seasonings. Thyme, savory, garlic, onions, lemon juice, olive oil, cayenne.
black-eyed peas	no	1–1½ hrs.	African and Southern U.S. Excellent in salads and combined with steamed greens. Tomatoes, garlic, onions, lemon juice, cider vinegar, olive oil, black pepper.
chick peas (garbanzos)	yes	2½–3 hrs.	Middle Eastern, Mediterranean, North African, Indian. Base for falafel and hummus. Tahini, lemon juice, garlic, cumin, coriander, curry.

Bean	Pre-Soak	Cooking Time	Comments and Complementary Seasonings
great northern beans	yes	1½–2 hrs.	Italian cannellini. Mild flavor, creamy texture. Tomatoes, garlic, molasses, honey, mustard.
kidney beans	yes	1½–2 hrs.	Hardest to digest. Good in chilies, minestrones, marinated in salads. Take spicy seasonings well.
lentils	no	30–45 min.	Easily digested. Popular in Indian cuisine. Brown and red are similar in flavor. Good in dals, soups, salads, stews, and with noodles and many vegetables. Curry ginger, peppers, tomatoes, olive oil, lemon juice, garlic, onions.
limas			
large	yes	1–1½ hrs.	Frozen are most flavorful, but they are salted. Use dried and frozen interchangeably, except use dried in purees. Good with corn and other vegetables. Tomatoes, bay leaf, thyme, garlic, olive oil, basil.
baby	yes	45 min.–1 hr.	
mung beans	no	45 min.–1 hr.	Popular in Asian and Indian cuisines. Sprouted for bean sprouts. Flavor similar to peas. Season with curry spices, ginger, garlic, tomato, green chilies, spinach, cilantro.
navy beans	yes	1–1½ hrs.	Traditional in baked beans. Similar to great northerns in creamy texture and mild flavor. Molasses, tomatoes, mustard, onions, paprika.
(split) peas	no	1–1½ hrs.	Highly digestible. Yellow are milder than green, but can be used interchangeably. Combine with many vegetables in soups. Potatoes, rice, tomatoes, onions, garlic, miso, green chilies, lemon, dill, curry spices, thyme, dill.
pinto beans	yes	1½–2 hrs.	Traditional bean for refried beans in Southwestern and Mexican cooking. Good with hot peppers, tomatoes, garlic, onions, cilantro, cumin, rice, avocado, oregano, chili powder.

Easy Fried Rice

15 minutes

A great way to use up leftover rice, especially if you have kids. The mung bean sprouts make it moist. Serve with Kids' Favorite Salad (page 146) and Baked Spring Rolls (page 323).

4 cups mung bean sprouts
½ cup diced carrot
3 tablespoons low-sodium soy sauce
2 tablespoons tamari
½ teaspoon ground ginger
1 teaspoon light miso
4 tablespoons safflower oil
¾ cup diced tofu (optional)
¼ cup thinly sliced green onions
½ cup finely chopped onion
2 cups coarsely chopped bok choy (use mostly greens)
6 cups cooked short-grain brown rice
Freshly ground pepper

1. Blanch bean sprouts in boiling water for 1 minute, drain, and set aside. Blanch carrot in boiling water for 2 to 3 minutes, drain, and set aside.

2. Combine soy sauce, tamari, ginger, and miso. Mix well and set aside.

3. Heat wok. Add 1 tablespoon oil and swirl to coat sides. Add tofu and stir-fry for 1 minute. Add 1 tablespoon sauce, then continue stir-frying for 2 additional minutes. Add green onions, onion, carrot, and bok choy and stir-fry for 2 minutes, or until bok choy is wilted. Turn vegetables out onto serving dish.

4. Wipe wok with paper towel. Return to heat and reheat. In a bowl, toss rice with 2 tablespoons oil and mix well. Add remaining tablespoon oil to wok and swirl to coat sides. Add rice to wok and heat through for 1 minute. Add remaining sauce and stir well.

5. Fold in vegetables and bean sprouts. Adjust seasonings to taste.

Serves 6.

Reheating Rice

Place cold, leftover rice in a steamer over boiling water for 5 to 10 minutes. Transfer to serving bowl, add seasonings, and mix well.

Basmati Rice with Spinach and Maui Onions

20 minutes

Serve this with Mushroom Ratatouille (page 168) and Greek Salad 2000 (page 146).

1½ cups brown or white basmati rice
3 cups water
2 teaspoons plus 2 tablespoons olive oil
Ground rock salt to taste
2 large Maui onions or Spanish onion
1 (10-ounce) box frozen chopped spinach, thawed

1. Bring rice, water, 2 teaspoons oil, and salt to a boil. Cover and simmer for 18 minutes for white basmati, 35 minutes for brown.

2. While rice is cooking, heat 2 tablespoons oil in a medium skillet. Add onion and sauté, adding 1 to 2 tablespoons water to prevent scorching. Add spinach and cover skillet with lid, allowing spinach to heat through.

3. When rice is ready, combine with spinach-onion mixture. *Serves 4.*

Perfect Spanish Rice

25 to 40 minutes

This is a wonderful party dish or an easy-to-make lunchbox item. Serve with Easy Tostada (page 162).

2 teaspoons olive oil
½ cup chopped onion
½ teaspoon ground coriander
¼ (scant) teaspoon ground cumin
1 tablespoon dehydrated vegetables (optional)
2 teaspoons powdered vegetable broth, 1 vegetable bouillon cube, or 2 teaspoons yellow miso (light)
2 cups white or brown basmati rice, washed and drained
4 cups water
¾ teaspoon salt-free seasoning
1 medium tomato
1½ cups frozen petite peas
Freshly ground pepper

1. Heat oil in a medium saucepan with a lid. Add onion and sauté until translucent over medium-low heat. Add the coriander and cumin, and sauté, stirring constantly, for 1 minute.

2. Add dehydrated vegetables, broth powder, and rice to saucepan. Mix thoroughly. Add water and 1/2 teaspoon salt-free seasoning, then increase heat to high and bring to a boil, stirring frequently. Cover and reduce heat to low. Simmer 20 minutes for white basmati, 35 for brown basmati.

3. Plunge tomato into boiling water for 30 seconds or until skin loosens. Peel and chop or puree with hand blender or in food processor. When rice is ready, stir in peas and tomato. Add remaining salt-free seasoning and pepper to taste. Mix thoroughly but gently, cover and cook over low heat an additional 3 minutes to cook peas. *Serves 6.*

Baked Rice

25 to 45 minutes

When you bake rice in the oven, it is exposed to an even heat that cooks it through, rather than the intense heat at the bottom of a pot on the stove, which causes sticking and uneven cooking. This dish is handy when you are doing other cooking and need to free up burners on your stove. It is excellent for entertaining. Serve with Carrots Vichy (page 229), Tofu Meunière (page 117), and Classic Green Salad (page 140).

1 to 2 tablespoons olive oil
1 large white onion, chopped (1¼ cups)
2 cups white or brown basmati rice
4 cups water or rich vegetable stock
Ground rock salt to taste
Freshly ground pepper to taste

1. Preheat oven to 375°F. Heat olive oil and onion in a medium saucepan and sauté until onion is tender. Add rice and sauté, stirring, for 1 to 2 minutes.

2. Add water, salt and pepper, bring to a rolling boil, stir, and cover with a round of oiled parchment. Place in oven and bake for 20 minutes for white basmati and 40 minutes for brown rice.

3. Remove rice from oven. Remove parchment and fluff with a fork.

Serves 6 to 8.

Variations:

(1) dissolve a pinch of saffron in stock before adding it to rice for a rich yellow color;

(2) add ¾ cup frozen petite peas to rice when you have removed it from the oven. They will cook from the heat of the rice.

Rice and Peas with Pesto

20 to 45 minutes

Serve this with Broiled Yam Chips (page 263) and English Cucumbers with Lime Juice and Mint (page 150).

1 cup short-grain brown rice
1 teaspoon olive oil
2 cups petite peas
¼ cup pesto
Freshly ground pepper
Salt-free seasoning

1. Bring 2¼ cups water to boil in medium saucepan. Stir in rice and oil. Cover and simmer over low heat for 40 minutes. Remove from heat, but do not lift cover for 10 minutes.

2. Steam peas, reserving ¼ cup steaming water.

3. Combine pesto with pea-steaming water and mix well. Combine rice and peas, then add pesto and mix again. Adjust seasonings to taste.

Serves 2.

Baked Rice Loaf

1 hour, 15 minutes

½ cup water
¼ cup rolled oats
1½ tablespoons olive oil
½ Spanish onion, diced
¾ cup diced celery
¾ teaspoon dried sage
1 tablespoon tamari
½ cup whole-wheat bread crumbs
¼ cup potato flour
½ teaspoon baking powder
1 tablespoon egg replacer mixed with ¼ cup water
1 8 ounce-package rice pilaf mix, cooked according to package directions
1 tablespoon nutritional yeast
1½ teaspoons salt-free seasoning
1½ teaspoons granulated onion
1½ teaspoons powdered vegetable broth
Ketchup or barbecue sauce

1. Preheat oven to 350°F. Bring water and oats to a boil and cook until oatmeal is soft, approximately 10 minutes.

2. Heat 1 tablespoon oil in a skillet with the onion and celery and sauté until soft. Add the sage, tamari, bread crumbs, yeast, potato flour, and baking powder. Stir well to combine and set aside.

3. Add egg replacer mixture to bread crumb mixture and combine entire mixture with rice pilaf. Mix well. Stir in salt-free seasoning, granulated onion, and powdered vegetable broth.

4. Use remaining teaspoon oil to coat loaf pan. Pour mixture into pan and bake for 30 minutes. Generously brush top of loaf with ketchup or barbecue sauce, and bake 30 minutes longer.

5. Remove loaf from oven and cool in pan on wire rack. Unmold, wrap, and refrigerate before slicing for best slicing results. May also be sliced warm and served with gravy.

Serves 6 to 8.

Green Chard Rolls of Rice and Vegetables

1 hour, 50 minutes

Serve with Broccoli and Bowties (page 226) and French Green Salad with Cottage Tofu (page 141).

Rolls

⅓ cup short-grain brown rice
⅓ cup long-grain brown rice
⅓ cup wild rice
2 cups water
½ teaspoon sea salt (optional)
2 teaspoons safflower oil
20 large green chard leaves
1 medium onion, chopped
1 medium carrot, diced
⅓ cup minced fresh dill, or 1 tablespoon dried
1 tablespoon olive oil
Seasoned salt or salt-free seasoning

Brown Onion Sauce

1 tablespoon olive oil
2 medium white onions, sliced into rings
1 small carrot, finely diced
1 tablespoon soy miso (dark)
1 tablespoon barley miso (light)
2 tablespoons lemon juice
1 teaspoon dried summer savory, or ¼ cup chopped fresh
½ cup minced fresh parsley
3 paper-thin lemon slices
2 bay leaves

1. Soak rice for several hours, drain well, and add to boiling water with sea salt and safflower oil. (If there is no time for soaking, which makes the rice a lot fluffier and less starchy, increase the water by ¼ cups.) Bring to a boil, stir briefly, cover, and simmer over *very* low heat for 45 minutes *without* lifting lid. Remove from heat, covered, and allow to rest for an additional 10 minutes. Lift cover and fluff with a fork.

2. While rice cooks, prepare chard leaves. Cut heavy stems from leaf, finely chop stems, and set aside. Place leaves, one on top of the other, in a large steamer or pasta pot over boiling water. Steam 1 to 2 minutes, or until they just begin to soften but are still strong and resilient. (Do not oversteam, or leaves will tear during rolling.) Remove from steamer, reserving liquid for sauce, and drain on cookie sheet or board covered with towel until ready to use.

3. Heat olive oil in a medium skillet. Sauté 1 cup chard stems, onion, and carrot until soft, adding 1 to 2 tablespoons of chard water to prevent scorching. Stir in dill. Mix into finished rice and stir well, adding salt and pepper to taste.

4. When you are ready to prepare rolls, place a heaping tablespoon of filling at the base of a chard leaf. Fold up once, fold in sides, and then roll, eggroll style. Repeat until all leaves and rice are used, arranging rolls in shallow ovenproof casserole.

5. Preheat oven to 350°F. Heat oil for sauce. Sauté onions and carrot, and remaining chard stems, until onion begins to soften. Add 2 to 3 cups of the chard-steaming water and the misos. Bring to a boil and simmer over medium heat to reduce sauce slightly, about 5 to 7 minutes.

6. Stir in lemon juice, savory, and parsley. Cook 1 to 2 minutes longer, then spoon over chard rolls. Garnish with lemon slices and bay leaf. Cover with aluminum foil lined with parchment, and bake for 45 minutes.

Serves 6 to 8.

Three-Grain Pilaf

1 hour

1 tablespoon olive oil
1 onion, minced
2 garlic cloves, minced
3 cups vegetable stock
½ cup bulgur
½ cup long-grain brown rice
½ cup pearl barley
Dash of cayenne or Tabasco
¼ cup minced fresh parsley

1. Place oil, onion, and garlic in a large skillet with a lid. Cook 5 minutes, stirring occasionally.

2. Add stock, bulgur, rice, and barley, then bring to a boil. Add cayenne and parsley, reduce heat to low, cover, and simmer 40 minutes.

3. Allow pilaf to stand, covered, for 10 minutes. Lift cover, fluff with fork, and adjust seasonings.

Serves 4 to 6.

Baked Brown Rice with Herbs

30 to 60 minutes

This is an easy and elegant rice dish that you can pop into the oven in no time flat. While it bakes, you'll have plenty of time to prepare the other dishes for the meal. Use a heavy, enameled, ovenproof casserole with lid or a heavy, covered skillet for best results. Serve with Green Pea Soup with Cashew Cream (page 196) or Sweet and Sour Eggplant (page 235), and Classic Green Salad (page 140).

White basmati rice takes only 20 minutes; brown rices require 50 minutes. Double this recipe so you will have leftover rice to put into salads or soups.

1 tablespoon olive oil
½ cup diced onion
1 teaspoon minced garlic (optional)
2 cups long-grain brown rice
4½ cups chicken-flavored vegetable broth, boiling
2 teaspoons dried thyme
1 bay leaf
1 teaspoon dried marjoram
½ cup minced fresh parsley
Tabasco sauce to taste
Ground rock salt
Freshly ground pepper

1. Preheat the oven to 375°F.

2. Heat the oil in a heavy saucepan, add the onion and garlic, and sauté for 2 minutes.

3. Stir in rice and mix well. Add boiling broth and remaining ingredients. Stir well, cover, and bring to a boil.

4. When rice is boiling, cover with a circle of oiled parchment and place on center rack in oven. Bake 50 minutes.

5. Remove from oven. Remove and discard bay leaf. Season to taste.

Serves 6.

Note: This dish can be prepared in advance and reheated gently on the stove.

Variation: For curried rice, add 2 teaspoons curry powder to onion mixture before adding the rice and cooking liquid.

Easy Broccoli Pilaf

15 minutes

1 tablespoon safflower oil
½ teaspoon cumin seed (optional)
½ teaspoon mustard seed (optional)
1 teaspoon ground coriander
1 teaspoon turmeric
Pinch of asafetida (optional)
¼ teaspoon ground cinnamon (optional)
2 bay leaves
1 teaspoon minced garlic
½ cup minced onion
1 bunch broccoli, cut into small florets, stems peeled and cut crosswise into ⅓-inch slices
⅓ cup water
3 cups steamed brown rice
Juice of a small lemon (2 to 3 tablespoons)
2 tablespoons chopped cilantro (optional)
1 teaspoon sea salt

1. Prepare rice. (Measure 1 cup into 2¼ cups boiling water, with 1 teaspoon olive oil. Cook, covered, over very low heat for 40 minutes. Remove from heat and allow to rest 10 minutes before lifting cover.)

2. While rice cooks, heat the oil in a large skillet with lid. Add the cumin and mustard seed and sizzle the seeds briefly. Stir in the coriander, turmeric, asafetida, cinnamon, and bay leaves.

3. Add the garlic and onion and cook the mixture, stirring, until the onion is soft and begins to brown. Add the broccoli and cook, stirring, for 5 minutes over medium heat.

4. Add water, cover, and steam the mixture over medium-low heat for 5 minutes, or until the broccoli is tender.

5. Stir in the rice and cook, stirring frequently, until the mixture is hot. Stir in the lemon juice and the salt. Mix well.

Serves 5 to 6.

Traditional Couscous and Vegetables

vegetables: 45 minutes
couscous: 15 minutes

For the most appetizing effect, cut vegetables in generous bite-size pieces. Vegetables should be in soupy broth, since couscous soaks up the liquid.

Vegetables

2 tablespoons olive oil
½ teaspoon grated nutmeg
¼ teaspoon ground cinnamon
1½ teaspoon ground cumin
½ teaspoon turmeric
Cayenne pepper to taste (optional)
2 teaspoons minced garlic
3 cups cubed potatoes
3 cups thickly sliced carrots
2 cups coarsely chopped onions
3 to 4 cups water
3 cups thickly sliced zucchini
1 tablespoon light miso
Ground rock salt (optional)
Freshly ground pepper (optional)

Couscous

2 cups quick-cooking couscous
4 cups water

1. Heat oil in a heavy pot. Add nutmeg, cinnamon, cumin, turmeric, cayenne to taste, and garlic. Sauté briefly. (Change amounts of spices to suit your taste.) Add all the vegetables to the spice mixture, except the zucchini. Sauté, stirring continuously, for 3 minutes.

2. Add water, bring to a boil, and cook for 20 minutes, covered, over medium heat until vegetables are almost soft. Stir in zucchini and cook an additional 5 to 10 minutes, allowing mixture to bubble, uncovered to preserve bright color of the zucchini. Stir frequently and add additional water, if necessary.

3. Remove ½ cup of water from the pot, add miso, and stir to dissolve. Return miso broth to stew and stir well. Season to taste with salt and pepper, if desired. Let sit and mellow in flavor while you prepare couscous. (Vegetable mixture can be prepared hours or a day in advance and allowed to sit for flavors to deepen.)

4. Bring water for couscous to a boil. Add couscous and boil 1 minute, stirring frequently. Remove from heat, cover tightly, and allow to sit for 10 to 15 minutes. Remove cover and fluff immediately with a fork.

5. Spoon vegetables and sauce over couscous in individual bowls.

Serves 6 to 8.

Rice and Spinach Mold

50 minutes

Serve this with Marinated Paintbox Vegetables (page 167) and Grilled Asparagus (page 221).

1 (10-ounce) pkg frozen chopped spinach
3 tablespoons olive oil
¼ teaspoon turmeric
1 small white onion, finely chopped
4 green onions, finely chopped
8 ounces firm tofu
¼ teaspoon seasoned salt
½ teaspoon salt
Freshly ground white pepper
2 cups cooked basmati rice

1. Preheat the oven to 325°F. Defrost the spinach, reserving 2 tablespoons of liquid.

2. Heat 2 tablespoons of oil in a skillet. Add turmeric and let sizzle briefly. Add white and green onions and sauté until soft. Remove from heat and set aside.

3. Blend tofu, remaining oil, spinach juice, seasoned salt, salt, and pepper to taste until smooth and creamy.

4. In large bowl, combine sautéed vegetables, rice, and tofu mixture with spinach. Mix well. Bake in an oiled 1½ quart soufflé dish for 30 minutes.

Serves 6.

Kasha and Noodles with Onion-Mushroom Gravy

40 minutes

This is the traditional way to prepare kasha, although the egg (used to ensure separation of the grains) is omitted. Artichoke noodles work very well in lieu of the traditional bowties. The onion-mushroom gravy is a breeze. In just 40 minutes, you will have a hardy cold-weather entrée to accompany Steamed Beets and Chard (page 224) and a green salad.

2 cups roasted medium buckwheat kernels (kasha)
4 cups boiling water mixed with 2 vegetable bouillon cubes, or 4 cups heated vegetable stock
1 bay leaf
1½ cups artichoke noodles
1 tablespoon olive oil
1 medium white onion, peeled and sliced
½ pound mushrooms, stems removed and caps sliced
1 tablespoon whole-wheat pastry or amaranth flour
1 teaspoon dried thyme
3 cups water mixed with 1 tablespoon powdered vegetable broth

1. Heat a heavy skillet with a lid. Add buckwheat and pan roast briefly, stirring constantly until its nutty aroma begins to fill the kitchen. Add boiling water and bouillon cube or heated stock. Add bay leaf. Cover and bring to a boil. Stir, cover again, and cook over very low heat for 15 to 20 minutes, or until kasha is soft and fluffy.

2. While kasha is cooking, prepare noodles according to package directions for al dente. Drain, rinse, and set aside.

3. Place oil and onion in a skillet and sauté until soft, adding a little water or broth to keep onion from scorching. Add sliced mushroom caps. (Reserve stems for your stockpot!) Add flour and thyme and sauté, stirring, until mushrooms are soft and flour is lightly browned. Add vegetable broth and bring to a boil, whisking periodically. Boil until gravy is reduced by one-third and approximately 2 cups remain.

4. Combine noodles and kasha in a heatproof serving dish. Mix well over very low heat, then ladle 1 cup of gravy over mixture, reserving remainder to be poured separately at table.

Serves 4 generously.

Note: Kasha reheats beautifully. Just add a little liquid and stir well.

Linda's Millet-Stuffed Cabbage

2 hours

This hearty dish is one of my sister's solutions for cold winter nights. It's an easy version of stuffed cabbage and well worth the preparation time. Try it!

1 cup millet
2½ cups water or vegetable stock and 1 cup water
2 celery stalks, minced
2 carrots, grated
1 large onion, minced or grated
3 garlic cloves, minced or crushed
⅓ cup chopped fresh parsley
½ cup pine nuts or cooked chickpeas (optional)
1 small tomato, peeled, seeded, and chopped (optional)
1 large Savoy cabbage, leaves removed
1 (11-ounce) can tomato sauce
1 (14½-ounce) can plum tomatoes
3 tablespoons lemon juice
2 teaspoons honey
¼ cup dried currants (optional)
1 bay leaf
½ red onion, sliced
Seasoned salt
Freshly ground pepper

1. Toast millet lightly in a dry skillet and then add it to 2½ cups boiling water or vegetable stock. Cover and simmer over low heat for 35 to 40 minutes. Lift cover and fluff with fork.

2. Add celery, carrots, onion, garlic, parsley, pine nuts, and tomato to millet and mix well.

3. Separate cabbage leaves carefully. Steam leaves briefly in water, about 3 minutes.

4. Preheat oven to 375°F. Fill each leaf with ⅓ cup millet mixture. Roll, folding up bottom and turning in sides to make neat rolls. Place seam side down in an ovenproof casserole.

5. Combine tomato sauce, plum tomatoes, and water. Add lemon juice and sweetener. Pour over cabbage rolls and sprinkle with currants. Top with bay leaf and sliced red onions. Add seasoned salt and pepper to taste.

6. Cover and bake for 45 minutes to 1 hour, or until aroma fills the kitchen.

Serves 6.

Easy Baked Beans

1 hour, 10 minutes

This is a perfect accompaniment to Spicy Tofu Tacos (page 186), Corn on the Cob with "Stedda" Butter Sauce (page 233), and Deli-Style Cole Slaw (page 151).

¼ cup diced onion
2 tablespoons crumbled firm tofu (optional)
1 tablespoon olive oil
1 14-ounce jar Great Northern or pinto beans, undrained
2 tablespoons ketchup
1 tablespoon tomato paste
2 tablespoons sorghum molasses or maple syrup
1 teaspoon dried mustard
Ground rock salt to taste (optional)
Fresh ground pepper to taste
Dash of red pepper

1. Preheat oven to 350°. Sauté onion and tofu in olive oil over medium heat for 2 minutes.

2. Combine beans, ketchup, tomato paste, sorghum, dried mustard, salt and pepper and red pepper in an ovenproof casserole dish. Stir in onion and tofu.

3. Cover and bake ½ hour. Uncover and bake an additional ½ hour.

Serves 4.

Armenian Kufta

1 hour, 10 minutes

These can be served with a small mound of finely chopped parsley and green onions to be used as a dip. Serve with Mediterranean Rice Salad (page 160).

5 cups water
2 cups red lentils
4 tablespoons safflower oil
2 medium onions, coarsely chopped
1 to 1½ cups fine bulgur
½ cup chopped fresh parsley
⅓ cup finely chopped green onions
Ground rock salt
Dash of cayenne

1. Bring water to a boil in a heavy saucepan. Add lentils, return to a boil, and simmer, stirring frequently, until mixture is thick and mushy, approximately 1 hour.

2. While lentils are cooking, heat oil in a heavy skillet. Add chopped onions and sauté until they begin to brown on the edges, but do not let them burn. Set aside.

3. When lentil mixture is thick, remove from the heat and stir in bulgur. Mix well. Bulgur will begin to swell. Add sautéed onions to mixture. It should be thick enough to form into balls. If too stiff, add a little hot water. Stir in parsley and green onions, salt to taste, and cayenne.

4. Roll mixture into balls the size of a large walnut. If desired, make a tiny indentation in the top with your thumb and sprinkle with cayenne.

Serves 7.

Stewed Pinto Beans

3½ hours

2 cups pinto beans, soaked overnight
10 cups water
2 tablespoons olive oil
1 medium onion
1 teaspoon minced garlic
3 tomatoes, peeled and coarsely chopped, or 1 (17-oz) can tomatoes, drained and chopped
½ teaspoon dried oregano
½ teaspoon ground cumin
Ground rock salt

1. Drain beans and place in water in a large pot. Bring to a boil and simmer 2 to 3 hours, until very tender.

2. Drain beans and reserve the bean water for soups. Heat oil with onion and garlic; sauté until translucent. Stir in tomatoes, oregano, and cumin. Simmer 2 to 3 minutes, then add to drained beans. Add salt to taste.

Serves 4.

Corn, White Beans, and Green Beans in Green Onion Sauce

25 minutes

A simple, but hearty side dish of nice colors, especially tasty because of its sauce. Serve with a finger food like Potato Burek (page 312) and a beautiful green salad.

2 medium green onions
1/3 cup extra-virgin olive oil
1/2 teaspoon crushed garlic
Salt-free seasoning
Freshly ground black pepper
2 cups green beans, trimmed and cut in 1-inch segments
3/4 cup chicken-flavored vegetable stock, or 2 teaspoons light miso, dissolved in 3/4 cup boiling water
4 ears fresh corn, cut from cob (approximately 4 cups)
2 1/4 cups cooked Great Northern or navy beans (or flageolets)

1. Place green onions, oil, garlic, and seasonings to taste in a food processor and process until you have a smooth sauce. Set aside.

2. Bring plenty of water to a boil in a large saucepan. Add green beans and boil until tender, uncovered, approximately 5 minutes. Drain and set aside.

3. Heat broth in same saucepan. Add corn and simmer 5 minutes or until tender.

4. If using prepared beans from a jar or can, rinse under cold water. Add to corn with green beans and bring to a boil. Add sauce and heat mixture over medium heat, stirring for several minutes, until well blended and heated through. Adjust seasonings.

Serves 6.

Note: Use white corn, if available.

Blue Ribbon Chili

45 minutes to 1½ hours

Include in any picnic buffet.

2 teaspoons safflower or sunflower oil
1 large garlic clove, minced
1 large onion, finely chopped
1 medium carrot, finely chopped
2 cups crumbled tofu (optional)
3 cups cooked pinto beans
2 cups fresh or canned tomatoes, seeds and juice squeezed out
¼ cup ketchup or tomato sauce
1½ cups fresh or frozen corn
3 teaspoons paprika
1 teaspoon ground cumin
¾ teaspoon chili powder
½ teaspoon ground rock salt
4 tablespoons masa (optional)

1. Heat oil, garlic, onion, and carrot in a Dutch oven. Sauté until onion begins to soften, then add tofu and sauté several minutes.

2. Add beans, tomatoes, tomato sauce, and corn. Mix well. Stir in spices and masa. Cover and simmer over very low heat until flavors have combined, 45 minutes to 1 hour.

Serves 8.

Note: If you are rushing, cook the chili for a much shorter time (15 to 30 minutes), and it will still be wonderful. The longer cooking time allows the flavors to come through.

Spicy Lentil Chili

1 hour, 15 minutes

1½ cups chopped onions
3 celery stalks, diced
2 carrots, diced
½ cup chopped green bell pepper
2 garlic cloves, chopped
1 cup bulgur
2 tablespoons olive oil
1 large can chopped tomatoes
1 pound lentils
2 quarts water
1 teaspoon powdered vegetable broth
1 teaspoon Mexican seasoning
¼ teaspoon ground cumin
½ teaspoon dried basil
Ground rock salt to taste
½ teaspoon Hungarian sweet paprika

1. Sauté onions, celery, carrots, green pepper, and garlic in oil until soft.

2. Add remaining ingredients and simmer for 45 minutes to 1 hour, covered. Add extra liquid if necessary.

Serves 8.

White Bean Casserole

2½ hours

Use tiny white beans for this dish. Soak them overnight or use the quick-soak method on page 291. This is a good dish for a buffet because it is so easy to prepare.

2 cups small white beans (navy beans or French flageolets), presoaked
4 carrots, diced
1 celery stalk, diced
1 tomato, peeled, seeded, and diced (optional)
1 small red bell pepper, seeded and diced
2 onions, sliced
3 garlic cloves, minced
1 bay leaf
½ teaspoon dried rosemary
½ teaspoon dried thyme
2 tablespoons olive oil
1½ teaspoons ground rock salt
Freshly ground pepper
1 vegetable bouillon cube (optional)

1. Drain beans and place in a heavy pot with 10 cups of water. Add the carrots, celery, tomato, red pepper, and onions. Bring to a boil and stir in the garlic, bay leaf, rosemary, thyme, and oil.

2. Bring to a boil, then simmer over low heat for 1 hour and 40 minutes.

3. Add salt and pepper to taste and bouillon cube, if desired. Cook an additional 30 to 40 minutes.

Serves 10.

French Vegetable Mélange

2 hours with dried beans
25 minutes with prepared beans

Mélange means "mixture," and this is a successful one. The greens complement the beans. This can be served with crusty bread and a Main-Course Salad.

2 cups dried white beans, either Great Northerns or navy, or 4½ cups cooked white beans, drained and rinsed
1 garlic clove (optional)
1 bay leaf (optional)
8 cups fresh green chard (leaves only), thoroughly washed, or spinach
2 tablespoons olive oil
¾ cup chopped onions
2 teaspoons minced garlic
3 cups tomatoes, peeled, seeded, and coarsely chopped
¼ teaspoon dried basil
¼ teaspoon dried thyme
Salt-free seasoning
Freshly ground pepper

1. If using dried beans, soak them overnight, drain, and cook in plenty of water with garlic and bay leaf. Or use the quick-soak method on page 291. Drain beans and proceed with recipe.

2. Cook chard in its own juices in a large saucepan over medium-high heat, stirring continuously. Drain well and coarsely chop.

3. Heat oil, onions, and garlic in a large skillet over medium heat. Sauté until soft, approximately 7 minutes, then stir in beans, chard, tomatoes, herbs, and seasonings to taste. Reduce heat to low and simmer 10 minutes to blend flavors, stirring frequently. Adjust seasonings.

Serves 8.

14

Savories in Crusts and Wrappers

These are the foods that are among the most exciting to make and eat. They take their inspiration from many of America's national favorites and from cuisines from around the world. Yet they remain true to the dietary goals we uphold in this book.

I use these recipes for everyday meals and for entertaining. Most are easy to prepare, but have that touch of specialness that makes them appropriate for feasts and celebrations.

Fit for Life Pizza

15 to 20 minutes

In their original form, from Italy and southern France, pizzas were made without cheese. This surprisingly easy and heathful version will give you the opportunity to see how fresh-tasting and delicious pizza without cheese can be and how it will totally satisfy pizza lovers.

Dough

1 package dry active yeast
1 cup whole-wheat pastry flour
1½ cups unbleached white flour
1 cup hot water (120°F to 130°F)
3 tablespoons olive oil
Ground rock salt to taste

Filling

⅓ cup olive oil
4 small Japanese eggplant, thinly sliced lengthwise
2 medium or 4 small zucchini, thinly sliced lengthwise
½ pound mushrooms, thinly sliced
Several thin rounds of red onion
1 teaspoon crushed garlic
1 teaspoon corn meal
½ cup pesto (see page 270)
1 cup Roasted Red Pepper strips (page 184), or 1 cup sun-dried tomatoes, or both
2 large tomatoes, thinly sliced
½ cup chopped Greek olives
¼ cup fresh basil, chopped, or 1 teaspoon dried basil
¼ teaspoon oregano (optional)

1. In large bowl, combine yeast and half a cup of each of the flours. Stir in hot water and olive oil. Stir in additional half cup of each of the flours and salt, if desired. Knead until smooth and elastic, adding additional flour if dough remains too sticky. Knead for at least 5 minutes. Cover dough and allow to rest while you prepare filling.

2. Preheat oven to 500°F. Lightly oil two cookie sheets with olive oil. Arrange eggplant, zucchini, mushrooms, and onion slices on cookie sheet. Combine remaining olive oil with crushed garlic and brush sliced vegetables well. Place in oven and grill for 5 minutes.

3. While vegetables are grilling, flour work surface and roll dough into a large, thin sixteen-inch round to be baked on a pizza pan, or for a change of pace, roll dough into a thin rectangle to fit a cookie sheet. Brush cookie sheet or pan lightly with olive oil and dust with corn meal. Transfer dough to backing pan.

4. Remove grilled vegetables from oven. Brush crust generously with pesto. Layer vegetables on pesto, beginning with eggplant slices, topping with zucchini, and then adding mushrooms and onion rings. Top with Roasted Red Pepper or sun-dried tomatoes. Add slices of fresh tomato. Sprinkle with chopped olives, fresh or dried basil, and oregano.

5. Place pizza on bottom rack of 500°F oven and bake for 15 to 20 minutes, or until crust is lightly browned. Remove from oven and cut into slices or squares.

Serves 4 to 6.

Shepherd's Pie (New and Improved)

1½ hours

This is a wonderful holiday dish that I used to think required butter and cream, but not so! This version is ever-so-wonderful. Who doesn't like stuffing and mashed potatoes? Everyone loves Shepherd's Pie! Serve this with Creamy Mushroom-Onion Gravy (page 251), along with Exotic Mushrooms and Vegetables in a Salad (page 164), Christmas Casserole of Whipped Yams and Winter Squash (page 262), Lebanese Green Beans (page 238), and Holiday Pumpkin Pie (page 355) with Cashew Cream (page 96).

Stuffing

¼ cup olive oil
1 shallot, finely chopped (2 teaspoons)
1 large white onion, finely chopped (1¼ cups)
1½ cups finely chopped celery
12 cups stale whole-grain bread, cut in ½-inch cubes
2 teaspoons ground sage
½ teaspoon dried marjoram
½ teaspoon dried thyme
½ teaspoon ground celery seed
½ teaspoon paprika
Freshly ground pepper
1 tablespoon chicken-flavored vegetable stock dissolved in 2¼ cups boiling water, or 2¼ cups other strong vegetable stock, heated

Mashed Potato Crust

10 small White Rose potatoes, peeled and quartered (approximately 8 cups)
1 celery stalk
1 large garlic clove
1 bay leaf
8 peppercorns
1 scant tablespoon light miso
1 to 2 tablespoons olive oil
Freshly ground pepper
Paprika

1. Heat the oil, shallot, onion, and celery in a heavy pot. Sauté until the vegetables begin to soften, then add bread cubes, sage, marjoram, thyme, celery seed, paprika, and pepper to taste. Mix well. Cook, stirring frequently, for 5 minutes over medium-low heat.

2. Add hot vegetable stock to pot and mix well. Cover and cook over low heat for 30 minutes or longer, stirring frequently, until bread cubes have broken down. (The secret to a good stuffing is in the slow cooking and the frequent stirring.)

3. Place potatoes, celery stalks, garlic, bay leaf, and peppercorns in a large pot of cold water. Bring to a boil, cover, and simmer for 15 to 20 minutes, or until tender. Potatoes are ready when they pierce easily, but do not fall apart.

4. Use a slotted spoon to remove potatoes from water, reserving water for mashing and gravy; leave peppercorns behind. Combine ½ cup potato water with the miso and stir to completely dissolve.

5. Begin mashing potatoes, incorporating miso mixture and adding oil and pepper to taste. Add additional potato water in small increments if potatoes appear too dry.

6. Preheat oven to 375°F. Oil a deep casserole and press stuffing down gently into bottom. Top with mashed potatoes and smooth the crust with a spatula. Dust top of potatoes with paprika.

7. Bake for 45 minutes or until potatoes have formed a golden crust.

Serves 6 to 8.

Tamale Pie

1 hour, 20 minutes

A spicy casserole with South of the Border flavors, this combines chili and cornbread. Make the chili hours or even a day in advance and assemble the casserole right before baking. This pie freezes well.

Chili

1 tablespoon safflower oil
1 teaspoon minced garlic
1¼ cups finely chopped onions
¾ cup finely chopped carrots
2 cups crumbled firm tofu, wrapped for 30 minutes or frozen
2 cups chopped canned tomatoes
3 cups cooked pinto beans
¼ cup ketchup or tomato sauce
1½ cups fresh or frozen corn
3 teaspoons paprika
1 teaspoon ground cumin
¾ teaspoon chili powder
⅛ to ¼ teaspoon cayenne
½ teaspoon salt-free seasoning or salt
2 tablespoons masa

Cornbread

1 cup yellow cornmeal
1 cup whole-wheat flour
1 teaspoon baking powder
1 teaspoon baking soda
¼ cup honey
⅓ cup soft tofu
1⅞ cups Almond Milk (page 60)
1 teaspoon sunflower oil
Pinch of salt (optional)

1. Heat oil, garlic, onions, and carrots in a Dutch oven. Sauté until onions begin to soften, then add tofu and sauté 4 minutes. Add tomatoes, beans, tomato sauce, and corn. Mix well. Stir in spices and masa. Cover and simmer over medium-low heat until chili is heated through and flavors have combined, stirring occasionally, about 30 minutes.

2. Preheat oven to 375°F. Combine all the dry ingredients for cornbread in a medium bowl In a blender, combine the tofu with the liquid ingredients until creamy. Stir liquid ingredients into dry ingredients. Batter will be a little lumpy.

3. Place chili in a deep casserole. Spread batter on top of chili gently, taking care to cover chili entirely. Bake uncovered for 30 to 45 minutes. Test cornbread for doneness after 30 minutes. If a toothpick inserted in center comes out clean, casserole is ready. Cool slightly before serving.

Serves 8 to 10.

Note: For a thinner crust, cut recipe in half and bake for 25 to 30 minutes.

Potato Burek

50 minutes

This light, savory potato strudel creates such a stir every time I serve it, I can't resist including it. This recipe seems complicated. When you bite into these rolls, you feel you are eating a creation. But it is in fact among the easiest recipes in this chapter.

4 large White Rose or Idaho potatoes, peeled and coarsely grated
1 small onion, finely minced
Ground rock salt (optional)
Freshly ground pepper
2 teaspoons olive oil
1 package phyllo dough (preferably whole-wheat)
¼ cup sunflower oil combined with ¼ cup olive oil

1. Place potatoes in a colander and squeeze to press out moisture. Transfer to a medium bowl and combine with onion, salt and pepper to taste, and olive oil. Mix well and prepare to use immediately, before potatoes begin to discolor.

2. Preheat oven to 425°F. Place 1 phyllo sheet, with short side facing you, on work surface. (Cover remaining dough with slightly damp towel to prevent drying.) Fold sheet one-third up from the bottom to create a double thickness where you will place potato filling. Brush phyllo immediately with oil mixture. Spread approximately ½ cup filling along folded edge, leaving 1-inch margins along bottom and sides. Fold phyllo over filling and fold in sides. Roll burek in neat strudel-like log from bottom to top.

3. Place burek on a oiled baking sheet and immediately brush with oil. With a sharp knife, cut diagonal shallow slashes across the top of the dough—4 for dinner burek, 6 for appetizers. Repeat until filling is used up.

4. Sprinkle burek sparingly with water and bake 20 to 25 minutes, until golden.

Yields approximately 10 burek rolls.

Variation: Substitute 2 medium carrots, peeled and coarsely grated, for one of the potatoes.

Dolmas (Stuffed Grape Leaves)

90 minutes

Here's a marvelous buffet item of Middle Eastern origin.

1 (8-ounce) jar grape leaves
9 tablespoons olive oil
1 small onion, minced
1 teaspoon dried dill
3 tablespoons dried currants (optional)
1 teaspoon grated nutmeg
¼ teaspoon ground cardamom
2 cups cooked basmati rice (omit salt, since leaves are salty)
Juice of one lime (2–3 tablespoons)
Several thin slices of lemon
2 to 3 bay leaves

1. Remove grape leaves gently from the jar and rinse under cold water to remove some of the salt. Drain on layers of paper towel in a colander. If there is a stem protruding from leaf, cut it off.

2. Heat 5 tablespoons of olive oil in a large skillet. Add the onion and sauté until transparent but not brown. (Add a tablespoon of water to prevent browning, if necessary.) Add the dill, currants, nutmeg, and cardamom. Remove from heat and combine with rice. Mix thoroughly.

3. Preheat oven to 350°F. Place 1 heaping teaspoon to 2 heaping tablespoons of filling in the center of each grape leaf, depending on size of the leaf. Fold the sides of the leaves over the filling and roll gently from the bottom to the top. Arrange dolmas in a baking dish.

4. Mix the lime juice, remaining olive oil, and water to equal 1 cup of liquid. Pour over the dolmas. Top with lemon slices and bay leaves. Cover casserole with a sheet of parchment and secure with a sheet of aluminum foil. Bake for 45 minutes or until liquid is almost completely absorbed.

Serves 6 to 8.

Samosas

1 hour, 20 minutes

These spicy Indian turnovers are surprisingly easy to make.

Dough

1 cup whole-wheat pastry flour
1 tablespoon safflower oil
¼ teaspoon sea salt
½ cup water
¼ cup unbleached all-purpose flour

Filling

3 cups White Rose or red potatoes, steamed, peeled, and cubed
½ cup frozen peas
2 teaspoons sunflower oil
1 teaspoon black mustard seeds
¼ teaspoon cumin seeds
⅓ cup diced onion
1 tablespoon grated fresh ginger
2 teaspoons curry powder
½ teaspoon ground cumin
¼ teaspoon turmeric
½ teaspoon ground coriander
Dash of cayenne (optional)
¼ to ½ teaspoon sea salt
½ cup chopped fresh cilantro (optional)
1 tablespoon lemon juice
½ to 1 cup oil, for brushing and frying

To Cook

1. Combine pastry flour, oil, and salt to form a grainy mixture. Work oil into flour with your fingers. Add water and mix with fork to form a dough.

2. In 1-tablespoon increments, add all-purpose flour and knead into dough until smooth and elastic. Knead dough until it is no longer sticky, reserving any white flour you don't use for coating rolling pin and board when you are ready to roll dough. Cover dough with a cloth.

3. Steam, peel, and cut potatoes in ½-inch cubes. Set aside. Blanch peas in boiling water for 1 minute; remove from water and set aside.

4. Heat oil in a large skillet, add mustard and cumin seeds, and sizzle them until they crackle and pop. Just when they begin to jump out of the skillet, add onion and ginger, and sauté until onion begins to soften, stirring constantly.

5. Add curry powder, cumin, turmeric, coriander, cayenne, and salt and cook 2 minutes, stirring continuously. Add potatoes and peas, and mix well to coat thoroughly with spices. Stir in cilantro and lemon. Cook 2 minutes and remove from heat. Let cool.

6. Divide dough into 12 individual balls. Coat board and rolling pin with flour and roll each ball of dough into a 5-inch disk. Brush disk with oil. Add 2 tablespoons of filling to half of a disk, fold second half over filling, and squeeze edges together. Assemble remaining samosas.

7. Pour enough oil into skillet to cover bottom to a ⅛-inch depth. Heat oil and fry samosas for 2 to 3 minutes per side, or until dough is golden brown. Drain on paper towels.

Yields 12 samosas.

Tortilla Sit-Down Shuffle

35 to 40 minutes

This is not a recipe. It is a concept for a mainly vegetable meal—and a very useful one at that. We once called this the Boogie, because people would get up and down from the table to heat tortillas on the stove as they were needed. Then we devised ways to heat the tortillas right on the table, in an electric frying pan or crepe-maker. The former had the slight disadvantage of throwing off more heat than those present required to be comfortable, and the latter would turn itself off and on periodically, which delayed the heating process. Now we have discovered the perfect solution: a terra-cotta tortilla steamer.

We added "Sit Down" and "Shuffle" to the title to represent the infinite combinations that can come from the concept.

To use the terra-cotta tortilla steamer, soak the base in water for a few moments; the water is absorbed by the unglazed pottery inside the steamer. Then fill the base with tortillas, cover, and heat in your oven for 10 to 15 minutes. The damp heat permeates the tortillas. At the table, in the covered steamer, they remain hot and soft throughout the meal.*

The Tortilla Sit-Down Shuffle is an innovative way to arrange a meal around lots of steamed vegetables, raw vegetables, and whole grains (in the form of the tortillas). Corn tortillas lend a special flavor to the meal. Soft and hot, they can't be beat.

Hot corn tortillas
Steamed vegetables (one or more of the following: broccoli, cauliflower, asparagus, zucchini, Brussels sprouts, green beans, yellow squash, carrots)
Sautéed mushrooms (optional)
Raw vegetables (one or more of the following: shredded carrots, cucumber spears, avocado slices, tomato slices, shredded lettuce, sprouts, sliced pickle), or a vegetable salad with dressing, or cole slaw

1. Cut and steam an assortment of the vegetables your family enjoys. Workable lengths are about ½ inch thick by 2 inches long. Create a steamed vegetable platter. Grate carrot, slice tomatoes, cut cucumbers into spears, shred lettuce, and add some sprouts to create your raw vegetable platter (or use your favorite salad in place of the raw vegetables).

2. Mash avocado in a bowl for a spread. Also place mustard, mayonnaise, or Almonnaise (page 98) in bowls.

3. When everyone is seated, give each person a tortilla. (Be sure to have heated at least 3 per person.) Everyone then selects and spreads his or her tortilla with condiments and a line of the vegetables, steamed or raw. Children tend to keep it simple; don't be surprised if they choose only cucumbers or steamed green beans. On the other hand, men usually pile it *all* on. Once the vegetables are in place, the tortillas are rolled tightly around the filling, held in the hand, and enjoyed like a burrito or taquito.

*Treasure Craft makes a handy tortilla steamer.

Mushroom-Leek Crepes

crepes: 45
filling and baking: 30 minutes

Crepes

1 cup unbleached white flour
1 cup whole-wheat pastry flour
¼ cup nutritional yeast (omit if unavailable and reduce water to 3 cups)
½ teaspoon baking powder
Dash of salt (optional)
3½ cups water
2 tablespoons sunflower oil
1 cup silken tofu
Oil to coat pan

Filling

2 to 3 tablespoons olive oil
1 pound fresh mushrooms
1 cup thinly sliced leeks
1 teaspoon dried thyme
2 tablespoons whole-wheat pastry flour
½ teaspoon ground coriander
½ teaspoon curry powder
1½ cups water (or potato broth, if you have some on hand)
1½ tablespoons light miso
2 teaspoons lemon juice
1 tablespoon minced fresh parsley
Freshly ground pepper
Additional minced parsley, for garnish

1. Puree all ingredients except tofu in a blender. Add tofu and blend until smooth.

2. Heat a 9-inch nonstick crepe pan over medium-high heat until a drop of water sizzles. Coat pan with oil and pour in ¼ cup of batter. Tilt and swirl the pan so that the batter forms an even layer over the whole surface. Cook until the edges loosen from the side of the pan and the top starts to bubble. Flip crepe over and cook on other side until flecked with gold. Stack finished crepes in a dish to cool. You should have about 24 crepes.

3. Heat oil in a large skillet with mushrooms, leeks, and thyme. Sauté for 2 to 3 minutes, stirring continuously, over medium-high heat, then stir in flour and continue sautéing for 1 to 2 minutes longer. Add coriander and curry powder and sauté briefly.

4. Dissolve miso in water and add to mushroom mixture. Bring to a boil over high heat and simmer, stirring, to allow sauce to thicken. Stir in lemon juice, parsley, and pepper to taste. Remove from heat and allow to cool slightly.

5. Preheat oven to 375°F. Remove ½ cup of sauce from filling, taking care not to remove mushrooms. Set aside. Place crepes on a work surface. Fill each crepe with 2 to 3 tablespoons of filling. Roll and place seam side down in a lightly oiled baking dish. Drizzle filled crepes with reserved sauce and bake for 20 to 30 minutes, or until sauce is slightly bubbly and crepes are golden. Garnish with additional minced parsley, if desired.

Serves 4.

Note: The filling can be prepared 24 to 48 hours in advance. Crepes can also be used for Winter Squash Blintzes (page 317).

Winter Squash Blintzes

1 hour, 15 minutes

The delicate flavor and texture of the filling for these blintzes are nicely complemented by the moist, eggless crepes, tangy "Stedda" Sour Cream, and snipped chives.

4 pounds butternut squash
4 ounces tofu (soft or firm)
2 teaspoons FruitSource
4 tablespoons orange juice
¼ to ½ teaspoon salt
Freshly ground pepper
¼ teaspoon grated nutmeg
¼ teaspoon ground coriander
24 crepes (page 316)
2 tablespoons sunflower oil or soy margarine
¼ to ½ cup "Stedda" Sour Cream (page 105)
2 tablespoons snipped chives

1. Peel and seed the squash. Cut in 1-inch chunks and place in a covered steamer over boiling water. Steam for 20 minutes or until soft. Cool squash for 10 to 15 minutes.

2. Puree squash with tofu, FruitSource, and orange juice (in several batches, if necessary) in a food processor or blender. Gently process in salt, pepper to taste, nutmeg, and coriander. (Mixture can be refrigerated for up to 4 days if you are not going to make blintzes immediately.)

3. Arrange crepes on work surface, cooked side down. Spoon ¼ cup filling into center of each crepe. Fold bottom and top flaps over puree, then fold in side flaps. You will have a 2½-inch package. (At this point, blintzes can be placed in freezer on a foil-lined cookie sheet. When they are partially frozen, wrap them tightly. They will keep up to 2 months. When ready to use, brush with oil and bake frozen for 30 minutes in preheated 350°F oven.)

4. Preheat oven to 400°F. Arrange blintzes in a shallow baking dish in one layer. (You may need 2 dishes.) Brush with oil and bake until puffy and lightly browned, approximately 20 minutes.

5. Top with tiny dollops of "sour cream" and a dusting of chives.

Yields 24 blintzes.

Potato, Cauliflower, and Onion Fajitas

25 minutes

Fajitas are a very popular dish in the southwestern United States. They require tortillas and a good salsa, mild or spicy, according to your taste.

1 tablespoon safflower oil
2 to 3 medium red-skinned potatoes, thinly sliced
1/2 small cauliflower, thinly sliced
1 large onion, coarsely chopped
1/4 to 1/2 cup teriyaki sauce
Juice of one small lime
Water as necessary to prevent scorching
6 flour tortillas, whole wheat, if available
Salsa
Sliced avocado

1. Sauté onions, potatoes, and cauliflower in oil for 3 minutes. Add teriyaki sauce and lime juice and continue sautéing vegetables for 15 minutes, adding small increments of water as necessary to prevent scorching. Set filling aside when vegetables are tender.

2. Heat 6 tortillas in a dry skillet. Spoon a line of filling onto the center of each tortilla. Top with a tablespoon or two of salsa and sliced avocado. Roll crepe-style.

Serve with a vegetable soup for a hearty lunch.

Serves 3.

Spinach Pie

1 hour

Whole-Wheat Crust

1¼ cups whole-wheat pastry flour
Pinch of salt
6 tablespoons soy or safflower margarine
3 to 4 tablespoons ice water

Filling

1 tablespoon olive oil
1 cup minced onions
2 cups finely chopped fresh spinach, or 1 10-ounce package frozen chopped spinach, thawed
¼ teaspoon grated nutmeg
1 pound firm tofu
2 tablespoons brown rice vinegar
1 tablespoon light miso
1 tablespoon tahini
1 teaspoon Dijon-style mustard
1 garlic clove, pressed

1. Prepare crust. Sift flour and salt into a deep bowl. Add cold margarine, cut into small bits. Cut margarine into flour with pastry cutter or two knives, until mixture resembles coarse meal. Stir in ice water with a fork and mix until dough forms into a ball. Turn out onto floured board and knead briefly. Form into a ball, flatten with the palm of your hand, wrap in waxed paper and refrigerate while you prepare filling. (Pastry can actually be prepared several hours in advance and refrigerated until you are ready to use. If prepared well in advance, bring to room temperature for an hour before rolling.)

2. Prepare filling. Heat oil and onions in a medium skillet and sauté until translucent. Add spinach and nutmeg, and sauté one minute.

3. Combine tofu, vinegar, miso, tahini, mustard, and garlic in a food processor or by hand and puree until creamy. Combine with spinach in a bowl and mix well by hand.

4. Preheat oven to 400°F. On a floured board, gently roll out pie crust to fit a 9-inch pie plate. (Any cracks in the crust can be repaired once you have transferred it to the pie plate.) Crimp or flute edges. Pour filling into crust and bake for 30 minutes. Serve chilled.

Serves 6 to 8 as a main course or 12 as an appetizer.

Variation: Substitute 2 cups chopped asparagus for spinach.

Note: For a crustless pie pour mixture into a lightly oiled 9-inch baking dish and bake as above.

Country Pot Pie

1 hour, 20 minutes

Serve this with Spinach and Sun-dried Tomato Salad (page 147) or Classic Green Salad (page 140), Lemon Beets (page 223), and Corn on the Cob with "Stedda" Butter Sauce (page 233).

Pie

½ cup whole-wheat pastry flour
2 tablespoons nutritional yeast
Ground rock salt (optional)
Pinch of ground sage
1 teaspoon garlic powder
1½ cups firm tofu, cut in ½-inch cubes
1 tablespoon olive oil
1 cup diced onions
1 cup diced celery
1 cup diced carrots
1¼ cups petite peas
1½ cups diced potatoes
2 to 3 tablespoons water
2 tablespoons soy sauce
1 double recipe whole-wheat crust (page 318)

Gravy

½ cup nutritional yeast
¼ cup whole-wheat pastry flour
⅓ cup olive oil
1½ cups water
2 to 3 tablespoons soy sauce
Ground rock salt (optional)
Freshly ground pepper

1. Combine flour, yeast, salt, sage, and ½ teaspoon garlic powder in a small brown paper bag. Add tofu cubes, shake well to coat thoroughly, and set aside.

2. Roll out 60 percent of crust on a floured surface. (Crust will be thin.) Place in 9-inch pie plate, leaving edges uncut. Cover with a damp towel and set aside. Wrap remaining dough and refrigerate.

3. Heat oil, onions, and celery in a large skillet. Sauté until translucent, then add carrots, peas, and potatoes. Sauté 3 to 4 minutes, stirring frequently. Add water, cover, and steam over medium-low heat until carrots are slightly tender. Remove cover and stir in tofu. Sauté until tofu is browned, adding remaining ½ teaspoon garlic powder and soy sauce.

4. Preheat oven to 400°F. Prepare gravy. Combine yeast and flour in a medium skillet and toast until aromatic. Add oil and whisk until smooth, then add water slowly, stirring with a whisk until gravy begins to thicken. Stir in soy sauce and salt and pepper to taste.

5. Combine gravy with tofu-vegetable filling and mix thoroughly. Pour into pie shell. Roll out remaining dough to cover pie. Crimp edges and prick top with a fork. Bake for 30 to 40 minutes, or until top is golden.

Serves 6 to 8.

Spanokopita

45 minutes

Here are the triangular cheese and spinach pies so popular in Greece.

2 packages frozen spinach, or 2 pounds fresh
1 large onion, chopped
1 tablespoon olive oil
1 cup chopped green onions
2½ to 3 cups "Stedda" Ricotta (page 106)
¼ teaspoon grated nutmeg
Freshly ground pepper
3 tablespoons chopped fresh dill, or 2 teaspoons dried
½ cup chopped fresh parsley
1 package phyllo dough (preferably whole-wheat)
Olive oil

1. Steam frozen spinach until tender; chop fresh spinach coarsely (discarding stems) and steam in a large covered pot until juices run out. Press in a colander to remove as much juice as possible. Set aside.

2. Heat onion and oil in a large skillet. Add green onions and sauté over medium heat for 5 minutes, stirring frequently.

3. Combine tofu "ricotta," nutmeg, pepper to taste, dill, parsley, and onion mixture with spinach in a medium bowl. Mix well and set aside.

4. Preheat oven to 375°F. Cut phyllo sheets into three 5 × 12-inch strips. Stack on work surface and cover with slightly moistened kitchen towel. Take 1 strip from stack, cover stack, and immediately brush strip with oil. Fold one-fourth of strip up and brush again. Place generous 2 tablespoons of filling at bottom of folded strip. Fold end of strip up diagonally over filling, forming a triangle. Fold up once again until you have reached top and have a triangular shape in front of you. (Fold and tuck any edges that distract from triangle.) Brush with oil and place on a lightly oiled cookie sheet. Continue until you have used all the "ricotta." Bake for 20 minutes or until spanokopita are golden. Transfer to rack to cool.

Yields 16–20 spanokopita.

HOW TO FOLD SPANOKOPITA

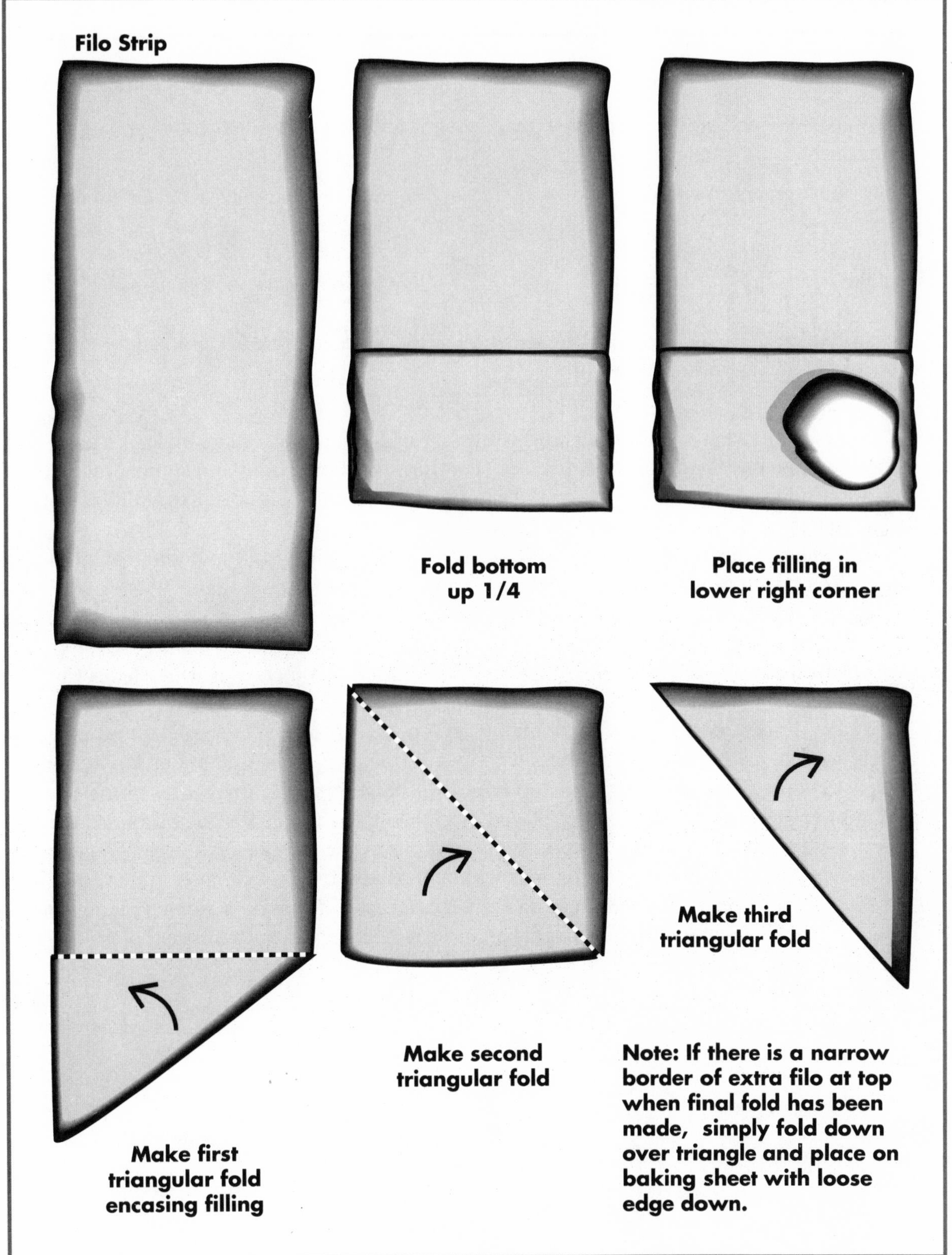

Filo Strip
Fold bottom up 1/4
Place filling in lower right corner
Make first triangular fold encasing filling
Make second triangular fold
Make third triangular fold
Note: If there is a narrow border of extra filo at top when final fold has been made, simply fold down over triangle and place on baking sheet with loose edge down.

Superb Vegetable Sushi

1 hour, 20 minutes

A favorite—and so much easier to make than it appears. A handy bamboo rolling mat helps enormously.

1 cup short-grain brown rice
2¼ cups water
1 teaspoon sunflower oil
2 tablespoons brown rice vinegar
8 round, crisp green beans
8 carrot strips, in ½-inch lengthwise pieces
8 strips cucumber, in ¼-inch lengthwise pieces
Handful of fresh chives, cut in 2-inch lengths (optional)
8 strips firm tofu, cut ¼ inch thick
½ cup tofu sauce, barbecue sauce, or tamari
4 sheets nori
Black sesame seeds (optional)

1. Measure rice into a bowl, fill bowl with some water, and wash rice well for 1 minute. Drain. Bring 2¼ cups water to a boil, add rice and oil, return to a boil, cover, and simmer over very low heat for 40 minutes. Remove from heat and allow to sit, without lifting lid, for 10 additional minutes. Stir in vinegar and turn out onto a platter to dry and cool.

2. Blanch beans and carrot strips in plenty of boiling water for 3 to 4 minutes, or until just tender. Remove from water with slotted spoon and shock under cold running water.

3. Arrange cucumber strips, carrot strips, beans, and chives on a platter with tofu strips. Measure tofu sauce into a small bowl and set near work area.

4. Toast nori. Turn a burner to high and hold nori 2 to 4 inches over heat, sheet by sheet, turning, allowing nori to change from black to bright green but taking care not to char.

5. Lay 1 sheet of nori on a sushi mat. Place one-fourth of rice, covering two-thirds of nori closest to you, patting it firmly to the side edges and leaving 1 inch empty at top bottom edge closest to you and 2 inches empty at top edge (see illustration). In the center of the rice, place a strip of vegetables and tofu, evenly placed close together, and dab a line of tofu sauce on the rice along the line of vegetables. Begin to curl mat up over nori, rice, and vegetables, guiding it to roll over the filling. Press firmly on nori with mat as you roll so that sushi roll is tight.

6. Cut each nori roll into 8 slices with a serrated knife. Place on a serving platter and dust lightly with black sesame seeds or dulse flakes, if desired, taking care not to cover colorful vegetable pattern in center of roll.

Serves 2.

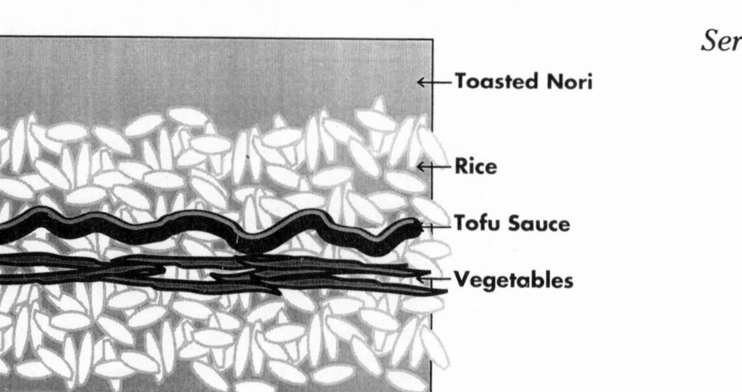

Cucumber-Avocado Roll

1 hour, 10 minutes

These are even easier than Vegetable Sushi because there is no blanching.

8 thin lengthwise slices firm avocado
8 thin slices cucumber
Alfalfa or sunflower sprouts
4 teaspoons Umeboshi plum paste or tofu sauce
4 sheets nori

Follow process for arranging slices of avocado and cucumber in line on top of rice, as for recipe on page 322. Top with sparse, but even, line of sprouts and paint a line of plum paste along filling. Roll and slice.

Serves 2.

Baked Spring Rolls

1 hour, 15 minutes

Rolls

1 white onion
1 bunch green onions
1 tablespoon safflower oil
1 teaspoon minced fresh ginger, or ½ teaspoon ground
2 cups shredded carrots
4 cups shredded green cabbage
2 cups bean sprouts
¼ cup tamari
2 teaspoons roasted sesame oil
Black pepper
1 package whole-wheat phyllo dough
¼ cup sesame or sunflower oil
Sesame seeds

Hot Chinese Mustard

½ cup Dijon-style mustard
2 teaspoons dry mustard
2 teaspoons raw honey

1. Using the coarse shredding blade of food processor, shred the onion. Cut the green onions into very thin lengthwise slivers.

2. Heat wok. Add safflower oil, then add ginger, green onions, and white onion. Stir-fry several minutes, then add carrots and cabbage. Stir-fry briefly until colors turn bright. Stir in bean sprouts.

3. Add the tamari, roasted sesame oil, and pepper to taste to the vegetable mixture. Mix well and set aside to cool completely.

4. Preheat oven to 500°F. Working quickly to prevent drying out, cut entire batch of phyllo sheets in half, forming 2 stacks approximately 8 by 13 inches. Place one stack on top of the other, and cover immediately with slightly dampened kitchen towel.

5. Remove a sheet of dough from the stack. Fold it to form a square. Brush square lightly with sesame oil, then place a heaping tablespoon of filling in a line along folded edge of square closest to you. Gently fold dough and filling toward single edge. After 2 folds, fold sides in over filling. Continue folding up toward single edge until filling is completely encased in neat roll. Any tears in phyllo will be covered as you continue rolling.

6. Place roll on a lightly oiled cookie sheet. Brush immediately with oil. Repeat process, taking care to keep unused dough covered with damp cloth. Sprinkle rolls with sesame seeds. Bake for approximately 10 to 15 minutes, or until rolls are golden. (These may be made in advance and reheated at high temperature [475°F] briefly before serving.)

7. Mix ingredients for mustard sauce, and pass as a dip.

Yields approximately 40 small spring rolls.

15

Baking with Love

The recipes in this chapter are personal, time-tested favorites that I think you will enjoy. Baking is a homey art. With simple techniques, anyone can make wonderful cookies, cakes, and pies. Your choice of ingredients, of course, makes a difference, but the love you put into what you bake is the ingredient that people feel the most. Just caring enough to do it says a lot!

THESE BAKED SWEETS ARE FOR YOUR HEALTH

Perhaps you have noticed that this book draws heavily on personal experience. What I have found to be true about food in my own efforts to define a healthful life-style, and what has supported and substantiated that experience in the work of others I have studied, has defined the contents. Likewise, in this final chapter, I would be doing you a disservice if I did not include my own experiences.

Sweet is one of the palate's natural cravings. (If you taste mother's milk, our first and primary food, you find that it is inordinately sweet, which is precisely what Nature intends for us.) That craving for sweets has by and large been satisfied for me and my family by fresh, natural sweet and luscious fruit—so much so, that we indulge in baked sweets only on occasion.

As a cook, I have not put the bulk of my efforts into preparing sweet, baked foods. When I turned my attention to this subject, to perfect the recipes I had long used and develop new ones, like a little messenger from the gods my daughter Lisa came to work with me full time. She brought with her a flair, a natural talent and creativity for baking. With self-assurance and enthusiasm she turned her attention toward sweet treats and began to pull one sweet-smelling, mouth-watering creation after another from our ovens. Many of these recipes are the result of this collaboration between mother and daughter, which has greatly enhanced our baking perspective.

Fresh baked goodies have played a vital part in nearly everyone's experience. Many people have fond memories of the sweet aroma of fresh bread, cookies, or muffins wafting through the house. No one who has ever experienced this particularly human pleasure would deny its emotional benefits. However, there has been debate lately regarding the physical benefits of sweets.

Baked goodies *can* be wholesome and pure. They can be perfectly legitimate food choices in a healthful diet. On a cold winter day, a hot muffin with a cup of peppermint tea may be just what is necessary to smooth you out, ground you, and leave you feeling satisfied and ready to get on with the rest of your life. But the ingredients of that muffin are very important. They determine whether it is a threat to your health or a delicious food of high nutritional integrity. The truth is that baked foods have become more and more suspect only because of the ingredients usually chosen. These have been highly processed materials, stripped of nutritional value that, in turn, strip the body of its nutrient reserves. They usurp body energy and give back none.

JUST CHANGE THE INGREDIENTS

We can return to the basics our grandmothers and great-grandmothers relied on before everybody jumped on the refined-food bandwagon. *And* we can begin to take advantage of breakthrough ingredients that are available to fill this very need. We will want to reassess the value of the "white and light" we have come to expect with highly refined materials, and reacquaint ourselves with the down-to-earth look and feel of cakes or cookies made from wholesome, wholefood ingredients. With the first bite, the more homey taste of this food will make sense to you. It will taste real. You will sense that it will do "good" in your body, and you will be perfectly happy that it will also look real!

The recipes on the following pages redefine what "good" really means in baking. The key, of course, is that the food is so delicious that it really does satisfy. Fortunately, since much of the inherent damage from refined baked food results from the addictive quality of some of its ingredients, it is less likely that people who eat *wholesome* baked foods will experience the need to continuously maintain or increase their consumption. The best way to enjoy homebaked goodies is to have them on days when the bulk of your food intake is fresh fruit, salads, and light vegetable dishes or soups. If, instead, you are eating complex starches and heavy proteins, avoid baked foods; they will make you feel as if you have overeaten.

There is a new psychology here. Now that you are making foods that are truly good for you, you no longer have to treat them as contraband or feel guilty. That guilt, you realize, is nothing more than an emotional manifestation of the body's instinctive cringe from the harm being inflicted on it. You can make baked foods a more central part of the meal, rather than something everybody pines over. Make fresh baked breads, muffins, and biscuits the main event. Surround them with wholesome soups, salads, and vegetables. Giving them a stamp of approval relieves any tendency to be compulsive about them.

Avoiding Refined White Sugar

In my early adult years, I was a victim of refined sugar. Like William Dufty, author of *Sugar Blues,*[1] my moods swung from roaring high to reeling low; my energy soared one moment and

[1]Warner Books; New York, 1976. This book should be required reading for everyone, from policemen and teachers to mothers and grandmothers, from politicians to doctors and nurses.

plummeted the next; my mind was confused and clear decisions were hard to make. My weight fluctuated, my diet became erratic, I was frequently depressed, and symptoms of ill health were increasingly serious rather than merely chronic. I was, like billions of people worldwide, feeling the impact of a product that is among the most widely distributed and least understood. As Dr. John Yudkin said,

> **If only a fraction of what is already known about the effects of sugar were to be revealed in relation to any other material used as a food additive, that material would promptly be banned. . . .** [1]

When I read *Sugar Blues,* and I saw my own life described on its pages, I began to understand the history and politics of refined sugar, as well as its nearly universal effect. Abruptly, I made the decision that it would never cross my lips again, and (with a few exceptions in fifteen years) it never has. I also resolved to do everything in my power to keep it from my children. That wasn't as easy as it sounds, however, since refined sugar can be found in many unsweet places, from spaghetti sauce to crackers, from salad dressings to gravy enhancers. In fact, sugar is overtly and covertly included in almost everything Americans eat. As a nation we consume an average of 140 pounds per person per year. That's ¾ cup a day! If you think you don't use that much, remember that a 12-ounce can of soda contains 9 teaspoons of refined sugar. One 8-ounce serving of fruit-flavored yogurt contains almost as much. No wonder we're practically a nation of sugar addicts!

The Effects of Refined White Sugar

Refined white sugar is an empty food, a simple carbohydrate derived from sugarcane or sugar beets. But in the processing, it is completely stripped of all fiber and nutrients. When refined white sugar is eaten in any quantity, the body sets in motion its blood-sugar regulating system. Because sugar is a simple carbohydrate that does not have to be converted and has no fiber to slow the process, the bloodstream is suddenly overloaded with glucose. This forces the pancreas to pump out larger amounts of insulin to metabolize the glucose. The extra insulin very quickly burns off the extra glucose, and then remains in the bloodstream for hours, continuing to burn glucose and causing low blood-sugar levels, or "sugar blues." The initial surge of energy felt after the sugar is eaten is quickly replaced by a tired, unsatiated state (reflecting the body's depleted blood sugar level) and a craving for more sweets. A vicious cycle is set in motion, where blood sugar and insulin levels are continuously out of balance, leading to hypoglycemia or diabetes (one of the ten leading causes of death in the United States). Additionally, these continuous chemical changes in the body contribute to obesity, as the individual overconsumes sweets to satisfy the cravings caused by low blood sugar. What a depressing scenario! All due to refined sugar consumption!

[1]Dr. John Yudkin, Physician Biochemist and Emeritus Professor of Nutrition at London University, quoted in Kathy Hishijo, *The Art of Dieting Without Dieting* (Glendale, CA.: The Self-Sufficiency Association, 1986).

THE "BAKING WITH LOVE" SOLUTION

To ensure that your sweet treats are health supportive, these recipes incorporate sweeteners other than refined white sugar, along with whole-grain and low fat ingredients. We are also using, whenever possible, a *lower ratio* of sweetener to other ingredients to make the product healthier overall. You will probably find that these baked foods have a more subtle, mellower sweetness compared to those that are made with refined white sugar. In our opinion, they are *perfectly* sweet, not too sweet. Their sweetness harmonizes with, rather than dominates, other flavors in the food.

Speaking as a mother who has witnessed with distress the refined sugar highs and lows in her own children, I can attest that when I watch children bite into a cookie, muffin or other baked food from this group of recipes, I am confident and happy in a very deep gratifying way. I hope you will feel that way too!

THE BEST TIME TO EAT SWEETS

Certainly, not for dessert, when the stomach is already hard at work on foods of different natures. Instead, let's resurrect the traditional tea meal when the occasion warrants. At tea, which comes several hours after lunch, when your stomach is registering "empty" and dinner is still several hours away, have your chosen sweet with a cup of herbal tea. Without other foods to work on simultaneously, your stomach will focus on the sweet. When you have dinner, eat a little lighter than usual, feeling satisfied with salad and some soup. For some people, even a fruit meal is sufficient.

MODERATION IS THE KEY

When you choose to satisfy a sweet craving with baked food, be aware that you will not always experience the vibrant, full-of-life feeling you get from fruit. Baked sweets create a different kind of energy. It is more mellow, slower, and, if you overeat or indulge too often, can make you feel quite heavy. The rule of thumb with baked sweets is to *eat them in moderation* and when the stomach does not have other food in it. Unlike fruit, sweets *can* be eaten with other foods, but they digest better when eaten alone.

Baked sweets are also better in cool weather, when the body can benefit from their warming qualities. The calories they contain will help generate the heat the body needs. In warm weather, sweet fruit is a better choice because it's low in fat; its high water content helps cool the body and keeps it feeling light and energetic.

Use Aluminum-Free Baking Powder

When baking quick breads and muffins or cookies, use baking powder that is *aluminum free.*

> **Studies have shown that aluminum salts can be absorbed from the intestines and concentrated in various human tissues, and that high aluminum levels are found in the brains of patients with Alzheimer's and Parkinson's diseases. In addition, aluminum is linked to bone degeneration and kidney dysfunction.**[1]

With all this known, you probably would wonder why aluminum is allowed in baking powder and why anyone would use it. The baking powders that contain aluminum are "double-acting," indicating that although some of the leavening power is released when the mix is prepared, the greater leavening takes place when the item is baked. This produces a very fine, light texture, and is appreciated particularly in commercial baking, where mixes often sit for long periods before they go into the oven. But it isn't necessary for your baking. For a lighter texture, bake the mix immediately.

If you wish to be sure your baking powder is aluminum free, you have two choices:

- Make your own baking powder from:

2 parts cream of tartar
1 part baking soda
2 parts arrowroot

Prepare ahead of time and keep on hand. Store in an airtight container.

- Rumford baking powder contains no aluminum. It is made from calcium phosphate (extracted from phosphate rock), bicarbonate of soda, and cornstarch. It is double-acting, so it reacts both in the bowl and in the oven.

[1]*Shoppers Guide to Natural Foods* (Garden City, NJ: Avery Publishing Group, 1987), p. 33.

THE *FIT FOR LIFE* BAKING PANTRY

There are many healthful, good-tasting products you can use in baking. Since some of them may be unfamiliar, refer to this section when you need information about new ingredients.

Sweeteners

Honey is the product of the blossom nectar gathered by bees and converted into a sweet, sticky liquid. It takes one bee its *entire lifetime* to make one teaspoon of honey, so this is a food that should be consumed with a certain amount of awe. Honey is primarily a simple carbohydrate, which is absorbed rapidly into the bloodstream, immediately raising the blood-sugar level. As such, it is not a balanced sweetener. Honey is sweeter than other sweeteners so less is always better than more. Use mild-flavored honey in baking.

Maple syrup is produced in a brief yearly season when sugar maple sap is tapped. About 40 gallons of sap must be boiled down to make 1 gallon of syrup, which is why pure maple syrup is so expensive. Maple syrup is valued for its exquisite flavor rather than its nutritive qualities, of which it has few. It is composed primarily of simple carbohydrates and some traces of minerals. If using maple syrup, only use pure or fancy; "maple-flavored" syrups contain mostly additives and as little as 3 percent real syrup. Maple syrup should be refrigerated after opening. Maple sugar is the crystalline form of maple syrup.

Brown rice syrup is a *balanced* sweetener. It is primarily a complex carbohydrate, which enters the bloodstream more slowly than honey or maple syrup. Brown rice syrup does not contain as high a concentration of nutrients as does barley malt syrup, but it contains enough trace minerals and B-vitamins to make it a valid choice when available. It is less concentrated in flavor than other sweeteners and adds a mild, rather than a bold, sweetness.

Sorghum molasses is sometimes called Chinese sugarcane. Sorghum is a plant related to millet. Sorghum molasses was a common sweetener in eighteenth and nineteenth century America, particularly in the South. The stalks of the plant are crushed, and the sweet syrup released is cooked and clarified into a dark syrup rich in minerals such as potassium, iron, calcium, and the B-vitamins. Blackstrap molasses is an acceptable substitute. Use sorghum molasses in place of cane molasses in any recipe.

Barley malt syrup is less sweet than both molasses and honey, and on a fairly even par with brown rice syrup. High in complex carbohydrates, it enters the bloodstream slowly and can be considered a *balanced* sweetener that will not upset blood-sugar levels. The malting process increases the level of B-vitamins in this product. It also contains some trace minerals.

Date sugar is ground from dehydrated dates and cannot be considered a sugar, since it is actually a food. It is high in fiber and rich in a wide range of vitamins and minerals, including iron. Date sugar can be used interchangeably with FruitSource in cakes, muffins, and batter breads. It does not dissolve, however, when added to liquids. Date sugar's most limiting factor is its high price.

Flours

Whole-wheat flour comes in varying grinds, but is not always labeled accordingly, except in the case of stone-ground flour. This latter label implies a coarse grind, and is generally considered the finest choice. Stone grinding exposes the grain to less heat, thus protecting the nutrients, notably the B-vitamins and vitamin E. Keep in an airtight container and store in the refrigerator or freeze if you don't use often. Good for breads, rolls, crackers, and pancakes.

Whole-wheat pastry flour is made from a softer wheat with a lower gluten content than regular whole-wheat flour. It has a finer texture than whole-wheat flour and retains the germ and bran. It gives baked food a lighter texture. If a recipe calls for whole-wheat flour, use whole-wheat flour, not whole-wheat pastry flour. Use whole-wheat pastry flour for cakes, pastries, cookies, and muffins.

Unbleached all-purpose flour is a refined, enriched wheat flour that has not been bleached. It is most useful when combined with other flours, to produce finer textures or lighter risings. Germ and bran have been removed.

Oat flour retains most of the nutrients present in whole oats, such as seven B-vitamins plus significant amounts of iron, calcium, and phosphorus. The bran and germ remain intact in oat flour since the oats are not refined before processing. It can be used interchangeably with whole-wheat pastry flour in some recipes and in combination with white flours in many others.

Brown rice flour contains a wide range of B-vitamins and minerals as well as vitamin E. Most successfully used when combined in low ratios with other flours. Adding brown rice flour to baked food usually results in a drier product.

Soy flour, like soybeans, is 20 percent fat (a small percentage of which is saturated) and 34 percent protein. It retains most of the original nutrients, notably the B-complex vitamins, vitamin E, phosphorus, calcium, and iron. It's made from raw soybeans that have been dehulled, cracked, and finely ground. Soy flour contributes to a tender, moist, and nicely browned finish in baked goods, but it has an assertive flavor, so always use in moderation. It can successfully replace up to 25 percent of all-purpose flour in baked goods. Even when used in small amounts, soy flour increases the usability of the proteins in accompanying grain flours, which is why it is considered a nutritional booster.

Millet flour is a nutritious, easily digested grain flour that provides high-quality protein, a wide range of B-vitamins, and calcium, potassium, and particularly iron. Millet flour cannot be used on its own, as the results are slightly bitter. Combine with other flours for a fine texture and highly nutritious product.

Leavening Agents and Binders

Tofu. Use as substitute for eggs and other dairy products in many baking recipes. The results are truly miraculous. Tofu is high in protein, vitamins, minerals, and polyunsaturated fat (including omega-3 fatty acids), low in saturated fat with no cholesterol, and imparts a light, moist texture yet does not alter the flavor of the product.

Egg replacer is a powdered formula consisting of potato starch, tapioca flour, leavening, and carbohydrate gum. Combined with water, it achieves an egglike consistency, and the solution can then be added to batters as an egg would be. Available in natural foods stores.

Banana. Half of a small banana will bind a batter and create a lighter, moister result.

Baking soda is also known as bicarbonate of soda. It is used to neutralize and leaven batters with acid ingredients.

Baking powder gives volume and lighter texture to the product. Only *aluminum-free* baking powders are recommended (see page 329). "Double-acting" indicates that the product will rise both when batter is prepared and during baking. Aluminum-free baking powder contains calcium phosphate, bicarbonate of soda, and cornstarch.

Successful Baking with Wholefood Ingredients

1. When making cake batter, use a food processor, hand blender, electric mixer, or whisk to incorporate air into the wet mixture. The final product will have a lighter texture.
2. When using a food processor to add dry ingredients to a creamed mixture, use the pulse button and process just to blend. Overprocessing will result in a tough cake.
3. Always preheat your oven, so it is the correct temperature when ready to bake. Some ovens are slower than others, and preheating instructions in individual recipes cannot take into account these differences. Normally, ovens need 10 to 15 minutes to preheat, and most recipes allow that much time. If your oven takes longer, set it sooner. Batters that wait while the oven preheats will not rise fully and the product will be dense.
4. If a recipe calls for a 9 × 13 × 2-inch baking pan, you can divide the batter between two 9-inch round pans or two 8-inch square pans; baking time is then slightly reduced. Another alternative is to make cupcakes. An 8-inch cake will yield approximately 24 cupcakes; baking time is usually 20 to 30 minutes for cupcakes.
5. To test for doneness, insert a metal cake tester or wooden toothpick in the center of the cake. If it comes out clean, the cake is done. Another test is to lightly touch the top of the cake. If it springs back, it is done.
6. Oven temperature specifications for baking are not flexible. Use an oven thermometer to check your oven temperature, and adjust the setting to ensure the exact temperature indicated in the recipe.
7. Cakes and breads made from unrefined ingredients should be stored in the refrigerator if not used within the first day or two after baking. Most cookies can be stored at room temperature for extended periods of time, owing to their low moisture content. It is very disappointing to create something delicious, only to have it spoil a few days later because it should have been refrigerated.
8. Most baked foods can be frozen, but the longer they remain in the freezer, the greater the loss of flavor and texture. Wrap well to prevent freezer burn.
9. If you are dividing or multiplying a recipe, increase or decrease the number of baking pans you use. When dividing, use a smaller pan.
10. Stainless-steel bakeware is recommended for cakes and cookies. Tinned steel is also acceptable. Pyrex can be used for some recipes, but be aware that the recipe will brown faster in glass. If using Pyrex, lower the oven temperature a few degrees.
11. Keep maple syrup refrigerated after opening. Sorghum or unsulphured molasses can be used whenever a recipe calls for molasses.
12. Use a mildly flavored honey to avoid overpowering the other flavors in your recipe. To measure honey, first measure your oil or rub a little oil inside the measuring cup, then use the same cup to measure the honey; the oily coating allows the honey to slide out without sticking.

Agar-agar flakes are a seaweed product used for gelling. At 75 percent carbohydrate, it is high in a form of fiber that passes through the body undigested; it adds bulk to the diet and has a beneficial laxative effect. Agar-agar contains iron, calcium, potassium, and iodine as well as a number of vitamins, including B_6, B_{12}, C, D, and K. A highly recommended ingredient.

Arrowroot is derived from the root of a tropical plant. It's a silky white thickening agent that works quickly, without the gummy texture that flour sometimes imparts. One tablespoon of arrowroot thickens 1 cup of liquid; it should be dissolved first in cold water. Arrowroot is interchangeable with cornstarch in terms of culinary properties, but higher in nutritional value.

Flavorings

Pure vanilla extract is achieved by soaking the vanilla bean in water or alcohol. Imitation vanilla is a product of synthetic, chemical ingredients and is not recommended.

Carob is a powder that is ground from the pods of the evergreen carob tree. It is most commonly used as a substitute for cocoa, owing to the similarity of color, texture, and cooking properties. Carob, *unlike chocolate,* contains a negligible amount of fat, *no* caffeine, and encourages, rather than inhibits, absorption of calcium. Carob contains calcium, phosphorus, and iron.

Carob chips are made from barley malt, corn malt, carob powder, and lecithin. Since they contain no refined sugar or dairy solids, they are preferred for baking.

Coffee substitutes are made from a varying combination of roasted rye, barley, chicory, beetroot, and other ingredients. They contain no caffeine, and are useful in baking where a mocha taste is desired, in conjunction with carob powder. Carob and coffee substitutes give us a pleasing chocolate taste.

Oils and Butter Substitutes

Pure soy margarine contains liquid soybean oil, soybeans, salt, vegetable lecithin, and water. It's an optional substitute for butter in baking, in that it contains no cholesterol and has a lower ratio of saturated fat, but because the hydrogenated oil molecules are difficult for the body to break down and eliminate, use it only occasionally, in small quantities.

Olive oil is used in savory pastries and breads in place of shortening, butter, or margarine.

Safflower oil is a fine, all-purpose oil, 90 percent polyunsaturated fat containing lineolic acid, both of which are said to lower blood cholesterol. It's an excellent replacement for butter, margarine, or any of the higher fat content oils in baking.

Sunflower oil is another popular all-purpose oil, ranking second to safflower in polyunsaturated fat content, at 65 to 70 percent. It has a sweeter flavor than safflower oil and a slightly buttery quality that makes it an excellent replacement for butter or other higher fat oils in baking.

Milks

Almond Milk, made in the blender from raw almonds and water (see page 60), can be used as a substitute for dairy milk in most baking recipes. A high calcium food.

Cashew Milk can be used as a replacement for dairy cream since it is richer in flavor and thicker than Almond Milk. Made in blender like Almond Milk, from raw cashews and water (page 63).

Soymilk is expressed from soybeans that have been soaked, boiled, and pureed. Soymilk compares favorably to dairy milk in nutritional value. It can be used in baking for convenience, since soymilk is available ready-made in containers, but almond milk is preferable and will give you a lighter, tastier product.

***Remember*, if the nondairy replacements for dairy products used in these recipes are not available or you do not choose to use them, you may use traditional low fat dairy products instead with successful results.**

Spices

Cinnamon is available ground or you can buy cinnamon sticks and grind them yourself in a spice grinder for better flavor.

Nutmeg is available ground or you can grind the whole nutmeg by hand on a fine grater. Fresh ground nutmeg has a far deeper flavor.

Ginger is the root of a tropical plant. The ground ginger is more appropriate for baked foods.

Allspice is the berry of an evergreen tree. Its name reflects its flavor, which is a hint of several spices, including cinnamon, nutmeg, and cloves. Ground allspice enhances apple desserts, banana breads, spice cakes, cookies, and pumpkin and squash recipes.

Mace is the red encasement surrounding the nutmeg kernel. The flavor is similar to that of nutmeg, but milder. It's particularly popular in pumpkin recipes.

Cloves are the buds of the evergreen clove tree. I have found that many people really don't appreciate their flavor. Ground cloves are often used in conjunction with cinnamon. Use sparingly; too much will leave a bitter aftertaste.

BREAKFAST FOODS THAT MAINTAIN YOUR ENERGY

Since the *Fit for Life* program so avidly espouses fresh fruit until noon, people have asked what to do about the breakfast foods they enjoy. Unless you are a professional athlete in heavy competitive training (some of whom need 16,000 calories a day), you know the drop in energy that comes from eating concentrated carbohydrates in the morning. So when *do* we eat these foods?

Many people have found the perfect solution to be the weekend midday brunch or occasional "breakfast" supper consisting of, for example, French Toast (page 335), Scramblers (the zero-cholesterol substitute for eggs [page 108]), and hash browns. Or go for pancakes or waffles with maple syrup. When you eat these breakfast foods for lunch or dinner, you are getting a very concentrated meal, so the trick is to make your other meals that day fruit or vegetables with no concentrated food. You can toss lightly steamed vegetables into the vegetable salad at one meal. That will give you a good "veged-out" feeling, and then the concentrated "breakfast" meal will be a welcome change. In the case of a "breakfast" supper, eat it early so that your body has plenty of time to digest the meal before you retire, *and* take a short walk after dinner. If you satisfy your craving for breakfast foods at a midday brunch lunch on the weekend, have a light supper at night (soup and salad) or make supper a fruit meal to help wash out all the concentrated food from brunch.

If hot or cold breakfast cereals (granola, corn flakes, bran flakes, farina, oatmeal, amaranth flakes, rice nuggets, and so on) are foods you miss most, a brunch or dinner of cereal and whole-grain toast may be just the answer from time to time. Just keep the other meals of the day fruit or vegetable-laden.

What to pour on your cereal? There's soymilk for simplicity or sunflower or Almond Milk for its irresistible and luxurious flavor. Just be sure your boxed cereal is whole grain in nature. Commercial cereals, in which the box is more nutritious than its contents, are not acceptable choices. You and your loved ones are too important and too valuable to be eating empty foods.

Whole-Grain Pancakes or Waffles

20 minutes

These dairy-free pancakes are light and tasty. They are an adaptation from *The Cookbook for People Who Love Animals* by Gentle World.

1 cup buckwheat, oat, or whole-wheat flour
¾ cup whole-wheat pastry flour
¾ teaspoon baking soda
2 tablespoons soy powder diluted in 4 tablespoons water
2 tablespoons barley malt, sorghum molasses, honey, or maple syrup
⅓ cup sunflower oil
1⅔ cups soymilk or Almond or Cashew Milk (pages 60, 63)
Oil, for griddle

1. Combine the dry ingredients in a medium mixing bowl. Combine the liquid ingredients in a large bowl. Add the dry ingredients to the liquid ingredients and stir lightly to form a thick, lumpy batter.

2. Brush a nonstick griddle or waffle iron lightly with oil. Heat to medium-high and pour ⅓ cup of batter onto griddle or waffle iron. Cook 3 minutes per side or until golden. Serve with warmed maple syrup.

Serves 4.

Very Easy French Toast

15 minutes

8 slices whole-grain bread
2 cups Almond Milk (page 60) or soymilk
2 to 4 tablespoons maple syrup
1 teaspoon ground cinnamon
Pinch of salt
2 tablespoons sunflower oil
Maple syrup

1. Cut bread diagonally into triangles. Arrange on a cookie sheet.

2. Combine milk, maple syrup, cinnamon, and salt with a hand blender or whisk. Pour over bread and allow to stand for 5 to 30 minutes; bread will absorb liquid.

3. Brush a nonstick skillet with oil. Fry bread slices until browned and slightly crusty, turning once. Serve with maple syrup.

Serves 4.

MUFFINS AND BISCUITS

Blueberry Oat Muffins

40 minutes

Moist, like miniature cakes.

2 tablespoons tofu
3 large ripe bananas, mashed (1 1/2 cups)
Egg replacer for one egg
3 tablespoons sunflower oil
1/3 cup honey
1 cup whole-wheat pastry flour
1/2 cup oat flour
1/2 cup oat bran
1 tablespoon soy flour
2 teaspoons baking powder
1/2 teaspoon baking soda
1 teaspoon ground cinnamon
Pinch of salt
2 cups fresh or frozen blueberries

1. Preheat oven to 375°F. Cream the tofu, bananas, egg replacer, oil, and honey with a blender or in a food processor

2. Combine dry ingredients in a large bowl. Make a well in the center and fold in creamed mixture with a spatula until dry ingredients are moistened. Gently fold in blueberries.

3. Oil muffin cups. Spoon batter into cups and bake 25 to 30 minutes, or until toothpick inserted in center comes out clean. Cool briefly and turn out to finish cooling on wire rack.

Yields 12 muffins.

Apple Pie Muffins

40 minutes

This moist, flavorful muffin is bound to be the favorite of those who love apple pie.

2 tablespoons tofu
3 large ripe bananas mashed (1 1/2 cups)
Egg replacer for 1 egg
3 tablespoons sunflower oil
1/3 cup honey
1 cup whole-wheat pastry flour
1 scant cup oat flour
1 tablespoon soy flour
2 teaspoons baking powder
1/2 teaspoon baking soda
2 teaspoons ground cinnamon
Pinch of salt (optional)
2 cups sliced, peeled apples, cut in 1/2-inch dice
1 teaspoon lemon juice
1/2 cup presoaked raisins

1. Preheat oven to 375°F. Cream tofu, bananas, egg replacer, oil, and honey with a hand blender or in a food processor

2. Combine flours, baking powder and baking soda, 1 teaspoon cinnamon, and salt in a large bowl. Make a well in center and fold in creamed mixture with a spatula until moistened.

3. Combine apples, remaining teaspoon cinnamon, lemon juice, and raisins. Add to batter.

4. Oil muffin cups, then spoon batter into cups and bake 25 to 30 minutes. Muffins are ready when toothpick inserted in center comes out clean. Cool briefly and turn out to finish cooling on wire rack.

Yields 12 muffins.

Peach Cobbler Muffins

40 minutes

Perfectly textured muffins, studded with spicy fresh peaches, create a mouth-watering aroma while they bake. Serve with jam for a treat that will have them swooning!

1/3 cup tofu
Egg replacer for 3 eggs
3 tablespoons sunflower oil
1/2 cup honey or maple syrup
1/2 cup unsweetened applesauce
1 1/2 cups whole-wheat pastry flour
3/4 cup oat flour
1 tablespoon soy flour
Dash of salt
2 1/2 teaspoons baking powder
2 ripe peaches, peeled and cut in 1/2-inch cubes
1/2 teaspoon nutmeg
3/4 teaspoon cinnamon

1. Preheat oven to 375°F. With a blender or in a food processor, cream tofu, egg replacer, oil, sweetener and applesauce.

2. In a large bowl, combine flours, salt, and baking powder. Make a well in the center of the dry ingredients and add blended mixture. Fold in with a spatula until dry ingredients are thoroughly moistened.

3. Toss peaches in nutmeg and cinnamon, and then fold mixture into batter, scraping bowl with rubber spatula so you don't lose any of the spices.

4. Oil muffin cups. Spoon batter into cups and bake 15 to 20 minutes, or until lightly browned and a toothpick inserted in the center comes out clean. Cool briefly and turn out to finish cooling on a wire rack.

Yields 12 muffins.

Banana-Bran Muffins

35 to 40 minutes

Light and sweet, like small, individual cakes.

2 tablespoons tofu
Egg replacer for 1 egg
3 large ripe bananas (1 1/2 cups)
3 tablespoons sunflower oil
1/3 cup honey or maple syrup
Dash of salt (optional)
1 cup whole-wheat pastry flour
1 tablespoon soy flour
Scant 3/4 cup oat bran
2 teapoons baking powder
1/2 teaspoon baking soda
1 teaspoon ground cinnamon
1/2 teaspoon ground nutmeg

1. Preheat oven to 375°F. With a hand blender or in a food processor, cream tofu, egg replacer, bananas, oil, and sweetener.

2. In a separate bowl, combine salt, flours, oat bran, baking powder, baking soda, cinnamon, and nutmeg. Make a well in the center and add banana mixture, folding in with a spatula until dry ingredients are thoroughly moistened.

3. Oil 10 to 12 muffin cups, depending on desired size. Spoon batter into cups and bake for 20 to 25 minutes, or until muffins are lightly browned and a toothpick inserted in the center comes out clean. Cool briefly and turn out to finish cooling on wire rack.

Yields 10 large or 12 regular muffins.

Zucchini-Carrot Muffins

30 minutes

1 2/3 cups whole-wheat pastry flour
1/2 teaspoon baking soda
1/4 teaspoon sea salt
1 teaspoon ground cinnamon
1/4 teaspoon grated nutmeg
1/2 cup safflower oil
1/4 cup Almond Milk (page 60)
Egg replacer for 1 egg
2/3 cup FruitSource or generous 1/2 cup honey
1/4 cup soft tofu
1 1/4 cups finely shredded peeled carrots, loosely packed
2/3 cup finely shredded unpeeled zucchini, loosely packed
1 cup presoaked raisins (optional)

1. Preheat oven to 425°F. In a medium bowl, combine flour, baking soda, salt, cinnamon, and nutmeg. Mix thoroughly and set aside.

2. With a blender or food processor, combine oil, milk, egg replacer, sweetener, and tofu. Add to dry ingredients and stir until just moistened. Fold in carrots, zucchini, and raisins.

3. Turn batter out into 12 oiled muffin tins for small muffins, filling two-thirds full; for larger muffins, fill 8 muffin tins three-fourths full.

4. Bake for 20 minutes for smaller muffins, 20 to 25 for larger, or until a pick inserted in center comes out clean. Serve warm.

Yields 8 to 12 muffins.

Sweet Potato Biscuits

30 minutes

Very flaky and moist.

2 cups sifted whole-wheat pastry flour
4 teaspoons baking powder
Pinch of salt
⅓ cup soy margarine
⅓ cup sunflower oil
1 rounded cup mashed sweet potatoes or yams
2 tablespoons soymilk, Almond Milk (page 60), or Cashew Cream (page 96)

1. Preheat oven to 400°F. Sift dry ingredients, then cut in margarine and oil. Blend in potatoes. Add milk to make a moist (slightly sticky) dough.

2. Drop in ¼-cup measures on a dry cookie sheet. Bake for 15 to 20 minutes.

Yields 12 to 16 biscuits.

Note: Unbaked biscuits can be frozen on cookie sheet for several hours and then stored in freezer in airtight container until needed. Bake frozen for 20 to 25 minutes at 400°.

Flaky Biscuits

20 minutes

10 tablespoons pure soy or safflower margarine, softened
3 cups less 1 tablespoon whole-wheat pastry flour
1 tablespoon soy flour
2 teaspoons baking powder
2 teaspoons baking soda
Dash of salt
2 tablespoons honey
1 teaspoon egg replacer
½ cup Almond Milk (page 60)

1. Preheat oven to 400°F. In a food processor or by hand, combine margarine, flours, baking powder, baking soda, and salt.

2. Combine egg replacer with milk and honey. Pour into dry mixture and mix until dough forms into a ball. Drop batter on a lightly oiled cookie sheet in ⅓-cup rounds. Bake 10 to 12 minutes, then cool on wire rack.

Yields 10 to 12 biscuits

Chili Corn Muffins

40 minutes

1 cup cornmeal
1 tablespoon soy flour
1 scant cup whole-wheat pastry flour
Dash of sea salt
1 teaspoon baking powder
1 teaspoon baking soda
1/4 cup tofu
1 cup fresh or frozen corn
1 cup Almond Milk (page 60)
1/4 cup honey
Egg replacer for 1 egg
2/3 diced red and green bell pepper
1 tablespoon sunflower oil
2 tablespoons diced Spanish onion
1/4 teaspoon sea salt (optional)
1/4 to 1/2 teaspoon ground cumin
1/8 to 1/4 teaspoon chili powder
1/4 teaspoon garlic powder

1. Preheat oven to 375°F. Combine cornmeal, flours, salt, baking powder, and baking soda in a large mixing bowl. Set aside.

2. In a blender or food processor, combine tofu, 1/2 cup corn, milk, honey, and egg replacer. Pour mixture through sieve and reserve creamy mixture. Set aside.

3. Heat oil and onion in a medium skillet. Add peppers and sauté, stirring, for 3 minutes. Drain off oil and add salt and spices. Cool briefly.

4. Gently stir liquid ingredients into dry ingredients. Do not overmix. Fold in sautéed vegetables and remaining 1/2 cup uncooked corn; mixture should be lumpy. Oil muffin cups and fill three-fourths full with batter. Bake for 15 to 20 minutes, or until toothpick inserted in center of muffin comes out clean.

Yields 12 medium muffins.

COOKIES

Peanut Butter and Jelly Cookies

Who doesn't love these two flavors? Designed around the Thumbprint principle, this is a truly heavenly cookie. Try them when they are warm, right from the oven, with a glass of almond milk. These are moist, delectable cookies that are packed with nutrition!

1 cup peanut butter
1/2 cup soy margarine
1/2 cup maple syrup
1 cup mashed banana
2 1/2 cups whole-wheat pastry flour
Dash of sea salt
1 1/2 teaspoons baking powder
1 1/2 cups ground almonds
1 cup raspberry preserves

1. Preheat oven to 375°F.
2. Cream peanut butter, margarine, and maple syrup until fluffy. Blend in mashed banana.
3. Sift together dry ingredients and combine with ground nuts.
4. Fold dry mixture into wet and mix until incorporated.
5. On a dry cookie sheet, place golf-ball size nuggets about 3 inches apart. Press down with the palm of your hand and make an indentation in the centers with your thumb. Fill with raspberry preserves and bake 15 minutes. Cool on racks.

Yields 2 dozen cookies.

Thumbprints

30 minutes

A round, flavorful cookie with a dollop of jam in the center. Kids just love thumbprints! Here's a wheat-free option.

1 cup raw almonds
1 cup rolled oats
1¼ cups oat flour, or 1 cup whole-wheat pastry flour
½ teaspoon ground cinnamon
½ cup maple syrup or brown rice syrup
½ cup sunflower oil
½ cup pineapple-apricot or strawberry jam, preferably fruit juice or honey sweetened

1. Preheat oven to 350°F. Place almonds in a food processor and grind to a meal. Place oats in food processor and grind to a meal. Add flour, cinnamon, maple syrup, and oil. Pulse to combine.

2. Wet hands and form dough into walnut-size balls. Place on an oiled cookie sheet. Press an indentation in center of each with your thumb. Fill with jam. Bake for 10 to 15 minutes, or until golden.

Yields approximately 24 cookies.

Variation: Fill the thumbprint with Creamy Carob Frosting (page 353).

Oat Chewies

30 minutes

A great "giant size" cookie. These are absolutely mouth-watering with cold Almond Milk!

¾ cup sunflower or safflower oil
1 cup FruitSource or date sugar
¾ cup honey or brown rice syrup
½ cup Almond Milk (page 60)
2 teaspoons vanilla extract
2½ cups whole-wheat flour
½ teaspoon baking soda
½ teaspoon sea salt
3 cups rolled oats
½ cup raisins
½ cup carob chips
¾ teaspoon ground cinnamon

1. Preheat oven to 350°F. In a large mixing bowl, beat oil, sweetener, honey, milk, and vanilla until smooth. Add remaining ingredients one at a time and mix well after each addition.

2. With lightly floured hands roll batter into balls the size of golf balls. Place on an ungreased cookie sheet and press down with a spatula to a ⅜-inch thickness. Bake for 20 minutes, or until cookies are lightly browned on the bottom.

Yields 2½ dozen cookies.

Linda's Choco-Nutties

20 minutes

These are *so easy* to make. The coffee substitute deepens the flavor of the carob.

½ cup sunflower or safflower oil
½ cup FruitSource or ⅓ cup honey
Egg replacer for 1 egg
½ medium banana
⅔ cup whole-wheat pastry flour
¼ cup carob powder
1 tablespoon coffee substitute (optional)
1 cup coarsely ground walnuts
1 teaspoon vanilla extract
Pinch of salt

1. Preheat oven to 350°F. Combine oil, sweetener, egg replacer, and banana in food processor.
2. Mix in flour, carob, and coffee substitute. Stir in walnuts, vanilla, and salt.
3. Drop by teaspoonfuls onto an oiled cookie sheet. Bake 10 to 12 minutes.

Yields 18 to 20 cookies.

Banana Chippers

30 minutes

An easy-to-make, delicious cookie that whips up in minutes.

3 large ripe bananas (1 1/2 cups)
1 teaspoon vanilla extract
1/3 cup safflower oil
3/4 cup Almond Milk (page 60) or soymilk
1/2 cup honey
1/2 cup maple syrup
2 1/2 cups oat flour
1 tablespoon soy flour
1 1/2 cups whole-wheat flour
1 teaspoon baking soda
1 teaspoon baking powder
2 teaspoons ground cinnamon
1/4 teaspoon ground cardamom
1/8 teaspoon sea salt
1 1/2 cups carob chips

1. Preheat oven to 350°F. In a food processor, combine bananas with liquid ingredients. Mix well.

2. Combine dry ingredients except chips in large bowl. Add liquid ingredients and stir in the chips.

3. Drop by teaspoonfuls onto a lightly oiled cookie sheet. Bake for 20 to 25 minutes, or until lightly browned.

Yields 36 cookies.

Banana, Date, and Oatmeal Jumbles

45 minutes

A soft, fruity confection with a very special sweetness and texture. Couldn't be easier to make. Reserve two cookies for yourself before the aroma pulls everyone else into the kitchen!

3 large bananas, mashed
2 cups rolled oats
1 cup chopped dates
⅓ cup oil
Dash of salt
1 teaspoon vanilla extract

1. Preheat oven to 350°F. Combine bananas, oats, dates, oil, salt, and vanilla. Allow to rest 15 minutes to let flavors mingle.

2. Drop by teaspoonfuls onto an ungreased baking sheet and bake for 20 minutes or until brown.

Yields 24 jumbles.

Pumpkin Squares with Cashew Whipped Cream

1 hour, 45 minutes

A holiday favorite that has been enthusiastically anticipated by friends and family for the last several years, these are remarkably easy to make. Everything is mixed together in the food processor and poured into a simple crumb crust. Serve with Cashew Whipped Cream (page 96).

Cookie Crust

5 tablespoons margarine
1/3 cup maple syrup or honey
1 cup whole-wheat pastry flour

Filling

3¼ cups cooked or baked or canned pumpkin, mashed
1 cup Cashew Milk (page 63)
¼ cup arrowroot powder
¼ cup cashew butter
1/2 cup honey and 1/2 cup maple syrup
1 teaspoon vanilla extract
2 teaspoons ground cinnamon
1 teaspoon ground coriander
1 teaspoon mace
¼ teaspoon ground allspice
Dash of ground ginger (optional)
1½ tablespoons sorghum molasses
Dash of salt

1. In a food processor, combine cold margarine, sweetener, and flour. Process until blended by pulsing 20 to 30 seconds. Press remaining crumbs into a 9 x 9 x 2-inch pan. Set aside. Preheat oven to 425°F.

2. Place the pumpkin and milk in a food processor. Puree, then add remaining ingredients and process to a smooth, thick cream.

3. Pour filling into crust. Bake for 15 minutes at 425°F, then reduce oven temperature to 250°F and continue baking for 1¼ hours. Place on rack to cool and then chill before cutting. When completely chilled, squares will be firm.

Yields 16 squares.

Fooled You! Brownies

2⅓ cups whole-wheat flour
1 cup water
½ cup margarine
⅔ cup carob powder
1 heaping tablespoon grain coffee
1½ cups honey or maple syrup
1 teaspoon vanilla
½ teaspoon sea salt
2½ teaspoons baking powder

1. Preheat oven to 350°F. Mix ⅓ cup flour with 1 cup water. Cook until thick and cool completely.

2. Melt margarine and sift in carob powder and grain coffee. Whisk mixture thoroughly to avoid lumping. Cool.

3. Beat together sweetener, flour and water mixture, and vanilla. Add to carob mixture.

4. Combine remaining 2 cups flour, sea salt, and baking powder. Add to above ingredients. Bake in 8-inch-square oiled pan for 35 minutes, or until inserted knife comes out clean.

Yields 25 brownies.

To Bake Pumpkin

To cook pumpkin, wash and cut it in half crosswise. Remove seeds and strings. Place it in a pan, cut side down, and bake in a 325°F oven for 1 hour or more, depending on size, until it is tender and begins to fall apart. Scrape the pulp from the shell and put it through a ricer or strainer, or puree in a blender.

Carrot-Cake Cookies

30 minutes

1 cup safflower or sunflower oil
1 cup FruitSource, or ¾ cup honey or sorghum molasses
Egg replacer for 1 egg
½ medium banana
1 cup rolled oats or oat bran
2 cups whole-wheat flour
½ cup soy flour
1 teaspoon baking powder
3 teaspoons ground cinnamon
¼ teaspoon grated nutmeg
1 teaspoon vanilla extract
2 cups finely grated carrot, packed
1 cup presoaked raisins or currants, or ½ cup raisins or currants and ½ cup carob chips

1. Preheat oven to 375°F. Cream oil, sweetener, egg replacer, and banana in a food processor. Add oats, flours, baking powder, cinnamon, nutmeg, and vanilla. Stir in carrot. Mix well, then stir in raisins.

2. Drop by tablespoonfuls on lightly oiled cookie sheets. Bake for 15 minutes or until soft and chewy.

Yields 36 cookies.

"Cheesecake" Bars

35 minutes

½ cup soy or safflower margarine, chilled
½ cup FruitSource, or ⅓ cup maple syrup or honey
1½ cups plus 1 tablespoon whole-wheat pastry flour
8 ounces firm tofu, wrapped for 30 minutes
⅓ cup honey
1 teaspoon vanilla extract
Egg replacer for 1 egg
½ cup carob chips, fresh cut strawberries, or blueberries

1. Preheat oven to 350°F. In a food processor, combine margarine, sweetener, and 1½ cups flour until mixture resembles coarse crumbs. Reserve ¾ cup of mixture and with floured hands press remainder into a 9 x 9 x 2-inch pan. Bake on middle shelf for 10 minutes.

2. In blender or food processor, puree the tofu, honey, vanilla, egg replacer, and remaining tablespoon flour. Spread mixture on top of crust. Sprinkle with carob chips and reserved crumb topping. Bake 20 minutes.

Yields 9 squares.

BREADS AND TEA CAKES

Onion Piazettes

1 hour, 20 minutes

Individual garlic breads, topped with grilled onions. Great with soup and salad.

Bread

1 package active dry yeast
¼ cup hot water (105–115°F)
4 tablespoons honey
½ cup olive oil
⅔ cup water
½ teaspoon salt
2½ cups whole-wheat flour
1½ cups whole-wheat pastry flour or unbleached all-purpose flour

Topping

½ cup olive oil
3 garlic cloves
3 teaspoons dried sage or basil
1 large onion, very finely sliced

1. In a small bowl, combine yeast, hot water, and 1 tablespoon honey. Mix well and allow to stand for 5 minutes or until bubbly.

2. Combine olive oil, remaining honey, and water with yeast mixture. Add dry ingredients and knead for 7 minutes. Place in an oiled bowl and allow to rise for 45 minutes to 1 hour.

3. While dough is rising, prepare topping. Liquefy the oil, garlic, and sage with a hand blender. Combine in a small bowl with the sliced onions. Set aside.

4. Preheat oven to 500°F. When dough has risen, do *not* punch it down. Separate it with your hands into 6 equal pieces. Using your hands, roll each piece into a ball and press onto an oiled baking sheet to form six 1-inch-thick flatbreads. Brush with oil mixture and top with onion rings.

5. Bake for 10 minutes. Onions will be slightly crisped. Cool briefly on racks before serving.

Yields 6 individual breads.

Note: If smaller piazettes are desired, form 8 or 10 piazettes and reduce baking time slightly.

Easy Banana Bread

1 hour, 10 minutes

1/2 cup soft tofu
3/4 cup honey
1/4 cup sunflower or safflower oil
1 teaspoon vanilla extract
1 cup mashed ripe banana
Egg replacer for one egg
2 cups whole-wheat pastry flour
½ teaspoon baking powder
½ teaspoon baking soda
Dash of salt
1 tablespoon poppy seeds

1. Preheat oven to 350°F. In a food processor, cream tofu, sweetener, oil, vanilla, egg replacer and banana.

2. In a bowl, combine flour, baking powder, and baking soda. Add to food processor along with salt and process until creamy.

3. Pulse in poppy seeds. Pour into an oiled 9 x 5 x 3-inch loaf pan. Bake for 30 to 35 minutes, or until toothpick inserted in center of bread comes out clean. Cool on a wire rack for 30 minutes before removing from pan.

Yields 1 loaf

Gingerbread Tea Cake with Cashew Cream

1 hour, 20 minutes

This cake improves as it sits, so wrap in plastic wrap when cool and store in the refrigerator. It will keep up to 10 days, if it lasts that long.

4 tablespoons sunflower oil
1½ tablespoons soy lecithin (available in natural foods stores) (optional)
½ cup FruitSource or date sugar
Egg replacer for 1 egg
½ cup sorghum or blackstrap molasses
½ cup boiling water
1½ cups sifted whole-wheat pastry flour
2½ tablespoons grated fresh ginger
½ teaspoon ground cinnamon
¼ teaspoon ground cloves
¼ teaspoon mace
Dash of salt
1 teaspoon baking powder
½ teaspoon baking soda
½ cup dried currants

1. Preheat the oven to 350°F. Oil and flour a 9 × 5 × 3-inch loaf pan.

2. Combine the oil, lecithin, and sweetener in the work bowl of a food processor. Add egg replacer, molasses, and boiling water; process until creamy.

3. Add flour, ginger, cinnamon, cloves, mace, salt, baking powder, and baking soda. Process batter until just blended. Pulse in currants; do not overmix.

4. Pour batter into prepared tube pan. Bake for 50 to 55 minutes, or until a toothpick inserted in center comes out clean. Cool cake in pan on wire rack for 5 minutes. Remove cake from pan and finish cooling on rack. Serve it warm with Cashew Cream (page 96).

Yields 1 loaf.

"Cheese" Strudel

50 minutes

8 ounces firm tofu
1½ tablespoons honey
1 teaspoon lemon juice
¼ teaspoon vanilla extract
¼ to ½ teaspoon grated nutmeg
Dash of ground cardamom
2 teaspoons soy flour
3 sheets whole-wheat phyllo dough
2 tablespoons sunflower oil
3 tablespoons pineapple-apricot jam
Dash of ground cinnamon

1. Preheat oven to 400°F. Mash tofu and mix with sweetener, lemon juice, vanilla, nutmeg, cardamom, and flour.

2. Fold sheet of phyllo up one-third. Brush with oil, then spread 1 tablespoon jam on the double thickness. Add a line of filling, using one-third of what you have. Fold in sides of sheet, fold bottom over filling, and roll up.

3. Place on an oiled cookie sheet, brush with oil, and sprinkle with cinnamon. Repeat twice. Bake for 20 to 25 minutes, or until lightly brown and crisp.

Yields 12 individual strudels.

Spicy Zucchini Bread

1 hour, 30 minutes

2¾ cups whole-wheat flour
1½ teaspoons baking powder
1 teaspoon baking soda
1 tablespoon ground cinnamon
½ teaspoon ground nutmeg (optional)
¼ teaspoon salt (optional)
¼ teaspoon ground cardamom
⅓ cup soft tofu
¼ cup soymilk
Egg replacer for 3 eggs
¾ honey
¾ cup sunflower or safflower oil
3½ cups coarsely grated zucchini, firmly packed
1 cup presoaked raisins (optional)

1. Preheat oven to 350°F. Combine dry ingredients in a large bowl. Liquefy tofu in soymilk and combine in a separate bowl with remaining liquid ingredients.

2. Make a well in center of dry ingredients and stir in liquid ingredients. Stir in zucchini and raisins. Pour into oiled loaf or bread pan.

3. Bake for 1 hour to 1 hour and 15 minutes, or until bread tests done and toothpick inserted in center comes out clean. Cool on rack before cutting.

Yields 1 loaf.

PUDDINGS

Mocha Parfait

10 minutes

Inspired by a recipe from Bill Shurtleff and Akiko Aoyagi of the Soyfoods Center in Lafayette, California, this mocha parfait gets high ratings!

10 1/2 ounces silken tofu, or 9 1/2 ounces firm tofu blended with 1 tablespoon water
2 tablespoons honey and 2 tablespoons maple syrup
1 tablespoon carob powder
1 tablespoon soy margarine, softened
1 tablespoon sunflower oil
½ teaspoon vanilla extract
Dash of salt
¼ teaspoon coffee substitute (optional)

1. Combine ingredients in a blender and puree until smooth.
2. Serve chilled.

Serves 3 to 4.

Baked Indian Pudding

3 hours, 15 minutes

This sweet, dark breadlike pudding takes less than 15 minutes to prepare and then bakes slowly for 3 hours while you do other business. Have a salad meal and then have it warm for dessert. Or serve it warm at tea time or brunch. For a richer version, serve with Cashew Cream (page 96).

5 cups soymilk
¼ cup soy margarine
⅔ cup sorghum or cane molasses
5 tablespoons honey
1 cup cornmeal
¾ teaspoon ground cinnamon
¾ teaspoon grated nutmeg

1. Preheat oven to 300°F. Heat 4 cups of the milk in a 2-quart saucepan. Stir in margarine, molasses, and sweetener. In a bowl, combine cornmeal with spices, then stir gradually into warm milk mixture, using a wire whisk to avoid lumps. Cook over low heat, stirring constantly, for about 10 minutes, or until thick.

2. Turn pudding into an oiled 2-quart casserole or soufflé dish. Pour remaining cup of milk over top (do not stir), and bake for 3 hours. Serve warm.

Serves 6 to 8.

Brown Rice Pudding

1 hour

1 cup short-grain brown rice, soaked overnight
2¼ cups water
1 teaspoon sunflower oil
Dash of sea salt
1½ cups soymilk or Cashew Milk (page 96)
⅓ cup presoaked raisins
1 teaspoon ground cinnamon
Dash of ground cardamom
Dash of ginger (optional)
½ cup maple syrup

1. Drain rice and combine in a saucepan with water, oil, and salt. Bring to a boil, stir briefly, cover, and simmer over low heat for 40 minutes. Remove rice from heat and allow to sit without lifting cover for 10 minutes. Lift cover and fluff with a fork.

2. Gently heat milk. Drain raisins and add to milk along with seasonings. Add rice and sweetener and mix thoroughly. Cook 5 minutes, stirring frequently to prevent sticking. Serve warm or cold.

Serves 6.

Creamy Rice Pudding

1 hour, 45 minutes

A baked rice pudding, ideally used as a follow-up to a salad meal. The baking time is extensive, but the actual preparation time is minimal. It's a good reason to keep cold brown rice on hand.

3 cups cooked short-grain brown rice
2⅓ cups water
1 cup raisins or dried currants (optional)
⅔ cup honey
½ teaspoon ground cinnamon
1 teaspoon vanilla extract
1 teaspoon lemon juice
1 cup soymilk
½ cup soft tofu
2 tablespoons tahini
Ground cinnamon

1. Preheat oven to 325°F. Place rice, water, raisins, sweetener, cinnamon, vanilla, and lemon juice in a large saucepan. Bring to a boil and simmer, uncovered, over medium-low heat for 5 minutes.

2. While rice cooks, combine milk, tofu, and tahini in a blender and liquefy. Stir into rice mixture, and cook until mixture is thick.

3. Oil an 8- or 9-inch casserole. Spoon rice mixture into casserole and dust top with cinnamon. Bake 1 hour and 30 minutes.

Serves 8.

CAKES AND PIES

Applesauce Cake

1 hour, 10 minutes

3/4 cup applesauce
3/4 cup honey
1/2 teaspoon almond or vanilla extract
1/4 cup soft tofu
Egg replacer for 2 eggs
2 tablespoons oil
2 tablespoons orange juice
1 teaspoon cinnamon
1 7/8 cup whole-wheat pastry flour
2 tablespoons soy flour
1 teaspoon baking soda
2 teaspoons baking powder
1 cup raisins, soaked and drained
1/2 cup chopped walnuts (optional)

1. Preheat oven to 350°F. Combine first eight ingredients with a hand blender, mixer, or in a food processor until smooth and creamy.

2. Lightly oil a 9-inch tube pan.

3. Combine the flours, soda, and baking powder. Make a well in the center of the dry ingredients. Add the liquid ingredients and mix only until moistened.

4. Immediately stir in raisins and walnuts. Pour into prepared pan, and bake for 40 minutes or until a toothpick inserted near the center comes out clean.

5. Cool cake on wire rack before removing from pan. Serve warm or room temperature.

Serves 8.

Variations: Substitute 3/4 cup whipped banana or 3/4 cup drained crushed pineapple for the applesauce.

Banana-Chip Cake

50 minutes

2/3 cup maple syrup or honey
1/2 cup sunflower oil
Egg replacer for 2 eggs
1 tablespoon soy lecithin (optional)
3 ripe bananas, mashed
2 cups whole-wheat pastry flour, or 2 1/2 cups oat flour
1 teaspoon baking soda
Pinch of salt
1/2 cup carob chips

1. Preheat oven to 350°F. Cream together the syrup, oil, and egg replacer. Add lecithin and bananas.

2. Combine flour, baking soda, and salt. Add carob chips, then fold dry ingredients into creamed mixture, stirring just to moisten and combine. Do not overmix.

3. Pour batter into an ungreased 8-inch cake or Bundt pan. Bake approximately 40 minutes, or until cake tests done with a wooden toothpick. Cool on wire rack.

Serves 8.

Variation: Double this recipe, bake in two 8-inch cake pans, and frost with this Creamy Carob Frosting for a winning birthday cake.

Creamy Carob Frosting

3 tablespoons soy margarine
½ cup carob chips
½ cup FruitSource, or ¼ cup honey
¼ cup Almond Milk (page 60)
1 teaspoon vanilla extract

In a saucepan, combine the ingredients and warm over medium-low heat while stirring continuously with a wooden spoon. Drizzle over cake.

Yields ¾ cup.

"Chocolate" Carrot Cake

1/2 cup sunflower oil
1/2 cup unsweetened applesauce
1 cup maple syrup
1/3 cup carob powder
2 tablespoons coffee substitute
1 cup tofu, soft or firm
2 cups grated carrot, lightly packed
2 cups whole-wheat pastry flour
2 tablespoons baking soda
1/4 teaspoon salt
1 teaspoon ground cinnamon

1. Preheat oven to 350°F. In a food processor, blend oil, applesauce, and sweetener for 1 minute. Add carob powder, coffee substitute and tofu. Continue to process. Add carrot and pulse several times.

2. In a large mixing bowl, combine dry ingredients. Make a well in center and add carob mixture. Beat thoroughly to combine.

3. Oil a 8 to 10 cup bundt or tube pan. Spoon batter into pan and bake for 50 to 55 minutes, or until a toothpick inserted in center comes out clean. Cool on wire rack before removing from pan.

Serves 8 to 10.

Variation: Top with Creamy Carob Frosting, if desired.

Apple Cream Pie

45 minutes

We had a difficult time deciding whether to name this Apple Cream Pie or Apple Dream Pie. The creamy filling is an innovation in this double-crust pie.

Sweet Crust

1 cup whole-wheat pastry flour
1 cup unbleached white flour
7 to 7½ tablespoons soy margarine, cut into bits
½ teaspoon grated nutmeg
Dash of salt (optional)
6 tablespoons ice water

Filling

3 cups coarsely grated peeled apples
3 tablespoons lemon juice
3 tablespoons sunflower oil
2½ teaspoons ground cinnamon
½ cup soft tofu
½ cup maple syrup
⅔ cup raisins, soaked and drained
½ cup whole-wheat pastry flour
1½ teaspoon soy or safflower margarine, melted
Ground cinnamon

1. Place flours, margarine, nutmeg, and salt in a food processor and process 10 seconds to a cornmeal texture. With processor running, add 3 tablespoons ice water. Add remaining water slowly, and stop the machine as soon as the dough begins to form a ball. Tiny pieces of margarine should be visible in dough.

2. Form the dough into 2 equal balls and flatten one into a thick disk. Flour your work surface and rolling pin, and roll dough from center out to sides, turning into a perfect circle about 10 inches in diameter.

3. Place the rolling pin in the center of the dough. Fold half over the pin and transfer to a 9-inch pie plate. Press the dough gently into the pie plate, fold the rough edges under neatly or trim them. Wrap second ball of dough in waxed paper and refrigerate. Cover pie plate with a slightly damp kitchen towel and place in the refrigerator.

4. Preheat oven to 450°F. Toss apples with lemon juice to prevent oxidization. In a blender or food processor, combine oil, cinnamon, tofu, and ½ cup FruitSource; whip until creamy. Pour creamed mixture into apples and mix thoroughly. Add remaining ½ cup FruitSource to raisins and flour. Stir into apple mixture. Pour filling into pie crust.

5. Roll out remaining pie crust into a 9-inch round. Place over apples, trim, and crimp edge with thumb and forefinger or flute with a fork. Brush top with melted margarine and dust with cinnamon. Bake for 25 to 30 minutes, or until crust is golden. Cool on wire rack.

Serves 8.

Cold Yam Pie

1 hour, 35 minutes

For this pie to be most successful, use the deep orange yams. The problem is that from the outside skin you can't tell the difference. I ask my produce man to trim the ends of those I have selected, to see what color they are.

3 large yams, baked and peeled (approximately 4 cups)
3 tablespoons soy powder or soy flour
1 tablespoon barley malt syrup
2 tablespoons honey or date sugar
3½ teaspoons ground cinnamon
½ teaspoon ground allspice
¼ teaspoon ground cardamom
¼ to ½ teaspoon sea salt
1 unbaked Sweet Crust (page 354)
Cashew Whipped Cream (page 96)

1. Preheat oven to 350°F.

2. Combine ingredients for filling in a food processor and puree with the steel knife. Pour into pie crust and bake 1 hour and 15 minutes. Cool to room temperature or chill. Top with Cashew Whipped Cream.

Serves 8 to 10.

Holiday Pumpkin Pie

1 hour, 20 minutes

Thanks to tofu, you can easily whip up a perfect pumpkin pie with no cholesterol and no saturated fat.

¾ pound firm tofu
2 cups cooked or baked pureed pumpkin
¾ cup FruitSource, or ⅔ cup honey or maple syrup
⅓ cup oil (¼ if you use liquid sweetener)
2 tablespoons sorghum or cane molasses
1 teaspoon vanilla extract
1½ teaspoon ground cinnamon
¾ teaspoon grated nutmeg
¾ teaspoon powdered ginger
½ teaspoon mace
¼ teaspoon sea salt
1 unbaked Sweet Crust (page 354)
Cashew Whipped Cream (page 96)

1. Preheat oven to 350°F.

2. Blend ingredients for filling until smooth and creamy in a blender or food processor. Pour into pie shell and bake for 1 hour.

3. Chill and serve with Cashew Whipped Cream.

Serves 8 to 10.

THE NO-BAKE PIES

Fresh-fruit, no-bake pies are the epitome of fruit creativity. They totally satisfy the sweet craving, and they are unusual and beautiful to see. The taste is unique, so very different from anything most people have eaten. But the truly important attribute is that these pies are totally *fresh,* and therefore good for us from the very first bite.

Whenever we have one of these pies on hand, I hate to eat anything cooked, because then I'll have to wait hours before I can have my pie. It's important *not* to eat these no-bake pies *after eating cooked food.* They must be treated just like fruit. That's because fruit's nature, even in a no-bake pie, requires that it be eaten on an empty stomach. Raw (living foods) leave the stomach more quickly than cooked foods. If you eat them on top of cooked food, you are asking for trouble. Since they are a combination of dried and fresh fruit, they *demand* an empty stomach, or at least nothing heavier than a salad. In fact, sometimes we make a meal of a fruit pie and a big salad.

The recipes begin with a standard no-bake pie crust, then follow with our favorite pies.

Lisa's Standard Fruit Pie Crust

10 minutes

⅓ cup sunflower seeds
½ cup sesame seeds
⅓ cup pecans or almonds
⅓ cup dried, unsweetened, shredded coconut
½ to 1 cup raisins (enough to make mixture gluey)
1 cup soft dates, seeds removed

1. Grind the seeds, nuts, and coconut to a fine meal in a food processor. Add the fruit and process, adding additional raisins, as necessary, until mixture forms a ball.

2. Press mixture into a 9-inch pie plate. The crust will be nearly ¼-inch thick. Flute the edges with your thumb and forefinger. Crust is ready to be filled.

Yields 1 crust.

Note: (1.) You can substitute any combination of seeds and nuts to equal quantities given in recipe.

(2.) If mixture does not ball up, add a few tablespoons of apple juice, Almond or Cashew Milk, or water.

Variation: For a delicious high-energy treat, roll this fruit-and-nut mixture into walnut-size balls or logs, roll in coconut, and freeze.

Peaches and Cream Pie

45 minutes

1 Lisa's Standard Fruit Pie Crust (page 356)
5 to 6 large peaches, peeled
3 tablespoons fresh orange juice
½ cup raw cashew pieces
3 tablespoons maple syrup
½ cup water
1 teaspoon vanilla extract
⅓ cup sunflower oil
Fresh mint leaves, for garnish

1. Prepare crust and set in refrigerator or freezer to chill.

2. Slice peaches in thin half-moons. In a mixing bowl, combine peaches with orange juice and set aside.

3. Place cashews in a blender with sweetener, water, and vanilla. Blend until creamy and smooth. While blender is running on low, add oil in a thin stream through opening in lid until mixture thickens but is still slightly runny.

4. Coat bottom of crust with a thin layer of cashew mixture. Add a layer of peach slices in flower-petal fashion, spread with cashew again and continuing layering, ending with top layer of peaches. Garnish with mint leaves in center of peach "flower."

5. Refrigerate for at least 2 hours before serving.

Serves 8.

Fresh Persimmon Pie

30 minutes

This is a very seasonal fresh pie, since it is made from Hychia persimmons, which are available only in the fall. The persimmons must be very soft and ripe. If the skin comes off easily, peel them; otherwise, they can be blended with the skin.

1 Lisa's Standard Fruit Pie Crust (page 356), made with more pecans and no sesame seeds
7 medium persimmons, stems removed
3 large dates
3 tablespoons psyllium husks
1 teaspoon ground cinnamon
¼ teaspoon grated nutmeg
1 tablespoon shredded coconut

1. Prepare crust and set in refrigerator or freezer to chill.

2. Place filling ingredients in a blender and blend on high speed until a thick pudding forms. Pour into prepared pie crust.

3. Chill and serve cold.

Serves 8 to 10.

Note: The husk of the psyllium seed is used occasionally as a thickener. Available at natural food stores.

Piña Colada Pie

30 minutes

1 Lisa's Standard Fruit Pie Crust (page 356)
1 teaspoon grated nutmeg
4 large ripe bananas
⅓ cup shredded coconut
1 small pineapple, cored and peeled
2 teaspoons honey
2 tablespoons agar-agar
⅓ cup water
1 ripe kiwifruit
Shredded coconut

1. Prepare crust and set in refrigerator or freezer to chill.

2. Sprinkle crust with nutmeg. Slice bananas in ⅛-inch diagonals and layer them over crust.

3. Blend coconut, pineapple, and honey until smooth in a blender.

4. Heat agar-agar with water in a small saucepan over low heat until bubbly and gelatinous, about 3 to 4 minutes. Stir mixture constantly.

5. Add agar-agar mixture to pineapple mixture immediately and blend for 20 seconds. Pour over banana then allow to cool for several minutes.

6. Peel kiwifruit, cut in half lengthwise, and slice. Place slices with flat side adjacent to crust in a scallop fashion. Dust with shredded coconut. Chill for several hours before serving.

Serves 8 to 10.

Orange-Ginger Spice Pie

30 minutes

1 Lisa's Standard Fruit Pie Crust (page 356)
½ cup dried, unsweetened, shredded coconut
6 navel oranges, peeled
6 teaspoons grated fresh ginger
1 teaspoon ground cardamom
Dash of grated nutmeg
1 non-stringy mango, peeled, or 1 small papaya, peeled and seeded
3 tablespoons agar-agar
⅓ cup water
Fresh mint leaves
Orange zest for decoration

1. Prepare crust and set in refrigerator or freezer to chill.

2. Place coconut in a blender and grind to a fine powder. Add oranges, ginger, cardamom, nutmeg, and mango or papaya. Blend for 2 or 3 minutes until smooth.

3. Heat agar-agar and water in a saucepan over low heat. Stir constantly to keep mixture smooth for 3 to 4 minutes, until it becomes gelatinous. Immediately pour mixture into fruit mixture and blend for 45 seconds.

4. Pour filling into pie crust, decorate with mint leaves and orange zest, and chill for several hours before serving.

Serves 8 to 10.

Strawberry-Banana Pie

35 minutes

This fresh fruit pie with a creamy dried fruit and nut crust is a treat beyond description. You can vary the crust ingredients to your taste as long as the consistency is thick enough to hold.

Crust

⅔ cup sesame seeds
⅓ cup sunflower seeds or almonds
¼ cup pecans or walnuts
1 cup raisins or Black Mission figs
¾ cup pitted dates
1 to 2 tablespoons Almond Milk (page 60) or water
Ground cinnamon

Glaze

3 cups strawberries
1 to 2 tablespoons psyllium husks (available in natural food stores)
3 tablespoons FruitSource, or 2 tablespoons maple syrup

Filling

3 medium bananas
3 cups strawberries
Shredded coconut

1. Grind seeds and nuts to a meal in a blender or food processor. Add raisins and dates and enough milk to make a thick paste. Press "crust" into a 9-inch pie plate. Flute the edges with forefinger and thumb. Dust with cinnamon.

2. Blend 3 cups of strawberries with psyllium and sweetener. Pour two-thirds of glaze into crust, reserving one-third for the top.

3. Thinly slice the bananas on the diagonal (scant ⅛-inch slices). Slice strawberries as thin as possible. Cover the bottom of the pie plate, first with a layer of half the strawberries, then with the banana slices. Top with a final layer of strawberries and remainder of glaze. Sprinkle with coconut. Refrigerate at least 3 hours before serving.

Serves 8 to 10.

Lemon Cream Pie with Blueberry Cream Topping

30 minutes

Crust

¼ cup sesame seeds
½ cup raw almonds
½ cup shredded coconut
4 large dates
½ to 1 cup raisins

Filling

2 tablespoons agar-agar
½ cup water
½ cup lemon juice
1½ cups water
1½ cups pineapple juice
1¾ cups cashews
⅓ cup maple syrup
⅓ cup shredded coconut
4 tablespoons arrowroot
Dash of salt

Topping

½ cup frozen blueberries
⅓ cup cashews
½ cup fresh orange or apple juice
2 ripe peaches, cut in chunks

1. Place seeds, almonds, and coconut in a food processor and process into a meal. Add dates and enough raisins so that mixture forms a ball. Turn out into a 9-inch pie plate and pat into an even crust. Flute the edges with thumb and forefinger.

2. Combine agar-agar in a saucepan with water. Soak for 10 minutes.

3. In a blender, combine remaining ingredients and blend on high until smooth and creamy.

4. Heat agar-agar mixture for 5 minutes, allowing to boil and stirring until smooth. Add agar to filling and blend for an additional minute.

5. Pour filling into pie crust. Chill several hours to allow to set.

6. Place ingredients for topping in blender and blend until smooth, thick, and creamy. Pour over chilled pie.

Serves 8.

Peanut Butter–Banana Pie

35 minutes

This one is sinfully good! But then again, we all deserve a little something sinful now and then. Allow it to sit for 5 minutes after cutting before serving; the texture becomes creamier.

Crust

1 cup raisins
½ cup sunflower seeds
½ cup sesame seeds
½ cup almonds
1 cup dates, seeds removed
Ground cinnamon
Grated nutmeg
A few tablespoons Almond Milk, water, or apple juice

Filling

10 frozen bananas
3 tablespoons lemon juice
3 tablespoons maple syrup
1½ cups crunchy peanut butter

Topping

⅓ cup coarsely ground roasted peanuts
Ground cinnamon

1. Place raisins in a food processor with sunflower and sesame seeds, and process until coarsely chopped. Add almonds and process briefly to chop coarsely. Add dates and process until mixture forms a ball. Use Almond Milk, water, or juice to add moisture if a ball doesn't form readily.

2. Turn crust into a 9-inch pie plate and gently flatten and form to the plate. (If it sticks to your fingers, wet them with a little water.) Push crust up to extend slightly over the top of the pie plate so it forms a nice ledge to contain filling. Crimp edge in a scalloped fashion with thumb. Sprinkle with cinnamon and nutmeg and set in freezer.

3. Wash food processor and dry it well. Place frozen bananas in work bowl and process to break up into chunks. Add lemon juice, maple syrup, and peanut butter and process until creamy and smooth. Immediately spoon mixture into cold pie crust, smoothing and swirling top. Place immediately back in freezer.

4. Coarsely chop peanuts in blender. Dust top of pie with cinnamon, then sprinkle evenly with peanuts. Dust again with cinnamon. Return pie to freezer.

Serves 10.

Note: Frozen bananas are fragile. Air turns them brown quickly. To keep this pie looking its best, cut and quickly return remainder to the freezer.

Afterword

AT the beginning of every new year, many of us find ourselves forgetting how far we have come on the calendar, and it takes weeks to become accustomed to writing the new year correctly. That's a harmless habit. But as we become accustomed to a new decade and approach a new century, there is a far more serious danger of not realizing and not taking advantage of how far we have come with respect to our own bodies and our planet.

The last paragraph of our original *Fit for Life* book states that with respect to how you look and how you feel, you deserve what you have achieved. All of us deserve to benefit from the years of painstaking research, experimentation, study, and growth to which so many dedicated men and women have committed their lives. Some are well known through deed and position. Others are anonymous but their findings are famous.

We now have every opportunity to prepare better foods in a better way than ever before in our society. We now have unprecedented access to information to guide us in achieving and preserving wellness individually and for our planet. The gains we have made are the very foundation of what we will need to ensure our success and survival in the years ahead. There is a danger in the tendency many of us have to become too busy to follow through even when we know what is best for ourselves, our families, and our neighbors.

This book, I truly believe, can help you to help yourself. Feeling better, looking better, functioning better are the most admirable of human goals. With what lies ahead of us, they become prerequisites. If we are to have a chance to reverse some of the unfortunate environmental trends that threaten our planet, we must have our own personal environments in order. We must have the energy and clarity, to say nothing of the dedication to a positive outcome.

I have had the unique pleasure and privilege of meeting people all over the United States and throughout the world. Regardless of their background or their views, despite the differences that divide them, I have always sensed passion for the human family. There really is a worldwide concern about our collective future. I would hope that this book helps you to do more for yourself so that you will be able to do more for others.

A friend reading a draft of this book and these closing comments told me that my dreams are rosy visions and that I am an optimist. I took that as a compliment. Perhaps what he was describing is the tendency to focus on the happiest outcome for all as the only outcome possible, and then to move resolutely toward it. Perhaps what he sensed is the unshakable viewpoint that SUCCESS IS OUR ONLY ALTERNATIVE.

Appendix: Tables, Charts, and Other References

QUICK-REFERENCE NUTRITION CHART

This nutrition chart is designed to give you an answer, at a glance, to the simple question: "What can I *eat* to get more vitamin A?" and so forth. To make the data more understandable and useful, I have supplied a brief description of each nutrient, the role it plays in your body, and the "enemies" that reduce its effectiveness or destroy it.

You are probably going to find this chart different from others you have seen. The listed foods are nonmeat, nondairy food sources of each nutrient. They are truly usable sources of these nutrients (not foods with nearly negligible trace amounts). Where there are exceptionally high sources of any nutrient, they are listed first, for your convenience.

This nutrient chart is taken from references chiefly on raw foods, including the USDA's *Handbook of the Nutritional Contents of Foods.* Of course you must realize that when any raw food is heat-processed or cooked, there is chemical alteration of many nutrients. If you check the "enemies" columns, you will see which nutrients are notably damaged by heat (cooking).

The chart is in three sections: vitamins and minerals, fiber, and protein. I hope you find it useful in this Age of Nutrition, when any 3-year-old is likely to ask you, "Hey, does this have any vitamin C in it?"

Vitamins and Minerals

Note: On the Subject of RDAs. Because each nutrient on this chart cites a Recommended Daily Allowance, you should consider this information first. The Food and Agriculture Organization of the World Health Organization has set its own standards for nutrient intakes, as have the Canadian Department of National Health and Welfare and the U.S. government. The standards differ. In some cases, they differ widely. For instance, the U.S. requirement for vitamin C is set at twice the amount of the Canadian standard. Many critics of our high RDAs are quite vocal. For instance, Dr. Ray Walford:

> **The recommended daily allowance for instance, which we are always hearing so much about, is at an unnecessary high level. Three-thousand calories per day for men—twenty-two hundred for women—*too high*. It's a diet 50,000 years out of date; a diet that might have been good when we were in caves, hunting and running, never living long enough to fall victim to old-age diseases, but a diet that's unnecessary and dangerous now.**[1]

The figures given on this chart are the U.S. RDAs for adults (not pregnant or lactating). Please be aware that RDA amounts can be broken down into many smaller categories (for age groups of children and of adults, for males versus females, and so on). Detailed information of that variety is available in many nutrition texts. But overall, keep in mind Dr. Walford's warning and the arbitrary variables in the system.

[1]Ray Walford, M.D., gerontologist, professor of pathology, UCLA, author of *Maximum Life Span;* chairman, National Institute of Arizona Task Force on Immunology; member, National Academy of Sciences Committee on Aging.

VITAMIN A

RDA*	Major Functions	Enemies
Vitamin A		
U.S. RDA 4,000 to 5,000 IU (International Units)	Immunity builder.	Air Pollutants
	Infection fighter, esp. respiratory.	Alcohol
	Aid to protein synthesis.	Coffee
	Aid to bone growth, healthy skin, sexual functioning.	Cortisone
	Air pollution fighter.	Excess Iron
	Aid to eyesight, esp. night blindness.	Mineral Oil
	Assists gall bladder function.	Vitamin D Deficiency (not enough sun)

SAMPLE SELECTION

IU per 100 g (about 3½ ounces) edible portion

Dried Apricots
10,000 IU

Dandelion Greens
14,000 IU

Dock (Sorrel)
12,900 IU

Carrots
11,000 IU

Collards
9,300 IU

COMPLEMENTARY NUTRIENTS

Plant Protein
B-Complex Vitamins
Choline
Vitamins C, D, E, F (Essential Fatty Acids)
Calcium
Zinc

BEST FOOD SOURCES	OTHER GOOD SOURCES	
Dried Apricots	Fresh Apricots	Fennel
Dandelion	Cherries, Sour Red	Lettuce
Dock (Sorrel)	Mango	Mustard Greens
Carrots	Cantaloupe	Green Onion
Seaweeds especially Nori	Nectarine	Parsley
Collards	Papaya	Sweet Red Pepper
Kale	Peach	Pumpkin
Hot Red Peppers	Prunes	Spinach
	Asparagus	Winter Squash: Acorn
	Beet Greens	Butternut
	Broccoli	Hubbard
	Swiss Chard	Sweet Potato
	Chicory Greens	Turnip Greens
	Chives	Watercress
	Endive (Escarole)	

*United States Recommended Daily Allowance of this nutrient.

VITAMIN B_1: THIAMINE

RDA	Major Functions	Enemies
Vitamin B_1	Aids in maintaining healthy nervous system.	Alcohol Coffee Fever
U.S. RDA 1.0 to 1.6 mg	Needed for normal growth.	Heat Excess Sugar
	Appetite enhancer and aids carbohydrate digestion.	Stress Surgery Tobacco
	Aids muscle building, including healthy heart.	Raw Clams

SAMPLE SELECTION

mg per 100 g
(about 3½ ounces)
edible portion

Rice Bran
2.26 mg

Wheat Germ
2.01 mg

Sunflower Seeds
1.96 mg

Nutritional Yeast
56.63 mg

Major Functions (continued)

Aids cell respiration (oxidation).

Assists liver health.

COMPLEMENTARY NUTRIENTS

B Complex and B_2 (Riboflavin)
Folic Acid
B_3 (Niacin)
Vitamins C & E
Manganese
Sulphur

BEST FOOD SOURCES	OTHER GOOD SOURCES	
All whole grains, esp. Brown Rice, Millet, Whole Wheat, Rye	Avocado	Asparagus
All legumes, esp. Soybeans, Pintos, Red Beans, White Beans, Dried Peas	Cherimoya	Bamboo Shoots
Pecans	Figs, dried	Beet Greens
Pine Nuts (Piñon)	Oranges	Broccoli
Brazil Nuts	Pineapple	Brussels Sprouts
Sunflower Seeds	Prunes	Cauliflower
Sesame Seeds	Raisins	Collards & Kale
	Pumpkin	Corn
		Garlic
	Almonds	Leek
	Cashews	Mushrooms
	Chestnuts	Mustard Greens
	Filberts	Okra
	Macadamias	Parsley
	Walnuts	Potato With Skin
	Water Chestnuts	Spinach
		Sweet Potato
	Nutritional Yeast	Turnip Greens
		Yam
		Soymilk

VITAMIN B_2: RIBOFLAVIN

RDA	Major Functions	Enemies
Vitamin B_2 U.S. RDA 1.2 to 1.7 mg **SAMPLE SELECTION** mg per 100 g (about 3½ ounces) edible portion Hot Red Pepper, Dry 1.33 mg Almonds .92 mg Wheat Germ .68 mg Wild Rice .63 mg Mushrooms .46 mg	Aids protein metabolism. Aids metabolism of fats. Essential for health of skin, liver, eyes, nails, hair. Promotes cell respiration. Promotes formation of red blood cells and of antibodies. Raises resistance to disease. Assists health of kidneys and heart.	Alcohol Caffeine Coffee Sugar Tobacco Oral Contraceptives Ultraviolet Lights **COMPLEMENTARY NUTRIENTS** B Complex B_6 Niacin (B_3) C (Ascorbic Acid) Phosphorus

BEST FOOD SOURCES	OTHER GOOD SOURCES	
Almonds Wild Rice Mushrooms Wheat Germ Hot Red Peppers	Avocado Banana, esp. Dried Peach, esp. Dried Prunes Pumpkin Sesame Seeds Sunflower Seeds Cashews Chestnuts Water Chestnuts Asparagus Beet Greens Broccoli Collards Kale Cress Mustard Greens Okra	Parsley Kelp Spinach Turnip Greens Legumes, esp. Mung Beans Pinto Beans Red Beans Soybeans White Beans Broadbeans Split Peas Whole Grains, esp. Millet Brown Rice Whole Wheat Rice Bran Wheat Bran Nutritional Yeast

VITAMIN B_3: NIACIN

RDA	Major Functions	Enemies
Vitamin B_3	Aids carbohydrate metabolism.	Alcohol Antibiotics
U.S. RDA 13 to 20 mg	Promotes healthy circulatory system.	Caffeine Sugar
	Necessary for healthy skin.	Excess Starches Sleeping Pills
SAMPLE SELECTION	Aids health of the nervous system.	Estrogen

COMPLEMENTARY NUTRIENTS

B-Complex
Vitamin C (Ascorbic Acid)
Phosphorous

SAMPLE SELECTION

mg per 100 g
(about 3½ ounces)
edible portion

Rice Bran
29.8 mg

Wheat Bran
21.0 mg

Hot Red Pepper, Dry
10.8 mg

Wild Rice
6.2 mg

Peach, Dried
5.3 mg

Sesame or Sunflower
Seeds 5.4 mg

BEST FOOD SOURCES	OTHER GOOD SOURCES	
Rice Bran	Apricots	Asparagus
Wheat Bran	Bananas	Corn
Hot Red Pepper, Dry	Peaches	Mushrooms
Wild Rice		Peas, Green
	Sesame Seeds	
	Sunflower Seeds	Legumes:
	Almonds	Mung
	Cashews	Beans
	Pine Nuts (Piñon)	Limas
		Pintos
	Buckwheat	Red Beans
	Whole Wheat	Soybeans
		White
		Beans
		Broadbeans
		Cowpeas
		Split Peas

VITAMIN B_5: PANTOTHENIC ACID

RDA	Major Functions	Enemies
Vitamin B_5 U.S. RDA 10 mg	Promotes antibody production. Aids functioning of gastrointestinal tract. Assists building of body cells. Promotes healthy skin and hair. Promotes adrenal gland function, helping to handle stress. Thought to protect against radiation. Aids development of central nervous system. Aids liver health.	Alcohol Antibiotics Caffeine Coffee Estrogen Heat Sleeping Pills Stress **COMPLEMENTARY NUTRIENTS** B-Complex B_6 and B_{12} PABA Biotin Folic Acid Vitamin C (Ascorbic Acid)

GOOD FOOD SOURCES

Rice Polish
Sunflower Seeds
Buckwheat Flour
Wheat Germ

Papaya

Legumes, such as
- Mung Beans
- Broadbeans
- White Beans
- Red Beans
- Pinto Beans
- Split Peas

Green vegetables, such as
- Kelp (Sea Vegetable)
- Broccoli & other Cabbages
- Artichokes
- Asparagus
- Celery
- Collards
- Kale
- Lettuce(s)
- Spinach
- Swiss Chard

Whole grains, such as
- Whole Wheat
- Buckwheat

VITAMIN B_6: PYRIDOXINE

RDA	Major Functions	Enemies
Vitamin B_6 U.S. RDA 2 mg	Aids in digestion and food assimilation. Promotes hormone production (adrenaline and insulin). Aids in antibody production. Aids in production of red blood cells. Helps in prevention of nausea. Assists RNA and DNA synthesis. Thought to assist weight control.	Alcohol Antibiotics Anticonvulsants Caffeine & Coffee Cooking (Heat) Cortisone DES Estrogen Isoniazid Oral Contraceptives Radiation Sugar Tobacco **COMPLEMENTARY NUTRIENTS** B_1, B_2, B_5, B-Complex Vitamin C Magnesium Potassium Linoleic Acid Naturally occurring Sodium

BEST FOOD SOURCES	OTHER GOOD SOURCES	
Rice Polish Wheat Germ Whole Grains like Brown Rice Whole Wheat Oats Rye especially Buckwheat Cabbage Beets Oranges Lemons	Avocados Bananas Cantaloupe Papayas Walnuts Filberts Sunflower Seeds Carrots Green Peppers Legumes, such as Broadbeans Red Beans White Beans Split Peas Pinto Beans	Green Leafy Vegetables, such as Celery Collards Kale Lettuce(s) Swiss Chard Spinach Nutritional Yeast

VITAMIN B_9: FOLIC ACID

RDA	Major Functions	Enemies
Vitamin B_9 U.S. RDA 0.4 mg	Essential for cell growth. Essential for RNA and DNA synthesis. Aids in formation of red blood cells. Important for protein metabolism. Aids in the production of antibodies.	Alcohol Anticonvulsants Barbiturates Caffeine & Coffee Dilantin Oral Contraceptives Sleeping Pills Stress Sulfa Drugs Sunlight, Heat, and Cooking Tobacco **COMPLEMENTARY NUTRIENTS** B-Complex B_{12} Biotin Pantothenic Acid (B_5) Vitamin C PABA

GOOD FOOD SOURCES

Asparagus
Beet Greens
Broccoli
Dark Green Leafy Vegetables, such as
- Kale
- Endive
- Spinach and
- Swiss Chard

Lima beans

Irish Potatoes

Mushrooms

Turnips

Nuts, such as
- Almonds
- Cashews
- Filberts
- Walnuts

Nutritional Yeast

Wheat Germ

VITAMIN B_{12}: COBALAMIN

RDA	Major Functions	Enemies
Vitamin B_{12}	Formation and maintenance of healthy nervous system.	Alcohol Antacids Antibiotics
U.S. RDA 3 mcg	Blocks nerve cell degeneration.	Aspirin Caffeine
(Whereas other nutrients are measured in millionths of a gram, B_{12} is measured in **billionths**.)	Red blood cell formation. Essential for growth in children.	Diuretics Estrogen Laxatives Oral Contraceptives
	RNA and DNA synthesis.	Sleeping Pills
	Aids carbohydrate metabolism. Needed during pregnancy.	**COMPLEMENTARY NUTRIENTS** B_6 and B-Complex Vitamin C Choline and Inositol Cobalt Potassium Naturally occurring Sodium

IMPORTANT NOTE	GOOD FOOD SOURCES	
The American Dietetic Association (ADA) support paper on vegetarianism* (see p. 19) states that there is no B_{12} in anything that grows out from the soil. Other sources, however, do name these foods.** and ***	Bean Sprouts *Other Sprouts:** Alfalfa Clover Sunflower & Buckwheat Bananas Concord Grapes Papaya Peaches Sunflower Seeds Nuts, esp. Almonds Peas Alfalfa Comfrey Burdock Capsicum Catnip Chickweed	Dandelion Dong Quai Eyebright Fenugreek Ginger Ginseng Hops Licorice Mullein Red Clover Sea Vegetables Kelp Dulse Spirulina Chlorella Nutritional Yeast, if grown on B_{12}-enriched medium (check the label)

*American Dietetic Association, *Position of the American Dietetic Association*: "Vegetarian diets"—technical support paper, ADA REPORTS, March 1988, Volume 88, Number 1.

**Louise Tenney, *Today's Healthy Eating* (Provo, Utah: Woodland Books, 1986), pp. 66–67, 120.
Dr. John R. Christopher, *Regenerative Health* (Springville, Utah: Christopher Publications, 1982), pp. 73–81.

***Robert A. Kreucher, D.C., Hippocrates Health Institute, West Palm Beach, FL 33411

VITAMIN B_{15}: PANGAMIC ACID

RDA	Major Functions	Enemies
Vitamin B_{15} No RDA is currently established for this nutrient. B_{15} is not widely recognized, and at least one textbook lists it as *not* a vitamin while others beg to differ!	Increases oxygen levels in the blood, muscles, and tissues. Stimulates glandular and nervous systems. Increases circulation. May prevent premature aging factors. Protects against carbon monoxide poisoning.	Alcohol Caffeine Most Laxatives Sunlight Water **COMPLEMENTARY NUTRIENTS** B-Complex Choline Inositol Vitamin C Potassium Naturally occurring Sodium

GOOD FOOD SOURCES

Sesame Seeds
Sunflower Seeds
Black Walnut
Rice Bran
Brown Rice
Nutritional Yeast

VITAMIN B_{17}: LAETRILE

RDA	Major Functions	Enemies
Vitamin B_{17}	May reduce risk of cancer.	Alcohol
No RDA established.	Not legal in the United States.	Caffeine

COMPLEMENTARY NUTRIENTS
B-Complex
Choline and Inositol
Vitamin C
Potassium
Naturally occurring Sodium

FOOD SOURCES

Whole seed (kernel) of such fruits as
- Apples
- Apricots (especially)
- Peaches
- Plums
- Nectarines

Also in
- Mung Beans
- Garbanzos
- Millet
- Buckwheat

VITAMIN B COMPLEX GROUP VITAMINS
Choline and Inositol

RDA

Choline:
No RDA established.

Major Functions

Helps fat metabolism.

Aids healthy hair, thymus gland and liver.

Aids immunity build-up.

Essential ingredient of the nerve fluid acetylcholine.

Assists in maintaining healthy arteries.

Enemies

Alcohol
Coffee
Estrogen
Food Processing (Heat)
Sugar
Sulfa Drugs
Water Contact

COMPLEMENTARY NUTRIENTS

Vitamins A, B-Complex, B_{12}
Folic Acid, Inositol, and Linoleic Acid

GOOD FOOD SOURCES

Turnips
Many Herbs, like
Anise, Burdock
Capsicum
Eyebright
Fenugreek
and Ginger
Kelp

Most Fruit

Nuts, such as
Almonds
Brazil Nuts
Cashews
Walnuts

Peanuts (raw)
Soybeans and other Legumes

Green Leafy Vegetables, such as
Celery, Collards, Kale, Lettuce(s), Spinach, and Swiss Chard
Snap Beans
Peas
Cabbage(s)

Wheat Germ
Nutritional Yeast

RDA

Inositol:
No RDA established.

Major Functions

Aids hair growth.

Vital to healthy heart muscle.
Found in high concentrations in the human brain, kidneys, liver, spleen, & stomach.

Enemies

Alcohol
Antibiotics
Coffee
Estrogen
Food Processing
Sugar
Water Contact

COMPLEMENTARY NUTRIENTS

Vitamin B_{12} & B-Complex
Choline, and Linoleic Acid

GOOD FOOD SOURCES

Citrus Fruits
Cantaloupe
Papaya
Raisins

Molasses
Nuts, like
Almonds
Brazil Nuts
Cashews
Walnuts

Many Herbs, like
Burdock
Eyebright
Fenugreek
Kelp
Dandelion

Brown Rice
Corn
Oats
Wheat Germ
Bulgur Wheat
Nutritional Yeast

VITAMIN C: ASCORBIC ACID

RDA	Major Functions	Enemies
Vitamin C U.S. RDA 60 mg	Helps prevent infection and promote healing. Aids in maintaining healthy sex organs and adrenal glands. Promotes healthy formation of connective tissue. Aids tooth formation. Strengthens capillary tissue. Promotes healthy gums and bones.	Alcohol Antibiotics Aspirin Barbiturates Cooking (Heat) Cortisone Diuretics High Fever Pain Killers Stress Tobacco

SAMPLE SELECTION

mg per 100 g
(about 3½ ounces)
edible portion

Acerola Juice
1600 mg

Acerola Cherry
1300 mg

Hot Red Pepper, Raw
369 mg

Common Guava
242 mg

Sweet Green Pepper
128 mg

Broccoli
113 mg

Brussels Sprouts
102 mg

Strawberry
59 mg

COMPLEMENTARY NUTRIENTS

Bioflavonoids
Calcium
Magnesium

GOOD FOOD SOURCES

Acerola Cherry or Juice
Black Currant
Guava
Fresh Orange Juice
Fresh Lemon Juice
Strawberries
Tomatoes

Alfalfa Sprouts
Broccoli
Brussels Sprouts
Other Cabbages:
- Red and Savoy
- Cauliflower

Chives
Collards
Cress

Dock (Sorrel)
Kale
Kohlrabi
Mustard Greens
Parsley
Sweet Green Pepper
Sweet Red Pepper
Spinach
Turnip Greens
Watercress

Hot Peppers, Red and Green

Raw Horseradish

VITAMIN D

RDA	Major Functions	Enemies
Vitamin D U.S. RDA 200 IU	Ultraviolet rays from the sun change an oily substance on our skin (ergosterol) into Vitamin D. Regulates the use of calcium and phosphorous in the body. Essential to healthy teeth and bones and nervous system. Aids thyroid function. Assists blood clotting.	Anticonvulsants Barbiturates Cortisone Dilantin Doriden Mineral Oil Primidone Sleeping Pills Smog **COMPLEMENTARY NUTRIENTS** Vitamins A and C Vitamin F (Essential Fatty Acids) Choline Calcium Phosphorous Magnesium Naturally occurring Sodium

BEST SOURCE	GOOD FOOD SOURCES
Sunshine!	Alfalfa Chickweed Eyebright Fenugreek Mullein Papaya Red Raspberry Rosehips

VITAMIN E

RDA	Major Functions	Enemies
Vitamin E U.S. RDA 10–30 IU	Keeps oxygen in cells from combining with wastes to form toxic compounds (antioxidant). Aids health of red blood cells. Improves circulation. Helps to prevent blood clots: dissolves fibrin and reduces thrombin formation. Protects lungs against air pollution. Helps health of reproductive system. Helps to prevent sterility. Assists selenium and phosphorous absorption.	Chlorine Heat Mineral Oil Rancid Fat & Oil Oral Contraceptives **COMPLEMENTRY NUTRIENTS** Vitamins A, B_1, B-Complex Inositol Vitamin C Vitamin F (Essential Fatty Acids) Manganese Selenium Phosphorous

GOOD FOOD SOURCES

Blackberries
Pears

Sesame Seeds
Sunflower Seeds

Almonds
Brazil Nuts
Filberts
Walnuts

Asparagus
Beet Greens
Broccoli
Brussels Sprouts
Corn
Leeks
Spinach
Sweet Potato
Turnip Greens

Watercress

Barley
Brown Rice
Buckwheat
Oats
Quinoa
Rye

Wheat Germ

VITAMIN F: ESSENTIAL FATTY ACIDS
Linoleic and Linolenic Acids

Major Functions	Enemies
Helps in the prevention of cholesterol build-up and hardening of the arteries.	Heat Light Contact Oxygen Contact Rancid Oils
Aids growth.	Radiation, including X-Rays
Promotes healthy hair and skin.	**COMPLEMENTARY NUTRIENTS** Vitamins A, C, D, & E
Contributes to normal glandular activity.	Phosphorous Calcium
Called "essential" because they cannot be manufactured in the body.	

BEST FOOD SOURCES	OTHER GOOD SOURCES	
Soybeans	Butter	Seaweeds
Pumpkin Seeds	Avocados Sunflower Seeds	Spinach Parsley
Walnuts	Nuts, especially Almonds Cashews Pecans Pistachios Walnuts Millet Corn Oats Rice Bran Wheat Germ Coconut	Broccoli Olive Oil Dark-bottled, cold-pressed flaxseed oil

VITAMIN H: BIOTIN

RDA	Major Functions	Enemies
Vitamin H U.S. RDA .15 mg	Assists the metabolism of carbohydrates, proteins, and unsaturated fatty acids. Needed for normal growth. Aids in vitamin B utilization. Important to kidneys, liver, and pancreas. Involved in the maintenance of bone marrow, hair, sex glands, and skin.	Alcohol Coffee Estrogen Food Processing Raw Egg White Sugar Sulfa Drugs **COMPLEMENTARY NUTRIENTS** B-Complex and B_{12} Vitamin C Folic Acid (B_9) Pantothenic Acid (B_5) Sulphur

GOOD FOOD SOURCES

Asparagus	Brown Rice
Beet Greens	Oats
Endive	
Kale	Wheat Bran
Spinach	Nutritional Yeast

CALCIUM

RDA	Major Functions	Enemies
Calcium U.S. RDA 800 mg **SAMPLE SELECTION** mg per 100 g (about 3½ ounces) edible portion Sesame Seeds 1160 mg Kelp 1093 mg Pressed Tofu 377 mg Dulse 296 mg Almond 234 mg Fig, Dried 126 mg Broccoli 103 mg	Promotes health of teeth and bones. Aids in blood clotting. Strengthens nervous system. Aids heart rhythm. Helps in muscle function (contraction). Normalizes metabolism. Activates some enzymes.	Aspirin Chocolate Mineral Oil Oxalic Acid* Phytic Acid** Stress Tetracyclines **COMPLEMENTARY NUTRIENTS** Vitamins A, C, D, & F Iron Magnesium Phosphorous, and Manganese Amino acid Lysine Exercise!

BEST FOOD SOURCES	OTHER GOOD SOURCES	
Sesame Seeds Figs, esp. Dried Almonds Beet Greens Broccoli Seaweeds: Kelp, Agar, Irish Moss, and Dulse Turnip Greens Watercress	Apple, esp. Dried Banana, esp. Dried Dates Peach, esp. Dried Pear, esp. Dried Prunes Raisins Raspberries, Black Citrus Peel Squash: Pumpkin Yellow Squash Scallop Zucchini Brazil Nuts Filberts Sunflower Seeds Tofu Miso Artichokes Brussels Sprouts Cabbage(s) Celery	Swiss Chard Cress Fennel Kale Parsley Spinach Legumes, especially Dried Lima Beans Mung Beans Pinto Beans Soybeans Red Beans White Beans Garbanzos Lentils Split Peas Amaranth Barley Buckwheat Brown Rice Millet Oats Rye Rice Bran Wheat Bran

*Oxalic acid is concentrated in beet greens, spinach, rhubarb, and swiss chard, but may be counter-balanced by their calcium content.
**Phytic acid is in wheat and other glutinous grains. Again, may be counter-balanced by calcium content of whole grain.

CHROMIUM

RDA	Major Functions	Enemies
Chromium	Promotes healthy blood circulation.	Refined carbohydrates
U.S. RDA 125 mg	Assists energy by affecting glucose tolerance.	Sugar
	Increases insulin effectiveness.	**COMPLEMENTARY NUTRIENTS** Zinc Vitamin C
	Aids in synthesis of fatty acids, cholesterol and protein.	
	Affects health of thyroid and spleen.	

GOOD SOURCES

Potatoes with Skins

Kelp

Whole Grains, like
- Whole Wheat
- Brown Rice
- Rye
- Oats

IODINE

RDA	Major Functions	Enemies
Iodine U.S. RDA .15 mg usually stated as 150 mcg	Regulates metabolism Stimulates circulation. Promotes healthy thyroid. Aids energy production. Promotes healthy hair, nails, skin, and teeth. Aids oxidation of fats and proteins.	Cooking (Heat) Food Processing Soaking in Water **COMPLEMENTARY NUTRIENTS** Vitamin E Vitamin F (Essential Fatty Acids) Iron Magnesium Phosphorous Potassium

SAMPLE SELECTION

mg about 100 g (about 3½ ounces) edible portion

Kelp
150,000 mg

Dulse
8,000 mg

Swiss Chard
.099 mg

Turnip Greens
.076 mg

Summer Squash
.062 mg

BEST FOOD SOURCES	OTHER GOOD SOURCES	
Seaweeds Dulse Kelp	Bananas Blueberries Peaches Strawberries Watermelon Black Walnuts Artichokes Asparagus Chinese Cabbage Carrots Swiss Chard Collards Cucumber with Skin Eggplant Green Beans Kale Lettuces, Boston & Bibb Mustard Greens Okra Sweet Green Pepper Potato with Skin Rutabaga Other Seaweeds, esp. Agar	Raw Mushrooms Summer Squash Yellow Scallop Zucchini Snap Beans Spinach Sweet Potatoes Tomatoes Turnip and Turnip Greens

IRON

RDA	Major Functions	Enemies
Iron U.S. RDA 10–18 mg	Aids in hemoglobin formation (carries oxygen from lungs to every body cell). Promotes resistance to disease. Assists energy level. Contributes to health of bone, brain, and muscle.	Coffee Some Food Additives Tetracyclines Excesses of Phosphorous and Zinc

SAMPLE SELECTION

mg per 100 g
(about 3½ ounces)
edible portion

Dulse
150 mg

Kelp
100 mg

Rice Bran
19.4 mg

Wheat Bran
14.9 mg

Sesame Seeds
10.5 mg

White Beans, Dried
7.8 mg

Apricots, Dried
5.5 mg

COMPLEMENTARY NUTRIENTS

Vitamin B_{12}

Vitamin E

Calcium
Cobalt
Copper

Folic Acid (B_9)

Phosphorous

BEST FOOD SOURCES

Seaweeds: Dulse and Kelp
Rice Bran
Wheat Bran & Germ
Legumes
- Lima Beans
- Mung Beans
- Pintos
- Red Beans
- White Beans
- Soybeans
- Lentils
- Split Peas

Apricots, Dried

OTHER GOOD SOURCES

Figs, esp. Dried
Dates
Peaches, Dried
Prunes
Raisins
Pumpkin

Sesame Seeds
Sunflower Seeds

Almonds
Brazil Nuts
Coconut, esp. Dried
Filberts
Walnuts

Tofu
Blackstrap Molasses

Seaweeds in addition to Dulse and Kelp:
- Agar and
- Irish Moss

Spinach
Squash

Amaranth
Millet
Quinoa
Rice Bran
Rye
Wild Rice
Whole Wheat
Wheat Germ

MAGNESIUM

RDA	Major Functions	Enemies
Magnesium U.S. RDA 300–350 mg	Assists acid-alkaline balance in body. Aids energy level by affecting blood sugar metabolism. Assists metabolism of calcium and vitamin C. Natural tranquilizer. Promotes healthy functioning of arteries, heart, bones, nerves, muscles, and optimum health of teeth. Affects utilization of fats. Conditions liver and glands. Stimulates elimination.	Alcohol Diuretics Food Processing Refined Flour Sugar Excess Protein

SAMPLE SELECTION

mg per 100 g
(about 3½ ounces)
edible portion

Kelp
760 mg

Wheat Bran
490 mg

Wheat Germ
336 mg

Almonds
270 mg

Cashews
267 mg

Dulse
200 mg

Peas, Dried (Split Pea)
180 mg

Banana, Dried
132 mg

Figs, Dried
71 mg

Dates
58 mg

COMPLEMENTARY NUTRIENTS

Vitamin B_6
Vitamin C
Vitamin D
Calcium
Phosphorous

BEST FOOD SOURCES	OTHER FOOD SOURCES	
Kelp Almonds Cashews Legumes, such as: Red Beans Soybeans White Beans Cow Peas Pinto Beans Lentils Split Peas, etc. Dried Fruit, esp. Figs Bananas Wheat Bran Wheat Germ	Apples Avocado Apricots Coconut, Dried Dates Nuts, like Almonds Cashews Filberts Beet Greens Sweet Corn Spinach Garlic Lima Beans Millet	Brown Rice Wild Rice Rye Whole Wheat Honey

MANGANESE

RDA	Major Functions	Enemies
Manganese U.S. RDA 3.750 mg	Aids in digestion of fats Promotes production of sex hormones. Affects enzyme activation. Assists tissue respiration. Involved with B_1 metabolism and utilization of vitamin E. Formation of urea. Assists carbohydrate metabolism. Strengthens tissue and bones. Important to kidneys, liver, lymph system, pancreas, and spleen, as well as brain and heart.	Excesses of Calcium and Phosphorous **COMPLEMENTARY NUTRIENTS** B-Complex Vitamin E Calcium Zinc

GOOD FOOD SOURCES

Apricots
Bananas
Grapefruit
Oranges

Outer coating of nuts, like
- Almonds
- Filberts
- Pecans
- Walnuts

Beets
Carrots
Celery
Chives
Cucumber

Green Leafy vegetables like
- Collards
- Kale
- Lettuce(s)
- Spinach
- Swiss Chard

Parsley
Peas
Sweet Potatoes

Outer Coating of Whole Grains like
- Whole Wheat
- Brown Rice
- Buckwheat
- Rye

Wheat Germ

PABA (VITAMIN)
Para-Amino-Benzoic Acid

RDA	Major Functions	Enemies
PABA U.S. RDA None established.	Natural sunscreen; aids health of skin. Promotes blood cell formation. Stimulates intestinal flora to produce folic acid. Assists protein metabolism (coenzyme). Promotes utilization of pantothenic acid. Believed to help maintain the natural color of one's hair.	Alcohol Coffee Estrogen Food Processing Sulfa Drugs **COMPLEMENTARY NUTRIENTS** B-Complex Vitamin C Folic Acid (B_9) Pantothenic Acid (B_5)

GOOD FOOD SOURCES

Papaya

Alfalfa

Kelp

Leafy Green Vegetables, like
- Collards
- Kale
- Lettuce(s)
- Spinach
- Swiss Chard

Rice Bran
Wheat Germ
Nutritional Yeast
Blackstrap Molasses

PHOSPHOROUS

RDA	Major Functions	Enemies
Phosphorous	Promotes healthy growth of bones and teeth.	Sugar
U.S. RDA 800 mg	Works with calcium to help in the metabolism of fats and carbohydrates.	Excesses of Aluminum Iron and Magnesium
SAMPLE SELECTION	Aids in growth and repair of cells and nerves.	**COMPLEMENTARY NUTRIENTS** Vitamins B_3 and B_{12}
mg per 100 g (about 3½ ounces) edible portion	Assists healthy muscle activity.	Vitamins D, E, and F (Essential Fatty Acids)
Rice Bran 1386 mg	Key in maintaining appropriate acid-alkaline balance.	Calcium Iron
Wheat Bran 1276 mg	Builds blood, brain, and hair.	Magnesium
Wheat Germ 1118 mg		
Sunflower Seeds 837 mg		
Brazil Nuts 693 mg		
Sesame Seeds 616 mg		
Pinto Beans, dried 457 mg		

BEST FOOD SOURCES	OTHER GOOD SOURCES	
Rice Bran Wheat Bran and Germ Almonds & Brazil Nuts Pine Nuts (Piñon) Walnuts Sesame Seeds Pinto Beans Red Beans Soybeans White Beans	Apple, esp. Dried Apricots, esp. Dried Bananas, esp. Dried Dates Figs, esp. Dried Peaches, esp. Dried Prunes Raisins Cashews Coconut, esp. Dried Pumpkin Seeds Miso Tofu Artichokes Sweet Corn Celeriac Garlic Mushrooms	Seaweeds: Dulse Irish Moss Kelp Yams Many Herbs, like Capsicum Chicory Ginger Hawthorne Parsley Other Legumes, like Lima Beans Mung Beans Garbanzo Beans Lentils Split Peas Barley Millet Brown Rice Quinoa Wild Rice Whole Wheat

POTASSIUM

RDA	Major Functions	Enemies
Potassium U.S. RDA 1875 mg–5625 mg	Aids in ph balance in blood and tissues. Assists kidney function of detoxifying blood. Stimulates endocrine hormone production. Assists regulation of heartbeat. Regulates nervous and muscular irritability. Aids elimination.	Alcohol Caffeine Coffee Cortisone Most Laxatives and Diuretics Stress Excess Salt

SAMPLE SELECTION

mg per 100 g (about 3½ ounces) edible portion

Dulse
8060 mg

Kelp
5273 mg

Lima Beans, Dried
1529 mg

Rice Bran
1495 mg

Bananas, Dried
1477 mg

White Beans, Dried
1196 mg

Apricot, Dried
979 mg

COMPLEMENTARY NUTRIENTS

Vitamins B_6 and B_{12}

Naturally occurring Sodium

BEST FOOD SOURCES

Seaweeds
- Kelp
- Dulse
- Irish Moss

Almonds
Apricots, esp. Dried
Apples, esp. Dried
Bananas, esp. Dried
Dates
Figs, esp. Dried

Dried Legumes
- Lima Beans
- Mung Beans
- Soybeans

Rice Bran
Wheat Bran

OTHER GOOD SOURCES

Avocados
Currants, Black
Nectarines
Orange Juice
Passion Fruit
Peaches, esp. Dried
Pears, esp. Dried

Sesame Seeds
Brazil Nuts
Chestnuts
Coconut, esp. Dried
Filberts
Pecans
Walnuts
Waterchestnuts

Miso
Soymilk

Artichokes
Asparagus
Bamboo Shoots
Beets
Beet Greens

Broccoli
Brussels Sprouts
Carrots
Celery
Swiss Chard
Cress
Fennel
Kale
Kohlrabi
Parsley
Radish
Spinach
Squash
- Acorn
- Butternut
- Hubbard

Yams
Other Legumes
- Pinto Beans
- Red Beans
- White Beans
- Lentils
- Split Peas

Millet
Quinoa
Rye

SELENIUM

RDA	Major Functions	Enemies
Selenium U.S. RDA .125 mg	Creates antioxidant effect similar to vitamin E. Protects against mercury poisoning. Preserves tissue elasticity. Promotes healthy function of testicles. Helps clean up free radicals.	Excess Fats Stress **COMPLEMENTARY NUTRIENTS** Vitamin E Zinc

BEST FOOD SOURCES	OTHER FOOD SOURCES	
Bran, such as Wheat Bran Rice Bran	Apples Cantaloupe Grapefruit	Legumes, like Navy Beans Garbanzos
Broccoli	Honeydew Melon Oranges Peaches	Whole Grains, like Whole Wheat Brown Rice Rye
Mushrooms	Pineapple Raspberries	
Garlic	Tangerines	
Onions	Brazil Nuts	
Kelp	Asparagus Cabbage(s)	
Wheat Germ	Winter Squash	

SULPHUR

RDA	Major Functions	Enemies
It is noted that a diet adequate in protein commonly contains enough sulphur. There is no recommended intake for sulphur and no deficiencies are known.[1]	Aids digestion. Counteracts acidosis. Assists maintenance of healthy hair, blood, nails, and skin. Purifies blood. May stop fermentation.	None **COMPLEMENTARY NUTRIENTS** B-Complex Biotin Pantothenic Acid Potassium

A WORD TO THE WISE

The inorganic, extracted sulphur used on some dried fruits is *not* a healthy source of this nutrient and is to be avoided.

GOOD FOOD SOURCES

Raspberries

Nuts, like
- Almonds
- Filberts
- Walnuts

Alfalfa
Brussels Sprouts
Cabbage(s)
Celery
Dandelion
Garlic
Kale
Kelp
Lettuce(s)

Onions
Parsley
Radishes
Snap Beans
String Beans
Turnips

Watercress

Soybeans and other Dried Legumes

Wheat Germ

[1]Whitney and Hamilton, *Understanding Nutrition*, Second Edition (Los Angeles: West Publishing Company, 1981), p. 435.

ZINC

RDA	Major Functions	Enemies
Zinc U.S. RDA 15 mg	Assists in healing wounds and burns. Aids protein and carbohydrate metabolism. Assists prostate gland function. Contributes to healthy reproductive organs. Essential for formation of RNA and DNA. Effects transfer of carbon dioxide from tissue to lungs. Important to brain, kidneys, liver, and thyroid.	Alcohol Food Processing Oral Contraceptives Stress Excessive Calcium Deficient Phosphorous

SAMPLE SELECTION

mg in 1 cup
edible portion

Pumpkin Seeds, Dried
10.30 mg

Peanut Butter, Chunky
7.17 mg

Refried Beans
3.45 mg

Tofu
3.96 mg

Dried Figs
1.00 mg

COMPLEMENTARY NUTRIENTS

Vitamin A
B Complex
Vitamin E

GOOD FOOD SOURCES

Wheat Germ
Wheat Bran
Sesame Seeds
Pumpkin Seeds
Sunflower Seeds
Sprouted Seeds

Nuts, like
- Almonds
- Brazil Nuts
- Cashews
- Filberts
- Pecans

Tofu
Tempeh
Mushrooms

Green Peas
Spinach (smaller amounts in other green leafy vegetables)

Lentils
Lima Beans
Split Peas

Outer Coating of Whole Grains, such as
- Brown Rice
- Quinoa
- Amaranth and
- Whole Wheat

Cornmeal

Fiber

Nutrient	Major Functions	Food Sources	
Fiber Note: Dietary Fiber is the residue of plant food resistant to hydrolysis by human digestive enzymes. Crude Fiber is what remains after extraction with dilute acid (laboratory procedure). For every gram of crude fiber in a food there tend to be 2 to 3 grams of dietary fiber. Whenever possible get your fiber from whole fruits and vegetables—the superior sources for human digestion.	To attract water into the digestive tract, thus softening the stools and preventing constipation. To exercise the muscles of the digestive tract for health and tone. To speed passage of food materials through the digestive tract, which is thought to be especially beneficial in limiting the presence of carcinogens (cancer-causing agents). To bind lipids such as cholesterol and carry them out of the body with the feces. Reduces risk of artery and heart disease.	Apples Apricots Currants Elderberries Figs Guavas Peaches Pears Sesame Seeds Sunflower Seeds Almonds Beechnuts Brazil Nuts Coconut Filberts Alfalfa Sea Vegetables, such as Kelp and Laver Carrots Corn Broccoli Brussels Sprouts Parsnips Peas Potatoes	Dried Legumes, such as Lima Beans Mung Beans Pintos Red Beans Soybeans White Beans Broadbeans Garbanzos Lentils Black-Eyed Peas Split Peas Carob Amaranth Barley Brown Rice Buckwheat Millet and Oats Quinoa and Rye Whole Wheat

Protein

Note: The chart that follows is built on three bases:

1. Protein in the human body is built from amino acids.
2. Every amino acid needed to build human protein is to be found in fruits, nuts, seeds, and vegetables (including legumes).
3. The medical journal *Lancet*, the American Dietetic Association, and the Food and Nutrition Board of the National Academy of Sciences, among others, are now advocating the benefits of protein from plant sources.

Of the twenty-three known amino acids, eight are called "essential" because the adult human body cannot synthesize them in amounts sufficient to meet physiological needs. These eight follow, with their common food sources listed for your reference.

PROTEIN

Essential Amino Acid	Functions in Body	Some Food Sources
Isoleucine (EYE-so-LOO-seen)	Regulation of the pituitary gland, spleen and thymus. Building of hemoglobin. Regulation of metabolism.	Avocados Papayas Olives Coconut Nuts, except Cashew and Chestnut Sunflower Seeds Nutritional Yeast Soymilk Tofu
Leucine (LOO-seen)	Counterbalances isoleucine.	Avocados Papayas Olives Coconut Nuts, except Cashew and Chestnut Sunflower Seeds Nutritional Yeast Soymilk Tofu

Essential Amino Acid	Functions in Body	Some Food Sources
Lysine or Lycine (LYE-seen)	Aids liver and gall bladder. Affects fats metabolism. Regulation of pineal and mammary glands and ovaries Prevents cell degeneration. Strengthens immune system. Helps calcium absorption. Helps body utilize and convert protein.	Apples Apricots Grapes Papayas Pears Alfalfa Beets Carrots Celery Cucumber Dandelion Parsley Soybean Sprouts Spinach Turnip Greens Nutritional Yeast Soymilk Tofu
Methionine (meh-THIGH-oh-neen)	Constituent of hemoglobin, tissues, and serum. Influences function of lymph system, pancreas, and spleen.	Apples Pineapples Brazil Nuts Filberts Brussels Sprouts Cabbage(s) Cauliflower Chives Dock (Sorrel) Garlic Horseradish Kale Watercress Soymilk Tofu

Essential Amino Acid	Functions in Body	Some Food Sources
Phenylalanine (fee-nul-AL-uh-neen)	Involved in elimination of waste; kidney and bladder functions.	Apples Pineapples Beets Carrots Parsley Spinach Tomato Nutritional Yeast Soymilk Tofu
Threonine (THREE-oh-neen)	Involved in exchange of amino acids to establish balance.	Papaya Alfalfa Carrots Green, leafy vegetables like Celery Collards Kale Lettuces (esp. Iceberg) Lima Beans Laver (Nori-Sea Vegetable) Spirulina Soybeans Soymilk Tofu
Tryptophane (TRIP-toe-fane)	Generation of cells and tissues, gastric juices, and pancreatic juices. Involved with the optic system.	Alfalfa Brussels Sprouts Carrots Celery Chives Dandelion Endive Fennel Snap Beans Spinach Turnips Nutritional Yeast Soymilk Tofu

Essential Amino Acid	Functions in Body	Some Food Sources
Valine (VAY-leen)	Involved in function of corpus luteum, mammary glands, and ovaries.	Apples Almonds Pomegranates Beets Carrots Celery Dandelion Lettuce(s) Okra Parsley Parsnip Squash Tomato Turnip Nutritional Yeast Soymilk Tofu
Arginine (AR-ga-neen) Sometimes found listed as "essential"	Muscle contracting. Cartilage constituent. Involved in health of reproductive organs. Thought to control body cell degeneration.	Alfalfa Beets Carrots Celery Cucumber Green Vegetables Leek Lettuce Parsnip Potato Radish Nutritional Yeast Soymilk Tofu

Amino Acid	Functions in Body	Some Food Sources
Sometimes listed as "essential," especially in the case of infants:	Assists in liver formation of glycogen.	Apples Papayas Pineapples
Histidine	Aids in mucus control.	Pomegranates
(HISS-tih-deen)	Component of hemoglobin and of semen.	Alfalfa Beets Carrots Celery Cucumber Dandelion Endive Garlic Horseradish Radish Spinach Turnip Greens Soymilk* and human Mother's Milk

*100 gms (about 3½ ounces) of soymilk contains 71 mg of histidine.

A General List of Protein Sources

To step away from the "fractionated" concept of this-amino-acid-here and that-amino-acid-there, I'm giving you a list of some very fine *foods of significant protein content.* Where the figure for the percentage of calories from protein for any given food was available, I have included it in parentheses.* Remember, our protein-need ranges from 2½ to 8% of daily caloric intake.

Avocado (5%)
Apricots (8%)
Bananas (5%)
Blackberries (*%)
Cantaloupe (9%)
Cherries (8%)

Grapes (8%)
Grapefruit (5%)
Figs (6%)
Honeydew (10%)
Papaya (6%)
Peaches (6%)
Pears (5%)
Oranges (8%)
Prunes (4%)

Strawberries (8%)
Watermelon (8%)
Sesame Seeds (13%)
Pumpkin Seeds (21%)
Almonds (12%)
Beechnuts
Brazil Nuts (9%)
Butternuts (15%)
Cashews (12%)
Chestnuts (6%)
Coconut, Fresh (4%)
Filberts (8%)
Hickory Nuts
Macadamias
Pecans (5%)
Pine Nuts (pinon) (8%)
Walnuts (13%)

Miso
Tofu (43%)
Soymilk
Dried Legumes:
Lentils (29%)
Limas (26%)
Garbanzos (23%)
Pintos (26%)
Red Beans (26%)
Soybeans (35%)
White Beans (26%)
Broadbeans (32%)
Split Peas (28%)
Legumes, Fresh:
Broadbeans
Lima Beans
Sprouts! }***
Sprouts! }
Mung Beansprouts (43%)
Artichoke (22%)
Asparagus (38%)
Bamboo Shoots (39%)
Beet Greens (37%)
Broccoli (45%)
Brussels Sprouts
Cabbage, Red (22%)
Cabbage, Savoy (22%)
Cabbage, Chinese (34%)
Cauliflower (40%)
Celery (21%)
Swiss Chard
Collards (43%)
Cucumbers (24%)
Corn, Sweet (12%)

Dandelion (24%)
Fennel
Garlic Clove (20%)
Green Beans (26%)
Green Peas (30%)
Hot Red Peppers (17%)
Kale (45%)
Kohlrabi
Leeks
Lettuce(s) (34%)
Mushrooms (38%)
Mustard Greens (39%)
Okra (27%)
Parsley (34%)
Pepper, Grn Bell (22%)
Sea Vegetables, like
Dulse, Kelp & Nori
Spinach (49%)
Turnip Greens (43%)
Watercress (46%)
Wild Rice (18%)
Zucchini (28%)
Amaranth (20%+)**
Barley (11%)
Buckwheat (15%)
Millet (12%)
Oats (15%)
Quinoa (20%+)**
Rice, Brown (8%)
Rye (20%)
Whole Wheat (17%)
Triticale
Wheat Germ (31%)

Source: **Nutritive Value of American Foods In Common Units,* USDA Handbook No. 456
Notes: **Amaranth and quinoa are the highest protein grains.
***Sprouted seeds, beans, grains, and nuts provide complete proteins—that is, they will give you all eight essential amino acids. Each sprout, however, has these nutrient components in differing proportions, so it is best to eat a variety of sprouts. (As per Ann Wigmore, *The Sprouting Book* [Wayne, NJ.. Avery Publishing Group, 1986], p. 8.)

SUBSTITUTIONS CHART

Item	Amount	Substitution Directions
Baking powder	1 teaspoon	1. Divide teaspoon in fifths; use 2 parts cream of tartar, 1 part baking soda, and 2 parts arrowroot. 2. Use ¼ teaspoon baking soda and ¼ to ½ cup molasses, reducing other liquids in the recipe equivalently.
Baking soda	1 teaspoon	Use ½ teaspoon baking soda and 1½ teaspoon lemon juice.
Butter as a spread		1. Use avocado, nut butters, or olive oil.
in baking and cooking		2. Use olive oil, safflower oil, or sunflower oil (in baking, use oil in 80% of butter amount).
in baking	1 tablespoon	3. Use applesauce in baking (up to ¼ cup only).
in mashed potatoes		4. Use 1 teaspoon light miso and 2 teaspoons olive oil for every 1 tablespoon butter.
in baking		5. Use equivalent of pure soy margarine.
Buttermilk	1 cup	Use 1 cup Almond Milk or Cashew Milk.
Cheese (dairy)		
cheddar		Use equivalent of soy cheese, cheddar style.
cottage		Use tofu. (See page 105.)
cream		Use equivalent of soy cream cheese; on sandwiches, use almonnaise.
mozzarella	8 oz.	Use equivalent of soy cheese, mozzarella style.
jack cheese		Use equivalent of soy cheese, jack style.
jalapeño pepper		Use equivalent of soy cheese, jalapeño pepper style.
ricotta		Use equivalent measure of tofu, ricotta. (See page 106.)
Chocolate (baking)	1 square	Use 3 tablespoons carob powder and 1 tablespoon oil, with 1 tablespoon water and 1 tablespoon coffee substitute.
Cocoa	1 cup	Use ¾ cup carob powder and ¼ cup coffee substitute or 1 cup carob powder.
Coffee or tea sweetener		1. Use FruitSource and stir well to dissolve (in hot liquid only). 2. Use honey or brown rice syrup.
Coffee		Use grain coffee substitutes; there are many.

Item	Amount	Substitution Directions
Cornstarch	1 tablespoon	Use 1 tablespoon arrowroot powder or kuzu. (Note: Kuzu and arrowroot may thin if stirred or heated excessively.)
Cream heavy	¼ cup	Use equivalent measure of Cashew Cream or 1 tablespoon tahini dissolved in ¼ cup water.
sour	½ cup	Use tofu.
Egg in baking	1 egg	1. Use 1 tablespoon defatted soy flour or 1 tablespoon water with 1 tablespoon powdered soy lecithin. 2. Use egg replacer as per package instructions. 3. Use half a ripe banana. 4. Use ¼ cup tofu.
salad		Use tofu.
scrambled	8 ounces	Use 8 ounces tofu along with tofu scrambler seasoning.
Flour all-purpose or white		Use 1 cup whole-wheat or other whole-grain flour.
Gelatin dessert	1 tablespoon	1. Use 1 tablespoon granulated agar-agar and 3½ cups liquid 2. Use 2 tablespoons flaked agar-agar and 3½ cups liquid.
Garlic, fresh	1 clove	1. Use 1 teaspoon minced garlic 2. Use ½ teaspoon garlic powder 3. Use ⅓ teaspoon crushed garlic (paste). 4. Use a pinch of asafetida.
Herbs, fresh	1 tablespoon	Use 1 teaspoon of dried herb.
Honey	1 cup	1. Use 1¼ cups FruitSource or brown rice syrup. 2. Use 1 cup barley malt syrup or sorghum molasses. 3. Use ¾ cup maple syrup.
Lard or shortening	1 cup	Use 1 cup soy margarine or ¾ cup vegetable oil.
Milk in baking	1 cup	1. Use 1 cup Almond Milk, Cashew Milk, or sunflower milk. 2. Use 1 cup soymilk, liquid or reconstituted from powder.

Item	Amount	Substitution Directions
Milk on cereals		Use 1 cup soymilk, Almond Milk, or other nut or seed milks.
Molasses, blackstrap	1 cup	Use 1 cup barley malt syrup (milder flavor), sorghum molasses, or rice bran syrup.
Potatoes, mashed	2 cups	Use rice flakes; 1 cup flakes cooked with 1¼ cups water yields 2 cups cooked flakes.
Salt (processed)	1 teaspoon	1. Use ground rock salt. 2. Use salt-free seasonings or herb blends. 3. Use sea vegetables such as powdered kelp, dulse, or miso. 4. Use umeboshi plum paste or tamari.
Soy sauce	1 teaspoon	Use ½ teaspoon low sodium tamari.
Sugar, brown	1 cup	1. Use ¾ cup maple syrup or honey; if maple syrup, reduce liquid in recipe by 2 tablespoons for every 1 cup sweetener (if honey, reduce liquid in recipe by ½ cup for every 1 cup sweetener and set oven 25° lower). 2. Use 1 cup date sugar or molasses.
Sugar, white	1 cup	1. Use 1 cup date sugar. 2. Use ¾ cup maple syrup (reduce other liquids in recipe by 2 tablespoons). 3. Use ¾ cup honey (reduce other liquids by ½ cup per 1 cup of honey and bake at 25° lower). 4. Use 1 cup sorghum molasses and ½ teaspoon baking soda (reduce other liquids in the recipe by ¼ cup per cup of molasses).
Coffee or tea sweetener		Use honey, brown rice syrup or maple syrup.
Tomatoes, cooked		Use fresh tomatoes, chopped, added in final step.
Water chestnuts		Use thin-sliced Jerusalem artichoke (in stir-fries).
Yogurt	1 cup	Use equivalent measure of soft tofu.

MAIL ORDER DIRECTORY

These fine companies may be contacted directly for their healthful products.

BRAUN DESIGN
P.O. Box 710477
Dept. C-143
El Paso, TX 88571-0477

EDEN FOODS, INC.
701 Tecumseh Road
Clinton, MI 49236
(800) 248–0301

FANTASTIC FOODS, INC.
HEALTH FOODS EXPRESS
P.O. Box 8357
Fresno, CA 93747
(209) 252–8321

GARDEN OF EATIN'
438 White Oak Road
New Holland, PA 17557
(717) 354–4936
In PA: (800) 292–9631

OASIS BREADS
440 Venture Street
P.O. Box 182
Escondido, CA 92025
(619) 747–7390

PITTMAN & DAVIS
801 North Express
Box 2227
Harlingen, TX 78551

TREASURE CRAFT
2320 N. Alameda Street
Compton, CA 90222-2803
(800) 828–7449
In CA: (213) 636–9777

WALNUT ACRES NATURAL FOODS
Penns Creek, PA 17862
(717) 837–0601

WATER FACTORY SYSTEMS
68 Fairbanks
Irvine, CA 92718
(800) 767–5511

SOME RECOMMENDED PERIODICALS

East West Journal
P.O. Box 6769
Syracuse, NY 13217

Health Freedom News
212 W. Foothill Boulevard
Monrovia, CA 91016
(818) 357–2181

Health Science
American Natural
Hygiene Society
P.O. Box 30630
Tampa, FL 33630

Newsletter of NCSFI
(National Coalition to
Stop Food Irradiation)
P.O. Box 59–0488
San Francisco, CA 94159–0488
(415) 626–2734

Nutrition Action Healthletter
Center for Science in
the Public Interest
1501 16th Street, N.W.
Washington, DC 20036–1499
(202) 332–9110

"Organic Advocate"
Albert's Organics
Publications Department
4605 S. Alameda Street
Los Angeles, CA 90058

Vegetarian Persuasion
The Canadian Natural Hygiene Society
P.O. Box 235, Station "T"
Toronto, Ontario M6B4A1
Canada

Vegetarian Times
P.O. Box 570
Oak Park, IL 60303
(800) 435–0715
in IL: (800) 892–0753

Bibliography

Acciardo, Marcia Madhuri. *Light Eating for Survival.* Woodstock Valley, Conn.: Omangod Press, 1977.

Atlas, Nava. *The Wholefood Catalogue: A Complete Guide to Natural Foods.* New York, N.Y.: Fawcett Columbine, 1988.

Baker, Elton and Elizabeth. *The UnCook Book.* Drelwood Saguache, Colo.: Drelwood Publications, 1980.

Bastyra, Judy. *Caribbean Cooking.* New York, N.Y.: Exeter Books, 1987.

Bond, Harry C. *Natural Food Cookbook.* No. Hollywood, Calif.: Wilshire Book Company, 1974.

Carrier, Robert. *Great Salads and Vegetables.* London: Angus and Robertson Publishers, 1965.

Chemical Additives in Booze. Report of the Center for Science in the Public Interest. Washington, D.C.: CSPI Books, 1982.

Christopher, John R. *Regenerative Health.* Springville, Utah: Christopher Publications, 1987.

Clare, Sally and David. *The Creative Vegetarian.* Wayne, N.J.: Avery Publishing Group, 1987.

The Complete Book of Vitamins. Staff of *Prevention Magazine.* Emmaus, Pa.: Rodale Press, 1977.

The Cookbook for People Who Love Animals, Third Ed. Umatilla, Fla.: Gentle World, Inc., 1986.

Crowley, Jerry. *The Fine Art of Garnishing.* Baltimore, Md.: Lieba, Inc., 1978, 1982.

Diamond, Harvey and Marilyn. *Living Health.* New York, N.Y.: Warner Books, 1987.

Dorland's Medical Dictionary. Philadelphia, Pa.: W.B. Saunders Company, 1977, 1980.

Duquette, Susan. *Sunburst Farm Family Cookbook.* Santa Barbara, Calif.: Woodbridge Press Publishing Co., 1976, 1978.

Erasmus, Udo. *Fats and Oils: The Complete Guide to Fats and Oils in Health and Nutrition.* Vancouver, B.C.: Alive Books, 1986.

Fathman, George and Doris. *Live Foods: Nature's Perfect System of Human Nutrition.* Beaumont, Calif.: Ehret Literature Publishing Co., 1967, 1973.

Freedman, Louise. *Wild About Mushrooms.* 1621 Fifth Street, Berkeley, Calif.: Harris Publishing Company, Inc., 1987.

Gerras, Charles, ed. and the staff of Rodale Press. *Rodale's Basic Natural Foods Cookbook.* Emmaus, Pa.: Rodale Press, 1984.

The Good Cook: Techniques and Recipes. Alexandria, Va.: Time-Life Books, 1980.

Guyton, Arthur C. *Physiology of the Human Body,* Sixth Ed. Philadelphia, Pa.: Saunders College Publishing, 1984.

Hagler, Louise. *Tofu Cookery.* Summertown, Tenn.: The Book Publishing Company, 1982.

———. *Tofu: Quick and Easy.* Summertown, Tenn.: The Book Publishing Company, 1986.

Haritage, Ford. *Composition and Facts About Foods.* Mokelumne Hill, Calif.: Health Research Publication, 1968.

Hirasuna, Delphine, et al. *Vegetables.* San Francisco, Calif.: Chronicle Books, 1985.

Horn, Jane, and Janet Fletcher. *Cooking A to Z.* San Ramon, Calif.: California Culinary Academy, 1988.

Hoshijo, Kathy. *The Art of Dieting Without Dieting!* Glendale, Calif.: Self-Sufficiency Association, 1986.

Hurd, Frank J., and Rosale. *A Good Cook . . . Ten Talents.* Chisholm, Minn.: Dr. and Mrs. F.J. Hurd, Publishers, 1968.

Johns, Leslie, and Violet Stevenson. *The Complete Book of Fruit.* North Ryde, Australia: Angus and Robertson Publishers, 1979.

———. *Fruit For the Home and Garden.* North Ryde, Australia: Angus and Robertson Publishers, 1985.

Katzen, Mollie. *The Moosewood Cookbook.* Berkeley, Calif.: Ten Speed Press, 1977.

Klaper, Michael, M.D. *Pregnancy, Children, and the Vegan Diet.* Umatilla, Florida: Gentle World, Inc., 1987.

———. Vegan Nutrition: Pure and Simple, Umatilla, Florida: Gentle World, Inc., 1987.

Kushi, Aveline. *Complete Guide to Macrobiotic Cooking.* New York, N.Y.: Warner Books, 1985.

Lappe, Frances Moore. *Diet for a Small Planet,* Tenth Anniversary Edition. New York, NY: Ballantine Books, 1982.

Leavy, Herbert T., and the editors of the *Vegetarian Times. Vegetarian Times Cookbook.* New York, N.Y.: MacMillan Publishing Co., 1984.

Lemlin, Jeanne. *Vegetarian Pleasures.* New York, N.Y.: Alfred A. Knopf, 1986.

Madison, Deborah, with Edward Espe Brown. *The Greens Cook Book.* New York, N.Y.: Bantam Books, 1987.

Mallos, Tess. *The Complete Middle East Cookbook,* New York, N.Y.: McGraw-Hill Book Company, 1979, 1982.

McDougall, John A. *McDougall's Medicine.* Piscataway, N.J.: New Century Publishers, Inc., 1985.

——— and Mary A. McDougall. *The McDougall Plan.* Piscataway, N.J.: New Century Publishers, Inc., 1983.

McNair, James. *Pizza.* San Francisco, Calif.: Chronicle Books, 1987.

———. *Power Food.* San Francisco, Calif.: Chronicle Books, 1986.

Migliace, Janice Cook. *Follow Your Heart's Vegetarian Soup Cookbook.* Santa Barbara, Calif.: Woodbridge Press, 1983.

Montagna, F. Joseph. *People's Desk Reference (P.D.R.): Traditional Herbal Formulas.* Lake Oswego, Oreg.: Quest for Truth Publications, Inc., 1980.

Moody, Agatha Thrash, and Calvin L. Thrash, Jr. *Nutrition for Vegetarians.* Seale, Ala.: New Lifestyle Books, 1982.

Morash, Marion. *The Victory Garden Cookbook.* New York, N.Y.: Alfred A. Knopf, 1982.

Murietta Hot Springs Vegetarian Cookbook. The Murietta Foundation. Summertown, Tenn.: The Book Publishing Company, 1987.

Nathan, Amy. *Salad.* San Francisco, Calif.: Chronicle Books, n.d.

"Organic Advocate," the monthly newsletter of Albert's Organics. Los Angeles, Calif.: May/June 1989, July/August 1989.

Puck, Wolfgang. *Modern French Cooking.* Boston, Mass.: Houghton Mifflin Company, 1981.

Robbins, John. *Diet For A New America.* Walpole, N.H.: Stillpoint Publishing, 1987.

Robertson, Laurel, Carol Flinders, and Brian Ruppenthal. *The New Laurel's Kitchen.* Berkeley, Calif.: Ten Speed Press, 1986.

Rombauer, Irma S., and Marion Rombauer Becker. *The Joy of Cooking.* Indianapolis, Ind.: The Bobbs-Merrill Company, Inc., 1975.

Sahni, Julie. *Classic Indian Cooking.* New York, N.Y.: William Morrow and Company, Inc., 1980.

Sandler, Sandra and Bruce. *Home Bakebook of Natural Breads and Goodies.* Harrisburg, Pa.: Stackpole Books, 1972.

Shannon, Sara. *Diet for the Atomic Age.* Wayne, N.J.: Avery Publishing Group, Inc., 1987.

Shelton, Herbert M. *Food Combining Made Easy.* San Antonio, Tex.: Dr. Shelton's Health School, 1951 (27th printing 1975).

Shopper's Guide to Natural Foods. Editors of *East West Journal.* Garden City Park, N.Y.: Avery Publishing Group, Inc., 1987.

Shurtleff, William, and Akiko Aoyagi. *The Book of Tofu.* Brookline, Mass.: Autumn Press, 1975.

Southey, Paul. *The Vegetarian Gourmet Cookbook.* New York, N.Y.: Exeter Books, 1980.

Tannahill, Reay. *Food in History.* New York, N.Y.: Stein and Day, 1973.

Tenney, Louise. *Today's Healthy Eating.* Provo, Utah: Woodland Books, 1986.

Thomas, Anna. *The Vegetarian Epicure.* New York, N.Y.: Vintage Books, 1972.

———. *The Vegetarian Epicure, Book Two.* New York, N.Y.: Alfred A. Knopf, 1979.

Tomlinson, H. *Aluminum Utensils and Disease.* Essex, England: L.N. Fowler & Co, Ltd., 1958. Reprinted 1978 by Eyre & Spottiswoode Ltd, Grosvenor Press, Portsmouth, England.

U.S. Department of Agriculture. *Handbook of the Nutritional Contents of Foods.* New York, N.Y.: Dover Publications, Inc., 1975.

Walker, N.W. *Fresh Vegetable and Fruit Juices.* Phoenix, Ariz.: Norwalk Press, 1986.

Waters, Alice. *Chez Panisse Pasta, Pizza and Calzone.* New York, N.Y.: Random House, 1984.

Webb, Tony, Tim Lang, and Kathleen Tucker. *Food Irradiation: Who Wants It?* Rochester, Vt.: Healing Arts Press, 1987, 1989.

Whitney, Eleanor, and Eva May Hamilton, *Understanding Nutrition,* Second Ed. St. Paul, Minn.: West Publishing Co., 1981.

Wigmore, Ann. *Recipes for Longer Life.* Wayne, N.J.: Avery Publishing Group, 1978.

———. *The Sprouting Book.* Wayne, N.J.: Avery Publishing Group, Inc., 1986.

Zamm, Alfred V., with Robert Gannon. *Why Your House May Endanger Your Health.* New York, N.Y.: Simon and Schuster, 1980.

Index